HEISEY GLASS

1896 – 1957
IDENTIFICATION & VALUE GUIDE

NEILA & TOM
BREDEHOFT

cb
COLLECTOR BOOKS
A Division of Schroeder Publishing Co., Inc.

The current values in this book should be used only as a guide. They are not intended to set prices, which vary from one section of the country to another. Auction prices as well as dealer prices vary greatly and are affected by condition as well as demand. Neither the authors nor the publisher assumes responsibility for any losses that might be incurred as a result of consulting this guide.

Front cover, left to right: No. 1552 Standing Pony, light amber; Moongleam and Flamingo No. 4035 Seven Octagon colognes, with No. 77 Duck Stopper; No. 134 Trident Candlestick, Flamingo; No. 1415 20th Century tumbler in Moongleam.

Cover design by Beth Summers
Book design by Beth Ray

Searching For A Publisher?

We are always looking for people knowledgeable within their fields. If you feel that there is a real need for a book on your collectible subject and have a large comprehensive collection, contact Collector Books.

COLLECTOR BOOKS
P.O. Box 3009
Paducah, Kentucky 42002-3009
www.collectorbooks.com

Contents

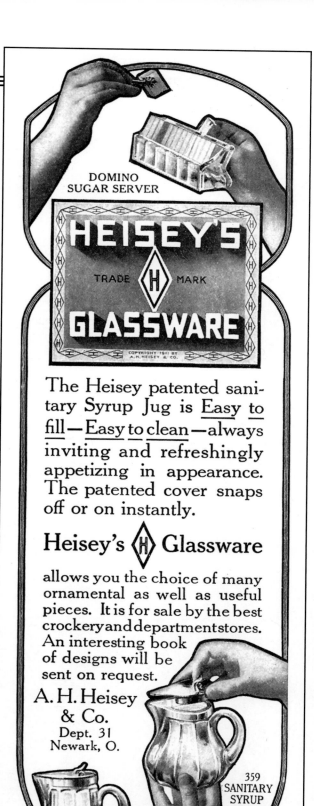

 Dedication

 Preface

This book is an overview of the A. H. Heisey & Co. of Newark, Ohio, comprising its history and production. Of necessity, it cannot include every pattern and every piece that the company made. However, all major patterns will be discussed and minor patterns will be included as space allows. All production colors are illustrated and many important decorations are also shown.

Heisey was an unsurpassed producer of high quality tableware for the middle-income and above-average-income housewife during its 62 years of production. The company pioneered many styles of glassware, colors, and decorations while in business. It was second to none in the production of artistic cut tableware, and its Orchid etching was one of the most popular decorations for stemware and tableware ever made in this country.

At the present time, there is no single book which presents the entire history and production of the Heisey company. We have often been asked to write a book about Heisey's entire production and we hope that this book will be of help and interest to both the beginning and the more advanced collector of Heisey glass. We feel that only in an overview-type book can anyone get a true picture of the Heisey company and its importance in American handmade table glassware.

The A. H. Heisey & Co. factory, circa 1913

As much as possible, we have listed patterns chronologically. Records are sometimes incomplete, so a "best guess" approach was done for some patterns. In those cases, we have placed them in numerical order, as this is probably the order in which these patterns were designed whether or not they were immediately placed on the market. Sometimes catalogs and price lists were not redone for up to four years. If a pattern was unsuccessful, it could easily have been introduced and dropped from the line within that time frame. The book is divided into chronological decades. Interestingly, this division is a good one as often differences in styles, colors, and other factors occurred over 10 year periods.

The following is an explanation of the small format used for each pattern entry and what you can expect to find in each listing.

Names and Numbers

The Heisey company did not name all its patterns, especially in the early years, but in later years almost all names are original with the company. Researchers are responsible for naming many of the early patterns. When we know the original Heisey company name, we use it, and so indicate it, in preference to other names applied later. Also, most of the numbers used are original with the company and are used in conjunction with the name.

Dates

We have attempted to date each pattern, sometimes only with an introduction date. Usually this is determined by the first mention of the pattern in a trade journal, an early ad, or the first catalog in which the pattern appeared. Patterns were developed continually but catalogs were printed only periodically, so there may be a span of three or four years when a pattern cannot be accurately dated. We have also included ending dates if known. These are primarily determined by the date of the catalog which first does *not* contain the pattern. Because of this, the patterns may have actually been discontinued months or even years before.

Colors

Almost all Heisey patterns were made in clear, colorless glass which we designate as crystal. Other known Heisey colors for patterns are included. If a pattern had a long life span, often the colored items were only made for a short period of time. Likewise, often only selected pieces of a pattern came in color. This is especially true of colored pieces of colonial styled glass. Most of these colonial pieces are scarce to rare. If you find a piece in a color not listed, first suspect it might be a reproduction.

Patents

The Heisey company protected many of their pieces and patterns by patents throughout the years they were in business. Heisey patents were of two types: design or mechanical. Most patents held by the company were design patents, but occasionally the method of manufacture or the manufac-

1913 ad

turing process was covered by a mechanical patent. Ray Cobel, head of Heisey's mold shop for many years, patented several processes or mold types and assigned the patents to the company,

In Heisey's earliest years, Andrew J. Sanford was the company's primary glass designer and he patented many patterns for the company. Many patents list either E. Wilson Heisey or T. Clarence Heisey as the designer. In reality, these men probably were not the true designers but simply signed the legal documents for the patents.

In this book, we have listed the patents held by the company and have listed the date on which the patent was granted. Patents could have been applied for weeks, months, or rarely, years, before the patent was granted and the pattern actually made.

Comments

Important information about patterns is included in this section. Whether or not a pattern is marked with the Diamond H is listed here. Unusual items may be discussed. Values for various colors are given in a percentage style. Imperial and other reproductions are mentioned here, but continued reproductions by the Heisey club in Heisey molds makes it difficult to list every item in every color currently being made or having been made in the last few years. So beware of unusual colors and strange pieces, i. e., baskets made from tumblers, etc.

Pieces and Prices

Most pieces in a pattern are listed. In some cases, patterns are known but not all items are known so the listings may be incomplete. Names of pieces are the ones Heisey used and not necessarily the names by which collectors today know them. Prices are given for each item in crystal glass, unless the pattern was not made in crystal or is usually found in another color. If this is the case, this is indicated in the Comments section. In an attempt to make the book more complete, we have used illustrations with Heisey decorations if possible. It is important to note that the prices listed are for *undecorated* pieces in all cases. Decorations can add as little as 25% to the price and up to 500% or more depending on the decoration and its scarcity and desirability.

All price guides are suspect. Prices can be arrived at in different ways. Some include auctions, shows, and educated opinions from knowledgeable people. Prices can also be a subjective matter depending on whether they are based on a seller's price, a buyer's price, an appraisal price, or some other category. Another factor is locale, although this is becoming less of a factor since the introduction of the Internet and auction sites such as eBay which have wide followings, and thus the information is available to people everywhere. We have attempted to list a fair value you might expect to pay for an item. You should be aware that if a rare or highly desirable item is available, prices may soar, especially at auctions. Eventually, the only true price of a piece is a price agreed to between buyer and seller.

1913 ad

Heisey's Numbering System

Heisey's numbering system is fairly consistent. The earliest pressed patterns of tableware begin with numbers in the 1200 series. For unknown reasons, this system was changed with Peerless in 1899 when the company began to use numbers in the 300 series. This continued through the 400s. In the 1930s this series for pressed tableware was replaced with a 1400 series which, with a few exceptions, continued to the end of the company. When the company began making blownware in the teens, the 3000 series was used for stemware. As a general rule of thumb, all items numbered from 1 to 1999 are pressed, while those from 2000 and above are blown. One exception is No. 7000 Sunflower which is pressed. Any numbers in the 8000 to 9000 listings are numbers assigned and not original with the Heisey company. Other series are evident when studying the Heisey pattern numbers. The following will give some idea of most of the major categories:

1– 136 Stoppers
1–13 Shades, gas or electric
1– 57 Salts & peppers
1– 209 Candlesticks
101– 237; 526–600 Tumblers or bars, pressed
325 – 527 Plate etchings
600 – 1104 Cuttings
700 – 716; 800 – 867; 900 – 917; 980 – 985;
  1049 –1056; 1109 –1114; 1183 – 1188;
  1212 – 1227 Stems, pressed
1020 – 1025 Creams & sugars
1122 – 1128; 1218 – 1254; 4182 – 4187 Plates
1122 – 1154 Puff boxes, ointments, pomades,
  toothbrush boxes, toothpowder boxes
1151 – 1175; 1185 – 1200; 1206 – 1212 Custards,
  pressed
1201 – 1206 Floral bowls
1401 – 1637A Pressed patterns, including
  some one or two item patterns
2028 – 3056; 3476 – 3483 Bar tumblers, sodas,
  ice teas, or tumblers, blown
3001 –3456; 4083 – 4094; 5009 – 5025; 5038 – 6009
  Stemware, blown

3947 – 3970 Comports, blown
4026 – 4039 Decanters, bar bottles
4071 – 4081 Finger bowls, blown
4156 – 4175; 5034 – 5036 Jugs, blown
4191 – 4233; 5034 – 5036 Vases, blown
4266 – 4269 Custards, blown
4291 – 4297 Candy jars, blown
5000 – 5020 Carvings

Within these categories not all numbers are used, and sometimes there are overlapping series. The early numbers from 1 to 20 seem to have been used as catchalls for many disparate items over the entire life of the company. For the most part, the sequential numbers also correspond to the time the patterns were first marketed. But this is not always true since patterns could be developed quite some time before they were actually put into the product line.

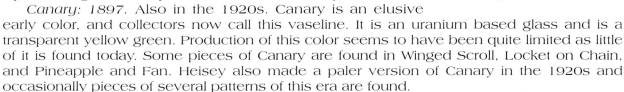

Emerald: 1897. Emerald became Heisey's first venture into making colored glass. It is a transparent vibrant, deep green often decorated with gold. It was made in several early patterns including Fancy Loop, Pineapple & Fan, and Winged Scroll.

Ivorina Verde: 1897. Ivorina Verde is the Heisey name for what collectors now call custard glass. It is an opaque, but sometimes somewhat translucent, medium yellow color. Some patterns made in Ivorina Verde include Winged Scroll and Ring Band.

Opal: 1898. Opal is Heisey's opaque milk glass. It is often quite translucent and exhibits a fiery opalescent quality when held to the light. Bead Swag is the primary pattern found in Opal although random pieces are found in other patterns.

Original Heisey label

Canary: 1897. Also in the 1920s. Canary is an elusive early color, and collectors now call this vaseline. It is an uranium based glass and is a transparent yellow green. Production of this color seems to have been quite limited as little of it is found today. Some pieces of Canary are found in Winged Scroll, Locket on Chain, and Pineapple and Fan. Heisey also made a paler version of Canary in the 1920s and occasionally pieces of several patterns of this era are found.

Rose: ca. 1900 – 1901. While never found in early catalogs, this color was listed in old inventory lists of the company. It apparently was an experimental color in this period and is a true, pale pink. It is unlike the later Flamingo which almost always has tints of orange or tan in it. Only a few items were listed in this color: No. 300 Peerless #1 candlestick (also called Georgian); No. 305 Punty & Diamond Point celery; several items in No. 325 Pillows-cream; 4", 5", 7", 8", and 9" nappies; three quart jug; egg cup; water bottle; tall celery; and "assorted vases." Also known in this color are several No. 300 Peerless swing vases and a No. 310 Ring Band spoon holder. Pieces of Pillows are also known other than those listed. Any Heisey collector is fortunate to own a piece of Rose as all are very scarce.

Moongleam: 1925. Heisey's first color made in the 1925 era was Moongleam. This is a transparent light green which often varies in shades and was made for about 10 years. At first the color was very similar to the old Emerald, but soon it was lightened to a more subtle shade of green. Many patterns are found in Moongleam, including Twist and Empress.

Flamingo: 1925. Flamingo was made at the same time as Moongleam and also for about 10 years. It is Heisey's pink color and usually contains a hint of orange, but some examples lack this. Flamingo can also vary in tint. Moongleam and Flamingo were Heisey's answer to the same type of colors being made by Fostoria and many Depression glass companies. Patterns made in Flamingo include Twist and Empress.

Hawthorne: 1927. Hawthorne was Heisey's first lavender color. It was made only during the year of 1927 – 1928, and so is difficult to find today. It is a delicate transparent lavender, but sometimes, unfortunately, has tints of brown. Apparently the color was not too popular, as it was replaced by Alexandrite. Patterns made in Hawthorne include Tudor and other miscellaneous items.

Marigold: 1929. Marigold is a transparent vibrant, brassy yellow-orange color — very like the flowers for which it is named. Marigold also has shades of yellow-green on the edges. It, too, was not made for a lengthly period (only about one year), probably because it is an unstable glass. Something in the formula caused the glass to develop crazing or even slivers, and sometimes surfaces are disintegrating. Marigold was made primarily in the Twist pattern.

Sahara: 1930. Sahara became Heisey's popular transparent yellow color. Unlike Marigold, it is an extremely stable color and the color was easily maintained so that few variations in shades are found. The glass trade was highly impressed by this color when it was new as it said it was the first true yellow color able to be made in lead glass. Sahara is easily found in Empress, and less easily in Ipswich and Old Sandwich.

Alexandrite: 1930. Heisey's second attempt at a lavender color is the very popular Alexandrite. This is an attractive lavender color with distinct red highlights on the edges. It was an expensive color in its time and is still so today. Unfortunately, fluorescent lighting makes the color turn an unattractive lavender green. This does not discourage collectors, however! Alexandrite is found primarily in the Empress pattern.

Stiegel Blue: 1932. This is Heisey's transparent cobalt blue color and is truly outstanding. It was often combined with crystal in a very pleasing effect. The most commonly found items are those in the Spanish stemware line.

Tangerine: 1932. Tangerine is very like the color of tangerines. It is a transparent, glowing orange color. It is a struck color, meaning it is reheated to bring out the true red-orange of the color. Unheated, it remains simply orange. Because of the heating process, several different shades of Tangerine can be found. The usual is the orange color as described, but other examples are almost entirely red. Tangerine can be found in the Empress pattern and occasionally in Duquesne stemware.

Zircon: 1936. Zircon is a blue-green color. It is transparent and very reminiscent of a greenish-blue sea. Zircon was developed very late in the color period and so is somewhat difficult to find today, having been made for only about three years. Patterns made in Zircon are Fern and Whirlpool.

Sultana: 1951. This is a deep, rich amber color made in only a few items for a short period of time. Cabochon is sometimes found in this color and also Suez and Legionnaire stemware. Heisey also made a pale amber, usually referred to by collectors today as honey amber. Heisey made amber for Fred Harvey restaurants as early as the 1920s.

Dawn: 1955. This was Heisey's charcoal gray color. It is a transparent deep gray-black with overtones of purple. Gray was an important decorating color in the 1950s. This color was used in Lodestar, Town & Country, and Roundelay.

Limelight: 1956. Late in the 1950s Heisey reintroduced their old Zircon color, but renamed it Limelight. It is likely that the same formula was used. The true collector can distinguish the color by the time frame in which the pieces were made. Early 1930s items are Zircon; late 1950s items are Limelight.

Several experimental or unusual colors are known in Heisey glass. Some of these include an experimental light blue similar to Cambridge's Moonlight Blue; a gold color similar to Marigold but lacking the green overtones and reacting orange under black light (also sometimes with opalescent edges); gold ruby; ultramarine blue, a transparent teal blue made in old patterns such as Pineapple & Fan; a deep, dark, almost black Emerald green found in Pineapple & Fan and Pointed Oval and Diamond Point; red, according to former factory workers made only as an experimental color but sometimes found in handles on beer mugs, so this was done in the early to mid 1930s; clear opalescent found in early patterns such as Punty Band and Peerless; and Canary opalescent found in Pineapple & Fan and Plaid vases along with a few other items.

1913 ad

The story of the A. H. Heisey & Co. actually begins many years before 1895 with the life and experiences of its founder, Augustus H. Heisey. He was born in Germany in 1842 and brought up in Merrittown, Pennsylvania, after his parents emigrated to the United States. As a young man, he was employed by Cascade Glass Company (subsequently King, Son & Co.) in Pittsburgh in 1861. During the Civil War he served with the 155th Infantry from Pennsylvania, and fought at Devil's Den and Little Round Top in the Battle of Gettysburg. After his discharge, he was employed by Ripley & Co. as a salesman.

In 1870 he married Susan Duncan, daughter of George Duncan, one of the owners of Ripley & Co. Soon Duncan became the sole owner of Ripley & Co. as the original investors either died or divested themselves of their interest in the firm. Duncan, a Pittsburgh financier, had his son, James, and son-in-law, Augustus Heisey run the new firm, which was renamed Geo. Duncan & Sons. James served as president while Heisey was in charge of sales. While at Duncan & Sons, Heisey patented several patterns for the company including Shell and Tassel, the umbrella vase, and others.

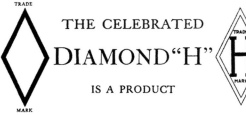

Diamond H

When Geo. Duncan & Sons joined the large U.S. Glass Co. combine, Heisey was a member of the original board of directors and became commercial manager (in charge of sales) for U.S. Glass. He stayed with the company until 1893 when he left to pursue his own interests and investments, primarily around Denver, Colorado. During the next two years, Heisey never completely gave up the idea of getting back into glassmaking. After investigating several potential sites, he eventually decided to erect his new factory in Newark, Ohio. The Newark Board of Trade gave favorable terms to Heisey if he would locate in Newark. In addition, Heisey was able to purchase a large tract of land, the Penney farm, east of Newark, on which to locate his factory and also to sell off tracts for houses for his employees. Heisey also took options on large areas in the vicinity for natural gas rights. His sons also formed a gas company which held options for gas not only on local land but as far away as Kentucky. Heisey was determined that his factory not suffer from lack of fuel (as had many others) so he established control of enough fuel rights to insure that he had sufficent supply.

Construction of the factory began in 1895 with the expectation of opening in January of 1896. However, due to several difficulties, including the collapse of an entire wall, the construction was not complete until several months later in 1896. The first glass was made in the new factory in April of 1896. Early samples and ware for sale were made by the Robinson Glass Co. of nearby Zanesville, Ohio.

Late in 1900, the company began using its well-known trademark, an H within a diamond. This design was the inspiration of Heisey's oldest son, George Duncan Heisey, and patterned after his fraternity pin. By 1901, the company had received its copyright for the trademark and then advertised that all pieces of Heisey glass were marked with the Diamond H. This remained the case for most of the time Heisey glass was made, although there are notable exceptions. Much blownware was never marked and some patterns and specific pieces in patterns seem to have never been marked. However, many of the "unmarked" pieces originally had paper labels affixed which used the Diamond H prominently in the design of the label.

Early production was mainly in crystal glass for which Heisey had an exceptional formula. Some production was done in early colors such as emerald, ivorina verde (custard), opal (milk glass), and canary (vaseline).

By 1914 or 1915, the company expanded its line to include blownware, etchings, and cuttings. These lines remained an important staple in the Heisey line (except for the years of World War II) until the factory went out of business.

A. H. Heisey died in 1922 and his second son, E. Wilson Heisey, succeeded him as president. Wilson had been educated in chemistry at Washington & Jefferson College in Washington, Pennsylvania, and almost immediately began to bring color into the Heisey line. The first colors were made in 1925 and various colors were made for the next 10 years.

In 1933 the company was fortunate to employ Emil Krall and his brother Willibald and their sons as engravers and cutters in the decorating department. Emil and his brother had been employed in Haida, Austria, in the court of Emperor Franz Josef. The quality of their designs put Heisey glass in the forefront of decorated tableware made for American households. Emil remained with the company until 1942 when Willibald succeeded him as head engraver and cutter.

In the mid to late 1930s, Heisey also had an association with Walter von Nessen, a nationally known designer who designed several lines and revamped other pieces for Heisey.

The end of Prohibition in 1933 allowed Heisey to expand its production into various bar ware and stemware lines helping the company survive the Depression. During the difficult days of World War II, the Heisey company managed to survive by producing the very popular lines of Crystolite and Lariat. In addition, the popularity of their new group of animal figurines, mostly designed by Royal Hickman, found immense favor with the buying public.

After the war's end, the Heisey company found it difficult to maintain its place in the market. One of the problems was the changing life style of the American family. Life became much more informal — the stylish dinner party giving way to the backyard barbecue. The company seemed to be out of step with this change, trying to continue selling sets of stemware and fancy party accessories when most hostesses were buying simpler styles. In addition, during the war years factory wages were frozen. At the end of the war, the union demanded increases in wages which the company could not meet and still make the margin of profit as before.

In an attempt to reach the new market, Heisey employed the noted commercial designer, Eva Zeisel, in 1954. Her designs won industry awards but proved to be unpopular to the buying public. Most are not easily found today. It is thought that her association with Heisey lasted for only about a year.

Eventually, all these things took their toll. The Heisey family sold the entire company, including trademark, accounts, molds, and all other assets to Imperial Glass Corporation of Bellaire, Ohio, in 1958. The company closed its doors permanently for Christmas vacation in 1957, and never reopened for business except to sell off remaining glass.

The factory buildings still stand at 301 Oakwood Avenue in Newark. They have lost much of their grandeur, now being used only as a warehouse. The molds, after Imperial's bankruptcy in 1984, were purchased by Heisey Collectors of America, Inc., the national collectors' club of Heisey Glass, and now are back in Newark, Ohio. (With the exception of the Old Williamsburg pattern and a few other colonial molds which Imperial had listed as belonging to the Old Williamsburg line. These molds were retained by Lancaster Colony who are still making some of the items, although the molds have been reworked or made new so that the glass is now machine made rather than handmade.)

Fighting Roosters, allover cranberry stain.

No. 1255 Pineapple and Fan vase, Ultramarine Blue.

 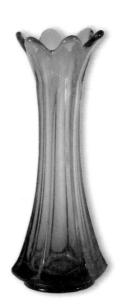 

No. 5082 Mid Century goblet, experimental light blue bowl, rare.

No. 300½ Peerless vases, Emerald and Rose.

Plaid vase, Canary opalescent, rare.

No. 1205 Rain Drop and No. 112 Mercury candlesticks, gold opalescent, experimental and rare.

No. 1 Madonna Limelight, No. 2 Madonna, crystal satin.

No. 3481 Glenford tumbler, Flamingo and Moongleam, rare.

No. 1506 Whirlpool plate, Limelight.

13

No. 1485 Saturn two-light candleblocks, Zircon.

No. 1193 Inside Scallop large nappy, Canary.

No. 1280 Winged Scroll 8" nappy, Canary.

No. 1280 Winged Scroll half-gallon jug, Canary.

No. 1184 Yeoman bouillon cup, Canary.

No. 6060 Country Club soda, No. 4054 Coronation old fashion, both with experimental screen optic in Dawn.

No. 6009A Roundelay ashtray, Dawn.

No. 1540 Oscar, light amber.

No. 1632 Lodestar celery, Dawn.

No. 3360 Penn Charter parfait, Hawthorne.

No. 1202 Paneled Octagon floral bowl with foot, No. 15 Flower Block and Duck insert, all Hawthorne.

No. 417 Double Rib and Panel basket, Hawthorne.

No. 411 Tudor mayonnaise, Hawthorne.

No. 1280 Winged Scroll oblong, Ivorina Verde with gold decoration.

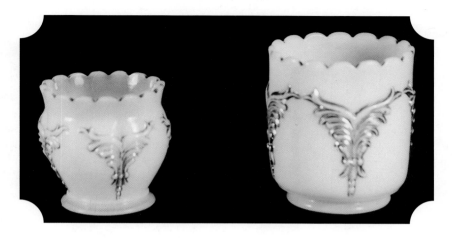

No. 1280 Winged Scroll toothpick and cigarette holder, Ivorina Verde with gold decoration.

No. 1280 Winged Scroll covered butter, Ivorina Verde with gold decoration.

No. 1255 Pineapple and Fan half-pint tankard, Opal and Ivorina Verde.

No. 310 Ring Band tumbler with center band, Ivorina Verde and tumbler, Opal.

No. 1220 Punty Band individual cream, mug, Opal.

No. 1295 Bead Swag spoon, Opal.

No. 300-2 Old Williamsburg 16" candelabrum, Sahara.

No. 1295 Bead Swag tankard, Opal.

No. 1401 Empress individual nut, Sahara.

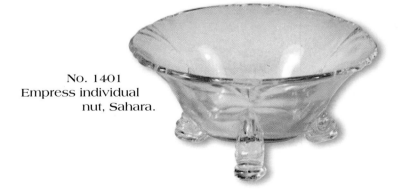

No. 1425 Victorian rose bowl, goblet, bar, Sahara.

No. 1447 Rococo sugar and cream, Sahara.

No. 1404 Old Sandwich whimsey cologne, Sahara.

No. 1430 Aristocrat high footed covered candy, No. 1428 Warwick vase, Sahara.

No. 1433 Thumbprint and Panel vase, Sahara.

No. 2516 Circle Pair
soda, Flamingo.

No. 1170 Pleat and Panel
compotier, Flamingo.

No. 1186 Yeoman puff box
and cover, Flamingo.

No. 417 Double Rib
and Panel mustard,
Flamingo.

No. 300 Peerless
Schoeppen, Flamingo.

Unknown Art Deco design
vase, marked with the Diamond H, Flamingo.

Unknown triangular ashtray, Flamingo.

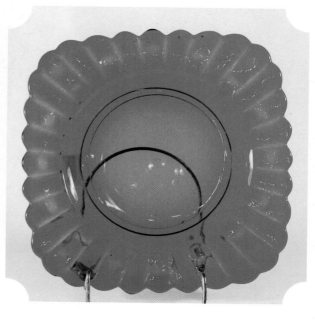

No.1404 Old Sandwich plate, Tangerine, rare.

No. 3360 Penn Charter parfait, Hawthorne and goblet, Flamingo.

No. 121 Pinwheel candlesticks, Flamingo.

Parade cane, carried by workers in Labor Day parades, Tangerine.

No. 4231 favor vase, No. 1401 Empress cup and saucer, No. 4227 favor vase, No. 4230 favor vase, Tangerine.

No. 3389 Duquesne goblet, parfait, cocktail, Tangerine.

No. 1776 Kalonyal covered butter, ruby stain.

No. 4027 Christos decanter, Tangerine on red side.

No. 1295 Bead Swag bud rose bowl, mug with applied handle, handled mug, ruby stain.

No. 365 Queen Anne tumbler, half-gallon jug, ruby stain.

No. 335 Prince of Wales, Plumes tumbler, tankard, ruby stain.

No. 335 Prince of Wales, Plumes oval, ruby stain.

No. 300 Peerless covered sugar, spoon, ruby stain, rare.

23

No. 1235 Beaded Panel and Sunburst nappy, amberette panels.

No. 1295 Bead Swag spoon, Emerald.

No. 1225 Plain Band toy sugar (no lid), toy butter, toy cream, ruby stain.

No. 1245 Star and Zipper nappy, Emerald.

No. 160 Locket on Chain salver, Emerald.

No. 1205½ Fancy
Loop bar, Emerald.

No. 1255 Pineapple and Fan table set, Emerald.

No. 42 Elegance salt,
Marigold.

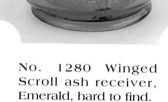

No. 1280 Winged
Scroll ash receiver,
Emerald, hard to find.

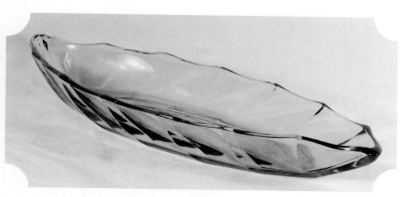

No. 3380 Old Dominion parfait,
Sahara; goblet, Marigold.

No. 1252 Twist celery, Marigold.

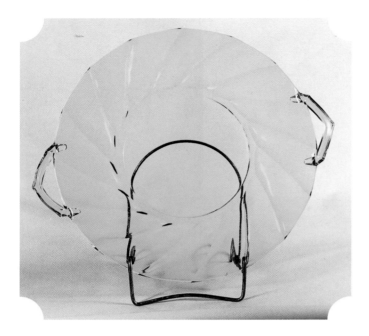

No. 1252 Twist sandwich plate, Marigold.

No. 3350 Wabash ice tea, Marigold.

No. 1210 relish, Marigold.

No. 2516 Circle Pair tumbler, Moongleam.

No. 1229 Octagon muffin plate, Moongleam.

No. 1170 Pleat and Panel oil,
Moongleam.

No. 1236 Eagle plate, Moongleam.

No. 105 Pembroke candelabra, Moongleam.

No. 3355 Fairacre goblets, Flamingo, Moongleam.

No. 357 Duck ashtray, Moongleam, Flamingo.

No. 1401 Empress footed mint, Moongleam.

No. 4157 Steele rose bowl, Moongleam.

No. 125 Leaf candlestick, Moongleam.

Nos. 1522, 1529, 1527 Ponies, standing, balking, kicking, Stiegel Blue, rare.

No. 1191 Lobe handled spice tray, Moongleam with silver band.

No. 3370 Gascony goblet, Stiegel Blue, rare.

No. 3404 Spanish cordial, goblet, cocktail, comport, Stiegel Blue.

No. 4044 New Era ice tea, claret, saucer champagne, Stiegel Blue, rare.

No. 1231 Ribbed Octagon rum pat, No. 1434 Tom and Jerry mug, Stiegel Blue.

No. 301 candelabrum, Stiegel Blue.

No. 1447 Rococo plate, Stiegel Blue, rare.

No. 1401 Empress dolphin footed candlestick, vase, No. 135 candlestick, Alexandrite.

No. 3381 Creole goblet, footed soda, cocktail, Alexandrite.

The new model glass works of A. H. Heisey & Co., located in this city (Newark, Ohio) are nearing completion, and when finished will deserve their name, as they will in plan, convenience, and equipment be second to none in the country. Mr. A. H. Heisey, the head of the firm, deserves the credit for all this, as he has drawn upon his knowledge of the business, the fruits of an experience of many years, to bring the new plant as nearly as possible to perfection. This same knowledge will come into advantageous play in the management of the new enterprise, which can be counted upon, under Mr. Heisey's direction, to win success by putting upon the market only first class goods in all lines covered by the output. Mr. Heisey is still young and vigorous, full of vim and energy, of well balanced judgment, and possessing every qualification necessary to win success. A brief description of the new factory will interest the readers of China, Glass & Lamps. The new factory building is in size 90x90 feet, the working floor being 12 feet above ground level. It will be equipped with one 16-inch pot furnace, arranged with 48-inch arches, and having four Nicholson gas producers connected with it. The stack is 112 feet high from ground to top. The lehrs and glory holes are connected with one of the improved Nicholson gas producers. There are six lehrs, 56 feet long, with 60-inch pans. The lehr and mold room will be 55x90 feet, with four brick arches underneath to be used for storage of materials, etc. The warehouse is 60x152 feet, three stories high, the mold shop 33x61 feet, three stories high. Fine offices will be located in a building separate from the factory. The roof of the factory, lehr, and mold rooms is of iron. All the lumber used, such as posts, joists, flooring, etc., are of native hard wood, principally oak, insuring the greatest security against fire. The entire plant will be heated by steam.

In 1895 A. H. Heisey started to build his new factory in Newark, Ohio, completely modern with the latest equipment and design then available. The factory was scheduled to open in early 1896; but set backs in construction, including the unfortunate collapse of an entire wall, delayed the opening until April 1896, when the first glass was actually made at the factory.

Despite this, A. H. Heisey & Co. had new samples on display at the Monongahela House in Pittsburgh in January of 1896. Heisey recognized that the success of his new company depended on the quick acceptance of new designs by the buyers who made the trip to Pittsburgh yearly. To miss the January show would effectively postpone his company debut for another year. In order to have samples on display, Heisey had the Robinson Glass Co. of nearby Zanesville, Ohio, produce the first pieces of No. 1200 Cut Block and No. 1201 Fandango.

Early trade journal accounts highly praise the new designs made by the Heisey company, and go into great detail to remark that all the patterns being brought out by the company were entirely new. No old molds are being worked, because the firm

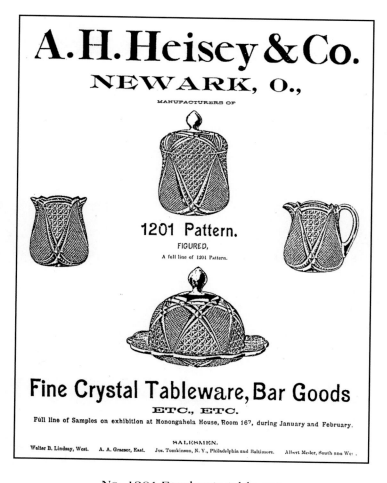

No. 1201 Fandango table set.

and lighted by electricity from a plant installed in the works. The entire works are being constructed under the supervision of John Nicholson, Jr., the original builder of the Nicholson gas producing furnaces. The works will be under roof by November 14, weather permitting, and are expected to be making glass by the middle of December. They will employ about 250 hands. The present mold shop is located in one of the machine works of Newark, where twelve mold makers are busy at work on two handsome lines of tableware for the spring trade. Everything about the works is conveniently arranged. The facilities for the receipt of raw materials and fuel and the shipment of ware are unsurpassed, a switch from the Panhandle Railroad reaching each side of the factory. The location is within the city limits, and is beautiful. Electric street cars run by the property, making it easy of access. China, Glass & Lamps, November 6, 1895.

A telegram of November 13 from Newark, Ohio, says: The northwest corner of the mammoth table glass factory, now being constructed in East Newark by Ferguson & Son, for A. H. Heisey, of Pittsburgh, collapsed about two o'clock this afternoon, burying four men under the debris. Samuel Cooper, aged 30, unmarried, who was working under an arch, is undoubtedly dead, but his body has not been found. Albert Boss, of Vail Street, and Wm. Brookins, of Riler Street, were rescued by their fellow workmen, who threw off the bricks and lumber that was crushing them. Both, however, are in a serious condition. Thomas Hastings and Addison Sidden, of Mansfield were covered with debris, but were only slightly hurt. The building was being roofed when the disaster occurred. It is thought that the recent copious rains weakened the walls. Mr. Nicholson, of Pittsburgh, representing Mr. Heisey, said tonight that the damage to the building would not exceed $2,000. China, Glass & Lamps, November 20, 1895.

has no old or second-hand molds, but proposes to put a new set on the market at least every six months, or as fast as new molds can be designed and executed in their shop, China, Glass & Lamps, September, 1896. Of course, in the early days, much of the production of the new company was in plain ware such as beer mugs, tumblers, salts and peppers, and other small items in good demand. Surely these plain items were the "bread and butter" production which made the introduction of new patterns possible.

The company was incorporated in West Virginia in 1896, with A. H. Heisey, George Duncan Heisey, Edgar Wilson Heisey, W. B. Lindsay, and D. C. Snyder listed as stockholders.

Many former workers from Geo. Duncan & Sons of Pittsburgh had followed A. H. Heisey to Newark to work in the new factory. The company started production with seasoned, knowledgeable workers — mold makers, hot metal workers, and even a designer, Andrew J. Sanford, who for many years was responsible for most of the new designs made by the fledgling company. Heisey personally was always held in high regard by his employees. Because of trouble in the glass world with the formation of the large combines (U. S. Glass and National Glass), many men happily relocated their families to Newark to work for a man they admired.

The famous Heisey trademark, the H within a Diamond was first put into use in November 1900 according to the patent application made in June of 1901. Prior to this no piece of Heisey glass had the trademark.

Rose, a color very similar to the later Flamingo, was made in very small quantities probably during 1901.

The following are the major patterns introduced by the Heisey company listed according to their first years of production.

1896:

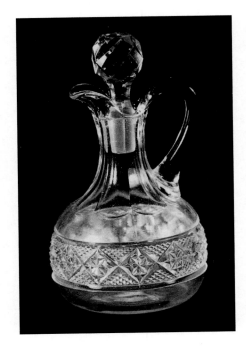

No. 1200 Cut Block oil, wrong stopper.

Cut Block, No. 1200
Date: 1896 to ca. 1899
Colors: Crystal, individual sugar and cream in Ivorina Verde

Comments: "The sets of tableware shown consist of No. 1200, an imitation of cut base and plain top, designed for plain and decorated sets, a combination of a cut star and diamond cut figure, which has been very favorably received by buyers, and has been praised by most of the salesmen of the older firms as a very meritorious production." *China, Glass & Lamps*, January 22, 1896.

    No. 1200 Cut Block was never marked with the Diamond H since production preceded the use of the famous trademark. The decorative band on the bottom portion of the pieces is made up of alternating areas of diamond point and a square filled with fine cut — both motifs borrowed from cut glass. A few of the pieces in the pattern survived until about 1898 or 1899 including the individual cream and open sugar. These two items are sometimes found in Ivorina Verde (custard) glass. Prices for these pieces in Ivorina Verde are $45.00 each. Late in the production of Cut Block, a berry set remained and was renumbered as No. 170. There have been no reproductions of this pattern. Decorations include ruby stain, amber stain in various styles, and Engraving No. 26 on more than 35 pieces. The small tankard cream was decorated with Elks etching. Prices are for crystal pieces. For engraved pieces, add 25%; for ruby stain or amber stain, add 50%+.

Bowl, 7" or 8" (comport)	$65.00
Bowl, footed, covered, 7" or 8" (comport)	130.00
Bowl, footed, shallow, 10" (comport)	75.00
Bowl, footed, straight or flared, 8" or 9" (comport)	80.00
Butter & cover	125.00
Celery, tall	65.00
Celery, tray, large	35.00
Celery tray, medium	30.00
Cracker jar & cover	175.00
Cream	65.00
Cream, individual	30.00
Cream, tankard, ½ pint	45.00
Custard (punch cup)	50.00
Finger bowl	30.00
Jelly, 4½" or flared, 5"	40.00
Jug, 1 quart	95.00
Jug, ½ gallon	150.00
Molasses can, 13 oz. (metal handle)	100.00
Nappy & cover, 7" or 8"	65.00
Nappy, crimped, 8"	45.00
Nappy, ice cream, 4" or 6"	22.00
Nappy, nut, 4" or 4½" (cupped)	20.00
Nappy, nut, 6", 7", or 8" (cupped)	45.00
Nappy, orange, 8"	45.00
Nappy, shallow, 5" or 6"	20.00
Nappy, shallow, 8", 10", or 11"	45.00
Nappy, straight or flared, 4" or 4½"	20.00
Nappy, straight or flared, 6" or 7"	35.00
Nappy, straight or flared, 8" or 9"	45.00
Oil & stopper	95.00
Olive, 5" or 6"	25.00
Oval, 6", 7", or 8"	25.00
Pickle tray	25.00
Pitcher, 3 pint (#1200½)	140.00
Plate, 4½", 5½", or 6½"	30.00
Plate, 9", 11", or 13"	70.00 – 100.00
Salt & pepper, pr.	110.00
Salt, individual	27.00
Salver, 9"	125.00
Spoon	65.00
Sugar & cover	75.00
Sugar, individual	27.00
Tankard, ½ gallon	140.00
Toothpick	80.00
Tumbler	35.00
Water bottle	95.00
Wine	70.00

No. 1200 Cut Block large nappy.

Original ad: No. 1200 Cut Block table set.

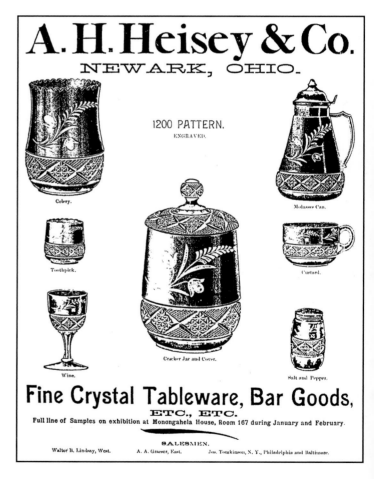

Original ad for No. 1200 Cut Block. Top: celery, molasses can. Middle: toothpick, cracker jar & cover, custard. Bottom: wine, salt. All with engraving.

Fandango, No. 1201
Date: 1896. By 1903 only 11 items remained.
By 1909 only the ice cream set was available.
Color: Crystal only

Comments: "The No. 1201 pattern is also an imitation cut figure and shows up especially well in the larger pieces and the shapeliness of the various pieces comprising the set." *China, Glass & Lamps,* January 22, 1896.

The firm of L. J. Rodgers (Pittsburgh) reported in 1896 that they were decorating both No. 1200 Cut Block and No. 1201 Fandango in "rich ruby" and amber. No. 1201 Fandango was the companion pattern brought out in 1896. Fancy figured, it was available only in clear and not marked with the Diamond H. Fandango is a more extensive pattern than Cut Block and easier to find. The pattern has not been reproduced. Most bowls have plain rims which follow the outline of the design, but they are also found with small scallops on the rim. Heisey called items with a gold rim the Klondike assortment. For gold decoration, add 10%+.

Bar tumbler or toothpick, 3 oz. $70.00
Bonbon, #1 or #2 ......20.00
Bowl, jelly, 6" 30.00
Bowl, 7" or 8" (comport) 65.00
Bowl, nut, 7" or 8" (comport) 70.00
Bowl, shallow, 9" or 10" (comport) 80.00
Bowl, flared, 8" or 9" (comport) 80.00
Finger bowl, straight, flared, or cupped 30.00
Butter, individual 30.00
Butter & cover 120.00
Cake basket, 9" 130.00
Celery (tall) 70.00
Celery tray, 11" 40.00
Cracker jar & cover, large 195.00
Cracker jar & cover, small 175.00
Cream 70.00
Cream, individual 45.00
Cream, hotel 40.00
Cream, ½ pint 55.00
Custard (punch cup) 25.00
Horseradish & cover 75.00
Ice tub with or without drainer 140.00
Ice tub with plate 140.00
Jelly, handled, 5½", or 3 corner, 5½" 30.00
Jelly, 4½" or 5" (tall) 60.00
Molasses can, #1, #2, #4, or #5, 7 oz. 120.00
Molasses can, 13 oz. 135.00
Nappy, 4", 4½", 5", or 6" 25.00
Nappy, 7" or 8" 55.00
Nappy, flared, 4½" or 5" 25.00
Nappy, flared, 7", 8", or 9" 55.00

Nappy, shallow, 5" or 6" 25.00
Nappy, shallow, 8", 9", or 10" 55.00
Nappy, nut, 6", 7" or 8" 55.00
Nappy, crimped or cupped, 6", 7", or 8" 55.00
Nappy, square ice cream, 5½" 25.00
Oblong, 7", 8", or 9" 40.00
Oil & stopper, 4 oz. or 6 oz. 90.00
Oil & stopper, 8 oz. 110.00
Olive, 4½" or 5" 25.00
Pickle tray, 6" 35.00
Pitcher, squat, ½ gallon 400.00
Plate, cheese, 8" 50.00
Rose bowl, 4" 55.00
Rose bowl, 7" 85.00
Salt & pepper, pr., #1, #2, or #3 ......90.00
Salt, individual 25.00
Salver, 9" 100.00
Spoon 65.00
Spoon tray 60.00
Sugar & cover 85.00
Sugar, hotel 40.00
Sugar, individual 45.00
Sugar sifter 125.00
Tankard, ½ gallon 225.00
Tankard cream 65.00
Toothpick 110.00
Tray, ice cream, 14" 125.00
Tumbler 45.00
Tumbler, champagne 55.00
Water bottle 95.00
Wine 65.00

No. 1201 Fandango hotel cream with gold.

No. 1201 Fandango covered horseradish.

No. 1201 Fandango celery.

No. 1201 Fandango large nappy.
Note finely scalloped or beaded rim.

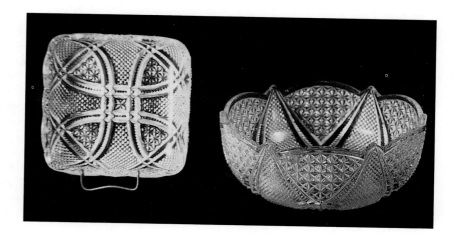

No. 1201 Fandango square
ice cream nappy and nappy.

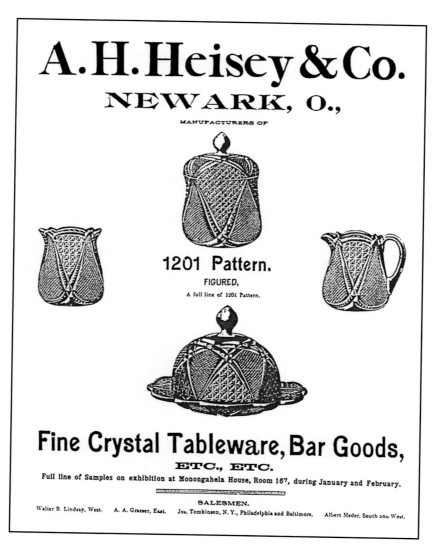

Original ad: No. 1201 Fandango table set, 1896 ad.

Fancy Loop, Nos. 1205, 1205½
Date: 1896. In 1903 12 items remained. Discontinued by 1909.
Colors: Crystal, Emerald

Comments: "Their new pattern, No. 1205, is an imitation cut, the characteristics of which are the beaded or pillar line of light, supplemented with diamond pointed double incut parallel and cross lines, filled in with faceted hobnails, and quartered faceted squares, which, by their deep cutting and angular structure, show off the crystal to fine advantage." *China, Glass & Lamps*, January 1897.

    A. H. Heisey amazed the glassware trade in late 1896 when he brought out a third pattern, No. 1205 now known as Fancy Loop. This became the most popular pattern so far and had many more pieces than either of its predecessors. Decorations include gold on crystal and Emerald, AA heavy gold and BB gold edge, and ruby stain and gold on crystal (rare). In addition, it was made not only in clear, but in Emerald green which is highly desirable today. Occasionally the small molasses can is found with fittings to make a miniature hand lamp. No. 1205½ pieces do not bear the distinctive loops of the pattern, but do still have all the major pattern elements such as the broad clear bars, cane, etc. Be aware that the correct lid for the mustard jar actually is a Fandango lid. The pieces are almost always unmarked with the exception of tumblers which occasionally are marked with the Diamond H. For Emerald, add 200 – 250%.

Bar tumbler, 2 oz. (#1205½)	$22.00
Basket, fruit	130.00
Bonbon, #1, #2, or #3	25.00
Butter & cover	120.00
Butter, individual	32.00
Celery dip	40.00
Celery tray, 11", A, B, or C shape	60.00
Celery tray, oval, 8", 9", or 10"	60.00
Celery (tall)	60.00
Claret, straight or cupped	40.00
Cocktail, large	35.00
Cocktail, small	35.00
Cologne & stopper, 1 oz.	200.00
Comport, footed, crimped, or cupped, 7" or 8" (bowl)	85.00
Comport, footed, flared, 8" or 9" (bowl)	85.00
Comport, footed, nut, 7" or 8" (bowl)	85.00
Comport, footed, square, 7" or 8" (bowl)	85.00
Comport, footed, straight, 7" or 8" (bowl)	85.00
Cracker jar & cover	200.00
Cracker jar & cover, medium	225.00
Cream	55.00
Cream, hotel	35.00
Cream, individual	50.00
Cream, tankard, ½ pint or pint	55.00
Custard (punch cup)	22.00
Dish, oval, 7", 8", or 9"	60.00
Dish, oval, A shape, 7", 8", or 9"	60.00

No. 1205 Fancy Loop cocktail.

No. 1205 Fancy Loop table set — sugar and cover, cream, spoon, and butter and cover.

Dish, square, 4½" 20.00
Dish, square, 9" 60.00
Finger bowl, straight, flared, cupped, or
    crimped...25.00
Goblet, straight or cupped...........................50.00
Ice tub & drainer, 9" 135.00
Jelly, handled, 5½", or 3 corner, 5½" 40.00
Jug, claret...165.00
Molasses can, 7 oz. 85.00
Molasses can, 13 oz. 145.00
Mustard & cover 90.00
Nappy, 3 cornered or straight, 4", 4½", or 6" ..25.00
Nappy, 3 cornered or straight, 7" or 8"..........50.00
Nappy, crimped, flared, or cupped, 6", 7", or 8"..50.00
Nappy, shallow, 5" or 6"............................25.00
Nappy, shallow, 8", 9", or 10"......................50.00
Nappy, square, 4"...................................20.00
Oil & stopper, 6 oz.................................60.00
Pickle tray 25.00
Pitcher, squat, quart 150.00
Pitcher, squat, 3 pint or ½ gallon 130.00
Plate, cheese, 8" or 9" 60.00
Plate, finger bowl 25.00
Potpourri jar & cover, medium or large........300.00
Punch bowl, 10" (no foot) 295.00

Punch bowl & foot, flared, 12"....................400.00
Punch bowl, crimped, or flared, with foot, 14"..400.00+
Punch glass (footed)................................35.00
Rose bowl, 4"......................................65.00
Rose bowl, 7"......................................85.00
Salt & pepper, pr, #1..............................90.00
Salt & pepper, pr. (#1205½)........................90.00
Salt, individual...................................20.00
Salver, 9" 100.00
Saucer champagne 45.00
Sherry 50.00
Spoon tray 30.00
Spoon 55.00
Sugar & cover......................................75.00
Sugar, hotel 35.00
Sugar, individual..................................50.00
Tankard, ½ gallon 125.00
Toothpick 85.00
Tumbler, 8 oz. 40.00
Tumbler, 8 oz. (#1205½) 45.00
Vase, #1 or #2, 10"................................110.00
Vase, #1, #2, or #3, 8"............................95.00
Water bottle, regular or squat 90.00
Wine, straight or cupped 50.00

No. 1205 Fancy Loop celery dip.

No. 1205 Fancy Loop cheese plate.

No. 1205 Fancy Loop square nappy.

No. 1205 Fancy Loop
7 oz. molasses can.

No. 1205 Fancy Loop handled jelly.

Vertical Bead & Panel, No. 8
Date: Ca. 1896, but uncertain. Discontinued before 1909.
Color: Crystal

Comments: This pattern is difficult to find and is never marked, indicating it was made prior to 1900. Most likely it was introduced in either 1896 or 1897. Prices are low due to the limited number of items and the plainness of the pattern.

Lily bowl	$22.00
Nappy, 4"	8.00
Nappy, crimped, 8½"	15.00
Nappy, flared, 9"	15.00
Nappy, shallow, 4½"	8.00
Nappy, shallow, 10"	15.00
Plate, 11"	18.00
Rose bowl, 7"	25.00
Shade, electric, 2½" ring	35.00
Shade, gas, 4" ring	35.00

No. 8 Vertical Bead & Panel
small nappy.

Single Slash & Panel, No. 9
Date: Ca. 1896, but uncertain. Discontinued before 1909.
Colors: Crystal, very rare in Canary

Comments: This pattern is difficult to find and is never marked with the Diamond H, indicating it was made prior to 1900. Most likely it was introduced in either 1896 or 1897. Prices are low due to the limited number of items and the plainness of the pattern. Any Canary item is valued at $300.00+.

Lily bowl...$22.00
Nappy, 4"..8.00
Nappy, flared, 9"............................15.00
Nappy, shallow, 10".......................15.00
Nappy, straight or crimped, 8".........15.00
Pitcher, 3 pint.................................45.00
Plate, 11".......................................18.00
Rose bowl, 6"..................................35.00
Shade, electric, 2½" ring.................35.00
Shade, gas, 4" ring..........................35.00

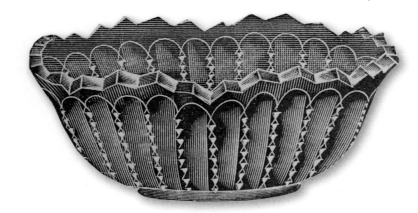

No. 9 Single Slash & Panel nappy.

Double Slash & Panel, No. 12
Date: Ca. 1896, but uncertain. Discontinued before 1909.
Color: Crystal

Comments: This pattern is difficult to find and is never marked with the Diamond H, indicating it was made prior to 1900. Most likely it was introduced in either 1896 or 1897. Prices are low due to the limited number of items and the plainness of the pattern.

Lily bowl $22.00
Nappy, 4"...8.00
Nappy, flared, 9"..15.00
Nappy, shallow, 4½".......................................8.00
Nappy, shallow, 10".....................................15.00
Nappy, straight or crimped, 8"......................15.00
Plate, 11"..18.00
Rose bowl, 6"...35.00
Shade, gas, 4" ring 35.00

No. 12 Double Slash & Panel nappy.

1897:

"Among American manufacturers who are fully up to date in their lines of pressed glassware, prominence must be given by virtue of merit, to the A. H. Heisey & Co. of Newark, Ohio. Mr. Heisey was for many years identified with the old house of Geo. Duncan & Sons, for whom he sold goods on the road before becoming an active partner and officer of the company, and the experience thus gained as to the taste, requirements, and demands of jobbers and consumers, has stood him in good stead ever since. The 16-pot factory built at Newark was started last spring, and one advantage of the new company consisted in the fact that there was an entire absence of old molds, patterns, and designs to work off and sandwich between a few new patterns. Every pattern put on the market since last spring has been of original design, and while some old glass men thought it a mistake in the management to spring its third new tableware line on the market early in the fall, it has been found that the line is of sufficient merit to hold its place among the finest patterns shown this year, while new pieces have been constantly added to round out and keep the pattern, No. 1205, fresh and brilliant as the best." *China, Glass & Lamps*, February 1897.

Punty Band, No. 1220

Date: 1897. Only a few items remained by 1909.

Colors: Crystal; individual cream, salt & pepper, mug in Ivorina Verde (custard); individual cream and mug in Opal (milk glass); a few very rare items in crystal opalescent.

Comments: "The exhibit contains a few advance pieces of the new No. 1220 pattern, a combination of plain and figured line, the plain surface predominating, making it available as plain set, or for engraving and decoration." *China, Glass & Lamps*, January 1897.

Pieces in this pattern are found both marked or unmarked with the Diamond H. Some pieces such as the toothpick and bowls are found with either a beaded top or a scalloped top. Decorations include engraving, ruby stain, decoration no. 20 gold bead, decoration no. 21 ruby ball, decoration no. 22 amber ball, or decoration no. 23 green ball (the wide band in which the punties are located). Occasionally pieces, especially stems, are found with an English registry number 310925 embossed. Made in over 70 items.

Bonbon, #1, #2, or #3.....................................$30.00	Comport, 6", 7", or 8" (bowl)............................55.00
Bowl, footed, covered, 5" or 6" (comport).......95.00	Comport, 9" or 10" (bowl).................................75.00
Bowl, footed, covered, 7" or 8" (comport).....135.00	Comport, crimped, 4" or 4½" (bowl)................22.00
Bowl, footed, crimped, 5" or 6" (comport).......70.00	Comport, crimped or straight, 6", 7", or 8"
Bowl, footed, crimped, 7" or 8" (comport).......95.00	(bowl)..55.00
Bowl, footed, shallow, 6" or 8" (comport)........70.00	Comport, shallow, 5" or 6" (bowl)...................45.00
Bowl, footed, shallow, 9" or 10" (comport)......95.00	Cream...55.00
Bowl, footed, straight or crimped, 5" or 6"	Cream, hotel..45.00
(comport)..70.00	Cream, individual...35.00
Bowl, footed, straight or crimped, 7" or 8"	Jelly, handled, regular, or 3 corner, 5½"..........45.00
(comport)..95.00	Molasses can, 13 oz. 150.00
Butter & cover...125.00	Oblong, 8"...50.00
Cake basket, 9" or 10"..................................150.00	Oil & stopper, 6 oz...65.00
Celery (tall)...50.00	Pickle, 6"...25.00
Claret..45.00	Pitcher, ½ gallon..165.00
Comport & cover, 6", 7", or 8" (bowl).............120.00	Plate, 5" or 6"...40.00
Comport, 4" or 4½" (bowl)................................22.00	Plate, 9", 10", or 11"...85.00

Salt & pepper, pr. (2 styles)............................90.00	Sugar, individual..75.00
Salt, individual...40.00	Tankard, ½ pint or pint 60.00
Salt, table (master)...60.00	Tankard, quart..180.00
Salver, 9" or 10"...110.00	Tankard, ½ gallon...155.00
Spoon...55.00	Toothpick 60.00
Spoon tray 35.00	Tumbler...50.00
Sugar & cover 85.00	Wine..50.00
Sugar, hotel...35.00	

No. 1220 Punty Band celery with amber stain and purple punties.

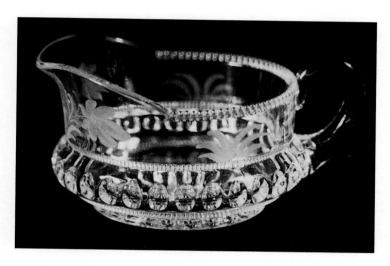

No. 1220 Punty Band hotel cream with engraving.

No. 1220 Punty Band covered sugar, spoon, cream, covered butter.

Plain Band, No. 1225
Date: 1897. Only a few pieces remained by 1909.
Colors: Crystal, sherbet (often mistaken for a toothpick) in Ivorina Verde (custard)
Patents: Given patent No. 28180 for cream and No. 28181 on 1-18-1898,
A. H. Heisey listed as designer

Comments: "A. H. Heisey & Co., of Newark, O., are getting out some very elegant gold edge decorations on their 1225 ware. ...The firm is making a strong bid for favor in the decorating line and the 1225 pattern is one which affords large scope for exertion in this direction. The outlines of the design are principally plain, but at the edges there is room for the introduction of an ornamentative feature and their decorator has availed himself of it to the fullest extent." *China, Glass & Lamps*, July 1897.

"They have the 1225 done in new decorations of gold band and engraved."... *China, Glass & Lamps*, January 1898.

The only Heisey pattern to have a toy table set. The toy spoon is the same as the toothpick. Do not confuse the true toothpick with the sherbet. The toothpick will have a beaded rim while the sherbet has a plain rim. This very large pattern was made for several years. Decorations include engraving, decoration no. 13 gold bead, decoration no. 16 green on ball, decoration no. 17 bronze on ball, and decoration no. 18 pink on ball (the plain "bulge" near the base), decoration no. 13, gold. Many items are marked, but some are not. Over 90 pieces made.

Berry, square, 4" or 4½"	$20.00
Berry, square, 7" or 8"	35.00
Bonbon, #1, #2, or #3 (rectangular)	22.00
Bowl & cover, footed, 5" or 6" (comport)	95.00
Bowl & cover, footed, 7" or 8" (comport)	120.00
Bowl, footed, regular or crimped, 5" or 6" (comport)	65.00
Bowl, footed, regular or crimped, 7" or 8" (comport)	95.00
Bowl, footed, shallow, 6" (comport)	70.00
Bowl, footed, shallow, 8", 9", or 10" (comport)	95.00
Butter & cover	95.00
Butter & cover, toy	125.00
Cake basket, 9" or 10"	110.00
Celery (tall)	40.00
Cheese & cover	145.00
Comport, 4" or 4½" (bowl or nappy, regular or crimped)	22.00
Comport, 6" or 7" (bowl or nappy, regular or crimped)	45.00
Comport, 8" (bowl or nappy)	55.00
Comport, shallow, 5" or 6" (bowl or nappy)	22.00
Comport, shallow, 8" (bowl or nappy)	45.00
Comport, shallow, 9" or 10" (bowl or nappy)	55.00
Comport & cover, 6" or 7" (bowl & cover)	75.00
Comport & cover, 8" (bowl & cover)	85.00
Cream	40.00
Cream, hotel	32.00
Cream, individual	40.00
Cream, toy	40.00
Decanter, individual	60.00
Jelly, handled, regular or 3 corner, 5½"	30.00
Molasses can, 13 oz.	100.00
Molasses can, hotel	75.00
Mustard & cover	125.00
Oblong, 8"	30.00
Oil & stopper, 4 oz. or 6 oz.	45.00
Pickle, 6" (rectangular)	20.00
Pitcher, ½ gallon	125.00
Plate, 5" or 6"	25.00
Plate, 9", 10", or 11"	65.00
Salt & pepper, pr. (3 styles)	80.00
Salt, individual	20.00
Salt, table (master)	55.00
Salver, 9" or 10"	80.00
Sherbet	22.00
Spoon	35.00
Spoon tray (rectangular)	25.00
Sugar & cover	65.00
Sugar & cover, toy	95.00
Sugar, hotel	32.00
Sugar, individual	40.00
Tankard, ½ pint or pint	45.00
Tankard, quart	145.00
Tankard, ½ gallon	125.00
Toothpick or toy spoon	45.00
Tumbler	30.00
Wine	35.00

No. 1225 Plain Band hotel molasses can, gold band with engraving.

No. 1225 Plain Band comport with No. 1220 Punty Band base.

No. 1225 Plain Band oil.

No. 1225 Plain Band covered sugar, cream, spoon, covered butter.

Beaded Panel & Sunburst, No. 1235
Date: 1897. Discontinued before 1913.
Colors: Crystal; punch set in Emerald, Ivorina Verde, and Opal, all rare

Comments: "They call it No. 1235 and it is the most elegant design we have yet seen in pressed glassware. The pieces are ornamented with fluting supplemented by chrysanthemums, which are as perfect representations of those pretty flowers as it is possible to make in glass.... about 65 pieces in all." *China, Glass & Lamps,* September 1897. (By January, 1898, mention was made of 80 pieces.) "This firm is making a magnificent 14-inch punch bowl in opal, with foot or without, which is having an excellent sale. They also make it in ivorina verde, emerald and crystal, plain and decorated." *China, Glass & Lamps,* August 1899.

Occasionally pieces are found marked with the Diamond H. This is a lengthy pattern of over 80 pieces. Decorations include decoration no. 25 gold, decoration no. 26 green, decoration no. 27 bronze, and decoration no. 28 ruby, decoration no. 29 green and gold and no. 30 ruby and gold, amberette stain on grooves, and blue and yellow enamel. Amber stained examples are desirable, commanding 100% over plain pieces.

Bar tumbler, 3 oz.	$40.00
Berry, 4" or 4½"	25.00
Berry, 7", 8", or 9"	75.00
Berry, flared, 8", 9" or 10"	75.00
Bonbon, #1, #2, or #3	45.00
Bowl, high foot, 8" or 9", (comport)	100.00
Bowl, low foot, 6", 7", or 8" (comport)	80.00
Bowl, low foot, crimped, 5", 6", 7", or 8" (comport)	75.00
Butter & cover	125.00
Cake basket, 9"	160.00
Catsup, 8 oz.	110.00
Celery dish, 11"	60.00
Celery, tall	60.00
Cracker jar & cover	175.00
Cream	60.00
Cream, hotel	35.00
Cream, individual	50.00
Custard (punch cup)	25.00
Decanter, handled	165.00
Jelly, handled, round or 3 corner, 5½"	45.00
Jelly, low foot, 5"	45.00
Molasses can, hotel	145.00
Mustard & cover	85.00
Nappy, 4½" or 5"	25.00
Nappy, 6", 7", or 8"	65.00
Nappy, crimped, 4½" or 5"	35.00
Nappy, crimped, 7" or 8"	70.00
Oil & stopper, 4 oz. or 6 oz.	90.00
Pickle tray	40.00
Pitcher, 3 pint	200.00
Pitcher, stuck handle, ½ gallon	200.00

Plate, 8" or 9"	50.00
Punch bowl & foot, 14"	350.00+
Salt & pepper, pr., #1, #2, or #3	150.00
Salt, individual	40.00
Salver, 9"	140.00
Salver, low foot, 7" or 8"	90.00
Salver, low foot, 10" or 11"	110.00
Shade, gas, 4" ring (#10)	95.00
Spoon	55.00
Spoon tray, 6"	40.00
Sugar & cover	100.00
Sugar, hotel	35.00
Sugar, individual	50.00
Tankard, 2 qt., plain rim, stuck handle	200.00
Toothpick	175.00
Tray, water, 10"	170.00
Tumbler, 8 oz. or 9 oz.	50.00
Water bottle	120.00
Wine	40.00

No. 1235 Beaded Panel & Sunburst hotel sugar with unusual blue enamel and yellow stain.

No. 1235 Beaded Panel & Sunburst covered sugar, covered butter, spoon, cream.

No. 1235 Beaded Panel & Sunburst oil.

No. 1235 Beaded Panel & Sunburst.
Top: Nappy. Bottom: Berry, wine, 10" tray, handled decanter.

Star & Zipper, No. 1245
Date: 1897 to 1903
Colors: Crystal, Emerald

Comments: Not marked with the Diamond H. This small pattern is a variation of No. 1250 Groove and Slash. For Emerald, add 150 – 200%.

Berry, 4½" $40.00
Berry, 9"..85.00
Jug 165.00

No. 1245 Star & Zipper berry bowl.

1896:

Emerald green was introduced in this year, Heisey's first attempt at making colored glass. Many patterns made in this year were made in the new color, as were previous patterns which were still popular, such as Star and Zipper, and Fancy Loop.

Groove & Slash, No. 1250
Date: 1898. Only 12 items remained in 1903. Discontinued before 1913.
Color: Crystal

Comments: "Their handsome imitation cut No. 1250 pattern has been the admiration of everybody who has seen it ever since it was placed on the market last winter." *China, Glass & Lamps,* August 1899.

Most pieces are not marked with the Diamond H. Pieces in this pattern may also be found with various silver-plated mountings. Price lists indicate that pieces were available "unfinished." This probably accounts for pieces which have been seen which were never fire polished.

Bonbon $25.00	Pickle tray 25.00
Bowl, high footed, 8" (comport)....................100.00	Pitcher, stuck handle, ½ gallon.....................185.00
Bowl, high footed, shallow, 9" (comport)......100.00	Plate, 5" or 6"..18.00
Butter & cover 110.00	Plate, bread, 10"..20.00
Celery 70.00	Puff, no cover..65.00
Condensed milk jar & cover or pickle jar......175.00	Rose bowl, 4", 5", or 7" 95.00
Cracker jar & cover....................................150.00	Salad, 8" or 9"..65.00
Cream 55.00	Salt & pepper, pr..90.00
Nappy, 4" or 4½"..18.00	Salver, 10"..125.00
Nappy, 7" or 8" 40.00	Shade, electric, flared (#3).............................80.00
Nappy, crimped, 7" or 8" 45.00	Shade, gas, straight (#3)................................80.00
Nappy, nut, 4" or 4½"..................................18.00	Spoon 50.00
Nappy, nut, or ice bowl, 7" or 8".....................45.00	Spoon tray 25.00
Nappy, shallow, 5" or 6" 18.00	Sugar & cover..85.00
Nappy, shallow, 8" or 9" 40.00	Tankard, ¼ gallon.......................................175.00
Oil & stopper, 6 oz......................................65.00	Tankard, ½ gallon.......................................165.00
Pickle jar, knob cover 90.00	Tumbler..30.00

No. 1250 Groove & Slash table set.

No. 1250 Groove & Slash oil, jug.

No. 1250 Groove & Slash pickle jar, cracker jar, pickle jar with knob cover.

Pineapple & Fan, No. 1255
Date: 1898 to 1907. Only 8 items remained in 1903.
Colors: Crystal, Emerald, small tankard cream in Ivorina Verde and Opal, rare pieces in Ultramarine Blue and Opalescent Canary

Comments: Most pieces are not marked with the Diamond H. This is a popular line made in over 85 pieces. Decorations include gold in two styles, one on plain top rims, the other in grooves; decoration no. 34 and 35; ruby stain on crystal is scarce. For Emerald add 200 to 250%. Rare colors are not found often enough to establish values.

Bowl, berry, oval, straight or shallow, 10" or 12"..$50.00
Bowl, berry, round, 4½" (straight sides) 20.00
Bowl, berry, round, 8" or 9" (straight sides).....50.00
Bonbon 25.00
Bowl, high foot, 7" or 8" (comport) 145.00
Bowl, high foot, flared, 8" or 9" (comport).....145.00
Bowl, high foot, nut or orange, 7" or 8"
    (comport) 145.00
Bowl, high foot, shallow, 9" or 10" (comport) ..155.00
Butter & cover 95.00
Celery, tall 55.00
Celery tray, 11" 45.00
Cracker jar & cover, #1, #2, or #3............195.00
Cream 60.00
Cream, hotel 35.00
Custard, handled (punch cup) 30.00
Jelly, footed, 5" 55.00
Jelly, handled, regular or 3 cornered, 5½".......30.00
Molasses can, 13 oz. 155.00
Mug, handled, 7 oz. 30.00
Nappy, 4" or 4½"..20.00
Nappy, 7" or 8" 55.00
Nappy, flared, 4½" or 5".............................20.00
Nappy, flared, 8" or 9"................................55.00
Nappy, nut or orange, 4" or 4½"...................20.00
Nappy, nut or orange, 7" or 8" 55.00
Nappy, shallow, 5" or 6" 20.00
Nappy, shallow, 9" or 10" 55.00
Oil & stopper, 6 oz......................................75.00
Pickle jar & cover 140.00
Pickle tray, 6" 30.00
Pitcher, ½ pint or 1 pint..............................45.00
Pitcher, 1 quart..130.00
Pitcher, 3 pint or ½ gallon...........................175.00
Plate, cheese, 7" 45.00
Rose bowl, bud, 2" 100.00
Rose bowl, 3"..100.00
Rose bowl, 4" or 5" 85.00
Rose bowl, 6" or 7" 95.00
Salt & pepper, pr., #1, #2, or #3 ....90.00

Salt, individual..50.00
Salver, footed, 10" or 11".............................155.00
Spoon 45.00
Sugar & cover 75.00
Sugar, hotel 35.00
Tankard, ½ pint 40.00
Toothpick 145.00
Tumbler, 8½ oz..35.00
Vase, 6" 35.00
Vase, 8" 40.00
Vase, 10" 50.00
Vase, 12" 60.00

No. 1255 Pineapple & Fan vase, gold decorated, Emerald.

No. 1255 Pineapple & Fan hotel cream and sugar, Emerald.

No. 1255 Pineapple & Fan pickle, Emerald.

No. 1255 Pineapple & Fan. Top: cream, No. 2 salt, spoon. Middle: toothpick, butter & cover, bud rose bowl. Bottom: covered sugar, No. 3 salt, molasses can.

51

Pointed Oval in Diamond Point, No. 150
Date: Exact date unknown, but 1898 is likely. In 1903 four items remained.
These were discontinued before 1909.
Colors: Crystal, Emerald, rare in a deep, almost black Emerald green

Comments: This short pattern is not marked with the Diamond H. Table set pieces are smaller than in most patterns. This pattern is relatively scarce except for the spoon. Add 200% for Emerald items.

Butter & cover $100.00	Nappy, 4" 18.00
Cream 75.00	Nappy, 8" 38.00
Jug, ½ gallon 140.00	Spoon 45.00
Jug & cover, ½ gallon 190.00	Sugar & cover 95.00

No. 150 Pointed Oval in Diamond Point spoon.

No. 150 Pointed Oval in Diamond Point cream.

No. 150 Pointed Oval in Diamond Point nappy.

No. 150 Pointed Oval in Diamond Point covered jug.

Locket on Chain, No. 160
Date: Exact date unknown, 1898 is likely. Discontinued by late 1906.
Colors: Crystal, scarce to rare in Emerald, Canary, and Opal,

Comments: Locket on Chain is a moderate length tableware pattern, but highly desirable. Pieces are not marked with the Diamond H. Pieces with allover ruby and gold are eagerly sought and prices are quite high (500%+). Allover light blue stain is rarely found. For Emerald add 200%, for Canary or Opal add 500%+.

Bowl, footed, 8" (comport)	$110.00
Butter & cover	145.00
Celery, tall	100.00
Cream	95.00
Custard (punch cup)	45.00
Goblet	300.00
Molasses can	265.00
Nappy, 4"	45.00
Nappy, 8"	100.00
Oil & stopper	225.00
Pitcher, 1 quart	295.00
Pitcher, ½ gallon	350.00
Plate, 8"	70.00
Salt & pepper, pr.	200.00
Salver, 9"	155.00
Shade, electric, flared (#4)	100.00
Shade, gas, straight (#4)	100.00
Spoon	90.00
Sugar & cover	150.00
Toothpick	950.00
Tumbler, 9 oz.	75.00
Wine	120.00

No. 160 Locket on Chain covered butter.

No. 160 Locket on Chain pitcher.

No. 160 Locket on
Chain footed bowl.

1899:

Ivorina Verde (custard) and Opal (milk glass) were probably introduced this year. Ivorina Verde immediately proved popular in two well-known Heisey patterns found most often in this color — Winged Scroll and Ring Band.

Winged Scroll, No. 1280
Date: 1899 to 1901
Colors: Ivorina Verde (Heisey sometimes called this Ivory), Emerald, scarce in Crystal, Canary, and Opal

Comments: This pattern is not marked with the Diamond H. Decorations include decoration no. 53 gold on figure; decoration no. 54, hand-painted roses on body on Ivorina Verde, Green, Lavender, and Brown on figure on Ivorina Verde. Winged Scroll contains many unusual pieces not found in other Heisey patterns. Heisey combined several pieces to make a dresser set and a smoking set. The trinket box and puff box were made later by Jefferson Glass in opaline (clambroth), black, and crystal, often with ruby stain or allover green stain which is often confused with true emerald glass. Heisey did not make either opaline or black. Authentic Heisey pieces have small recessed "dimples" above the winged scroll while Jefferson's is plain and flat in this area. Also, the real Heisey pieces have three dots in a row over the mid portion of the winged scroll while the Jefferson pieces have a single bar. The molasses can is sometimes found made into a hand lamp. Crystal is very difficult to find, but does not command the price of Ivorina Verde or Emerald. Prices listed are for Ivorina Verde or Emerald. For Crystal, deduct 50%. For Canary or Opal, add 100% to 200%.

Several sets were marketed by Heisey in Winged Scroll:

No. 1 Condiment set: tray, 8", oil bottle, No. 1 salt, pair
No. 2 Condiment set: tray, condiment, 10", oil bottle, salt bottle, pair
No. 3 Condiment set: tray, 8", oil bottle, No. 1 salt bottle, toothpick
No. 1 Smoker's set: tray, 8", cigar holder, match holder, ash receiver
No. 2 Smoker's set: tray, 13", cigar holder, cigarette holder, tobacco jar & cover, ash receiver, match holder
Toilet set: tray, 13", ring holder, cologne bottle, puff box & cover, trinket box & cover, pin tray, 4".

Ash receiver	$250.00
Bonbon, 5" or 6"	70.00
Bowl, footed, 8" or 9"	450.00
Bowl, footed, flared, 9"	450.00
Bowl, footed, shallow, 10"	450.00
Butter & cover	165.00
Cake basket, 9"	500.00
Card receiver, 5" or 6"	70.00
Card receiver, handled, 7½"	70.00
Celery, tall	225.00
Cigar holder	300.00
Cigarette holder	275.00
Cologne & stopper	450.00
Cream	95.00
Hair receiver & cover	185.00
Match holder	375.00
Molasses can, 7 oz.	350.00
Nappy, 4", 4½", or 5"	40.00
Nappy, 7" or 8"	100.00
Nappy, flared, 8" or 9"	120.00
Nappy, ice cream, 5" or 6"	40.00
Nappy, shallow, 9" or 10"	120.00
Nappy, 3 cornered, 5" or 6"	40.00
Oil & stopper, 6 oz.	220.00
Olive dish, 5" or 6"	55.00
Pickle, 5" or 6"	55.00

Pickle tray, 6" (oblong)	155.00
Pitcher, ½ gallon	450.00
Plate, 5" or 6"	75.00
Puff box & cover	185.00
Ring holder	450.00
Salt & pepper, pr. (#2 or #3, 2 styles)	220.00
Salver, 9"	275.00
Spoon	95.00
Sugar & cover	145.00
Tankard, ½ gallon	400.00
Tobacco jar & cover	400.00
Toothpick	230.00
Tray, 13"	195.00
Tray, condiment, 10"	250.00
Tray, pin, 4" or 5"	220.00
Tray, rectangular, 8"	180.00
Trinket box & cover	100.00
Tumbler, 8 oz.	95.00
Vase, 6"	225.00
Vase, 10"	400.00
Vase, handled, 10"	500.00

No. 1280 Winged Scroll puff box and trinket box, Emerald with gold decoration.

No. 1280 Winged Scroll small nappies and large nappy, Emerald.

No. 1280 Winged Scroll toothpick and celery, Ivorina Verde.

No. 1280 Winged Scroll cigarette holder, Ivorina Verde.

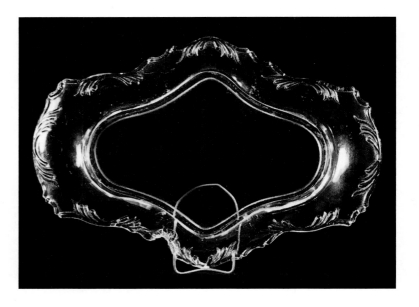

No. 1280 Winged Scroll 8" rectangular tray.

No. 1280 Winged Scroll toilet set.

Bead Swag, No. 1295
Date:1899 to 1903
Colors: Crystal, Opal, Emerald, a few items were made in Ivorina Verde

Comments: Bead Swag is a full tableware line, although it has somewhat fewer pieces than previous patterns. The egg-shaped plain pattern is particularly well suited for decorations. Decorations include: A variety of colored enamels on opal, sometimes above the beads or below the beads. Heisey price lists indicate "No. 40 Gold on edge and Pearls with broad Gold band and two narrow Green bands running around the plain portion, No. 56 Decoration is Wide Gold and two Narrow Gold Bands around plain portion and Gold Edge, No. 57 is Wide Gold and two Narrow Gold Bands around plain portion, and opal decorated No. 60, crystal amberette, and crystal engraved." Hand-painted roses or daisies on opal. Gold on Emerald and Crystal in several styles. Hand-painted florals on Emerald, sometimes combined with Gold. Ruby stain on Crystal. Many of these decorations were done by Oriental Glass of Pittsburgh. Bead Swag is not usually marked with the Diamond H, but occasionally marked pieces are found. The molasses can is sometimes found made into a hand lamp. This toothpick has been reproduced in an opaque dead-white milk glass which is very thick. These reproductions also have hand-painted decorations, but not similar to the old decorations. The original toothpick has thin sides throughout the piece, but the reproduction has very thick sides at the bottom. Prices are for pieces in Opal, the most common color found. Contrary to some opinions, original prices lists indicate that most of the pattern was made in Emerald, although it is difficult to find this color. For Crystal, deduct 50%. For Emerald or Ivorina Verde, add 100%. An exception is the Ivorina Verde goblet which is valued at $95.00.

Bonbon	$55.00
Bowl, nut, 8"	95.00
Bowl, salad, 8", 9", or 10"	95.00
Butter & cover	100.00
Celery, tall	80.00
Cream	60.00
Custard (punch cup)	30.00
Finger bowl, large	40.00
Finger bowl, small	35.00
Goblet	125.00
Jug, ½ gallon	140.00
Molasses can, 7 oz.	135.00
Mug, handled	50.00
Mug, applied handle	70.00
Nappy, 4½" or 5"	20.00
Nappy, 7", 8", or 9"	95.00
Nappy, shallow, 5" or 6"	20.00
Nappy, shallow, 9", 10", or 11"	95.00
Oil & stopper, 6 oz.	120.00
Pickle tray, #1 or #2	40.00
Plate, finger bowl, 7"	50.00
Plate, scalloped edge, 5" or 6"	30.00
Rose bowl, 2"	230.00
Salt & pepper, pr. (2 styles)	110.00
Salver, 9" or 10"	140.00
Spoon	45.00

Spoon tray (may be same as one of pickle trays)	40.00
Sugar & cover	90.00
Tankard, ½ gallon	140.00
Toothpick	135.00
Tumbler, 9 oz.	40.00
Tumbler, handled	60.00
Vase, 6"	110.00
Vase, 8"	140.00
Wine	90.00

No. 1295 Bead Swag spoon, Opal with hand-painted flower.

No. 1295 Bead Swag toothpick,
Opal with hand-painted decoration.

No. 1295 Bead Swag cream.

Peerless, Nos. 300, 300½

Date: 1899. By 1944 only a goblet, sherbet, three schoeppens, individual cream & sugar, and hotel cream & sugar remained.

Colors: Crystal. Rare in Crystal Opalescent. Candlesticks in Emerald, rare. The No. 300, 4½ oz. low-footed shallow sherbet and 8 oz. schoeppen were made in Flamingo. The No. 300 low-footed tumbler was made in Alexandrite, Moongleam, and Flamingo. The No. 300½, 2 oz. bar and the 8 oz. tumbler were made in Moongleam and Flamingo. The No. 300½ water bottle was made in Sahara. The No. 300½, 11" vase was made in Rose and Emerald. The No. 302 ice tea tumbler was made in Flamingo.

Patent: Patent No. 36400 was granted for the four light candelabrum on 8-18-1903 with A. H. Heisey listed as designer.

Comments: "A. H. Heisey & Co....have departed boldly and radically from the beaten path in designing their new line of crystal tableware, which they call No. 300. The line is severely plain being a reproduction of the old pure lead flint cut glassware of our fathers, with its limpid honest crystal, its broad cut flute, and regularly scalloped edge." *China, Glass & Lamps*, September 1899.

This is the first of Heisey's colonial-inspired patterns for which the company became so well known. This pattern name derives from Heisey's reference to it as "The Pattern Without a Peer." The base "petticoat" of Peerless is distinctive, made up of a series of small grooves just above the base. From this date until the factory closed, Heisey made at least one colonial pattern. Decorations include No. 1 gold on top plain portion with a line of gold around the base skirt, ruby stain done in the same manner as no. 1 gold is rare, no. 2 gold and engraved decoration. Other styles of gold decoration are also known. Also advertised in 1900 as decorated in "colors." Some pieces from Peerless were continued in later years as part of the No. 341 Old Williamsburg pattern. This is the first pattern in which most pieces are marked with the Diamond H. Some pieces also bear the English Registry number of 350676. It is unusual to find colonial patterns in colors, but company records indicate that at least some items were made in Flamingo and Moongleam around 1925. Tygart Valley Glass Co. made many pieces in very similar shapes to pieces of Peerless, but these are in an inferior glass.

Bar, 2½ oz. $15.00
Bitters bottle...50.00
Bonbon, #1, #2, or #3.................................25.00
Bowl, footed, 8" or 9" (comport) 90.00
Bowl, footed, flared, 8½" or 9½" (comport) 90.00
Bowl, footed, shallow, 9" or 10" (comport) 95.00
Brandy bottle 85.00
Burgundy, 3½ oz. 22.00
Butter & cover 85.00
Candelabra, 1 light, 9" pr. (#0) 200.00
Candelabra, 1 light, 12", pr (#1) 250.00
Candelabra, 2 light, pr (#2) 300.00
Candelabra, 3 light, pr. (#3) 550.00
Candelabra, 4 light, pr. (#4) 950.00
Candelabrum, 5 light, 1 only (#5) 2,000.00
Candle lamp, 1 only.................................200.00
Candlesticks, 9", pr. (#2) 225.00
Catsup & stopper, 10 oz. 80.00
Celery tray, 10" or 12".................................40.00
Celery, tall 45.00
Champagne, 6 oz...20.00
Champagne, tall, regular or flared, 3½ oz.......20.00
Claret, 4½ oz. 25.00
Cocktail, 2 oz. 20.00
Cordial, 1 oz. or ½ oz. sham 60.00
Cream 45.00
Cream, hotel 35.00
Cream, individual 38.00
Custard, 4 oz., plain or star bottom (punch cup) ..15.00
Decanter & stopper, individual 65.00
Decanter & stopper, 1 pint...........................70.00
Decanter & stopper, 1 quart 65.00
Decanter & stopper, handled, 1 pint..............70.00
Decanter, individual (no stopper)..................40.00
Dish, oval, 7"...25.00
Dish, oval, 9" or 10".....................................35.00
Dish, oval, 12"...45.00
Egg, footed, 5 oz...25.00
Egg, footed, 8 oz...30.00
Finger bowl 15.00
Goblet, 8 oz. or 10 oz. 25.00
Goblet, low footed, 8 oz................................18.00
Honey dish & cover 85.00
Ice tea (tumbler) 20.00
Ice tea (#302) 20.00
Ice tub..80.00
Jelly, footed, regular, flared or shallow, 4" or 5" ..45.00
Jelly, handled, regular, crimped, or 3
    cornered, 6" 25.00
Jug, claret...80.00
Molasses can, 13 oz. 75.00
Mustard & cover 55.00
Nappy, 4" or 4½"..12.00
Nappy, 6", 7", or 8" 35.00
Nappy, 9" or 10"...50.00

No. 300 Peerless tumbler, no. 1 gold decoration.

Nappy, berry, flared, 8½" or 9½".....................50.00
Nappy, berry, shallow, 8" or 9"........................50.00
Nappy, berry, shallow, 8½" or 10" 50.00
Nappy, flared, 4½" or 5"................................12.00
Nappy, flared, 7", 8", or 8½"..........................40.00
Nappy, flared, 9" or 11"................................50.00
Nappy, orange, 11".......................................55.00
Nappy, regular, flared, or shallow, 8" or 9" 50.00
Oil & stopper, 2 oz. or 4 oz...........................35.00
Oil & stopper, 6 oz. or 8 oz...........................45.00
Oyster cocktail, 5 oz.....................................10.00
Pickle tray, 6"...18.00
Pitcher, 1 quart..65.00
Pitcher, 3 pint 85.00
Pitcher, ½ gallon...125.00
Pitcher, 3 quart...200.00
Plate, 5" or 6"...10.00
Punch bowl & foot, 14"................................300.00
Salt & pepper, pr., #2 or #3 ....45.00
Salt & pepper, hotel, pr., #4.........................80.00
Salver, 9" or 10"...90.00
Saucer champagne, 4 oz. 20.00
Schoeppen, regular or flared, 5 oz. 15.00
Schoeppen, regular or flared, 7 oz. or 9 oz. 18.00
Schoeppen, regular or flared, 12 oz. 20.00
Sherbet 10.00
Sherbet, high footed, 4½ oz. 18.00
Sherbet, low foot, shallow, 4 oz. 15.00
Sherry, 1½ oz. 20.00
Soda, 5 oz. or 7 oz.......................................15.00
Soda, 9 oz. or 12 oz.....................................18.00
Spoon 40.00
Spoon tray 25.00
Sugar & cover 70.00

Sugar, hotel...25.00
Sugar, individual...40.00
Syrup, 5 oz. bar..60.00
Syrup, 7 oz. hotel..70.00
Toothpick 75.00
Tumbler, footed, 7 oz. 30.00
Tumbler, plain or star bottom, 7 oz. or 8 oz.
   (3 styles) 20.00
Vase, 6"..45.00
Vase, 8"..40.00
Vase, 10"..45.00
Vase, violet or small loving cup 60.00
Vase, violet, #1, #2, #3, or #4 ....45.00
Water bottle..50.00
Water ice, high footed, shallow, 4 oz.............20.00
Water ice, low footed, 5 oz.........................15.00
Wine, 2½ oz. or 3 oz. 25.00

No. 300 Peerless footed jelly, no. 1 gold decoration.

No. 300½ Peerless orchid vases.

No. 300-1 Peerless candlesticks.

No. 300-2 Peerless candlesticks.

No. 300 Peerless handled jelly.

No. 300 Peerless stemware, 1899 ad. Top: claret, sherry, burgundy. Middle: wine, egg glass. Bottom: goblet, champagne, footed tumbler.

No. 300 Peerless assortment, 1899 ad. Top: molasses can, covered butter, oil & stopper. Middle: flared nappy. Bottom: sugar, cream, spoon, honey dish & cover (honey dish and butter mislabeled in ad).

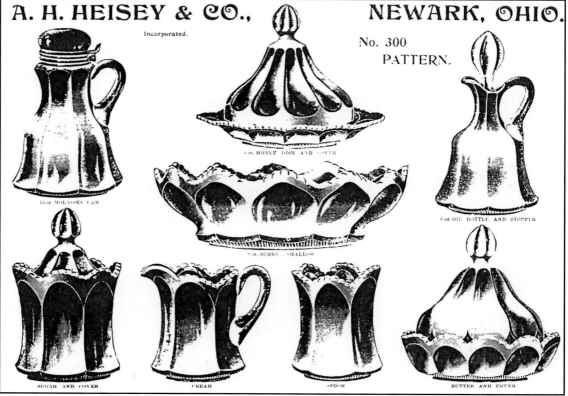

A. H. Heisey & Co., Newark, O.
(INCORPORATED)

No. 300
"THE PATTERN WITHOUT A PEER."

A Selection from the 30 new pieces recently added to our

300 Pattern

No. 300 Peerless 10 oz. goblet, 8 oz. goblet, 7 oz. goblet, tall champagne or parfait.

No. 300 Peerless ice tub.
Top: low sherbet,
saucer footed sherbet.
Bottom: cocktail, footed egg.

No. 300 Peerless assortment, 1900 ad. Top: individual sugar, No. 1 candlestick, cream. Middle: syrup, individual decanter. Bottom: No. 4 hotel salt, nappy.

No. 300½:

Bar, straight or flared, 2 oz.	$15.00
Berry, 7" or 8"	70.00
Berry, flared, 8" or 9"	70.00
Berry, shallow, 9" or 10"	80.00
Butter & cover	85.00
Communion cup, 2 handled, 13 oz.	90.00
Cream	35.00
Cream, hotel	25.00
Custard, handled (punch cup)	15.00
Finger bowl	15.00
Horseradish jar, mushroom stopper	75.00
Ice tea, 13 oz.	18.00
Jelly, footed, 6"	35.00
Jelly, low, 4½" or 5½"	30.00
Jug, stuck handle, ½ gallon	140.00

Loving cup, 3 handled, 13 oz.	125.00
Mug, 13 oz.	45.00
Nappy, fruit, 5"	12.00
Pickle jar, mushroom stopper	85.00
Pitcher, ½ gallon	120.00
Plate, finger bowl, regular (#1) or cupped (#2), 6"	20.00
Plate, ice cream, regular or shallow, 6"	20.00
Salt & pepper, pr., #2 or #3	45.00
Sherbet	10.00
Spoon	40.00
Sugar & cover	70.00
Sugar, hotel	25.00
Tea caddy, #1 or #2, mushroom stopper	85.00
Tumbler, 8 oz.	25.00

Tumbler, champagne, flared or straight,
5 oz., 7 oz., or 9 oz. 20.00
Vase, #1, 8" to 9½" tall (swing)......................45.00
Vase, #2, 10" to 11¾" tall (swing)..................60.00
Vase, #3, 12" to 15" tall (swing) 85.00
Vase, orchid, 5"...95.00
Vase, orchid, 6"...120.00
Vase, orchid, 7"...155.00
Water bottle, #1 or #2..................................50.00

No. 300½ Peerless hotel sugar.

No. 300½ Peerless covered sugar,
covered butter, spoon, cream.

No. 300½ Peerless. Top: low foot jelly,
loving cup. Bottom: berry, mug with
stuck handle, pitcher.

1900:

The company began using their well-known trademark, the Diamond H in November of this year.

Punty & Diamond Point, No. 305
Date: 1900 to 1907
Colors: Crystal, salt & pepper known in Opal
Patent: The claret jug was given patent No. 31078 on 6-27-1899 with A. H. Heisey listed as designer.

Comments: Many items are not marked with the Diamond H. This is a very popular pattern with a wide variety of pieces. The inspiration for this pattern came from several small items which Heisey made as early as 1896 for metal mounting companies. These were a mucilage bottle with brush, salt and pepper, claret jug, sugar shaker, and long neck cologne. All these were originally given no. 16 and had sterling tops. The salt and pepper, claret jug, and sugar shaker were continued in no. 305. Decorations include no. 3 frosted ending in curved outline about ½" above punty; no. 3½ same as no. 3 except that grinding runs up to the edge; no. 4 orange luster in punties; no. 5 amber in punties; no. 6 amber in punties and ground as in no. 3; no. 7 amber on plain flute, but not in punties and the amber with an engraved mark of circular form about ½" above punty; no. 8 amber allover plain portion except in punties and no. 9 gold in place of amber as in no. 8. Rare with ruby stain.

Bitters bottle	$120.00
Bowl, oval, 12"	70.00
Butter & cover	145.00
Cologne, sterling top (#16)	150.00
Comport, 6" (jelly)	75.00
Comport, 8"	140.00
Cracker jar & cover	230.00
Cream	95.00
Cream, individual	80.00
Custard, handled (punch cup)	25.00
Decanter & stopper	145.00
Jug, ½ gallon	250.00
Jug, claret	180.00
Mucilage bottle with brush top (#16)	155.00
Mustard & cover	195.00
Nappy, 4" or 4½"	25.00
Nappy, 8"	75.00
Oil & stopper, 6 oz.	120.00
Oval	55.00
Plate, 8"	60.00
Punch bowl & foot, 14"	400.00
Salt & pepper, pr., #2 or #3	145.00
Salver	185.00
Spoon	75.00
Sugar & cover	120.00
Sugar, individual	80.00
Sugar sifter	175.00
Syrup, 5 oz.	140.00
Toothpick	345.00
Tumbler	65.00
Vase, 6"	50.00
Vase, 8"	75.00
Vase, 10"	95.00
Water bottle	145.00

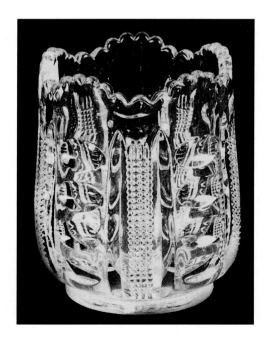

No. 305 Punty & Diamond Point spoon.

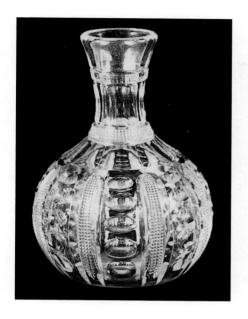

No. 305 Punty & Diamond Point water bottle.

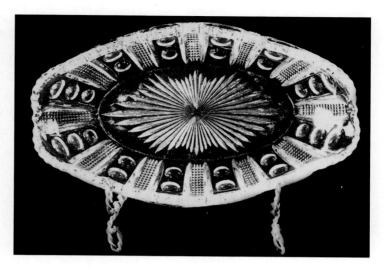

No. 305 Punty & Diamond Point oval.

Ring Band, No. 310
Date: 1900
Colors: Ivorina Verde, rare tumblers in Crystal and Opal,
a rare spoon is known in Rose

Comments: This pattern is marked with the Diamond H. Some tumblers are marked on both the interior and exterior of the base. Decorations known include gold, hand-painted roses and other florals, gold and green. There are two styles of tumblers. The original tumbler had a raised band around the middle. This tumbler is usually found without souvenir inscriptions. The second type has a plain top portion and is the one usually found with souvenir inscriptions. The No. 1 condiment set consists of the condiment tray, a salt and pepper, and a toothpick. For gold or gold and green decorations add 25%+. For hand-painted floral decorations, add 75% to 100%. Tumblers in Opal or Crystal are valued at $150.00 to $200.00 each.

Butter & cover	$145.00	Nappy, flared, 9"	110.00
Celery, tall	120.00	Nappy, shallow, 10"	120.00
Comport, 8"	165.00	Oil & stopper, 6 oz.	175.00
Cream	95.00	Pitcher, ½ gallon	175.00
Custard (punch cup)	50.00	Salt & pepper, pr.	125.00
Jelly, footed, 5"	80.00	Sugar & cover	135.00
Molasses can, 13 oz.	220.00	Toothpick	75.00
Nappy, 4½"	40.00	Tray, condiment, 8" (rectangular)	140.00
Nappy, 8"	110.00	Tumbler (2 styles)	65.00
Nappy, flared or shallow, 5"	40.00		

No. 310 Ring Band tumbler, Opal with Zanesville, OH, Y Bridge.

No. 310 Ring Band toothpick, Ivorina Verde with hand-painted rose buds.

No. 310 Ring Band oil & stopper.

1901:

Paneled Cane, No. 315
Date: 1901 to late 1906
Color: Crystal only

Comments: Usually marked with the Diamond H. Shapes of pieces are very similar to those of No. 300 Peerless. "No. 315 pattern is a modification of our famous No. 300 Colonial, the pattern without a peer, in which we have retained much of the richness and graceful dignity of that popular pattern, the 300, and added the sparkling brilliancy of the imitation cut, securing an effect that is truly 'a happy medium.' *House Furnisher,* January 1901.

Decorations known include no. 1 gold and rare with ruby stain. Heisey also made two lamp shades — a 7" stalactite globe and an electric shade similar to the Paneled Cane pattern but these were given no. 14 as a pattern number.

Bonbon, #1, #2, or #3	$25.00
Bowl, footed, 8" or 9" (comport)	110.00
Butter & cover	110.00
Celery, tall	75.00
Cream	70.00
Custard, handled (punch cup)	30.00
Jelly, handled, 5"	25.00
Jelly, footed, 5" regular or 6" shallow	65.00
Jug, ½ gallon	200.00
Molasses can, 13 oz.	190.00
Nappy, 4"	18.00
Nappy, 8"	75.00
Nappy, shallow, 5"	18.00
Nappy, shallow, 9"	75.00
Oil & stopper	150.00
Pickle tray, 6"	25.00
Plate, small	35.00
Salver, 9"	145.00
Spoon	65.00
Sugar & cover	110.00
Toothpick	130.00
Tumbler	75.00

No. 315 Paneled Cane foot-ed jelly, sugar & cover, nappy, shallow nappy, spoon, covered butter, cream, from *China, Glass & Pottery Review*, 1901.

No. 315 Paneled Cane oil.

Pillows, No. 325
Date: 1901 to 1910
Colors: Crystal, rare occasional pieces in Rose

Comments: A very desirable pattern that is quite similar to the old pressed glass pattern Westmoreland made by Gillinder. Each "pillow" in Westmoreland has two flat sides opposite each other. Heisey's are rounded on all four sides — making a "fluffy" pillow. Interestingly, while Heisey was involved with Geo. Duncan & Sons in Pittsburgh, they produced several sizes of colognes with the Pillows motif. It is likely that Heisey revived this motif and expanded it into a tableware line. The colognes were made only by Duncan, never by Heisey. The individual salt is oval in this pattern. Most pieces are marked with the Diamond H. Decorations known are gold on top plain area and ruby stain on top plain area which is rare.

Bowl, footed, 9" (comport)........................$200.00	Jelly, footed, shallow, 5" or 5½" 85.00
Butter & cover 185.00	Jelly, handled, 5" or 6" 50.00
Celery, tall 120.00	Molasses can, 13 oz. 250.00
Cracker jar & cover......................................275.00	Mustard & cover 140.00
Cream 90.00	Nappy, 4" or 4½"...25.00
Cream, hotel 65.00	Nappy, 7", 8", or 9" 95.00
Custard, handled (punch cup) 35.00	Nappy, crimped, 4" or 4½"............................25.00
Egg glass, footed 40.00	Nappy, crimped, 7", 8", or 9" 95.00
Finger bowl, straight or cupped 30.00	Oil & stopper, 2 oz......................................190.00
Fruit, footed (same as jelly but more flat).......85.00	Oil & stopper, 6 oz......................................155.00
Ice tub with drainer (frappe tub)..................240.00	

Oval, 9"	55.00	Salver, footed, 9"	200.00
Oval, 10½" or 12"	65.00	Spoon	80.00
Pickle tray, 6"	45.00	Sugar & cover	135.00
Pitcher, stuck handle, ½ gallon	290.00	Sugar & cover, hotel	120.00
Pitcher, stuck handle, 3 quart	310.00	Syrup, 7 oz.	180.00
Punch bowl & foot, 14"	450.00+	Tankard, stuck handle, ½ gallon	290.00
Rose bowl, 3" (footed, 9" tall)	270.00	Toothpick	375.00
Rose bowl, 7"	130.00	Tumbler	75.00
Salt & pepper, pr., #2 or #3	175.00	Water bottle	140.00
Salt, individual	75.00		

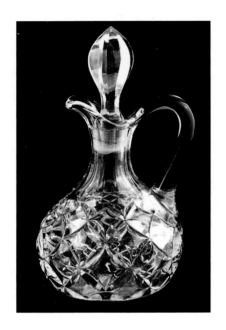

No. 325 Pillows oil.

No. 325 Pillows spoon, covered sugar,
covered butter, cream.

No. 325 Pillows rose bowl, nappy, frappe tub.

No. 325 Pillows tankard, half-gallon pitcher, three-quart pitcher.

1902:

Colonial Panel, No. 331
Date: Probably designed in 1902.
Not placed on the market until ca. 1907. In the line until 1929.
Color: Crystal only

Comments: A full pressed tableware pattern. Most pieces are marked with the Diamond H. The toothpick in this pattern is eight sided and is also used with pattern No. 400.

Bar $15.00	Nappy, shallow, 10" or 11" 45.00
Custard, 4½ oz. (punch cup) 15.00	Oil & stopper, 4 oz. or 6 oz. 35.00
Finger bowl...12.00	Oyster cocktail, 2 piece (bar & finger bowl)....30.00
Jug, stuck handle, 1 pint 70.00	Oyster cocktail, 3 piece
Jug, stuck handle, 1 quart.........................100.00	(bar, finger bowl & plate).........................40.00
Jug, stuck handle, 3 pint 135.00	Pickle jar, mushroom stopper 70.00
Jug, stuck handle, ½ gallon.......................145.00	Plate, finger bowl...10.00
Mustard & cover..55.00	Salt & pepper, pr. 55.00
Nappy, 4" or 4½" 10.00	Salt, individual, square.................................15.00
Nappy, 6" or 7" 25.00	Straw jar & cover 350.00
Nappy, 8" or 9" 35.00	Syrup, 13 oz. 65.00
Nappy, flared, 7" or 8" 35.00	Toothpick..140.00
Nappy, flared, 9" or 10" 40.00	Tumbler, 7 oz..30.00
Nappy, shallow, 4½" or 5"............................10.00	Water bottle, regular or squat......................75.00
Nappy, shallow, 7" or 9" 40.00	

No. 331 Colonial Panel. Top: pickle jar, tumbler. Middle: individual salt, toothpick. Bottom: straw jar, shallow nappy.

No. 331 Colonial Panel. Top: custard, mustard. Bottom: oil, molasses can, jug.

Waldorf Astoria, No. 333, 333½ — original name
Date: 1902 to 1917
Color: Crystal

Comments: A pattern presumably intended mainly for hotel use, most likely the famous Waldorf Astoria. The plain colonial style is relieved by the plain band around the middle of items. Pieces may be unmarked or marked with the Diamond H.

Bitters bottle or Worcester sauce $60.00
Decanter & stopper, 18 oz. or 20 oz..........170.00
Finger bowl...25.00
Oil & stopper, 2 oz. or 4 oz.......................55.00
Oil & stopper, 6 oz......................................50.00
Plate, finger bowl 12.00
Salt & pepper, pr. (#2) 80.00
Syrup, 9 oz. 110.00
Toothpick 120.00
Tumbler, 8½ oz., 9 oz. (#333½)..................45.00
Water bottle..85.00

No. 333 Waldorf Astoria toothpick.

No. 333 Waldorf Astoria bitters bottle.

Prince of Wales, Plumes, No. 335 — original name
Date: 1902 to 1912
Color: Crystal only

Comments: Pieces are marked with the Diamond H. Ruby stain items are very difficult to find. This pattern may have been adapted from a cut glass pattern. Decorations known are gold or ruby stain on plain top portions and elongated ovals. For gold decoration, add 25%. For ruby stain decoration, add 100%.

Berry, oblong, 11"	$135.00
Berry, oblong, shallow, 14"	185.00
Bitters bottle	225.00
Bonbon	45.00
Bowl, footed, 8" or 9" (comport)	185.00
Bowl, footed, flared, 9" or 10" (comport)	185.00+
Bowl, footed, shallow, 10" or 11" (comport)	185.00+
Brandy bottle & stopper	275.00
Butter & cover	140.00
Celery, tall	110.00
Celery tray, 10" or 12"	70.00
Cream	80.00
Cream, hotel	45.00
Custard, handled (punch cup)	20.00
Dish, oval, 7½" or 9"	65.00
Dish, oval, 10½" or 12"	75.00
Egg cup or sherbet, low footed	35.00
Finger bowl, cupped, straight, or flared	35.00
Jelly, footed, 5½" or 6"	110.00
Jelly, footed, shallow, 5" or 6"	110.00
Jelly, handled, regular or 3 corner, 5"	55.00
Molasses can, 13 oz.	250.00
Nappy, 4" or 4½"	30.00

Nappy, 7", 8", or 9"	80.00
Nappy, flared or orange, 10"	80.00
Oil & stopper, 4 oz. or 6 oz.	200.00
Pickle tray, 6"	50.00
Pitcher, ½ gallon	235.00
Plate, finger bowl	25.00
Punch bowl & foot, 10"	450.00
Punch bowl & foot, 14"	600.00
Rose bowl, footed, 3"	280.00
Salt & pepper, pr., #2 or #3	175.00
Salted almond tray	45.00
Salver, 9" or 10"	210.00
Salver, 12"	230.00
Spoon	80.00
Spoon tray	45.00
Sugar & cover	120.00
Sugar & cover, hotel	95.00
Syrup, 7 oz.	190.00
Tankard, stuck handle, ½ gallon	180.00
Toothpick	210.00
Tumbler	65.00
Water bottle	145.00

No. 335 Prince of Wales, Plumes custard.

No. 335 Prince of Wales, Plumes tumbler and half-gallon pitcher.

No. 335 Prince of Wales, Plumes covered butter, spoon, covered sugar, cream.

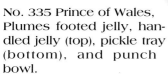

No. 335 Prince of Wales, Plumes footed jelly, handled jelly (top), pickle tray (bottom), and punch bowl.

Touraine, No. 337, 337½ — original name
Date: 1902 to 1909
Color: Crystal, in the 1930s stemware made in light amber

Comments: Most pieces are marked with the Diamond H. While this pattern is not easy to find, its severity and plainness cause it to have low values. The name Touraine is an industry term indicating the distinctive shape of the pieces with a narrow bottom portion flaring quickly to a wide, broad top which is slightly cupped. Decorations include ruby stain in various styles and green stain or gold in various styles, often in bands. Stemware was made in the 1930s in light amber with narrow optic for Fred Harvey's Harvey House Restaurants (associated with the Santa Fe Railroad). For amber stems, add 300% to 400%.

Bar $30.00	Butter & cover 50.00
Bowl & cover, footed, 7" (comport)..................85.00	Champagne, 5 oz..10.00
Bowl, footed, 6", 7", or 8" (comport) 60.00	Claret, 3½ oz. 10.00
Bowl, footed, flared, 6½", 7½", or 9" (comport) .60.00	Cocktail, 4½ oz. 10.00
Bowl, footed, shallow, 7", 8", or 10" (comport) .60.00	Comport & cover, 7" or 8" (nappy) 55.00
Burgundy, 2 oz..10.00	Cordial, ½ oz. 20.00

Cream 30.00
Crème de menthe, 2 oz. 10.00
Crushed fruit & notched cover, 8"...........200.00
Custard (punch cup)....................................12.00
Custard, handled, footed, 4½ oz. (punch cup).15.00
Egg, footed, 5 oz. 10.00
Goblet, 8 oz. or 10 oz. 10.00
Highball, 8 oz. 6.00
Ice cream, saucer footed, regular or cupped,
    4½ oz..12.00
Ice cream, saucer footed, regular or cupped,
    stuck handle, 4½ oz. 15.00
Jelly, handled, 5", regular or 3 cornered, 5½" ..16.00
Molasses can, 13 oz. 55.00
Nappy, 4" or 4½"...8.00
Nappy, 6" or 7" 12.00
Nappy, 8", 9", or 10" 25.00
Nappy, 11" or 12" 35.00
Nappy, flared, 6½" or 7½" 15.00
Nappy, flared, 9", 10", or 11" 25.00
Nappy, shallow, 4½", 5" or 6"....................10.00

Nappy, shallow, 7" or 8" 20.00
Nappy, shallow, 10", 11", or 12" 30.00
Oil & stopper, 2 oz. or 4 oz.........................65.00
Oil & stopper, 6 oz. or 8 oz.........................55.00
Oval, 7½" or 9" 18.00
Oval, 10½" or 12" 20.00
Oyster cocktail, 4 oz., 4½ oz., or 5 oz. 10.00
Pitcher, ½ gallon...70.00
Port, 3 oz. 10.00
Salt & pepper, pr., #3.................................145.00
Salver, 9" or 10"...75.00
Saucer champagne, 6 oz. 10.00
Sauterne, 5 oz..10.00
Sherbet, footed, 4 oz., also with stuck handle ..18.00
Spoon 25.00
Sugar & cover 45.00
Syrup, 5 oz..45.00
Toothpick..275.00
Tumbler, 8 oz., or 8 oz. footed 25.00
Water ice, footed, 4½ oz..............................10.00
Wine, 1½ oz. 10.00

No. 337 Touraine stemware. Top: saucer champagne, handled footed custard, egg cup. Middle: cordial. Bottom: tall champagne, goblet, hi-ball.

No. 337 Touraine toothpick.

No. 337 Touraine covered sugar, covered butter, cream, spoon.

No. 337 Touraine oil, salt, molasses can.

1903:

Continental, No. 339, 339½ — original name
Date: 1903 to 1910
Colors: Crystal. The water bottle is known in Flamingo.

Comments: Most pieces are marked with the Diamond H. There are two styles of table set pieces: flat (#339) and footed (#339½). "A. H. Heisey & Co.'s 'Continental' line is fully maintaining their reputation for high grade ware. It is in the purest metal, highly polished, and has a rich cut glass effect." *Crockery & Glass Journal,* January 1903. Known decorations are gold and rarely ruby stain.

Bonbon, #1, #2, or #3 (rectangular)............\$40.00
Bowl & cover, high footed, 7" or 8" (comport) .145.00
Bowl & cover, low footed, 7" or 8" (comport) ..125.00
Bowl, high footed, 7", 8", or 9" (comport).....110.00
Bowl, high footed, flared, 8", 9", or 10"
   (comport) 110.00
Bowl, low footed, 7" or 8" (comport)..............90.00

Bowl, low footed, flared 8" or 9" 110.00
Butter & cover 115.00
Butter & cover, footed (#339½) 130.00
Celery, tall 65.00
Celery tray, 10"..40.00
Cream 65.00
Cream, footed (#339½)..................................85.00

Cream, hotel 45.00
Crushed fruit & notched cover, 8" 250.00
Custard (punch cup) 22.00
Dish, oblong, 7½" 35.00
Egg cup...20.00
Finger bowl 15.00
Goblet 35.00
Jelly, 5" handled, or 5" handled 3 cornered ...35.00
Jelly, footed, 4½" or 5" 50.00
Jelly, footed, flared, 5" or 5½" 50.00
Molasses can, 13 oz. 100.00
Nappy & cover, 7" or 8" 130.00
Nappy, 4" or 5" 15.00
Nappy, 6" or 7" 20.00
Nappy, 8" or 9" 50.00
Nappy, flared, 5" 15.00
Nappy, flared, 7" or 8"..............................50.00
Nappy, flared, 9" or 10".............................65.00

Oil & stopper, 6 oz.....................................55.00
Pickle dish, 6"..25.00
Pitcher, 3 pint 140.00
Pitcher, ½ gallon 160.00
Pitcher, 3 quart 180.00
Salt & pepper, pr., #2 or #3........................60.00
Salver, 9" or 10".......................................85.00
Sherbet, footed 10.00
Spoon 60.00
Spoon, footed (#339½) 70.00
Spoon tray (rectangular) 40.00
Sugar & cover..90.00
Sugar & cover, footed (#339½)....................110.00
Sugar, hotel 45.00
Toothpick 135.00
Tumbler, 8 oz. or 9 oz................................35.00
Water bottle...55.00
Wine..35.00

No. 339 Continental covered sugar,
covered butter, cream, spoon.

No. 339 Continental molasses
can, oil, pitcher.

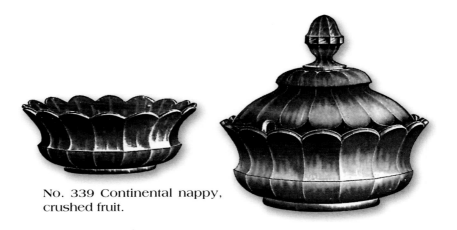

No. 339 Continental nappy,
crushed fruit.

Puritan, No. 341, 341½ — original name
Date: 1903 to 1938

Colors: Crystal. Rare sherbets in Ivorina Verde. The half-gallon tankard, three ounce low sherbet and custard were made in Flamingo. The No. 341½ pint squat jug is known in Crystal with a Moongleam handle. The finger bowl was made in Alexandrite.

Comments: "They are also showing a unique line of beautiful stemware, the 'Puritan' that is attracting special attention for its beauty and originality of design." *Crockery & Glass Journal*, January 1903.

This pattern is complicated for collectors because in 1939 Heisey reused the number and renamed the pattern Old Williamsburg. Some pieces (mainly stemware) were continued from Puritan, but Old Williamsburg also adopted pieces from many other colonial patterns. Puritan master table salts are sometimes found fully ground and polished on all surfaces. Most items are marked with the Diamond H and have ground and polished bottoms. Heisey combined several items to make various water sets: jugs, tumbler, trays, etc. These are rarely found intact today.

Bonbon, straight, cupped, or flared, 7" $140.00	Celery, tall 60.00
Bowl & cover, footed, 7" or 8" (comport) 110.00	Champagne, tall, 6½ oz. 15.00
Bowl, high footed, 6", 7", or 7½" (comport)......70.00	Cheese plate & cover..................................125.00
Bowl, high footed, 8" or 9" (comport)..............85.00	Claret, 4½ oz..20.00
Bowl, high footed, crimped, 7" or 8" (comport)..80.00	Cocktail, 2 oz. or 3 oz. 12.00
Bowl, high footed, crimped, 9" or 10" (comport) .95.00	Cordial, 1 oz...45.00
Bowl, high footed, shallow, 7½" or 8½" (comport) .90.00	Cream, footed 75.00
Bowl, high footed, shallow, 9½" or 11" (comport).100.00	Cream, hotel, oval..35.00
Burgundy, 3½ oz. 15.00	Crème de menthe, 2½ oz................................12.00
Butter & cover, footed 100.00	Crushed fruit & notched cover, 8"................225.00
Butter, individual 20.00	Custard, regular or flared, 3 oz., 4 oz., or
Candy jar & cover, 1 lb...................................100.00	4½ oz. (punch cup) 15.00
Candy jar & cover, 2 lb...................................250.00	Decanter & stopper, 24 oz............................140.00
Candy jar & cover, 3 lb...................................500.00	Egg cup, footed, 4½ oz. or 6 oz. or oyster
Candy jar & cover, 5 lb................................1,500.00	cocktail..15.00
Celery, oval, hotel, 12" or 13" 40.00	Finger bowl..15.00

Goblet, 9 oz. 20.00
Goblet, low footed, 8 oz. or footed tumbler 20.00
Horseradish, squat or tall, mushroom stopper..75.00
Ice cream, flared, 4½" or 5" 15.00
Ice cream, plain edge, 5½" 15.00
Ice cream, shallow, 4½" or 6" (#2)..................20.00
Ice tea, 13 oz. 25.00
Ice tub..100.00
Ice tub with drainer 145.00
Jar, cherry, or tea caddy, mushroom stopper,
    large 85.00
Jar, cherry, or tea caddy, mushroom stopper,
    small..75.00
Jar, cold cream, or squat horseradish,
    mushroom stopper..................................75.00
Jar, marmalade, mushroom stopper, medium ..70.00
Jar, marmalade, or pin pickle, mushroom
    stopper, small...70.00
Jelly, handled, regular or 3 corner, 5" 22.00
Jelly, high footed, 4½" or 5" 30.00
Jelly, high footed, crimped, 5½".....................30.00
Jelly, high footed, shallow, 5" or 5½"..............30.00
Jelly, low footed, 4" or 4½" 25.00
Jelly, low footed, crimped, 4½" or 5"...............25.00
Jelly, low footed, scalloped, 4" 25.00
Jelly, low footed, shallow, 4" or 5" 25.00
Jug, footed, ½ gallon 210.00
Mayonnaise..22.00
Molasses can, 13 oz. 90.00
Nappy & cover, 7" or 8" 90.00
Nappy, 4" or 4½"...10.00
Nappy, 6" or 7" 30.00
Nappy, crimped, 4½" or 5"..............................12.00
Nappy, crimped, 7" or 8" 40.00
Nappy, crimped, 9" or 10" 55.00
Nappy, ice cream, 6", #3 ....12.00
Nappy, ice cream, flared, 4½" or 5" 12.00
Nappy, shallow, 4½" or 5½"............................12.00
Nappy, shallow, 7½" or 8½"............................12.00
Nappy, shallow, 9½" or 11".............................12.00
Oil & stopper, 2 oz...12.00
Oil & stopper, 4 oz. or 6 oz............................35.00
Oval, 7", 8", or 9"...45.00
Oval, 10" or 12"..45.00
Oval, shallow or olive dish, 7".........................35.00
Oyster cocktail, 2 piece straight or flared 30.00
Oyster cocktail, 3 piece..................................40.00
Parfait, straight or flared, or tall champagne,
    3½ oz. or 4½ oz. 18.00

Pickle jar, knob cover 50.00
Pickle jar, mushroom stopper 75.00
Pickle tray, 6"..20.00
Plate, 5" or 6"..12.00
Plate, 9"...65.00
Plate, finger bowl, 6", #1 ....15.00
Plate, ice cream, shallow, puntied bottom, 6",
    #2...20.00
Plate, mayonnaise or olive dish, shallow 20.00
Port, 3 oz. 15.00
Punch bowl & foot, 13"; cupped, 12"; flared,
    14½" 300.00
Punch bowl & foot, shallow, 16" or 17" 350.00
Salt & pepper, pr., #1 or #2 ....40.00
Salt, individual..18.00
Salt, master table 50.00
Salver, 9" or 10"..85.00
Saucer champagne, 4½ oz..............................15.00
Schooner, footed, 10 oz. 35.00
Sherbet (flat) 10.00
Sherbet, high foot, straight, 4½ oz.,
    or scalloped, 5 oz.....................................18.00
Sherbet, high footed, shallow, 4½ oz. 18.00
Sherbet, low foot, straight, 3 oz.,
    or scalloped 3 oz or 4½ oz. 10.00
Sherbet, low footed, deep, 6 oz......................12.00
Sherbet, scalloped, high footed, 5 oz.............20.00
Sherry, straight or flared, 2 oz.......................20.00
Spoon, footed 65.00
Spoon tray, 6"...20.00
Sugar & cover, footed.....................................85.00
Sugar, hotel, oval 35.00
Tankard, 1 pint..60.00
Tankard, 1 quart..90.00
Tankard, 3 pint..100.00
Tankard, ½ gallon...110.00
Tankard & cover, 1 pint 85.00
Tankard & cover, 1 quart 120.00
Tankard & cover, 3 pint 145.00
Tankard & cover, ½ gallon 155.00
Toothpick, footed..135.00
Tray, ice cream, deep, 14" 120.00
Tray, ice cream, shallow, oval, 15" 120.00
Tumbler, 8 oz., 9 oz., or 10 oz. 22.00
Water bottle...50.00
Water ice, shallow, 4½"..................................12.00
Wine, 2 oz...20.00

No. 341 Puritan ice tub.

No. 341 Puritan cupped bonbon.

No. 341 Puritan finger bowl.

No. 341 Puritan flared toothpick, toothpick.

No. 341 Puritan covered sugar, covered butter, spoon, cream, all footed.

No. 341 Puritan candy jar, decanter.

No. 341 Puritan large marmalade jar, pin pickle jar, squat horseradish, pickle jar, horseradish jar.

No. 341 Puritan scalloped low footed sherbet, flared sherry, straight parfait, crème de menthe,
cocktail, saucer champagne.

No. 341 Puritan oil, molasses can, pickle jar.

No. 341 Puritan tankard, jug.

No. 341 Puritan nappy.

No. 341 Puritan. Top: nappy, individual salt. Bottom: individual butter, table salt, shallow high footed bowl, oval hotel cream and sugar.

No. 341½:

Butter & cover, squat.....................................$70.00
Creamer, squat..45.00
Custard, 3 oz. (punch cup) 15.00
Finger bowl, small, straight or flared 10.00
Finger bowl, large, straight or flared.............15.00
Jug, 1 pint 250.00
Jug, 1 quart 175.00
Jug, 3 pint 130.00
Jug, ½ gallon 160.00
Jug, 3 quart 250.00
Nappy, 4" or 4½"...10.00
Nappy, 7", 8", or 9" 30.00
Nappy, flared, 4½" or 5" 10.00
Nappy, flared, 8½", 9½", or 10½"..................30.00
Nappy, shallow, 5" or 5½" 10.00
Nappy, shallow, 9", 10", or 11" 40.00
Punch bowl & foot, regular, 10"; flared, 12";
    or shallow, 13"..250.00

Spooner, squat...45.00
Sugar & cover, squat 55.00
Tumbler, 8 oz. 22.00
Tumbler, footed, 8 oz. 28.00

No. 341½ Puritan jug.

No. 341½ Puritan cream,
spoon, covered butter,
covered sugar.

Paneled Colonial, No. 342
Date: Probably designed in 1903. Did not appear in a catalog until 1924.
Color: Crystal

Comments: A very short lived colonial pattern. Marked with the Diamond H. Difficult to find, but very similar to other Heisey colonials.

Butter & cover $70.00
Cream 45.00
Spoon 45.00
Sugar & cover..........................55.00

No. 342 Paneled Colonial covered sugar, covered butter, cream, spoon.

Sunburst, Nos. 343, 343½
Date: 1903. Discontinued before 1913.
Color: Crystal only

Comments: Most pieces are marked with the Diamond H. Unusual pieces are the footed rose bowl and the card suit bonbons. Sometimes decorated with gold.

Bonbon, card suit (club, diamond, spade, or
   heart) ea. $85.00
Bowl, footed, 8" or 9" (comport)...................165.00
Bowl, footed, flared or shallow, 9" or 10"
   (comport)..175.00
Butter & cover..145.00
Celery tray, 12"...95.00
Cream..95.00
Cream, hotel...75.00
Cream, individual...95.00
Custard (punch cup)......................................25.00
Egg cup 60.00
Finger bowl, straight or flared 25.00

Goblet...125.00
Jelly, footed, 5"; flared or shallow, 5½" 75.00
Jelly, handled, regular or 3 cornered, 5".........65.00
Jug, punty rim, stuck handle, 1 quart...........190.00
Jug, punty rim, stuck handle, 3 pint 210.00
Jug, punty rim, stuck handle, ½ gallon.........285.00
Jug, punty rim, stuck handle, 3 quart 295.00
Mayonnaise 60.00
Molasses can, 13 oz. 225.00
Nappy, 4", 4½", or 5" 20.00
Nappy, 6" or 7" 30.00
Nappy, 8", 9", or 10" 80.00
Nappy, crimped, 4½", 5", or 6"........................25.00

Nappy, crimped, 7", 8", or 9" 50.00
Nappy, crimped, 10", 12", or 14" 85.00
Oil & stopper, 2 oz. or 4 oz. 145.00
Oil & stopper, 6 oz. 120.00
Oval, 7" or 9" 45.00
Oval, 10" or 12" 70.00
Pickle jar, mushroom stopper 175.00
Pickle tray, 6" 35.00
Plate, 6" 35.00
Plate, mayonnaise 35.00
Punch bowl & foot, cupped, 12" 350.00
Punch bowl & foot, 14" 450.00

Punch bowl & foot, flared, 15" 450.00
Rose bowl, footed, 3" 375.00
Salt & pepper, pr., #1 or #2 ....225.00
Salver, footed, 9" or 10" 185.00
Spoon..85.00
Sugar & cover 125.00
Sugar, hotel...75.00
Sugar, individual 95.00
Toothpick...250.00
Tumbler, puntied.......................................60.00
Vase, orchid, 6" 225.00
Water bottle...145.00

No. 343 Sunburst individual sugar.

No. 343 Sunburst water bottle.

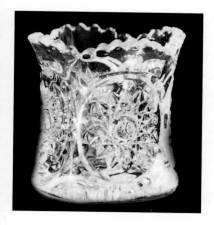

No. 343 Sunburst toothpick.

No. 343 Sunburst spoon, cream,
covered butter, covered sugar.

No. 343 Sunburst jug, pressed handle; tumbler; jug, stuck handle.

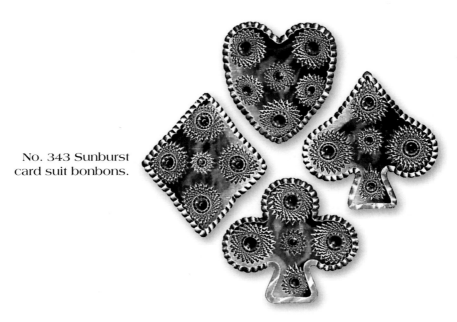

No. 343 Sunburst card suit bonbons.

No. 343 Sunburst. Top: nappy. Bottom: pickle jar, orchid vase, oil, molasses can.

No. 343½:

Custard (punch cup) 35.00
Jug, stuck handle, 1 quart.........210.00
Jug, stuck handle, 3 pint 225.00
Jug, stuck handle, ½ gallon 295.00
Jug, stuck handle, 3 quart 310.00
Nappy, regular or cupped, 4 or 4½".......20.00
Nappy, regular or cupped, 7", 8", or 9" .110.00
Nappy, flared or square, 4½" or 5" 40.00
Nappy, flared or square, 8", 9", or 10"..110.00
Nappy, shallow, 5" or 6".......................40.00
Nappy, shallow, 9", 10", or 11" 120.00
Punch bowl & foot, 10".......................350.00
Tumbler..60.00

No. 343½ Sunburst nappy, tumbler, jug.

1904:

Reports in July 1904, indicated that A. H. Heisey was asked to accept a nomination as congressman from the Newark district. He declined the offer.

In September, the Heisey plant had completed an addition including a new 16 pot furnace which would double the capacity of the plant, requiring the hiring of an additional 300 employees. At this time, Heisey also was able to secure gas from his own lands and leases sufficient to supply his factory with excess available to the town of Newark.

> **Patrician, No. 5; Skirted Panel, No. 33; Jack Be Nimble, No. 31**
> **Dates:** Patrician: 1905 to 1931. Skirted Panel: 1910 to 1939.
> Jack Be Nimble: 1908 to 1944.
> **Colors:** Patrician and Skirted Panel: Crystal only. Jack Be Nimble: Crystal, Moongleam, Flamingo, Sahara.
>
> **Comments:** Patrician and Jack Be Nimble are usually marked with the Diamond H on the base; Skirted Panel just below the candlecup. All were reproduced by Imperial Glass Corp. in Crystal. Patrician and Skirted Panel were made in several standard size candlesticks also.

Jack Be Nimble toy candlesticks, pr. $95.00
Patrician toy candlesticks, pr. 135.00
Skirted Panel toy candlesticks, pr. 110.00

Toy Candlesticks: No. 5 Patrician, No. 33 Skirted Panel, No. 31 Jack Be Nimble.

Priscilla, No. 351

Date: 1904. Discontinued sometime after 1929.
Colors: Crystal. The extra high footed bowl is rarely found in Canary.
The ales were made in colors: four ounce in Flamingo; 12 ounce in Moongleam,
Flamingo, Sahara, and Stiegel Blue; and the 14 ounce is known in Tangerine.

Comments: A full colonial styled tableware line, with most pieces marked with the Diamond H.

Ale, footed, straight or flared, 3 oz., 4 oz., 5 oz. or 6 oz. $20.00
Ale, footed, straight or flared, 8 oz. or 10 oz. ..30.00
Ale, footed, straight or flared, 12 oz. or 14 oz. ..35.00
Bar, 2 oz. 12.00
Bowl, extra high footed, puntied bottom, 10" ..275.00
Burgundy, 4 oz. 18.00
Butter & cover 85.00
Butter, individual 20.00
Catsup & stopper, 10 oz. 60.00
Celery tray, 9" 20.00
Celery tray, 13" 25.00
Champagne, 5½ oz. (tall) 15.00
Claret, 4½ oz. 15.00
Cocktail, 3½ oz. 12.00
Cordial, 1 oz. 40.00
Cream 45.00
Cream, hotel 30.00
Cream, hotel, cut shut and cut top & bottom .65.00
Crème de menthe, 2½ oz. 15.00
Decanter & stopper, 1 pint 135.00
Decanter & stopper, 1 quart 145.00
Finger bowl 10.00
Goblet, 8 oz. 22.00
Grapefruit, straight or flared (comport) 55.00
Jelly, low foot, 2 handled, puntied bottom 35.00
Jug, stuck handle, 1 pint 60.00
Jug, stuck handle, 1 quart 100.00
Jug, stuck handle, 3 pint 125.00
Jug, stuck handle, ½ gallon 145.00
Mayonnaise dish 20.00
Mustard & cover 45.00

Nappy, 4½", 5", or 6" 15.00
Nappy, 7" or 8" 25.00
Nappy, 9" or 10" 35.00
Oil & stopper, 2 oz. or 4 oz. 35.00
Oil & stopper, 6 oz. 30.00
Oyster cocktail, 2 piece 20.00
Plate, 6½" 15.00
Plate, 9" 35.00
Plate, mayonnaise (oval) 15.00
Salt & pepper, pr. 50.00
Salt, individual, cut top & bottom 25.00
Salt, oblong table, cut top & bottom 45.00
Saucer champagne, 4 oz. 15.00
Sherbet, high footed, scalloped, 4 oz. or 5 oz. ..20.00
Sherbet, low footed, straight or scalloped,
    3 oz., 4 oz, or 5 oz. 10.00
Spoon 45.00
Sugar, hotel 30.00
Sugar, hotel, puntied neck and cut shut 65.00
Sugar & cover 70.00
Sweetmeat, crimped (comport) 60.00
Toothpick 65.00
Tumbler, straight or flared 20.00
Water bottle, regular or squat 50.00
Wine, 2 oz. 22.00

No. 351 Priscilla footed ale.

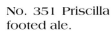

No. 351 Priscilla toothpick, cut.

No. 351 Priscilla decanter, extra high footed bowl.

No. 351 Priscilla. Top: cupped nappy, table salt, individual salt. Bottom: No. 351½ nappy, No. 351 low foot jelly.

No. 351 Priscilla hotel sugar and cream, cut shut; jug.

No. 351 Priscilla. Top: mustard. Bottom: high footed sherbet, wine, cordial, oil, catsup.

No. 351½

Nappy, 4½", 5", or 6"..$15.00
Nappy, 7" or 8" 25.00
Nappy, 9" or 10" 35.00

Flat Panel, No. 352

Date: Probably designed in 1904. Advertised for the first time in 1906. Discontinued sometime after 1929.

Colors: Crystal. The cigar jar was made in Moongleam and Zircon. The finger bowl was made in Flamingo. The lavender jar was made in Moongleam and Flamingo. The French dressing bottle was made in all Flamingo and in Crystal with a Moongleam or Flamingo stopper.

Patents: The crushed fruit jar was issued patent No. 39403 on 7-7-1908 and the spoon was given No. 39432 on 7-21-1908 with the designer listed as C. S. Whipple, one of Heisey's salesmen. The lavender jar was patented on 3-31-1914 and given No. 45542, designer, A. J. Sanford. The match stand with metal clip was assigned mechanical patent No. 952160.

Comments: One of several pressed colonial tableware patterns. Most pieces are marked with the Diamond H. The French dressing bottle was made under a license from T. G. Hawkes, Corning, New York, and can be found with Moongleam or Flamingo stoppers. See No. 500 for a lavender jar similar to the horseradish jar. Some of the cigar jars were made for Benson & Hedges (and are so marked). Flat Panel lavender jars are the same as the No. 356 lavender jars except that No. 356 jars have pointed stoppers while No. 352 have mushroom stoppers.

Ashtray	$125.00
Bowl, orange (same mold as flanged vase)	200.00
Butter & cover (oval flange)	80.00
Candy or cracker jar & cover, 1 pound	185.00
Candy or cracker jar & cover, 2 pound	210.00
Candy or cracker jar & cover, 4 pound	245.00
Celery, individual (tall) or small straw jar	90.00
Cheese & cracker plate, 2 piece	175.00
Cigar jar & stopper	250.00
Cologne, 8 oz.	100.00
Cream, hotel	25.00
Cream, individual	30.00
Crushed fruit jar, 1 quart	400.00
Crushed fruit jar, 2 quart	365.00
Finger bowl	15.00
French dressing bottle & stopper	70.00
Horseradish & stopper	70.00
Ice cream cone holder, straight or flared	70.00
Ice tub	85.00
Ice tub with drainer	160.00
Jelly, low foot, 5" (cheese & cracker center)	35.00
Jug, stuck handle, 1 pint	85.00
Jug, stuck handle, 1 quart	125.00
Jug, stuck handle, 3 pint	150.00
Jug, stuck handle, ½ gallon	185.00
Knife rest	80.00
Lavender jar, 1½ oz.	60.00
Lavender jar, 3 oz.	65.00
Lavender jar, 5 oz.	75.00
Lavender jar, 10 oz.	110.00

No. 352 Flat Panel toothpick.

No. 352 Flat Panel individual sugar, no cover.

No. 352 Flat Panel small straw jar or large spoon.

Lavender jar, 14 oz. 120.00
Lavender jar, 16 oz. 140.00
Lavender jar, 24 oz. 150.00
Marmalade & cover (similar to No. 358 hotel
    sugar) 100.00
Match stand, with metal clip..........................80.00
Mustard & cover...55.00
Nappy, 4½" or 5½" 10.00
Nappy, 7½" or 9"..25.00
Nappy, 10" or 11" 35.00
Oil & stopper, 2 oz. or 4 oz............................30.00
Oil & stopper, 6 oz...40.00
Oval 7½"..25.00
Pickle jar & cover 70.00
Plate, cantaloupe or grapefruit, 6½".............15.00
Plate, oyster cocktail, 8" 25.00
Sherbet, footed, 3½ oz. 10.00
Spoon, large..55.00
Spoon, small..45.00
Strawberry dish & drainer, 8".......................145.00
Strawberry dish & drainer, 10"......................160.00
Sugar sifter..50.00
Sugar, hotel...25.00

Sugar, hotel, with cover 35.00
Sugar, individual..30.00
Sugar, individual, with cover 40.00
Toothpick, puntied bottom 85.00
Tray, candy, 5⅝" x 8" 50.00
Tray, oval, 12" 95.00
Tray, oval, 13½"...110.00
Tray, oval, 15" 140.00
Tray, roll..40.00
Tray, round, 10"..75.00
Tray, round, 12"..85.00
Tray, round, 14"..110.00
Tumbler, 6½ oz...20.00
Vase, #1 with perforated cover 290.00
Vase, #2, medium flared.............................220.00
Vase, #3, wide flared 220.00
Vase, #4, drop flange..................................220.00
Vase, #5, tall 220.00
Vase, low, 2 piece (low bowl & perforated
    cover) 145.00
Vase, violet (same as flared ice cream
    holder) 70.00
Water bottle..50.00

No. 352 Flat Panel two-piece cheese & cracker.

No. 352 Flat Panel two quart crushed fruit.

No. 352 Flat Panel French dressing bottle, cut notches on edges of panels and crosshatched cutting around "Oil" and "Vinegar."

No. 352 Flat Panel marmalade and cover.

No. 352 Flat Panel cigar jar, 1-pound candy jar, cracker or candy jar.

No. 352 Flat Panel. Top: perforated cover. Bottom: no. 4 drop flange vase, violet vase, ashtray.

No. 358 hotel sugar & cream, similar to No. 352 marmalade.

No. 352 Flat Panel. Top: covered butter, oval. Middle: nappy. Bottom: strawberry plate & drainer, oil.

No. 352 Flat Panel. Top: knife rest. Bottom: sugar sifter, cologne, jug-stuck handle.

1905:

On December 30, 1905, George Duncan Heisey, A. H. Heisey's eldest son, became the acting president of the A. H. Heisey & Co. He remained as president until about 1912 when the West Virginia incorporation was canceled.

Medium Flat Panel, No. 353
Date: Probably designed in 1905, although not advertised until 1909.
Discontinued sometime after 1929.
Colors: Crystal. The toothbrush holder was made in Moongleam. The individual almond (same as #393) was made in Moongleam, Flamingo, Sahara, and Hawthorne while the large almond was available in Moongleam, Flamingo, and Hawthorne. The 8" vase was made in Flamingo, Hawthorne, and Canary. The 12" ice cream or candy tray was made in Flamingo.

Comments: Another pressed colonial tableware pattern with most pieces marked with the Diamond H. While similar pieces are included in most colonials, shapes often vary, especially in pieces other than bowls and plates. The sanitary syrup is shown in catalogs with a No. 1150 underplate. The No. 353 lavender jars are the same as the No. 357 lavender jars except that the No. 357 jars have pointed tops while the No. 353 have mushroom stoppers. The vases may have plain or rayed bottoms. Another similar vase has a scalloped base.

Almond, footed, 6" $30.00
Almond, footed, individual 15.00
Ashtray...20.00 – 35.00
Bowl, crushed ice..18.00
Butter & cover..80.00
Celery, individual 65.00
Celery, tall..55.00
Cheese & cracker plate (1 piece) 110.00
Cheese plate & cover, 10".........................135.00
Cologne, 8 oz. 95.00
Comport, low footed, 4½" or 5"...................10.00
Comport, low footed, 6" or 7" 20.00
Comport, low footed, 8" or 9" 35.00
Comport, low footed, cupped, 4½" or 5".......10.00
Comport, low footed, cupped, 6" or 7" 20.00
Comport, low footed, cupped, 8" or 9" 35.00
Cover, mushroom, 4½", 5½", or 6½"..............45.00
Cream..50.00
Cream, hotel, round.......................................35.00
Cream, hotel, oval 35.00
Crushed fruit & cover, 2 quart.....................250.00
Finger bowl, cupped or flared 10.00
Grapefruit..15.00
Jug, stuck handle, 1 quart............................90.00
Jug, stuck handle, 3 pint.............................100.00
Jug, stuck handle, ½ gallon........................125.00
Knife rest 125.00
Lavender jar, 2 oz. or 3 oz...........................65.00
Lavender jar, 6 oz...75.00

No. 353 Medium Flat Panel handled mug.

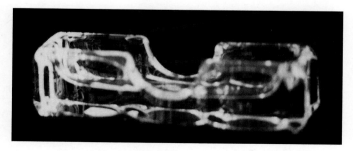

No. 353 Medium Flat Panel toothpick.

Lavender jar, 8 oz. 85.00
Lavender jar, 12 oz. 100.00
Lavender jar, 20 oz. 120.00
Lavender jar, 26 oz. (same as tobacco jar) .135.00
Lavender jar, 30 oz. 150.00
Marmalade jar & cover 55.00
Match stand 25.00
Mayonnaise 35.00
Measuring cup ....400.00+
Mug, handled..155.00
Nappy, berry, 7", 8", or 9" 35.00
Oil, 2 oz. or 4 oz. 35.00
Oil, 6 oz. or 8 oz. 45.00
Oil, 12 oz. 60.00
Plate, 7" or 8" 25.00
Plate, 10" 110.00
Plate, candy, 5⅝" x 8" 50.00
Plate, grapefruit 12.00
Plate, oyster cocktail, 9" 90.00
Salt, individual 60.00
Soap dish & cover 145.00
Soda, cupped, 8 oz. or 9 oz. (#353½) 12.00
Soda, cupped, 10 oz or 12 oz. (#353½) 15.00
Soda, flared, 8 oz. or 9 oz. 12.00
Soda, flared, 10 oz. or 12 oz. 15.00

Spoon 40.00
Straw jar, small 90.00
Straw jar, 4½" inside 60.00
Straw jar, 4½" inside, with cover 80.00
Sugar & cover 65.00
Sugar & cover, hotel, round 35.00
Sugar, hotel, oval 35.00
Syrup, sanitary, 5 oz. 65.00
Syrup, sanitary, 7 oz. 45.00
Syrup, sanitary, 12 oz. 55.00
Tobacco jar, 26 oz. 135.00
Toothbrush holder or individual straw jar ...110.00
Toothpick tray...85.00
Tray, 10" 80.00
Tray, ice cream or candy, 8" x 12"...............200.00
Tray, sanitary straw.....................................500.00+
Tray, spice, 10" 60.00
Tumbler, 8 oz...30.00
Vase, cemetery or automobile.......................125.00
Vase, plain or star bottom, 6" 30.00
Vase, plain or star bottom, 8" or 10" 45.00
Vase, plain or star bottom, 12" 55.00
Vase, plain or star bottom, 15" 75.00
Vase, plain or star bottom, 18" 125.00
Water bottle 50.00

No. 353 Medium Flat Panel cologne & stopper.

No. 353 Medium Flat Panel cheese & cracker, one piece.

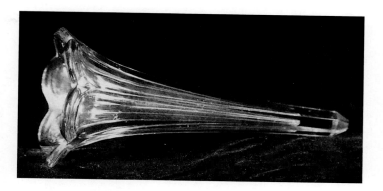

No. 353 Medium Flat Panel cemetery or automobile vase.

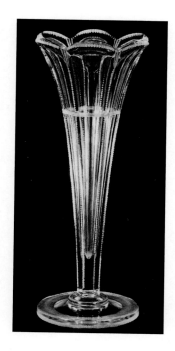

No. 353 Medium Flat Panel vase with cut notches and bands.

No. 353 Medium Flat Panel covered sugar, covered butter, cream, spoon.

No. 353 Medium Flat Panel tobacco jar, syrup, jug.

No. 353 Medium Flat Panel candy jar, two oils (different stoppers), crushed fruit.

No. 353 Medium Flat Panel hotel covered sugar and cream, oval hotel sugar and cream.

No. 353 Medium Flat Panel.
Top: marmalade, measuring cup, low footed comport, ashtrays, match stand. Bottom: ice cream or candy tray, sanitary straw tray.

Wide Flat Panel, No. 354

Date: Probably designed in 1905, but not advertised until 1910. Made until 1935.
Colors: Crystal. The stack set (cream, sugar, individual butter) was made in Flamingo. The footed oval hotel cream and sugar were made in Moongleam, Flamingo, and Hawthorne. The individual butter was made in Flamingo and Sahara. The 16 ounce sanitary syrup was made in Moongleam and usually has the patent date of 5-9-1909 in the base.
Patents: The oil was granted patent No. 42594 on 6-4-1912 with A. J. Sanford listed as designer. The sanitary straw jar was given patent No. 43108 on 10-8-1912 and the domino sugar was granted No. 43109 on the same date, both with A. J. Sanford given as designer. The domino sugar was given patent No. 43109.

Comments: This is a pressed colonial style pattern. Most pieces are marked with the Diamond H. Asterisks indicate items in the three-piece individual stack set. No. 356 is used for the stack set using the sugar with no handles. The No. 354 lavender jars are the same as the No. 358 lavender jars except the No. 358 jars have pointed stoppers while the No. 354 jars have mushroom stoppers.

Bowl, low foot, 6" or 7"	$35.00
Bowl, low foot, 8" or 9"	45.00
Bowl, low foot, cupped, 6" or 7"	35.00
Bowl, low foot, cupped, 8" or 9"	45.00
Butter & cover	50.00
Butter, individual *	20.00
Cream, hotel, oval	30.00
Cream, individual *	30.00
Crushed fruit, knob cover, 1 quart	250.00
Dish, fern with silver-plated liner, #1 (small)	50.00
Dish, fern with silver-plated liner, #2 (medium)	60.00
Dish, fern with silver-plated liner, #3 (medium)	70.00
Domino sugar	85.00
Domino sugar & spoon tray	95.00
Finger bowl, star bottom	8.00
Grapefruit with attached plate	35.00
Jug, ½ gallon	155.00
Lavender jar, 1 oz.	75.00
Lavender jar, 2½ oz.	65.00
Lavender jar, 4½ oz.	75.00
Lavender jar, 7 oz.	85.00
Lavender jar, 11 oz.	100.00
Lavender jar, 16 oz.	120.00
Lavender jar, 27 oz.	135.00
Match stand, individual	25.00
Nappy, 8"	30.00
Oil & stopper, 2 oz.	40.00
Oil & stopper, 4 oz.	25.00
Oil & stopper, 6 oz. or 8 oz.	45.00
Salt & pepper, pr.	60.00
Straw jar, sanitary	450.00
Sugar, hotel, oval	30.00
Sugar, individual, handled *	30.00
Sugar, individual, no handles	45.00
Syrup, sanitary, 12 oz.	55.00
Syrup, sanitary, 16 oz.	70.00
Vase, 10"	45.00

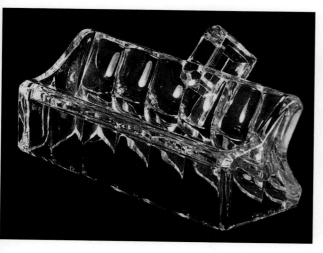

No. 354 Wide Flat Panel domino sugar.

No. 354 Wide Flat Panel sanitary syrup, oval hotel cream & sugar.

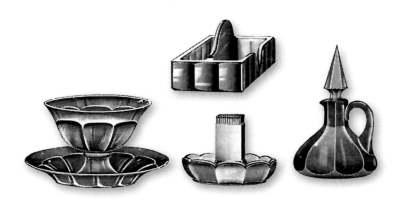

No. 354 Wide Flat Panel. Top: domino sugar and spoon tray. Bottom: grapefruit, match stand, oil.

No. 354 Wide Flat Panel. Top: mayonnaise. Bottom: sanitary straw jar, fern dish, crushed fruit.

Stack Sets. Top: No. 354 Wide Flat Panel. Bottom: No. 1184 Yeoman. 1914 ad.

No. 354 Wide Flat Panel vase, No. 391 vase, No. 387 vase.

1906:

After ten years in business, A. H. Heisey & Co. had firmly established itself as one of the premier high-grade glass tableware companies. With success came the impetus to improve both the factory and the lines for sale. A drawing of the factory was used as a frontispiece in Heisey's 1913 catalog, showing three tall smokestacks with Diamond H's built in. In 1914 the factory was expanded to house a new blownware department. Prior to this time, Heisey produced only pressed tableware and hotel ware. Many companies were developing blownware departments primarily to produce lightweight stemware, vases, and other articles which lent a more ethereal quality to glass for the home. Decorating departments were added — mostly producing etchings and cuttings.

This was also a period between pressed pattern glass and colonial styled glass, so both types were made. However, pressed pattern glass was waning in popularity and the colonial styles eventually took over the market. Colonial styles showed off Heisey's superior glass formula for clear glass; and the careful finishing of each piece, such as fire polishing and grinding and polishing of bases or base rims added to the quality of Heisey pieces. Heisey's popular baskets were introduced during this period. Many colonial styled candlesticks and candelabra were made during this period. Especially desirable are the candlesticks which were fully ground and polished on all surfaces!

Classic, No. 16
Date: Ca. 1906 to 1931
Color: Crystal

Comments: Made in several sizes of candlesticks and candelabra. May be marked on a panel at the top of the candlestick column.

Candelabrum, 16" $750.00
Candlesticks, 9" pr. 150.00

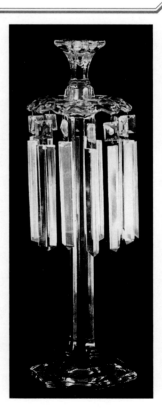

No. 16 Classic candelabrum.

Prison Stripe, No. 357
Date: 1906
Color: Crystal

Comments: "The other design, styled No. 357, is on the plain finger flute order and is really a close imitation of a certain old, effective and popular cut glass pattern." *Crockery & Glass Journal*, January 18, 1906.

Most pieces are marked with the Diamond H. A very interesting pattern with the plain colonial flutes enhanced by the horizontal flutes surrounding pieces.

Bonbon, #1, #2, or #3	$50.00
Bowl, high footed, 8" or 9"	200.00
Bowl, high footed, flared, 8½" or 9½"	200.00
Bowl, high footed, shallow, 9" or 10"	200.00
Butter & cover	195.00
Cream	110.00
Cream, hotel	90.00
Custard, 6 oz. (punch cup)	25.00
Goblet	160.00
Jelly, footed, 5"; flared or shallow, 5½"	95.00
Jelly, 2 handled, puntied bottom, low footed, 6"	95.00
Jug, quart	280.00
Jug, 3 pint	300.00
Jug, ½ gallon	325.00
Molasses can, 13 oz.	350.00
Nappy, 4" or 4½"	30.00
Nappy, 7" or 8"	65.00
Nappy, 9"	70.00
Nappy, 2 handled, 4", 4½", 5", or 6"	32.00
Nappy, flared, 7½", 8½", or 9½"	70.00
Nappy, shallow, 4½" or 5"	30.00
Nappy, shallow, 8", 9", or 10"	75.00
Oil & stopper, 6 oz.	250.00
Pickle tray, 6"	40.00
Plate, 5" or 6"	35.00
Punch bowl & foot, 10"	400.00
Punch bowl & foot, 12"	450.00
Punch bowl & foot, 14"	525.00
Punch bowl & foot, cupped, 10"	400.00
Punch bowl & foot, cupped, 12"	450.00
Punch bowl & foot, flared, 12"	450.00
Punch bowl & foot, flared, 14"	525.00
Punch bowl & foot, flared, 16"	575.00
Punch bowl & foot, shallow, 13"	450.00
Punch bowl & foot, shallow, 15"	550.00
Punch bowl & foot, shallow, 16"	575.00
Salt & pepper, pr., #3	275.00
Spoon	90.00
Spoon tray, 6"	50.00
Straw jar & cover	600.00
Sugar & cover	145.00
Sugar, hotel	90.00
Toothpick	400.00
Tumbler, 7 oz.	100.00

No. 357 Prison Stripe custard.

No. 357 Prison Stripe oil.

No. 357 Prison Stripe covered
sugar, covered butter, spoon, cream.

No. 357 Prison Stripe molasses, tumbler, jug.

Kalonyal, No. 1776 — original name
Date:1906 to 1909
Color: Crystal only
Patent: The scalloped edge nappy was granted patent No. 37203 on 11-1-1904 with
A. H. Heisey listed as designer.

Comments: Even though the pattern was patented late in 1904, an announcement of it as a new pattern was not made until January, 1906. "The Kalonyal is a panel pattern that possesses a sort of Colonial character." *Crockery & Glass Journal*, January, 18, 1906.

The panels of Kalonyal are embellished with long octagonal raised panels. Pieces are usually marked with the Diamond H and have ground and polished bottoms. Decorations sometimes found include gold, ruby stain, ruby stain with gold.

Bonbon, #1, #2, or #3 ....$40.00
Bowl, high footed, 8" or 9" (comport) 300.00
Bowl, high footed, shallow, 10" (comport)...330.00
Burgundy, 3 oz. 55.00
Butter & cover..185.00
Celery, tall...130.00
Champagne, 6½ oz. (tall)............................80.00
Claret, 5 oz. 65.00
Cordial, 1½ oz..350.00+
Cream...125.00
Cream, hotel..85.00
Custard, 3½ oz..35.00
Custard, 5 oz. 28.00
Egg cup, 9½ oz..65.00
Goblet, 9 oz. 110.00
Jelly, handled, round, 3 corner or crimped, 5" 55.00
Jelly, high footed, 6".....................................90.00
Jelly, high footed, crimped, 5½" 90.00
Jelly, high footed, flared, 5½".........................90.00
Jelly, high footed, shallow, 5½" 90.00

Jug, pressed handle, ½ gallon 210.00
Jug, stuck handle, ½ gallon.........................210.00
Molasses can, 13 oz. 275.00
Mug, handled..110.00
Mustard & cover...150.00
Nappy, 4½", 5", or 6" 30.00
Nappy, 7", 8", or 9"......................................90.00
Nappy, crimped, 4½" or 5" 30.00
Nappy, crimped, 8", 9", or 10" 90.00
Nappy, flared, 8", 9", or 10" 90.00
Nappy, high footed, 9" (crimped).................300.00
Nappy, shallow, 5", 5½", or 6".......................30.00
Nappy, shallow, 9", 10", or 11" 90.00
Oil & stopper, 2 oz. 225.00
Oil & stopper, 4 oz. or 6 oz. 195.00
Pickle dish 40.00
Pickle jar with knob cover............................175.00
Plate, 5½" or 6"..25.00
Plate, fruit, 11" 95.00
Punch bowl & foot, 12" 395.00

Salt & pepper, #2 or #3, pr. 175.00
Salver, high footed, 9" or 10" 325.00
Sherbet, 6 oz. 22.00
Sherbet, scalloped, 3½ oz., 4½ oz., or 5½ oz. .22.00
Sherbet, straight or flared, 5 oz. 22.00
Spoon tray..45.00
Spoon..95.00
Sugar & cover..155.00
Sugar sifter 175.00
Sugar, hotel 65.00
Toothpick 450.00
Tumbler 125.00
Water bottle 185.00
Wine, 2 oz. 85.00

No. 1776 Kalonyal tall compote.

No. 1776 Kalonyal spoon.

No. 1776 Kalonyal jug,
pressed handle; water bottle; jug, stuck handle.

No. 1776 Kalonyal handled mug, no. 2
salt, no. 3 salt, oil, molasses can.

1907:

Reports of the Heisey display at the Monongahela House in Pittsburgh in January commented that their line of colonial styles was immense. Mr. Cassel, Heisey's representative, said "If there is anything in colonial glassware we will make it if we are told what is wanted.'...Here is pattern after pattern in those pieces. It is a compliment to the line of this company that year after year they have to preserve lines of other years, and this gives them great variety which they possess."

Aristocrat, No. 21
Date: 1907 to 1935
Color: Crystal
Patent: No. 41590 granted 7-18-1911 to Andrew J. Sanford, designer

Comments: Made in several heights of candlesticks, including a short desk candlestick. Also used for several electroportable lamps. Marked with the Diamond H at the base of the candlecup.

Candlesticks, 7", pr......................................$130.00
Candlesticks, 9", pr......................................170.00
Candlesticks, 11", pr......................................345.00
Candlesticks, 15", pr......................................500.00+
Candlesticks, desk, pr. 175.00

No. 21 Aristocrat candlestick.

Windsor, No. 22
Date:1907 to 1933
Colors: Crystal

Comments: These candlesticks are usually marked at the top of the column just below the candleholder.

Candlesticks, 7", pr. $140.00
Candlesticks, 9", pr. 200.00
Candlesticks, 11", pr. 350.00

No. 22 Windsor candlestick.

Banded Flute, No. 150
Date: 1907 to 1932
Colors. Crystal. 10" trays are known in Flamingo and Moongleam.

Comments: This is the second pattern numbered 150. The two are not easily confused because of their great difference in style. See No. 150 Pointed Oval in Diamond Point in Chapter 1. The two ounce bar glass without sham is the same as the toothpick. Interestingly, catalogs also label punch bowls as orange bowls. Items are marked with the Diamond H and have ground and polished bottoms. Heisey combined several sets with pitchers, trays, candlesticks, tumblers, etc. to form various water sets. These are rarely found intact today.

Bar, water, 5 oz.	$20.00
Bar, with or without sham, 1½ oz., 2½ oz., or 3 oz.	30.00
Bowl, high footed, 8" or 9" (comport)	130.00
Burgundy, 3½ oz.	25.00
Butter & cover	145.00
Candlestick, saucer foot, handled	65.00
Celery tray, 12"	40.00
Claret, 4½ oz.	28.00
Cocktail, 3 oz.	20.00
Cordial, 1 oz.	85.00
Cream	60.00
Cream, hotel	45.00
Custard, 4 oz. (punch cup)	15.00
Egg cup, 5½ oz. (same as low foot sherbet or oyster cocktail)	15.00
Finger bowl	15.00
Goblet, 7 oz. or 9 oz.	40.00
Grape juice, 4 oz. (footed)	25.00
Horseradish jar & stopper, or mustard	95.00
Ice tea tumbler, 12 oz.	20.00
Jug, stuck handle, ½ pint or 1 pint	60.00
Jug, stuck handle, 1¼ pint or 1 quart	150.00
Jug, stuck handle, 1¼ quart or 3 pint	210.00
Jug, stuck handle, ½ gallon or 3 quart	260.00
Match box & cover	250.00
Match stand	50.00
Molasses can, 7 oz.	110.00
Mug, root beer, 16 oz.	200.00
Nappy, 4" or 4½"	15.00
Nappy, 7", 8", or 9"	45.00
Nappy, flared, 4½" or 5"	15.00
Nappy, flared, 8½", 9½", or 10½"	50.00
Nappy, shallow, 5" or 5½"	15.00
Nappy, shallow, 9" or 10"	50.00
Nappy, shallow, 12"	55.00
Oil & stopper, 4 oz. or 6 oz.	70.00
Oyster cocktail or low footed sherbet, 5½ oz.	15.00
Oyster cocktail, 2 piece	35.00
Oyster cocktail, 3 piece	45.00
Pickle jar & knob cover	95.00

Pickle tray, 7"	40.00
Plate, 5", 6", or 7"	20.00
Punch bowl & foot, straight 14", flared or shallow, 15", shallow 18"	395.00
Salt & pepper, pr.	75.00
Saucer champagne or high footed sherbet, 4½ oz.	20.00
Schoeppen, 5 oz. or 7 oz.	20.00
Schoeppen, 8 oz. or 9 oz.	25.00
Schoeppen, 10 oz. or 12 oz.	32.00
Schoeppen, 14 oz. or 16 oz.	45.00
Schoeppen, soda or lemonade, footed, straight, or flared 14 oz.	65.00
Sherbet, low foot, 3 oz. or 4½ oz.	15.00
Sherbet, saucer footed, 3 oz.	25.00
Soda, tapered 5 oz.	15.00
Soda, tapered, 8 oz. or 10 oz.	20.00

No. 150 Banded Flute
horseradish jar & stopper.

Soda, tapered, 12 oz. or 14 oz........................24.00
Spoon 55.00
Sugar & cover 85.00
Sugar & cover, hotel...70.00
Sugar sifter..120.00
Sundae, flared, handled, 4½"...........................25.00
Syrup, silver-plated top, 7 oz........................120.00
Tankard & cover, stuck handle, pint 250.00
Tankard, stuck handle, pint 120.00
Toothpick or 2 oz. bar 75.00
Tray, 10"...110.00
Tray, 13"...145.00
Tumbler 8 oz...45.00
Tumbler, footed, 9 oz. or low footed goblet 35.00
Water bottle, regular or squat 150.00
Wine, 2 oz. 40.00

No. 150 Banded Flute custard (punch cup).

No. 150 Banded Flute small nappy.

No. 150 Band-
ed Flute covered butter,
cream, spoon, covered
sugar.

No. 150 Banded Flute stemware: goblet, footed tumbler, claret, burgundy, wine, cordial, cocktail, saucer champagne, cupped goblet.

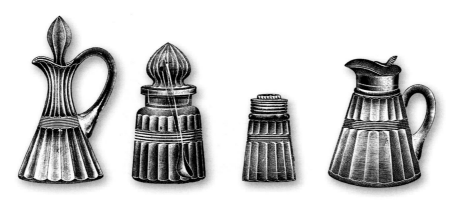

No. 150 Banded Flute oil, horseradish jar, salt, molasses can.

No. 150 Banded Flute high foot bowl, no. 2 bedroom set.

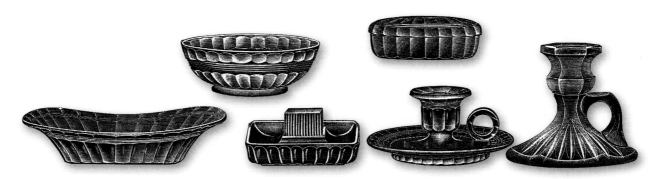

No. 150 Banded Flute. Top: nappy, match box. Bottom: pickle tray, match box stand, saucer foot candlestick, handled candlestick.

Queen Anne, No. 365 — original name
Date: 1907. Discontinued before 1913.
Color: Crystal
Patent: Design patent No. 38200 was given to the Queen Anne spoon on 8-28-1906 with A. H. Heisey listed as designer.

Comments: "The No. 365, or Queen Anne pattern, is one that needs to be seen and foolish is the buyer who misses any opportunity to look it over. It is a shield effect with mitered fluting decorations and is entirely out of the class of any similar productions of the kind in the past. It is a reproduction of a piece of cut glass and its scintillating beauty is marvelous." *China, Glass & Lamps*, January 19, 1907.

Queen Anne is the original company name. Pieces are marked with the Diamond H. Most have ground and polished bottoms. It is somewhat difficult to find and very attractive. It is very eye-catching in ruby stain. Do not confuse this with Heisey's later pattern named Queen Ann, No. 1509. Decorations occasionally found include gold, ruby stain on shields, ruby stain on shields outlined in gold. Add 100% for pieces with ruby stain.

Butter & cover	$180.00
Celery tray, 12"	80.00
Celery, hotel, 12"	90.00
Celery, tall	120.00
Cream	100.00
Cream, hotel	85.00
Custard (punch cup)	45.00
Dish, oblong, 8" or 10"	75.00
Goblet	125.00
Jelly, handled, 5"	70.00
Jug, 1 pint	120.00
Jug, 1 quart	175.00
Jug, 3 pint	210.00
Jug, ½ gallon	250.00
Molasses can, 13 oz.	245.00
Nappy, 4", 4½", or 5"	30.00
Nappy, 7" or 8"	70.00
Nappy, 9" or 10"	90.00
Nappy, crimped, 4½", 5", 5½", or 6"	30.00
Nappy, crimped, 9" or 10"	100.00
Nappy, shallow, 4½", 5", or 5½"	30.00
Nappy, shallow or flared, 8", 9", or 10"	100.00
Oil & stopper, 2 oz. or 4 oz.	165.00
Oil & stopper, 6 oz.	175.00
Pickle tray, 7"	65.00
Plate, 5"	25.00
Punch bowl & foot	500.00+
Salt & pepper, pr., #2 or #3	250.00
Salver, 10"	210.00
Sherbet, footed, 4 oz.	30.00
Spoon	95.00
Sugar & cover	150.00
Sugar & cover, hotel	110.00
Toothpick	750.00
Tray, fruit, oblong, 14"	125.00
Tumbler	90.00
Water bottle	185.00
Wine, 2 oz.	135.00

No. 365
Queen Anne covered sugar, covered butter, spoon, cream.

No. 365 Queen Anne salt shaker.

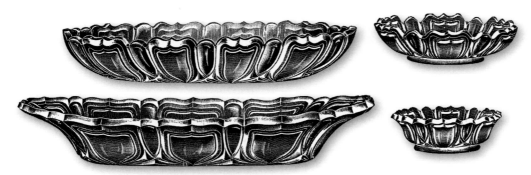

No. 365 Queen Anne. Top: celery tray, shallow nappy. Bottom: fruit tray, nappy.

1908:

The Heisey company built a new building of three stories to be used as a warehouse.

Skirted Panel, Handled, No. 33
Date: 1908 to 1928
Color: Crystal

Comments: May be marked with the Diamond H at the top of the base just under the candle cup. Made handled and without handle. See No. 5 Patrician for toy No. 33 candlestick.

Candlesticks, 5", handled, pr. $100.00
Candlesticks, 7", handled, pr. 110.00

No. 33 Skirted Panel handled candlestick.

Hartman, No. 369
Date: 1908, discontinued before 1924.
Color: Crystal only

Comments: Often found with narrow optic. Marked with the Diamond H. Usually have ground and polished bottoms.

Bar, plain or optic, straight or flared, 2 oz. or
  3 oz. $20.00
Bar, water, plain or optic, 6½ oz. 15.00
Finger bowl, straight or flared.......................10.00
Burgundy, 3½ oz. 20.00
Champagne, 7 oz. (tall)..................................22.00
Claret, 5 oz. 20.00
Cocktail, 3 oz...15.00

Cordial, 1 oz. 70.00
Goblet, straight or cupped, 9 oz. 30.00
Jug, 3 pint...145.00
Jug, ½ gallon...160.00
Nappy, 4" or 4½" 10.00
Nappy, 7", 8", or 9".......................................40.00
Nappy, flared, 4½" or 5" 10.00
Nappy, flared, 8½", 9½", or 10½" 40.00

Nappy, shallow, 5" or 5½" 10.00
Nappy, shallow, 9", 10" or 11".......................40.00
Oyster cocktail, 2 piece or 3 piece 35.00
Plate, 5" 8.00
Saucer champagne, 4½ oz. 20.00
Soda, straight or flared, 4 oz., 5 oz., or 6 oz...10.00
Soda, straight or flared, 7 oz., 8 oz., or 9 oz...15.00
Soda, straight or flared, 10 oz., 11 oz., 12 oz.,
   or 13 oz..20.00
Tumbler, 10 oz. 15.00
Tumbler, hotel, 8 oz.................................15.00
Wine, 2 oz. 35.00

No. 369 Hartman. Top: nappy. Bottom: flared bar, tumbler, jug.

No. 369 Hartman Stemware: goblet, champagne, claret, burgundy, wine, cordial.

1909:

During the latter part of 1909 and much of 1910, Andrew J. Sanford, Heisey's designer, patented at least 23 light shades, primarily for electric lights, for the Heisey company.

Criss Cross, No. 361
Date: 1909. The tumbler was made into the 1920s.
Colors: Crystal, tumbler in Flamingo made after 1925.

Comments: Marked with Diamond H. This pattern is uncommon. Nappies are sometimes found with gold decoration. The tumbler varies slightly from the nappies in that some of the woven bands do not have ridges on them. The tumbler in Flamingo is valued at $95.00+.

No. 361 Criss Cross nappy.

Nappy, regular, shallow, cupped, or flared, 4"
   or 4½"...$20.00
Nappy, regular, shallow, cupped, or flared,
   7", 8", or 10" 55.00
Nappy, shallow, crimped, 4" or 4½" 22.00

Nappy, shallow, crimped, 7", 8", or 10"..........60.00
Tumbler (Angular Criss Cross), Flamingo 80.00

Angular Criss Cross
tumbler, Flamingo.

Urn, No. 379, 379½
Date: 1909. Discontinued before 1913.
Color: Crystal

Comments: Most pieces were available with either fire-polished tops or full-ground tops. Be sure that your items have three tiny bands on tops and bottoms. If not, they have been repaired. Pieces are marked with the Diamond H. Gold is sometimes found on the small bands.

Bowl, orange, footed, flared, 13" (#379½) ...$140.00	
Bowl, orange, footed, shallow, 14" (comport) .140.00	
Bowl, orange, with foot, 12" 160.00	
Bowl, orange without foot, 12" 70.00	
Butter & cover...145.00	
Cream..70.00	
Cream, hotel...35.00	
Custard, 4½ oz. (punch cup) 25.00	
Egg, footed, 5 oz..30.00	
Finger bowl...35.00	
Goblet..75.00	
Goblet, 8½ oz. (#379½) 50.00	
Jug, ½ gallon...185.00	
Molasses can, 7 oz. 95.00	
Molasses can, 12 oz. 165.00	
Nappy, 4", 4½", or 5" 20.00	
Nappy, 6", 7", or 8"....................................55.00	
Nappy, 9" or 10"...90.00	
Oil & stopper, 4 oz. 120.00	
Oil & stopper, 6 oz. 150.00	
Oyster cocktail, 2 piece 55.00	
Salt & pepper, pr. 120.00	
Salt, individual 40.00	
Salt, large table (master)..............................45.00	
Salt, small table (master)..............................40.00	

Salver, 10"...165.00
Sherbet, footed, 4 oz. 25.00
Spoon...65.00
Sugar & cover 110.00
Sugar, hotel..60.00
Sugar & cover, hotel....................................75.00
Tankard, ½ gallon 195.00
Toothpick..200.00
Tumbler, 7 oz..50.00
Tumbler, 8 oz. (#379½)................................35.00
Water bottle 165.00

No. 379 Urn
toothpick.

No. 379 Urn covered sugar, covered butter, cream, spoon.

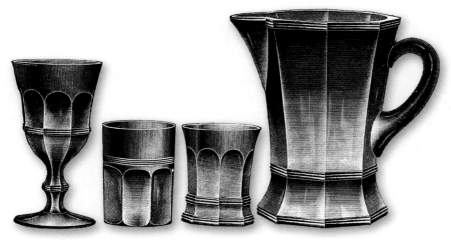

No. 379 Urn goblet, No. 379½ tumbler, No. 379 tumbler, tankard.

No. 379 Urn salver, hotel cream and sugar, covered hotel sugar.

Scalloped Octagon, No. 380
Date: 1909. Discontinued before 1913.
Color: Crystal only

Comments: A pattern only of nappies. Marked with the Diamond H. The bottom is ground and polished.

Nappy, 12".....................$150.00

No. 380 Scalloped Octagon nappy.

No. 381 Heisey Quilt nappy.

Heisey Quilt, No. 381
Date: 1909. Discontinued before 1913.
Color: Crystal only

Comments: Made only in nappies. Marked with the Diamond H. The pattern is difficult to find.

Nappy, 4"....................................$45.00
Nappy, 9"....................................140.00

Grid & Square, No. 385
Date: 1909. Discontinued by 1913.
Color: Crystal only

Comments: Made only in a water set. Marked with the Diamond H.

Jug, ½ gallon $350.00
Tumbler, 9 oz. 80.00

No. 385 Grid & Square tankard, tumbler.

Colonial Scalloped Top, Nos. 400, 400½
Date: 1909. Discontinued before 1924.
Color: Crystal

Comments: A colonial pattern similar to No. 300 Peerless. It is difficult to distinguish between the two except some of the items do not have the Peerless pleats around the bottom. Marked with the Diamond H.

Bowl, high footed, 8" or 9" (comport)...........$85.00
Bowl, high footed, flared, 9" or 10" (comport) ...90.00
Bowl, high footed, shallow, 10" or 11"
   (comport)...110.00
Bowl, high footed, shallow, 10" or 11"
   (comport, #400½) 110.00
Butter & cover 75.00
Celery, tall 45.00
Cream 40.00
Cream, hotel 30.00
Custard, 3½ oz. (punch cup).....................12.00
Egg cup...18.00
Goblet, 11 oz. 45.00
Jelly, footed, 5" or 5½" shallow 35.00
Jelly, low footed, 2 handled......................35.00
Jug, 1 quart 160.00
Jug, 3 pint 120.00
Jug, ½ gallon 120.00
Jug, 3 quart 130.00
Molasses can, 13 oz. 85.00

Nappy, 4" or 4½" 10.00
Nappy, 7½", 8½", or 9½".........................35.00
Nappy, shallow, 4½" or 5" 10.00
Nappy, shallow, 8", 9", or 10"....................35.00
Nappy, shallow, 10½" (#400½) 35.00
Oil & stopper, 6 oz................................55.00
Punch bowl & foot, cupped, flared, or shallow,
   12"...250.00
Salt & pepper, pr. no. 1 ....50.00
Salver, 9" or 10" 100.00
Sherbet, 4 oz......................................15.00
Spoon 35.00
Sugar & cover......................................60.00
Sugar, hotel 35.00
Toothpick 145.00
Tumbler, 8 oz. 20.00
Water bottle 65.00
Wine, 2 oz. 30.00

No. 400 Colonial Scalloped Top toothpick.

No. 400 Colonial Scalloped Top covered butter, covered sugar, cream, spoon.

No. 400 Colonial Scalloped Top salver, jug.

No. 400 Colonial Scalloped Top. Top: shallow nappy. Bottom: nappies, two-handled low footed jelly.

No. 400 Colonial Scalloped Top molasses, oil, hotel sugar and cream.

No. 400½ Colonial Scalloped Top shallow nappy, high footed shallow bowl.

1910:

During this year several of the Heisey syrups were patented. These included No. 353, 354, 355, 357, and 359 syrups. The company targeted the soda fountain industry with a special catalog of items suitable for soda fountains.

No. 16, No. 17, No. 25
Date: 1910
Color: Crystal
Patent: Patent No. 40640, filed 11-26-1909, designed by Andrew J. Sanford.

Comments: Pressed, with cut and polished tops and bottoms. Marked with the Diamond H. No. 17 is slightly larger than No. 16, and No. 25 even larger. These two styles are much more difficult to find than No. 16.

No. 16 hair receiver, cut top and bottom.

Hair receiver (#16)	$85.00
Puff & cover (#16)	85.00
Puff & cover (#17)	110.00
Puff & cover (#25)	145.00

No. 16, No. 25, and
No. 17 puff boxes and covers.

Pinwheel & Fan, No. 350
Date: 1910
Colors: Crystal. Large nappy in Flamingo, Moongleam, Marigold, and Canary. Custard and punch bowl in Moongleam. Four inch nappies are known in an odd shade of Moongleam and Canary while the tumbler is known in an off shade of yellow.

Comments: A limited line, not typical of Heisey's designs. Items in color are difficult to find and expensive. A basket pattern was made very similar in design to Pinwheel & Fan, but was given No. 460. It was made in 7", 8", and 9" sizes, marked with the Diamond H, and can have the patent date of 2-22-16 in the bottom.

Basket, 7" (#460)	$300.00
Basket, 8" (#460)	350.00
Basket, 9" (#460)	375.00
Cream, hotel	60.00
Custard, 4½ oz. (punch cup)	25.00
Hair receiver	100.00
Jug, stuck handle, 3 pint	175.00
Nappy, 4½"	20.00
Nappy, 8"	50.00
Nappy, shallow, 5"	20.00
Powder box & cover	100.00
Punch bowl & high foot, 14"	450.00
Sugar, hotel	60.00
Tumbler, 8 oz.	40.00

No. 350 Pinwheel & Fan nappy, hotel cream and sugar.

No. 350 Pinwheel & Fan tumbler, jug.

No. 460 basket.

Narrow Flute, Nos. 393, 393½ — original description
Date: 1910
Colors: Crystal. In the 1930s the bitter bottle was made in Stiegel Blue (cobalt), but this is very rare. The individual cream and sugar were made in Moongleam, Flamingo, and Sahara, and the individual sugar in Marigold. The individual cream is rare in experimental light blue. The individual salt and the salt shaker were made in Moongleam and Flamingo. The banana split was made in Flamingo.
Patents: The jug with stuck handle was given patent No. 42665 on 6-25-1912; the two-handled jelly was given patent No. 42711 on 7-2-1912; the #393½ nappy was granted No. 43852 on 4-15-1913; while the pressed handle jug was given No. 43854 on 4-15-1913. The parfait was granted patent No. 46733 on 12-8-1914. The patents were granted to A. J. Sanford for the jelly, nappy, and pressed handle jug, while T. C. Heisey was granted the patents for the jug with stuck handle and the parfait.

Comments: Narrow Flute is an original company description of this pattern. Heisey suggested that No. 393 or No. 394 sodas could be used as follows: 4 or 5 oz. for grape or orange juice; 6 or 7 oz. for hot whiskey (#393) or high ball; 12 oz. for ice tea. Heisey and Imperial were involved in a lawsuit regarding this pattern and a similar one Imperial was making. Heisey insisted it had a patent on the pattern while Imperial said that the simple panel motif was in common use. Heisey lost the suit. Heisey combined several items to make bedroom sets and water sets such as jugs, tumblers, candlesticks, match stands, etc. These are rarely found intact today.

Almond, footed, or low footed jelly	$22.00
Almond, individual (same as #353 individual almond)	15.00
Banana split, footed, 9"	30.00
Bar, 2½ oz.	10.00
Bitter bottle	55.00
Burgundy, 3 oz.	15.00
Butter & cover	65.00
Butter, individual	20.00
Celery tray, 9"	20.00
Celery tray, 12"	25.00
Champagne, 6 oz.	15.00
Champagne, hollow stem, straight or flared, 4½ oz.	28.00
Cheese & cracker plate, 2 piece, 10"	95.00
Claret, 5 oz.	20.00
Cocktail, 3 oz.	15.00
Cordial, 1 oz.	60.00
Cream	30.00
Cream, hotel, footed, oval	20.00
Cream, individual	30.00
Custard, 4½ oz. (punch cup)	18.00
Domino sugar, individual, footed	70.00
Egg, 5 oz. or 6 oz.	15.00
Finger bowl, medium or large, straight, cupped, or flared	12.00

No. 393 Narrow Flute assorted items.

No. 393 Narrow Flute individual domino sugar.

Goblet, 8 oz. or 9 oz.	25.00
Grapefruit, low footed	20.00
Hasty pudding (like a large creamer)	95.00
Ice tea, 12 oz. or 13 oz.	18.00
Ice tea, footed & handled, 12 oz.	25.00
Ice tub, hotel	130.00
Ice tub, individual	30.00
Jelly, 2 handled, 5½"	25.00
Jelly, handled, straight or 3 cornered, 5"	25.00
Jelly, low footed, 5½"	20.00
Jug, pressed handle, 8 oz. (straight sided)	35.00
Jug, pressed handle, 1 pint (straight sided)	45.00
Jug, pressed handle, 1 quart (straight sided)	75.00
Jug, pressed handle, 3 pint (straight sided)	85.00
Jug, pressed handle, ½ gallon (straight sided)	100.00
Jug, stuck handle, 1 pint	45.00
Jug, stuck handle, 10 oz. or 12 oz.	35.00
Jug, stuck handle, 1 quart	75.00
Jug, stuck handle, 3 pint	85.00
Jug, stuck handle ½ gallon	70.00
Jug, whiskey, & stopper, 24 oz.	150.00
Lemon dish, 4½" or 5" (no cover)	20.00
Lemon dish & cover, 4½" or 5"	45.00
Marmalade & cover	65.00
Mustard & cover	50.00
Oil & stopper, 2 oz. or 4 oz.	60.00
Oil & stopper, 6 oz.	45.00
Orange juice glass, 4 oz.	35.00
Oyster cocktail, 2 piece	30.00
Parfait, 4½ oz.	30.00
Pickle jar, mushroom stopper	85.00
Pickle tray, 7"	24.00
Plate, 4½", 5", or 5½"	8.00
Plate, 6", 6½", or 7"	12.00
Plate, 8" or 9"	18.00
Plate, 10"	80.00
Preserve & cover, low footed, 5½"	45.00

Punch bowl & foot, regular 14", flared 16", shallow 18"	300.00
Relish, combination, & cover	95.00
Salt & pepper, pr.	50.00
Salt, individual	25.00
Saucer champagne or high footed sherbet, shallow, 5 oz.	20.00
Sherbet, low footed, deep, 4 oz. or cupped or flared, 4½ oz.	10.00
Sherbet, shallow, footed, 5 oz.	15.00
Sherry, 2 oz.	30.00
Soda, footed & handled, 4 oz., 5 oz., or 6 oz.	18.00
Soda, footed & handled, 7 oz. or 8 oz.	22.00
Soda, footed & handled, 10 oz. or 12 oz.	28.00
Soda, straight or flared, 4 oz., 5 oz., or 6 oz.	12.00
Soda, straight or flared, 7 oz. 8 oz., or 9 oz.	15.00
Soda, straight or flared, 10 oz. or 11 oz.	20.00
Soda, straight or flared, 12 oz. or 13 oz.	25.00
Soda, straight or flared, 16 oz.	30.00
Spoon	30.00
Sugar & cover	40.00
Sugar & cover, hotel (round)	25.00
Sugar, hotel, footed, oval	20.00
Sugar, individual	30.00
Tankard, stuck handle, ½ gallon	140.00
Tray, biscuit, 9"	110.00
Tray, Japanese garden, 10" or 12"	130.00
Tray, Japanese garden, 14"	150.00
Tray, oval, 10"	50.00
Tray, oval, 10" with sherbet, 2 piece	65.00
Tumbler, 6½ oz., 8 oz., or 9 oz.	20.00
Tumbler, footed, 9 oz. or low footed goblet	25.00
Water bottle	45.00
Water ice, low footed, flared, 5 oz.	10.00
Wine, 2 oz.	25.00

No. 393 Narrow Flute low footed preserve & cover, gold decorated.

No. 393 Narrow Flute plate with enamel and gold decoration.

No. 393 Narrow Flute mustard & cover.

No. 393 Narrow Flute covered sugar, covered butter, spoon, cream.

No. 393 Narrow Flute Stemware: 9 ounce goblet, 8 ounce goblet, champagne, claret, burgundy, wine, cordial, sherry, cocktail.

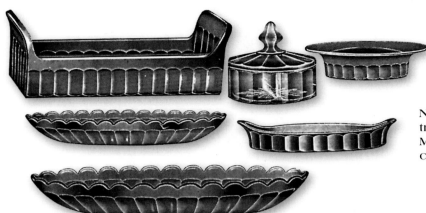

No. 393 Narrow Flute. Top: biscuit tray, combination relish, baked apple. Middle: 9" celery, pickle. Bottom: 12" celery.

No. 393 Narrow Flute. Top: custard. Bottom: stuck handle jug, orange juice, pressed handle jug.

No. 393 Narrow Flute. Top: oval hotel cream and sugar. Bottom: French dressing boat, round hotel sugar and cream.

No. 393 Narrow Flute
pickle jar, marmalade jar, decanter,
bitter bottle, oil.

No. 393½:

Oyster cocktail, 2 piece..............................$30.00
Nappy, flared, 4½" or 5"...................................8.00
Nappy, flared, 8"...25.00
Nappy, flared, 9½" or 10½" 30.00
Nappy, regular or deep, 4" or 4½"....................8.00
Nappy, regular or deep, 7", 8", or 9" 25.00
Nappy, shallow or flared, 4½" or 5".................8.00
Nappy, shallow, 8½"..25.00
Nappy, shallow, 10" or 11" 30.00
Sherbet, low footed, 4½", straight, cupped, or
    flared...9.00

No. 393½ Narrow Flute. Top: nappy. Bottom: shallow nappy, two-piece oyster cocktail.

Narrow Flute, Nos. 394, 395 — original description
Date: 1910

Colors: Crystal. The domino sugar was made in Flamingo, Moongleam, and Sahara. The 12" celery tray and the combination relish were made in Moongleam and Flamingo.

Patents: The domino sugar was assigned patent No. 45893. Patent No. 48612 was assigned on 2-22-1916 for the fruit dish (preserve) with A. J. Sanford as designer.

Comments: A continuation of Narrow Flute No. 393, but in slightly different forms. No. 394 sodas do not have handles as those of No. 393. Punch bowls are sometimes found with covers. Dr. Johnson refers to the shape of the punch bowl — tall and slender. Pieces are marked with the Diamond H, and most have ground and polished bottoms.

Boston egg cup or footed sherbet, 5 oz........$10.00
Celery tray, 12"...25.00
Chow chow dish, 4½".......................................15.00
Cottage cheese, 9"...35.00
Cracker & cheese & cover...............................85.00
Domino sugar..60.00
Domino sugar, individual 85.00
Goblet...25.00
Goblet, 10½ oz. (#395)...................................25.00
Lemon dish, 5"..15.00
Marmalade or horseradish & cover 50.00
Mustard & cover 90.00
Oil & stopper, 6 oz. 150.00
Orange juice glass, 4 oz..................................50.00
Pickle jar & cover 50.00
Preserve dish, 6"...20.00
Punch bowl, Dr. Johnson, footed 600.00
Relish dish, 3 compartment.............................30.00
Salted nut dish, 3½"..20.00
Schoeppen, straight or flared, 12 oz. 18.00
Sherbet, low footed, 3½ oz. 9.00
Soda, footed, 4 oz., 5 oz., or 6 oz. 12.00
Soda, footed, 7 oz. or 8 oz. 15.00
Soda, footed, 10 oz. or 12 oz. 17.00

Vase, bud, 4" or 5" 35.00
Vase, bud, 6" 40.00

No. 394 Narrow Flute oil & stopper.

No. 394 Narrow Flute covered mustard.

No. 394 Narrow Flute goblet, French dressing, marmalade jar, pickle jar.

No. 394 Narrow Flute. Top: salted nut, chow chow, cracker & cheese. Bottom: fruit, lemon, preserve.

No. 394 Narrow Flute. Top: individual domino sugar, orange juice, Boston egg. Middle: domino sugar, cottage cheese. Bottom: celery tray.

Colonial Cupped Scallop, No. 397
Date: 1910 to 1913
Color: Crystal

Comments: Rather difficult to find. Most pieces will be marked with the Diamond H. Gold is sometimes found on the scalloped band.

No. 397 Colonial Cupped Scallop tumbler.

Butter & cover $110.00
Celery tray, 13" 45.00
Cheese & cover 165.00
Cream 55.00
Jug, ½ gallon 145.00
Nappy, 4", 4½", or 5" 12.00
Nappy, 6", 7", 8", or 9" 35.00
Nappy, cupped, 7" or 8" 35.00
Nappy, shallow, 4½", 5½", or 6½" 12.00
Nappy, shallow, 7½" or 8½" 35.00
Nappy, shallow, 10" or 11" 40.00
Oil & stopper, 6 oz. 200.00
Pickle tray, 6" 25.00
Plate, 5", 6", or 7" 20.00
Salt & pepper, pr. 150.00
Spoon 60.00
Sugar & cover 85.00
Tray, candy, 5⅝" x 8" 50.00
Tumbler, 8 oz. 70.00

No. 397 Colonial Cupped Scallop large nappy.

Diamond Band, No. 423
Date: Exact date unknown. Likely 1910. Discontinued before 1913.
Color: Crystal

Comments: A rare pattern made for a short time. Marked with the Diamond H. Very attractive. Sometimes found with gold decoration. Goblets in the same design, but cut, were made by Val St. Lambert of Belgium.

Butter & cover..$200.00
Cream...145.00
Custard, handled, 4½ oz. (punch cup) 75.00
Finger bowl..60.00
Goblet...200.00

Jug, ½ gallon..450.00
Nappy, 4", or shallow, 4½"...............................35.00
Nappy, 8" straight, or 8½" shallow 75.00
Plate, 5"...25.00
Plate, 7" or 9" 35.00

Plate, 11" 100.00
Sherbet, footed, 4 oz. or 5 oz. 35.00
Spoon...145.00
Sugar & cover 180.00
Tumbler, 8 oz..150.00

No. 423 Diamond Band tumbler with gold.

No. 423 Diamond Band sherbet and custard.

1911:

Daisy & Leaves, No. 427
Date: 1911. Most pieces discontinued before 1913.
Color: Crystal only

Comments: Somewhat hard to find. Some items marked. Most items have ground and polished bottoms. Sometimes flowers are satin finished. A basket with a similar design was made (see page 160).

Cream, hotel...$75.00
Finger bowl 45.00
Ice tea, 12 oz..75.00
Jug, ½ gallon..325.00
Nappy, 4" or 4½" 30.00
Nappy, 8" 70.00
Nappy, shallow, 4½" or 5" 30.00
Nappy, shallow, 9½"..70.00
Sugar, hotel 75.00
Tumbler, 8 oz...125.00
Vase, cut top, 9" 225.00
Vase, plain top, 9"...195.00
Vase, swing, 7" to 48" (#54-440) price will vary
   due to height

No. 427 Daisy & Leaves tumbler, jug.

No. 54-440 Daisy & Leaves swing vase, made in several sizes.

Plain Panel Recess, No. 429
Date: 1911, still in 1924
Color: Crystal
Patents: The sugar was given patent No. 40686 on 5-10-1910. The tumbler
was given patent No. 43703 on 3-11-1913. Patent No. 43437 was
granted on 1-7-1913 for the crushed fruit. The oil was patented
on 4-15-1913 and given No. 43853. Andrew J. Sanford was listed
as designer on all patents.

Comments: The low footed sherbet was also used as a punch glass. Some items are
patent dated. Pieces are marked with the Diamond H, and have ground and polished
bottoms. This pattern always seems to have excellent, clear crystal glass.

Celery tray, 9".................................$20.00	Jug, ½ gallon 225.00
Celery tray, 12"...............................30.00	Nappy, 4" or 4½".............................12.00
Cream, hotel 45.00	Nappy, 7", 8", or 9" 40.00
Crushed fruit jar & cover, 1 quart.................270.00	Oil & stopper, 6 oz.............................65.00
Crushed fruit jar & cover, 1 quart (#429½).....325.00	Oval, 8", 9", or 10".............................32.00
Crushed fruit jar & cover, 2 quart.................300.00	Parfait................................30.00
Crushed fruit jar & cover, 2 quart (#429½).....350.00	Pickle tray, 6"................................15.00
Custard, handled, 4 oz. (punch cup) 18.00	Punch bowl & foot, regular 15", flared 16",
Egg, 5 oz......................................18.00	shallow 17" 325.00
Finger bowl...................................15.00	Salt & pepper, pr, #1 or #3 ....90.00
Goblet, 7 oz..................................85.00	Salt, individual, footed.................................35.00
Ice tea, 12 oz................................40.00	Sherbet, low footed, straight or flared, 4 oz. ..20.00
Jug, 1 pint 75.00	Sugar & cover, hotel.................................65.00
Jug, 1 quart 125.00	Tumbler, 8 oz. 50.00
Jug, 3 pint 175.00	

No. 429 Plain Panel Recess covered sugar.

No. 429 Plain Panel Recess tumbler and jug with Gravic-type engraving.

No. 429½ Plain Panel Recess one-quart crushed fruit jar.

Colonial Scallop & Angle, No. 430
Date: Uncertain. Probably 1911.
Discontinued before 1913.
Color: Crystal

Comments: Known only in a nappy.
Marked with Diamond H.

Nappy, 8" $60.00

No. 430 Colonial Scallop & Angle nappy.

Greek Key, No. 433 (Grecian Border)
Date: 1911. A few items remained until the late 1920s.
Colors: Crystal. Punch bowl & foot, underplate, and custard cup in Flamingo.
Patents: Three patents were granted to Greek Key, all listing A. J. Sanford
as designer: scalloped nappy No. 42110 on 1-23-1912; low footed
sherbet No. 41533 on 7-4-1911, and oval sugar
No. 41764 on 9-12-1911.

Comments: This is one of Heisey's most collectible patterns. Heisey called the pattern simply Grecian Border, but collectors widely know the name Greek Key. The bar glass without sham is the same as the toothpick. Marked with the Diamond H. Bottoms on pieces are ground and polished. Rarely found with ruby stain.

Almond dish & cover, 5" $120.00	Candy jar & cover, 1 lb. 220.00
Almond dish, 5" 55.00	Candy jar & cover, 2 lb. 325.00
Almond, individual......................35.00	Candy jar & cover, 4 lb. ....500.00+
Banana split, 9" (flat) 55.00	Celery, tall 135.00
Banana split, footed, 9"................35.00	Celery tray, 9" 55.00
Bar, sham 45.00	Celery tray, 12" 65.00
Bar, water, 5½ oz. 55.00	Cheese & cracker, 10" (1 piece) 155.00
Bowl, low foot, 7", 8", or 9" (comport)........100.00	Cherry jar or horseradish, small mushroom stopper 160.00
Bowl, low foot, shallow, 8", 9", or 10" (comport) 110.00	Cherry jar or pickle, large mushroom stopper 190.00
Bowl, orange, 12" 170.00	Claret, 4½ oz............................150.00
Bowl, orange, flared, 14" 250.00	Cocktail, 3 oz............................80.00
Bowl, orange, shallow, 14½"........250.00	Cordial, ¾ oz............................360.00+
Burgundy, 3½ oz.........................60.00	Cream......................................90.00
Butter & cover...........................195.00	Cream, hotel (oval).......................55.00
Butter, individual........................45.00	Cream, individual (oval) 90.00
Candy jar & cover, ½ lb. 165.00	

Cream, round 60.00
Crushed fruit jar & cover, 1 quart 400.00
Crushed fruit jar & cover, 2 quart 550.00
Custard, 4½ oz. (punch cup) 40.00
Egg cup, 5 oz. 60.00
Finger bowl 35.00
Goblet, 7 oz. or 9 oz. 150.00
Hair receiver & cover (small) 165.00
Ice tub, hotel...240.00
Ice tub, hotel, with cover 370.00
Ice tub, individual or butter & cover with
    plate 250.00
Ice tub, individual, with cover 125.00
Ice tub, large...175.00
Ice tub, small...150.00
Jelly, 2 handled (flat)...................................65.00
Jelly, 2 handled (flat), with cover, #2 ....125.00
Jelly, handled, 5"...65.00
Jelly, high footed, 5"....................................80.00
Jelly, high footed, 5" with cover 150.00
Jelly, high footed, shallow, 5½" 80.00
Jelly, high footed, shallow, with cover 150.00
Jelly, low footed, 2 handled 75.00
Jelly, low footed, 2 handled, with cover, #1 .150.00
Jelly, low footed, shallow, 4" or 4½" 30.00
Jelly, low footed, 5" 30.00
Jelly, low footed, with cover 95.00
Jug, 1 pint..120.00
Jug, 1 quart..200.00
Jug, 3 pint..240.00
Jug, ½ gallon..295.00
Nappy, 4", 4½", or 5" 40.00
Nappy, 7", 8", or 9" 85.00
Nappy, scalloped top, 4½" 40.00
Nappy, scalloped top, 8" 85.00
Nappy, shallow, 4½", 5½", or 6"...................50.00

No. 433 Greek Key (Grecian Border) hotel cream.

Nappy, shallow, 8½" or 9½" 95.00
Nappy, shallow, 11" 110.00
Oil & stopper, 2 oz. 150.00
Oil & stopper, 4 oz. 120.00
Oil & stopper, 6 oz. 135.00
Pickle jar, knob cover 185.00
Plate, 4½", 5", or 5½" 35.00
Plate, 6", 6½", or 7" 45.00
Plate, 8" or 9" 85.00
Plate, 10"..150.00
Plate, orange bowl, 16"..............................250.00
Puff & cover, #1 (small) 150.00
Puff & cover, #2 (large)..............................185.00
Punch bowl & stand, regular 15"; cupped
    12", shallow 18"..................................600.00+
Salt & pepper, pr. 225.00
Saucer champagne, 4½ oz. 70.00
Sherbet, high foot, 4½ oz. (also punch glass) ..45.00
Sherbet, low foot, 4½ oz., regular, cupped,
    flared, or shallow...................................25.00
Sherbet, low foot, 6 oz. 30.00
Sherry, 2 oz. 275.00
Soda, standard, 8 oz. or 12 oz. 70.00
Soda, straight or flared, 5 oz......................50.00
Soda, straight or flared, 7 oz, or 8 oz..........70.00
Soda, straight or flared, 10 oz., 12 oz., or
    13 oz. 85.00
Spoon..90.00
Spoon, large 110.00
Spoon, small, 4½" or straw jar 100.00
Straw jar & cover, tall 500.00
Sugar & cover..135.00
Sugar, hotel (oval) 55.00
Sugar, individual (oval)................................90.00
Sugar, round 60.00
Tankard, pint...110.00
Tankard, quart 185.00

No. 433 Greek Key (Grecian Border) cupped nappy.

Tankard, 3 pint...200.00
Tankard, ½ gallon 250.00
Toothpick or 2½ oz. bar 750.00
Tray, French roll, 12½" 145.00
Tray, oblong, 13".......................................155.00
Tray, oblong, 15".......................................225.00
Tumbler, 8 oz...75.00
Tumbler, footed or low foot goblet, 9 oz....125.00
Underplate for punch bowl 300.00
Water bottle 200.00
Wine, 2 oz..170.00

No. 433 Greek Key (Grecian Border) individual ice tub, cover, and underplate

No. 433 Greek Key (Grecian Border) cream, covered butter, covered sugar, spoon.

No. 433 Greek Key (Grecian Border). Top: almond and cover. Bottom: large ice tub, hotel ice tub and cover, oval hotel sugar.

No. 433 Greek Key (Grecian Border) goblet, tankard, jug, oil.

433½:

Nappy, 4", 4½", 5", or 5½"...........................$40.00
Nappy, 6", 6½", or 7" 80.00
Nappy, 8" or 9"...125.00
Jug, pint...110.00
Jug, quart..185.00
Jug, 3 pint...200.00
Jug, ½ gallon...250.00
Oil & stopper, 2 oz. 150.00
Oil & stopper, 4 oz. 120.00
Oil & stopper, 6 oz. 135.00
Puff & cover, #4 ....150.00
Puff, no cover, #4 ....90.00

No. 433½ Greek Key (Grecian Border)
oil, jug, nappy, no. 4 puff.

1912:

Ribbon Candy, No. 437
Date: Exact date of introduction not known, probably 1912.
Discontinued before 1913.
Color: Crystal

Comments: It is very difficult to find any piece in this pattern. Certainly it was made for only a short time. Pieces are marked with the Diamond H and are ground and polished on the base. Sometimes the band of ovals is satin finished. Little documentation is available for this pattern. Probably a full line was made.

Jug..$300.00
Oil & stopper..300.00
Tumbler 125.00

No. 437 Ribbon
Candy tumbler.

Raised Loop, No. 439
Date: 1912 to 1913
Color: Crystal only
Patents: The nappy was granted patent No. 42260 on 3-5-1912 with
A. J. Sanford listed as designer. E. W. Heisey was granted patent
No. 45044 on 12-16-1913 for the jug.

Comments: Difficult to find. Most items marked with the Diamond H. Most pieces have ground and polished bottoms.

Celery, 9"	$35.00	Jug, 1 quart	175.00
Celery, 12"	50.00	Jug, 3 pint	225.00
Cream	100.00	Jug, ½ gallon	275.00
Custard, 4½ oz. (punch cup)	25.00	Nappy, 4" or 4½"	20.00
Egg, straight or cupped, 5 oz.	25.00	Nappy, 7", 8", or 9"	35.00
Jug, 1 pint	100.00	Nappy, cupped, 4½"	20.00
		Nappy, cupped, 8"	35.00
		Nappy, shallow, 4½" or 5"	20.00
		Nappy, shallow, 8"	35.00
		Oil & stopper, 6 oz.	200.00
		Salt & pepper, pr, #1 or #3	130.00
		Sugar	100.00
		Tumbler	125.00

No. 439 Raised Loop
oil, jug, cream.

1913:

E. Wilson Heisey assumed the presidency of the company during this year while his father, A. H. Heisey remained as chairman of the board.

Quator, No. 355
Date: 1913 to 1935
Colors: Crystal, selected pieces in Flamingo, Moongleam, Marigold
Patents: The cream was granted patent No. 42752 on 7-9-1912 with T. C. Heisey listed as designer. The domino sugar was covered by patent No. 45138 on 1-6-1914 also with T. C. Heisey listed as designer.

Comments: This is a minor pattern with only a few pieces. However, pieces in this pattern continued into the color years. The bonbon was the first item in the pattern. Heisey revived the nappies in a later pattern, No. 1463 Quaker from 1935 to 1938. Quator nappies have ground and polished bottoms and a large Diamond H. Quaker items are not ground and have a small Diamond H. The original heavy, square cream and sugar were later redesigned with ridges and made part of the No. 1469 Ridgeleigh pattern. For Flamingo or Moongleam, add 100%. For Marigold, add 200%.

Ashtray & match holder (ground column)......$95.00
Bonbon...95.00
Cream..45.00
Cream, footed...30.00
Cream, individual..50.00
Domino sugar..95.00
Mustard & cover...160.00
Nappy..15.00
Nappy..35.00
Syrup, sanitary, 24 oz.....................................100.00
Syrup, sanitary, 32 oz.....................................135.00
Sugar..45.00
Sugar, footed or bonbon..................................30.00
Sugar, individual..50.00

No. 355 Quator large nappy and No. 1463 Quaker small nappy.

No. 355 Quator bonbon.

No. 355 Quator mustard & cover.

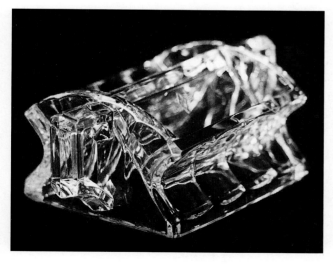

No. 355 Quator domino sugar.

No. 355 Quator ashtray and match-holder.

Nos. 500, 501, 502 Lavender Jars
Date: 1913
Color: Crystal

Comments: May be marked on the top neck portion of the bottle. These are similar in shape to the No. 352 horseradish jar, but it has a hollow top for a spoon handle. At least the small jar in this series has a solid stopper. We do not know if the larger two sizes have solid or hollow tops.

Lavender jar, 2 oz. (#500)...........................$100.00
Lavender jar, 5 oz. (#501)..............................70.00
Lavender jar, 7 oz. (#502)..............................95.00

Nos. 500, 501, and 502 lavender jars

Nos. 500 lavender jar and No. 352 horseradish jar.

Revere, No. 1183 — original name
Date: 1913 to 1957
Colors: Crystal, Flamingo, Moongleam, Sahara
Patents: The oval cream was given patent No. 52572 on 10-15-1918 with T. C. Heisey listed as designer. The candy jar was given patent No. 57275 on 3-8-1921 with A. J. Sanford as designer.

Comments: This is a transitional pattern developed between the heavy pressed patterns and the later dinnerware lines. Most pieces are severely plain, making them perfect for decorations, especially cuttings. The stemware was available both with and without optic. Due to its long life, the pattern items changed over the years. In later years, it was primarily a tableware pattern with a few serving pieces. Some of these were taken from other older plain Heisey patterns. The quality and simplicity were uppermost. Tiffany's of New York recognized this and sold Revere. Imperial Glass continued basic table setting pieces after 1957. Pieces are found both marked and unmarked.

    * items in the pattern from the late 1940s and 1950s

Ashtray, cigarette (small triangular)................$25.00	Bowl, low footed, 9"..30.00
Bonbon, 2 handled 35.00	Bowl, salad, 9" (#485) * 20.00
Bonbon, footed, 4½" or 6"..............................30.00	Burgundy, 3½ oz. 15.00
Bowl, gardenia, 13" (#485) * 20.00	Candy box & cover, 6" or 7" 35.00

Candy box & cover, 8".....................................40.00
Candy jar & cover, ½ lb. 70.00
Candy jar & cover, 1 lb. 75.00
Candy jar & cover, 3 lb. 225.00
Candy jar & cover, 5 lb. 450.00
Celery, 9"..12.00
Celery, 12"..22.00
Cheese & cracker, 2 piece 30.00
Claret, 5 oz..20.00
Coaster, 4½"...9.00
Cocktail, 3 oz. 15.00
Cologne & stopper 175.00
Comport, swirl optic, 6"..................................25.00
Cordial, ¾ oz. 30.00
Cream 22.00
Cream, individual...28.00
Cream, oval hotel...25.00
Cream soup, 2 handled (#1184) * 17.00
Crème de Coca, ¾ oz......................................30.00
Cup & saucer, after dinner (#1184) *...............35.00
Cup & saucer, tea (#1184) *............................18.00
Epergne with No. 1519 small epergnette,
    10" (#1187) * 95.00
Epergne with No. 4223 6" vase (#1187) *........95.00
Epergne with No. 5013 5" vase (#1187) *........95.00
Finger bowl..12.00
French dressing boat & plate 65.00
Goblet, 7 oz. or 8 oz.......................................20.00
Grapefruit, 6½"...15.00
Grapefruit, footed, for silver ring (#1184) *.......15.00
Grapefruit or baked apple, 6½" (#1184) *.........12.00
Hair receiver & cover 45.00
Honey & cover, square 75.00
Horseradish jar...55.00
Jelly, low footed, 5" 15.00
Jelly, low footed, 2 handled, 5" 18.00
Lemon dish & cover, 4½" or 5" 35.00
Lemon dish, no cover, 4½" or 5" 20.00
Manicure finger rest......................................150.00
Marmalade & cover or horse radish & cover. .65.00
Mayonnaise, round, 5½" * 25.00

No. 1183 Revere sugar shaker, late production.

Mayonnaise, round, 2 compartment, 5½" * 25.00
Mayonnaise, square, 4" (#1610) *....................15.00
Mint, 2 handled, 6" 18.00
Parfait, café, plain or optic, 5 oz.....................17.00
Pickle & olive, combination 24.00
Plate, bread & butter, 6" (#1184) *....................8.00
Plate, buffet, 16" (#1184) *..............................45.00
Plate, buffet, 18" (#1184) *..............................55.00
Plate, cheese & cracker, 2 piece, 12" 65.00
Plate, cheese, 2 handled................................10.00
Plate, mayonnaise, 7" (with or without ring)
    (#1184) * 10.00
Plate, mayonnaise, square (#1610) *...............15.00
Plate, oyster cocktail, 8½" (#1184) * 10.00
Plate, party (torte), 14" (#485) * 35.00
Plate, punch bowl, flat, 16½" (#1184) *............45.00
Plate, salad, 7" or 8" (#1184 or #1609) * 12.00
Plate, sandwich, 12" 35.00
Plate, service, 10½" (#1184 or #1609) *...........55.00
Plate, square, 8" (for honey dish)....................20.00
Puff box & cover...45.00
Punch bowl..225.00
Salt, individual...18.00
Salver, footed, 10" or 12"................................35.00
Sauce or nappy, star ground bottom, 4", 4½",
    or 5" (#398) * 5.00
Sauce or nappy, star ground bottom, 6" or 7"
    (#398) * 8.00
Sauce or nappy, star ground bottom, 8"
    (#398) * 20.00
Saucer champagne or high footed sherbet,
    shallow, 4 oz..8.00
Spice tray, divided...50.00
Sugar 22.00

No. 1183 Revere oval cream and sugar with No. 706 Warrick cutting

No. 1183 Revere mani-
cure finger rest.

Sugar & cover (#1183½) 25.00
Sugar, individual...25.00
Sugar, oval hotel 25.00
Sugar sifter * 55.00
Toast cover & plate 75.00
Tray, candy, 4½" x 7½".....................................20.00
Tray, oblong variety, 4 compartment, 13"
    (#500) * 65.00
Vase, candlestick, 2 piece, with prisms, pr. ..450.00
Wine, 2 oz. 20.00

No. 1183 Revere. Top: lemon dish with No. 679 Windsor cutting.
Bottom: basket, honey dish with No. 679 Windsor cutting, candy jar
with No. 679 Windsor cutting.

No. 1183 Revere: Top: pickle
and olive dish. Bottom: steak
plate and cover, candy box.

No. 1183 Revere. Top: cigarette box. Bottom: footed sugar and cream, toast cover and plate.

Top: Nos. 1181, 1182, 1181 — all similar to No. 1183 Revere; No. 1183 Revere individual cream. Bottom: No. 1183 Revere oval hotel sugar and cream with No. 679 Windsor cutting, No. 1183 Revere individual sugar & cover.

Yeoman, Nos. 1184, 1185, 1186, 1187, 1189
Date: 1913 to 1957
Colors: Crystal, Moongleam, Flamingo, Sahara, Marigold, Hawthorne
Patents: The stack set of sugar, cream, and butter was granted patent No. 47573 on 7-13-1915 with A. J. Sanford as designer. The oval nappy was given No. 50666 on 4-24-1917 with A. J. Sanford as designer.

Comments: Yeoman was an extensive pressed tableware line. Many pieces were made in plain or diamond optic. Selected pieces were made in other colors than those listed, and not all pieces were made in all colors listed. Over the years, Yeoman borrowed some pieces from other patterns which were added to its line. Original Heisey numbers are listed after these entries, but Yeoman is a name given by researchers. Pieces are often found with Heisey etchings. Cuttings on Yeoman blanks were usually done by decorating companies. Many pieces are marked with the Diamond H. Imperial Glass Corp. made most pieces of stemware and a few other pieces in crystal, some with diamond optic. Prices are for crystal pieces. For Moongleam, Flamingo, or Sahara, add 100%. For Marigold, add 150% to 200%. For Hawthorne add 200% to 300%.

Ashtray, 2 piece (#1187)	$45.00
Ashtray, cigar (large triangular)	35.00
Ashtray, handled, 4"	24.00
Ashtray, individual (#1186)	10.00
Ashtray and cigarette holder	24.00
Baker, oval, 9"	18.00
Banana split, footed	17.00
Bar, 2½ oz. (#236)	10.00
Bonbon, handled, 6½"	22.00
Bonbon, 2 handled, 5½"	18.00
Bouillon, footed	22.00
Bowl, floral, 12"	22.00
Butter, individual	10.00
Candy box & cover, 6"	38.00
Candy box & cover, deep, 6"	42.00
Candy dish, handled, 8½" (bow tie shape)	24.00
Candy jar & cover, ¼ lb.	95.00
Celery, 9"	10.00
Celery, 12" (#1185)	24.00
Celery, 13"	12.00
Celery tray, 9" or 12" (#1189)	22.00
Cigarette box & cover (#1185)	50.00
Cigarette box with ashtray cover	45.00
Claret	18.00
Coaster	9.00
Cocktail, 3 oz.	15.00
Comport, high footed, 5"	24.00
Comport, high footed, 6" & 7" (#1186)	30.00
Comport, low footed, deep, 6"	22.00
Cream	20.00
Cream (#1023)	24.00

Cream, hotel (#1185)	20.00
Cream, hotel, footed (#1188)	30.00
Cream, hotel, oval (#1186)	22.00
Cream, individual	20.00
Cream, individual (#1189)	55.00
Cream, individual (restaurant)	35.00
Cream, individual, round (#1185)	20.00
Cream soup	17.00
Cup & saucer (2 styles)	18.00
Cup & saucer, after dinner	35.00
Dish, berry, 2 handled, 8½"	24.00
Dish, lemon, oval, 5"	17.00
Dish, vegetable, 6"	8.00
Dish, vegetable & cover, 9"	50.00
Egg cup	30.00
Finger bowl	12.00
French dressing boat & plate	65.00
Fruit, oval, 9"	24.00
Fruit cocktail, 4 oz.	10.00
Goblet, 8 oz.	12.00

No. 1184 Yeoman pickle, diamond optic, Sahara.

Goblet, 10 oz. 15.00
Grapefruit, footed 18.00
Hi-ball, straight or cupped, 8 oz. 10.00
Hors d'oeuvre base, center & cover, 13"......145.00
Ice tea, straight or cupped, 12 oz. 12.00
Ice tub & butter, individual 30.00
Jelly, low footed, 5"......................................15.00
Jug, quart 75.00
Juice, straight 10.00
Juice, tapered (#527) 10.00
Marmalade & cover 30.00
Marmalade & cover (candy jar shape)...........55.00
Mayonnaise (#1189) 35.00
Mint, 3 compartment, center handled, 8".......28.00
Mixing glass & metal cover, 28 oz. (cocktail
    shaker)...120.00
Mustard & cover 65.00
Nappy, 4½" 8.00
Nappy, deep, 8"..18.00
Oil & stopper, 2 oz. 40.00
Oil & stopper, 4 oz. 35.00
Oyster cocktail, 2¾ oz. 10.00
Parfait, 5 oz. 17.00
Pickle & olive, 8"...27.00
Pickle & olive, 2 compartment, 13" (#1189) 24.00
Plate, 6" or 7"..8.00
Plate, 8" or 9"..10.00
Plate, 10½"...55.00
Plate, 14" 35.00
Plate, 4 compartment, 11"............................25.00
Plate, cheese, 2 handled 10.00
Plate, coaster, 4½" 10.00
Plate, crescent salad, 8" 30.00
Plate, grapefruit, 6½"......................................8.00
Plate, grill, 9"..25.00
Plate, oval, 7" 15.00
Plate, oyster cocktail, 8" or 9" 10.00

Plate, soup, 8" (bowl).................................20.00
Platter, 12" 22.00
Platter, 15" 32.00
Preserve, 6"..17.00
Puff box & cover with insert (#1186) 90.00
Puff box & cover (no insert) (#1186) 55.00
Relish, 3 compartment, 13" 17.00
Salver, low foot, 10"....................................38.00
Sandwich, handled, 10½".............................22.00
Saucer champagne, 6 oz.............................12.00
Sherbet, 3½ oz. or 4½ oz. 8.00
Smoking set, bridge-handled tray with 8 ash-
    trays 80.00
Soda, 4½ oz. 6.00
Soda, footed, 5 oz. 10.00
Soda, footed, 12 oz. 12.00
Soda, straight, 8 oz. 8.00
Soda, straight or cupped, 10 oz. or 12 oz. 8.00
Sugar & cover (#1023) 28.00
Sugar & cover, individual (#1189) 65.00
Sugar, hotel, footed (#1188)........................30.00
Sugar, hotel, oval (#1186) 22.00
Sugar, hotel, round (#1185) 20.00
Sugar, individual...20.00
Sugar, individual, round (#1185) 20.00
Syrup, saucer foot (attached), 7 oz. 60.00
Tray, 2 compartment, oval, 10½" 28.00
Tray, 3 compartment, handled, 11".................35.00
Tray, candy, 5¾" x 8" x 1".............................15.00
Tray, candy, 6" x 8" x 1" (#1185)...................15.00
Tray, oblong, 12"..23.00
Tray, relish, 7" x 10" with inserts 95.00
Tray, spice, 3 compartment, 12" 4 piece set
    (#1187) 45.00
Tumbler cover 35.00
Tumbler, cupped or straight, 8 oz...................8.00

No. 1184 Yeoman tumbler cover.

No. 1184 Yeoman stemware and jug.

No. 1184 Yeoman assortment.

No. 1184 Yeoman marmalade,
quarter pound candy, cream.

No. 1184 Yeoman comport, sand-wich plate, cologne, all with No. 657 Liberty cutting.

No. 1189 Yeoman individual cream & sugar.

No. 1186 Yeoman oval hotel sugar and cream, fruit, and bouillon cup and saucer. Fruit cut No. 657 Liberty. All others cut No. 693 Cloister.

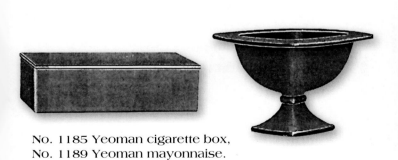

No. 1185 Yeoman cigarette box, No. 1189 Yeoman mayonnaise.

No. 1188 footed hotel sugar.

1914:

The most important change in the Heisey factory during this year was the beginning of blownware which became a mainstay for the company until its closing.

Cross Lined Flute, No. 451
Date: 1914 to ca. 1930, except for tumbler which was made longer.
Colors: Crystal, vase known in Canary
Patents: The jug was granted patent No. 45489 on 3-24-1914. The nappy was granted patent No. 48529 on 2-8-1916, designed by A. J. Sanford.

Comments: Only the tumbler was listed in price lists in 1913. Marked with the Diamond H. Most items have ground and polished bottoms.

Celery tray, 9" $25.00
Celery tray, 12" 35.00
Finger bowl 15.00
Goblet, 7 oz..45.00
Ice tea, 12 oz..25.00
Jelly, handled, 5"....................................25.00
Jelly, high footed, 5"................................35.00
Jelly, high footed, shallow, 4½" 35.00
Jug, pint..100.00
Jug, quart 180.00
Jug, 3 pint 210.00
Jug, ½ gallon..200.00
Nappy, 4" or 4½" 15.00
Nappy, 7", 8", or 9"..................................55.00
Nappy, shallow, 4½" or 5" 15.00
Nappy, shallow, 8½", 9½", or 10½" 60.00
Oil & stopper, 6 oz. 125.00

Oval, 8" or 9" 45.00
Plate, 6" 15.00
Plate, 8" 25.00
Salt & pepper, pr. 120.00
Saucer champagne, 5 oz...............................30.00
Sherbet, 5 oz..15.00
Tumbler, 8 oz. 40.00
Vase, regular or flared, 5" or 6"....................45.00
Vase, regular or flared, 7".........................55.00

No. 451 Cross Lined Flute half gallon jug.

No. 452 Cross Lined Flute. Top: goblet, hotel sugar. Bottom: tumbler, flared vase, oil.

1915:

Tea Drip, No. 1
Date: Ca. 1915, but actual date is uncertain
Color: Crystal

Comments: This is a specialty made for a company who applied the silver band around the top of the tea drip. This piece is not marked with the Diamond H. It is made to hold an old-fashioned tea ball for use with a silver tea service.

Tea drip..........$110.00

No. 1 Heisey tea drip without and with sterling silver band.

No. 356
Date: 1915 to 1919
Color: Crystal

Comments: Marked with the Diamond H. The lavender jars have ground bottoms and ground in stoppers. Jars are the same as No. 352 lavender jars except they have pointed stoppers.

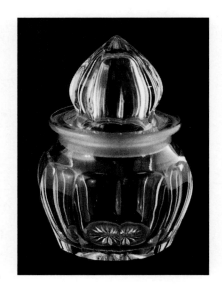

Ashtray & match holder $60.00
Lavender jar, 1½ oz. 80.00
Lavender jar, 3 oz..95.00
Lavender jar, 5 oz.......................................100.00
Lavender jar, 10 oz......................................150.00
Lavender jar, 14 oz......................................160.00
Lavender jar, 16 oz......................................180.00
Lavender jar, 24 oz......................................200.00

No. 356 lavender jar.

No. 357 lavender jar.

No. 357
Date: 1915 to 1919
Color: Crystal

Comments: Marked with the Diamond H. The lavender jars have ground bottoms and ground in stoppers. Jars are the same as No. 353 lavender jars except they have pointed stoppers.

Lavender jar, 2 oz. $95.00
Lavender jar, 6 oz. 110.00
Lavender jar, 8 oz. 125.00
Lavender jar, 12 oz. 150.00
Lavender jar, 20 oz. 180.00
Lavender jar, 26 oz. 200.00
Lavender jar, 30 oz. 225.00

No. 358
Date: 1915 to 1919
Color: Crystal
Patent: Assigned patent No. 455542.

Comments: The lavender jars have ground in stoppers. Marked with the Diamond H. Jars are the same as No. 354 lavender jars except they have pointed stoppers instead of mushroom stoppers.

No. 358 lavender jar.

Lavender jar, 1 oz......................................$110.00
Lavender jar, 2½ oz. 95.00
Lavender jar, 4½ oz. 110.00
Lavender jar, 7 oz. 125.00
Lavender jar, 11 oz. 150.00
Lavender jar, 16 oz. 180.00
Lavender jar, 27 oz. 200.00

No. 359
Date: Ca. 1915, although actual introduction may precede this by a few years.
Colors: Crystal, rare in Alexandrite

Comments: A colonial stemware line. Marked with Diamond H. The No. 348 Colonial Cupped and No. 363 Colonial shown were made in lines similar to No. 349 and have similar values. For No. 300 Peerless, No. 341 Puritan, No. 351 Priscilla, and No. 369 Hartman, please refer to the pattern lists for values.

Burgundy, 2½ oz. $20.00	Port, 3 oz. 20.00
Champagne, 5 oz. 15.00	Saucer champagne, 4 oz. 20.00
Claret, 4 oz. 20.00	Sherbet, 2½ oz., 3½ oz., or 4½ oz. 12.00
Cocktail, 3 oz. 15.00	Sherbet, high footed, 4 oz; or high footed
Cordial, ½ oz. 75.00	shallow, 4 oz. 15.00
Crème de menthe, 2½ oz. 18.00	Sherry, 2 oz. 22.00
Goblet, 7 oz. 25.00	Tumbler, 7 oz. 18.00
Ice tea, footed, 11 oz. 22.00	Wine, 1½ oz. 22.00
Pony brandy, ½ oz. 75.00	

No. 359 Stemware: goblet, champagne, claret, burgundy, wine, cordial, pony brandy, sherry, port.

No. 359 Stemware, optic: crème de menthe, cocktail, saucer champagne, high footed shallow sherbet, footed tumbler or low footed goblet, footed ice tea.

No. 300 Peerless, No. 341 Puritan, No. 348 Colonial Cupped, No. 351 Priscilla, No. 359 Colonial, No. 363 Colonial, No. 369 Hartman.

No. 360 Sanitary Syrup
Date: 1915
Color: Crystal

Comments: Has a ground and polished bottom.

Sanitary syrup...$75.00

No. 360 sanitary syrup.

No. 362 Earnshaw syrup with No. 679 Windsor cutting.

No. 362 Earnshaw
Date: 1915
Color: Crystal
Patent: No. 52347 was granted to A. J. Sanford on 8-27-1918 although it had been applied for in 1916.

Comments: Usually marked with the Diamond H on the side of the spout. Made primarily for decorating.

Sanitary syrup, 7 oz. $75.00
Sanitary syrup, 12 oz. 85.00

Prism Band, No. 367
Date: 1915 to 1957
Colors: Crystal, Moongleam, Flamingo

Comments: This decanter became part of No. 341 Old Williamsburg after 1939. Made in two sizes.

Decanter & stopper, 1 pint $120.00
Decanter & stopper, 1 quart 165.00

No. 367 Prism Band decanter & stopper.

No. 458 Picket basket with No. 604 Ornate Sprig cutting.

Picket, No. 458
Date: 1915 to 1933
Color: Crystal only

Comments: Marked with the Diamond H.

Basket, 8" $250.00

Round Colonial, No. 459
Date: 1915 to 1933
Color: Crystal only
Patent: Patent No. 47739 granted on 8-17-1915.
Andrew J. Sanford listed as designer.

Comments: Marked with the Diamond H.

Basket, 7" $240.00
Basket, 9" 260.00

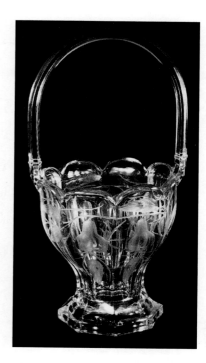

No. 459 Round Colonial basket with Gravic type deep engraving.

143

Banded Picket, No. 461
Date: 1915 to 1933
Colors: Crystal, Moongleam, Flamingo, Hawthorne

Comments: Marked with the Diamond H.

Basket, 7" $200.00

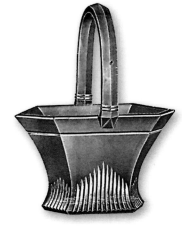

No. 461 Banded Picket basket.

Convex Circle, No. 461, 461½
Date: Ca. 1915. Due to its rarity it probably was only made for a year or less.
Color: Crystal only
Patent: No. 45127 for a bowl granted to Andrew J. Sanford. Interestingly, the patent was filed late in 1913.

Comments: Items are marked with the Diamond H and most have ground and polished bottoms. Difficult to find. The ad shown here labels the crushed fruit jar as a No. 803 three pound candy jar. This may have been directed to the soda fountain trade and had its own numbers assigned.

Crushed fruit jar, 1 quart. $300.00
Crushed fruit jar, 2 quart 375.00
Crushed fruit jar, 24 oz.
  (#461½).............................350.00
Crushed fruit jar, 48 oz.
  (#461½).............................400.00
Jug, ½ gallon (#461½) 350.00
Jug, 1 pint (#461½).................150.00
Jug, 1 quart (#461½) 250.00
Jug, 3 pint (#461½).................300.00
Nappy, 4½" 22.00
Nappy, 8" 60.00
Spoon, large 140.00
Spoon, small 90.00
Straw jar, individual 110.00
Tumbler 110.00

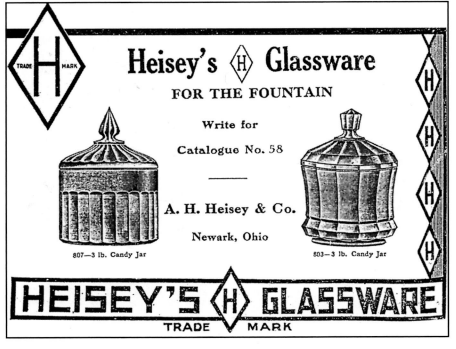

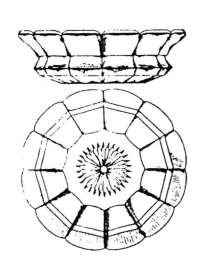

Patent drawing for No. 461 Convex Circle nappy.

No. 807 candy jar and No. 803 Convex Circle candy jar.

Plain Hexagon, No. 462
Date: 1915 to 1933
Color: Crystal only

Comments: Marked with the Diamond H.

Basket, 8" $200.00

No. 462 Plain Hexagon basket with non-Heisey cutting.

Nail, No. 462, 462½, 449, 450
Date: 1915. Discontinuation date uncertain, but it is difficult to find
so a year or two is likely.
Color: Crystal only
Patents: Square nappies were given patent No. 44938, round No. 44939. Both were
granted on 11-25-1913 with A. J. Sanford as designer.

Comments: Marked with Diamond H. The Nail motif was also used on the No. 449
and No. 450 vases. These vases were made in plain or optic.

Nappy, round, 4½" (#462½)..........................$40.00
Nappy, round, 8" (#462½) 120.00
Nappy, square, 4½" (#462)...........................40.00
Nappy, square, 8" (#462) 120.00
Vase, 8" (#449) 200.00
Vase, 10" (#450) 240.00

No. 462 Nail nappy (square).

No. 462½ Nail nappy (round).

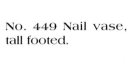

No. 449 Nail vase, tall footed.

No. 450 Nail vase.

Bonnet, No. 463
Date: 1915 to 1933
Colors: Crystal, Flamingo, Moongleam

Comments: Marked with the Diamond H. Add 100% for colors.

Basket, 7" $245.00

Lokay, No. 464
Date: 1915
Color: Crystal

Comments: A very plain fruit basket, primarily made for decorating. Marked with the Diamond H.

Basket, fruit, 8" $225.00

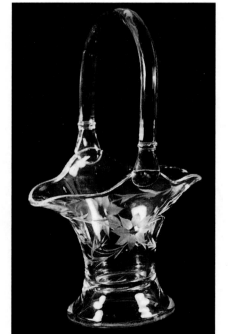

No. 463 Bonnet basket with No. 693 Cloister cutting.

No. 464 Lokay basket.

No. 464 Punty Row nappy.

Punty Row, No. 464
Date: 1915
Color: Crystal only

Comments: Known only in nappies. Ground and polished bottoms.

Nappy, 4½" $15.00
Nappy, 8" 45.00

Recessed Panel, No. 465
Date: 1915 to 1933
Colors: Crystal. The ½ pound candy jar was made in Moongleam and Canary.
Patents: The comport was assigned patent No. 46321 on 8-25-1914, while the tumbler was assigned 46449 on 9-22-1914. A. J. Sanford was the designer. The basket was patented on 8-17-1915 and assigned No. 47736 with A. J. Sanford as designer.

Comments: This pattern is relatively small, but has several sizes of Heisey baskets and candy jars, a complete set of which is difficult to assemble. Marked with the Diamond H. Sizes of the candy jars are as follows: quarter pound, 7½" tall; half pound, 9" tall; one pound, 10⅜" tall; three pound, 13" tall; five pound, 15½" tall; and eight pound, 18¼" tall.

Basket vase (side handles) (#456) $395.00
Basket vase, 7" 215.00
Basket vase, 8" 230.00
Basket vase, 9" 250.00
Candy jar & cover, ¼ lb. 100.00
Candy jar & cover, ½ lb. 75.00
Candy jar & cover, 1 lb. 110.00
Candy jar & cover, 3 lb. 250.00
Candy jar & cover, 5 lb. 2,000.00
Candy jar & cover, 8 lb. 3,000.00
Comport, shallow, footed, 8" or 9"..............100.00
Cream, applied handle (made from ¼ lb.
   candy base) 125.00

Nappy, 4" or 4½"..10.00
Nappy, 7", 8", or 9" 40.00
Sugar & cover (made from ¼ lb. candy
   base) 110.00
Tumbler, 8 oz. 20.00

No. 456 basket vase with side handles.

No. 465 Recessed Panel basket.

No. 465 Recessed Panel candy jar, footed sugar and cream.

Panel & Double Pleat, No. 466
Date: 1915
Color: Crystal

Comments: Only nappies made. Difficult to find. Marked with the Diamond H.

Nappy, 4" or 4½"......................................$15.00
Nappy, 7", 8", or 9" 45.00

No. 466 Panel & Double Pleat nappy.

No. 466 basket.

No. 466 Basket
Date: 1915
Color: Crystal
Comments: A semi-colonial design basket. Marked with the Diamond H.

Basket, fruit, 8"........................$235.00

Helmet, No. 467
Date: 1915 to 1933
Colors: Crystal, Moongleam, Flamingo
Patent: No. 51308 granted on 9-25-1917 with
Andrew J. Sanford listed as designer.

Comments: Marked with the Diamond H. Add 75% to
100% for colors.

Basket, 10"...$650.00

No. 467 Helmet basket.

Octagon with Rim, No. 468
Date: 1915 to the late 1920s
Colors: Crystal, Flamingo, Moongleam
Patent: The celery tray was given patent No. 47118 on 3-16-1915
with A. J. Sanford listed as designer.

Comments: A short line with ground and polished bottoms and marked with the Diamond H. Add 75% for colors.

Celery, 9"..$15.00
Celery, 12"..20.00
Nappy, 4½"...8.00
Nappy, 8"..25.00
Pickle tray, 7"..20.00

No. 468 Octagon with Rim nappy.

No. 468 Octagon with Rim celery tray.

Intercepted Flute, No. 470
Date: 1915 to 1924
Color: Crystal only

Comments: Heisey made at least three other tumblers very similar to No. 470 — No. 192, No. 193, and No. 194. All are valued the same as No. 470. In catalogs the tumbler is noted as "Patent Applied for."

Jug, 3 pint..$185.00
Nappy, 4" or 4½"...22.00
Nappy, 7", 8", or 9"......................................38.00
Nappy, flared, 4½" or 5½"..............................22.00
Nappy, flared, 8", 9", or 10".........................38.00
Nappy, shallow, 4½" or 5"............................22.00
Nappy, shallow, 8½", 9½", or 11"................38.00
Plate, 4½" or 5½"..15.00
Plate, 9½", 10", or 11½"..............................75.00
Tumbler, 8 oz. 38.00

No. 470 Intercepted Flute. Top: flared nappy. Bottom: tumbler, jug.

No. 192, No. 193, No. 194 tumblers — all similar to No. 470 Intercepted Flute.

Mentor Square, No. 471
Date: 1915
Color: Crystal

Comments: A pressed pickle tray only, marked with the Diamond H. Catalogs indicate it was cut top and bottom.

Pickle tray, 7".....................................$50.00

No. 471 Mentor Square pickle tray.

Nos. 602, 602½
Date: 1915 to ca. 1922. Designed in late 1913.
Color: Crystal only
Patents: The tumbler was given patent No. 46296. The crushed fruit jars were given patent No. 46870.

Comments: Marked with a Diamond H. This pattern is very similar to No. 393 Narrow Flute. This short line was made primarily for soda fountain use. Sodas were made both plain and optic. The No. 602½ crushed fruit jars are short and squat. The hollow covers on Heisey crushed fruit jars were made to accommodate spoon handles.

No. 602 straw jar, large spoon, small spoon, tankard.

Buttermilk, 9 oz.	$12.00
Crushed fruit, 1 quart.	300.00
Crushed fruit, 2 quart.	325.00
Crushed fruit, 24 oz. (#602½)	300.00
Crushed fruit, 48 oz. (#602½)	325.00
Mug, root beer, 16 oz., 18 oz., or 20 oz.	85.00
Soda, 4 oz., 5 oz., or 6 oz.	8.00
Soda, 7 oz or 8 oz.	10.00
Soda, 10 oz. or 12 oz.	12.00
Soda, 14 oz.	15.00
Spoon, large	55.00
Spoon, small	45.00
Straw jar (no lid)	110.00
Tankard, 18 oz. or 20 oz.	75.00
Tumbler, 8 oz.	12.00

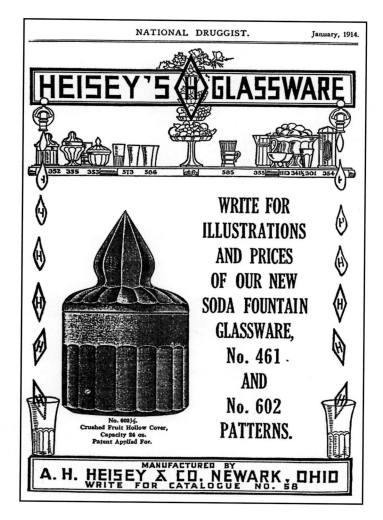

No. 602 crushed fruit, No. 602½ crushed fruit, No. 602 root beer mug.

No. 602½ crushed fruit. Note the small items at the top of the ad: No. 352, No. 355, No. 353, No. 573, No. 586, No. 46, No. 585, No. 355, No. 1113, No. 341½, No. 301, No. 354.

Nos. 804, 805, 806, 807
Date: 1915
Color: Crystal

Comments: Marked with Diamond H. Similar to No. 393 Narrow Flute. Any of these jars are difficult to find.

Candy or cracker jar, 1½ lb. (#806) (short) $250.00
Candy or cracker jar, 2 lb. (#804) (tall) 275.00
Candy or cracker jar, 3 lb. (#807) (short)....................275.00
Candy or cracker jar, 4 lb. (#805) (tall) 325.00

No. 804 2 pound candy or cracker jar.

No. 806 1½ pound candy or cracker jar.

No. 1000 Marmalade & cover.

No. 1000 Marmalade
Date: 1915
Colors: Crystal, rare in Alexandrite

Comments: Marked with the Diamond H.

Marmalade & cover.....................$175.00

Decorations Introduced in 1915:
Cuttings: No. 600 Mountain Laurel and No. 601 Myrtle on baskets.
Etchings: 9003 Oakwood plate etching and No. 9004 Iris plate etching.

Augustus H. Heisey

One of the leaders of the American flint glass industry, Maj. A. H. Heisey, of A. H. Heisey & Co., Newark, O., was laid to rest Saturday, February 18, following services at his home in Newark. The services were attended by a large concourse of friends and associates including many glass manufacturers. Maj. Heisey, who had been connected with the flint glass industry for nearly 60 years, died suddenly at his cottage in Atlantic City on Monday evening, February 13.

Born in Merritstown, near Brownsville, Pa., on August 3, 1843, Mr. Heisey graduated from the Merritstown Academy and then went to work for the King Glass Co., of Pittsburgh. He enlisted in the Union Army as a private in 1861 and served four years, being mustered out as a major of volunteers. Most of his service was with the 155th Pennsylvania (Zouaves) Volunteers. Maj. Heisey was cited for gallantry in several of the 22 engagements in which he

An important addition to the Heisey lines occurred about 1917 or 1918 when the company established a blown wake shop. From that date to the closing of the factory in 1957, blown items were a major sales line.

In 1919 Heisey applied for a patent for its Visible Cooking Ware. However, the patent was not granted, probably because of Corning's patent for Pyrex ware. In fact, Corning Glass sued the Heisey company, resulting in Heisey abandoning the plans for making glass cookware. Heisey had plans for a full line of 45 casseroles, baking dishes, and other oven-proof glassware; but only a few pieces were made prior to the lawsuit; these are rarely found

Copy of trademark for Heisey's Visible Cooking Ware

today. These items usually are marked with the Diamond H and are of a yellowish glass like a pale canary or a pale green.

The year 1922 became one of changes in the Heisey company beginning with the death of A. H. Heisey at his home in Atlantic City on February 13. E. Wilson Heisey, his second son, became president after his death. Emmett Olsen became chemist for the company. Wilson Heisey and Olsen were very interested in bringing color to the Heisey line, and the two are responsible for developing the new Heisey colors in the 1920s and 1930s. In 1922 Heisey sued Imperial Glass for infringement of their patents on No. 393 and No. 393½ Narrow Flute patterns, but the suit was eventually dismissed.

In 1925, the most momentous happenings were the introduction of the colors Moongleam and Flamingo late in the year. Also the Heisey company added another furnace to increase production and meet demand for glassware. During this year, the Heisey company acquired some of the original wooden models of the Sandwich glass company from a company salesman who had formerly been connected with them. Interest in these models was translated into glass copies with some of the patterns being added to the Heisey line, including Old Sandwich, Ipswich, the Beehive and Eagle plates, and the Sandwich Dolphin candlestick along with others.

1916:

Coffee Pot
Date: Ca. 1916 due to etching
Color: Crystal

Comments: A blown coffee pot of unknown number and indefinite date. This piece was purchased from the Tim Heisey estate and has a known Heisey etching. We have seen one other coffee pot, also bought from a Heisey relative, which was cut.

Coffee pot..$1,000.00+

participated. At the battle of Gettysburg, he was in command of his regiment and at the time of his death was the only surviving commissioned officer who helped defend Little Round Top at Gettysburg. It was the 155th Pennsylvania Zouaves who first received Lee's emissaries at Appomattox. Maj. Heisey was shot from his horse and slightly wounded at Gettysburg.

Returning to Pittsburgh after the war, Maj. Heisey resumed his position with the King Glass Co. at Pittsburgh. The South Side at that time had more than a score of glass factories. Later he was with Evans & Co., now the Macbeth-Evans Glass Co. He also was with the first Ripley & Co. and Challinor, Hogan & Co., all formerly well known names in the flint glass industry. The failure of Ripley & Co. led to the purchase of the factory by George Duncan & Sons, with whom Mr. Heisey was associated, he having married Miss Susan Duncan, daughter of George Duncan on May 15, 1871.

Mr. Heisey played a prominent part in the progress of George Duncan & Sons and was with that firm when the United States Glass Co. was formed in 1889 [sic-actually formed in 1891] by the consolidation of nearly a score of factories. Mr. Heisey was made commercial manager of the new glass combine.

In 1893, Mr. Heisey withdrew from the United States Glass Co., after several years in the mining business in Arizona, he broke ground, in 1895, for a complete, new tableware factory at Newark, O., where he planned to produce only glassware of the highest quality. The mammoth plant there was designed according to his own

Heisey coffee pot with No. 325 California Poppy etching.

plans and the eminence which its products have in the trade are due to Maj. Heisey's insistent demand for quality ware.

Maj. Heisey was the last survivor among the organizers of the Manufacturers' Bank, South Side, Pittsburgh, in 1899 and of which he had been a director. He was one of the founders of the Homeopathic Hospital, Pittsburgh, and the City Hospital and Y.W.C.A., Newark. He was a member of the Military Order of the Loyal Legion, the G. A. R., the National Republican Club, the Duquesne Club, Pittsburgh; the Columbus Country Club, Columbus, and the Mound Builders Country Club of Newark. He was an active participant in the activities of the American Association of Flint & Lime Glass Manufacturers.

In addition to his interests in the glass industry, Maj. Heisey had been for 30 years president of the Pittsburgh Clay Pot Co.; a founder and director of the Newark Heat & Light Co.; director of the Newark Consumers Gas Co.; formerly a director of the Franklin National Bank of Newark and for some years president of the Newark Trust Co. He was also vice president of the Ohio National Life Insurance Co., of Cincinnati. For three consecutive terms he was president of the American Protective Tariff League and was re-elected for another term on January 16.

Surviving are his widow, three sons and two daughters. The sons are George D., E. Wilson and T. Clarence Heisey, Mrs. Fred H. King, of Cleveland, and the wife of Col. O. K. Dockery, Jr., U. S. A., Seattle, Wash., are the daughters. E. W. and T. C. Heisey are officers in A. H. Heisey & Co. China, Glass & Lamps, *February, 1922.*

Salad Fork and Spoon, No. 2; Ice Tea Spoon, No. 3
Dates: Salad fork and spoon: 1913 to ca. 1944
Ice tea spoon: Ca. 1920s
Color: Crystal

Comments: The salad fork and spoon were made with plain handles as shown, and marked with the Diamond H. The other version, which has small sprays of tiny beads on the handles, is not marked. The ice tea spoon is marked with the Diamond H on the handle also. Heisey made a variety of marmalade spoons, mayonnaise ladles, and mustard spoons.

Ice tea spoon $65.00
Salad fork or spoon 90.00

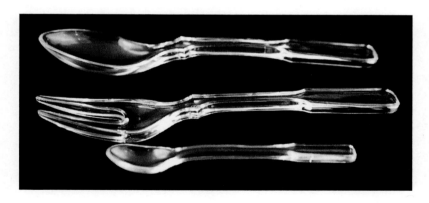

No. 2 salad fork and spoon, No. 3 ice tea spoon.

Narrow Flute With Rim, No. 472, 473, 474, and 475
Date: 1916 to 1931

Colors: Crystal. The No. 473 low footed comport and small oval plate were made in Canary. Several items were made in Moongleam and Flamingo. The No. 475 salted nut dish was made in Moongleam, Flamingo, and Hawthorne.

Patents: The No. 473 basket was patented on 8-17-1915 and given No. 47738 while the two-handled tray was patented on 6-20-1916 and given No. 49224 with A. J. Sanford listed as designer for both. The No. 475 oval dish was granted patent 48614 on 2-22-1916, again with A. J. Sanford as designer.

Comments: Most items have ground and polished bottoms. Most are marked with the Diamond H.

Almond, footed, individual (2 sizes)............$22.00	Griddle cake set, 4 piece (7" plate & cover,
Almond, footed, 5" 30.00	indiv. syrup, and butter, #473) ....450.00+
Baked apple, 6" 15.00	Hair receiver...120.00
Banana split, footed, 8" 55.00	Honey dish & cover, square (#473).............115.00
Basket, 8" 395.00	Jelly, high footed, 5", or 5", 2 handled (#473).55.00
Bowl, salad, 10½" or 11½" (#472) 35.00	Jug, 1 pint (#473) 60.00
Brush & comb tray, 10"................................65.00	Jug, 1 quart (#473) 130.00
Butter, individual...20.00	Jug, 3 pint (#473) 110.00
Cheese dish, 2 handled, 6" (#473)................30.00	Jug, ½ gallon (#473) 125.00
Cheese & cracker or strawberry & sugar,	Lemon dish, 5½" 20.00
individual..75.00	Loaf sugar & cream set, 2 piece, 8" (#473) 85.00
Cocktail, combination oyster 95.00	Marmalade & cover, square 85.00
Combination sugar, cream & butter (stack set).95.00	Mug (#473)..85.00
Cordial...60.00	Nappy, 4" or 4½" (#473) 12.00
Cream, individual, 3 oz. or 4 oz. (#473).........25.00	Nappy, 7" or 8" (#473) 35.00
Cream, hotel (#473) 30.00	Nappy, oval, 6", 7", or 8" (#473) 28.00
Cream, squat...30.00	Nappy, oval, 9" or 10" (#473) 32.00
Dice sugar & cream, 2 piece, 5" (#473)..........75.00	Nappy, shallow, 5½" or 6" (#474)....................15.00
Dish, chow chow, 4½" (#475) 15.00	Nappy, shallow, 4", 4½", or 5" (#474)............. 12.00
Dish, fruit, 9" (#475) 40.00	Nappy, shallow, 4½" or 5½" (#473) 12.00
Dish, lemon, 5½" (#475)................................15.00	Nappy, shallow, 5½" or 6" (#472)....................17.00
Dish, preserve, 6½" (#475)............................20.00	Nappy, shallow, 8½" or 10" (#473)..................35.00
Dish, salted nut, 3½" (#473) 15.00	Nappy, shallow, 10" or 11" (#472)..................45.00
Dish, salted nut, 3½" (#475) 25.00	Nappy, square, 4½" (#473) 18.00
Finger bowl 12.00	Nappy, square, 8" (#473) 45.00
French dressing dish (#473) 55.00	Nut dish, 3½" (#475)......................................20.00
Goblet 45.00	Oil & stopper, 2 oz. or 4 oz. (#473) 75.00
Grapefruit, 7" 30.00	Oil & stopper, 6 oz. (#473) 65.00

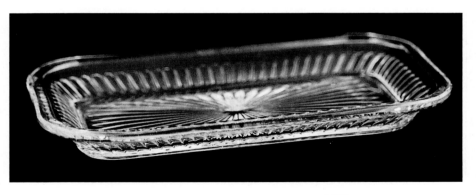

No. 473 Narrow Flute With Rim brush & comb tray.

Oval, 6", 7", or 8" (#473) 25.00
Oval, 9", 10", or 11" (#473) 30.00
Pickle, 6" (#473) 22.00
Pickle, 7" (#472) 22.00
Pickle, 8" (#473) 25.00
Pickle, 12" (#473) 35.00
Plate, 4½", 5", 5½", 6" or 6½" (#473)..................8.00
Plate, finger bowl, 6½" 8.00
Plate, square, 8" (#473) 35.00
Plate, sandwich 11" or 12" (#472) 35.00
Preserve, 6½"...22.00
Puff & cover (#473) 120.00
Relish, combination, 6" (#473) 30.00
Salt & pepper, pr. (#473)...............................70.00
Sardine dish & cover (#473) 180.00
Soap dish 180.00

Soda, 12 oz. 35.00
Sugar, hotel (#473) 30.00
Sugar & cover, hotel (#473) 40.00
Sugar, individual (#473).................................25.00
Sugar, individual squat..................................25.00
Sweetmeat, 8" 25.00
Tray, fruit, ice cream or comb & brush, 10"
    (#473)...60.00
Tray, Nabisco, 9" (#473) 40.00
Tray, oval, 9" (#472) 22.00
Tumbler, 8 oz. (#473) 35.00
Vase, 6" or 7", regular, flared, crimped, or
    cupped 60.00
Vase, 8", regular, flared, crimped, or cupped..75.00
Vase, with perforated cover, 2 piece, 7" 250.00

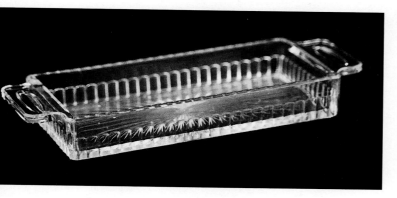

No. 473 Narrow Flute With Rim Nabisco tray.

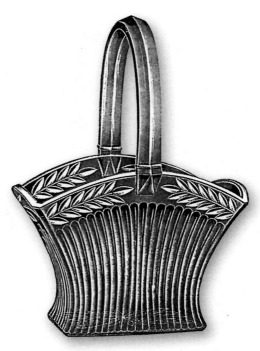

No. 473 Narrow Flute With Rim basket
with No. 600 Mountain Laurel cutting.

No. 473 Narrow Flute With Rim crimped vase, jug, sardine dish.

No.473 Narrow Flute With Rim. Top: dice sugar and cream, oil. Bottom: loaf sugar and cream, banana split, griddle cake set.

No. 473 Narrow Flute With Rim two-piece vase with perforated holder, ice tub.

No. 473 Narrow Flute With Rim.
Top: individual almond, individual nut.
Bottom: individual cheese and cracker, combination oyster cocktail, puff and cover.

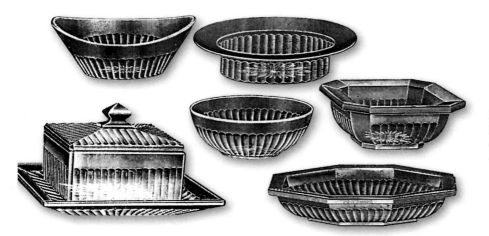

Narrow Flute With Rim. Top: No. 473 lemon, No. 473 baked apple. Middle: No. 473 nappy, square nappy. Bottom: No. 473 honey dish, No. 472 pickle tray.

Heisey Hairpin, No. 477
Date: 1916
Color: Crystal
Patent: Patent No. 48572 was given to the basket on
2-15-1916 with
A. J. Sanford as designer.

Comments: A very small pattern consisting of a handful of pieces. Pieces are marked with the Diamond H. The only pitcher and bowl set made by Heisey is in this pattern. Sometimes the loops are satin finished.

Basket $450.00
Bowl, wash 300.00
Jug...350.00
Tumbler 150.00

No. 477 Heisey Hairpin basket.

Decorations Introduced in 1916

Cuttings: No. 602 Leaf Band, No. 603 Sprig, No. 606 Scallop, No. 612 Leaf Swag, No. 613 Marjorie, and No. 614 Arlene — all on baskets.

Etchings: No. 1 Braid needle etching, No. 15 Spiral Band needle etching, No. 17 Zig Zag needle etching, No. 18 Spencerian needle etching, No. 19 Double Loop needle etching, No. 306 Spiral Vine plate etching, No. 325 California Poppy plate etching, No. 336 Rosette Band plate etching, No. 349 Margaret plate etching, No. 350 Mums plate etching, No. 352 Anne plate etching, No. 353 Susan plate etching, No. 366 Peacock plate etching, No. 370 Nile plate etching, No. 380 Cassandra plate etching, No. 384 Iroquois plate etching, and No. 9006 Cairo plate etching.

1917:

During this period of time, Heisey introduced many plain blown stem lines, most of which are like or extremely similar to those made by other companies. Since these are unmarked with the Diamond H, it is impossible to be certain these are of Heisey manufacture unless they have known Heisey decorations. Some of these lines include No. 3304 Universal, No. 3309 Petite, No. 3311 Velvedere, No. 3316 Biltmore, and others.

No. 517 tumble up jug.

No. 517
Date: 1917, made for many years.
Color: Crystal

Comments: A blown jug with pressed tumbler. The tumbler (#197) is marked with the Diamond H. The jug comes in two sizes.

Tumble up jug and tumbler $160.00

Daisy & Leaves, No. 480
Date: 1917 to 1923
Color: Crystal

Comments: Basket only. Marked with the Diamond H. Flowers sometimes have satin finish. There is also a small pattern line called Daisy & Leaves. See No. 427 Daisy & Leaves, Chapter 2.

Basket, fruit, 8"..$285.00

No. 480 Daisy & Leaves basket.

Dunham, No. 485
Date: 1917. Most items discontinued in a few years. The large nappy continued to be made into the late years as part of No. 1183 Revere.
Color: Crystal

Comments: A very plain pattern marked with the Diamond H. Except for nappies, most items are difficult to find.

Butter & cover $35.00
Cream...20.00
Jug, 3 pint...55.00
Nappy, 4½"...5.00
Nappy, 8" 15.00
Pickle jar, knob cover.......................25.00
Punch bowl and foot, 11" 95.00
Spoon 15.00
Sugar & cover 25.00

No. 485 Dunham covered sugar, covered butter, cream, spoon.

No. 485 Dunham pickle jar, footed punch bowl, nappy, jug.

Plain & Fancy, No. 2930
Date: 1917 to 1946
Colors: Crystal, Flamingo, Moongleam, Hawthorne, Marigold, Sahara

Comments: This tumbler is so plain that without a color, optic, or decoration, it is virtually impossible to identify this as Heisey. In various colors and decorations, value can vary considerably.

Tumbler $5.00

No. 2930 Plain & Fancy tumbler with No. 439 Pied Piper double plate etching.

Bob White, No. 3308 — original name
Date: 1917 to 1929
Color: Crystal only

Comments: A stemware line with blown bowl, pulled stem. Not marked with the Diamond H. Other companies made similar stem lines.

Burgundy, 3 oz.	$15.00
Claret, 4½ oz.	15.00
Cocktail, 3 oz.	15.00
Cordial, 1 oz.	25.00
Finger bowl	6.00
Goblet, 11 oz.	20.00
Goblet, 7 oz. or 9 oz.	15.00
Grape juice, 4½ oz.	15.00
Parfait, 4½ oz.	15.00
Pousse café	18.00
Saucer champagne, 6 oz.	10.00
Sherbet, footed, 6 oz.	8.00
Sherry, 2 oz.	15.00
Sundae, footed, 6 oz.	8.00
Wine, 2 oz.	20.00

No. 3308 Bob White goblet with No. 366 Peacock etching.

Gayoso, No. 3312 — original name
Date: 1917 to 1933
Colors: Crystal, Flamingo, Marigold. Finger bowl in Moongleam. Russian coffees with Moongleam foot and handle.

Comments: A stemware line with a blown bowl and pulled stem. Not marked with the Diamond H. While similar to stems of other companies, with study this line can be identified as Heisey by close comparison of the bowl shapes. Made plain, medium optic, wide optic, or diamond optic.

Burgundy, 3 oz..$10.00
Champagne, hollow stem, 4½ oz. or 5 oz.......15.00
Claret or grape juice, 4½ oz...........................10.00
Cocktail, 3½ oz..10.00
Cordial, 1 oz..30.00
Goblet, 8 oz. or 9 oz. 10.00
Goblet, 11 oz. 10.00
Parfait, 5 oz. 10.00
Pousse café 35.00
Russian coffee cup, 5 oz.................................35.00
Saucer champagne, 5½ oz...............................8.00
Sherbet, footed, 5½ oz. 5.00
Sherry, 2 oz. 30.00
Sundae, footed, 8 oz...5.00
Wine, 2½ oz. 15.00

No. 3312 Gayoso goblet with No. 387 Augusta double plate etching.

No. 3320 Ritz goblet with No. 403 Chartiers plate etching.

Ritz, No. 3320 — original name
Date: 1917 to 1929
Color: Crystal

Comments: A stemware line with a blown bowl and pulled stem. Very similar to stems made by other companies. Not marked with the Diamond H.

Burgundy, 3 oz. $10.00
Claret, 5 oz. 12.00
Cocktail, 3 oz. 10.00
Cordial, 1 oz. 35.00
Finger bowl..5.00
Goblet, 7 oz. 10.00
Goblet, 11 oz. 10.00
Pousse café 30.00
Saucer champagne, 6 oz. 7.00
Wine, 2 oz...12.00

No. 4121 Glenn marmalade &
cover, cut.

Glenn, No. 4121
Date: 1917 to 1946
Color: Crystal

Comments: A blown item and so not
marked with the Diamond H. Made
plain or diamond optic.

Marmalade & cover................$40.00

Weaver, No. 4122;
No. 4123 Marmalade
Dates: 1917 to 1928; 1934 to 1937
Color: Crystal

Comments: A blown item and so not
marked with the Diamond H. Made either
plain or with diamond optic.

Marmalade & cover (#4122 or
#4123) $40.00

No. 4122 Weaver marmalade
with No. 625 El Dorado cutting.

No. 4123 marmalade.

No. 4156
Date: 1917
Color: Crystal

Comments: A blown jug with applied handle, not marked with the Diamond H. Used primarily for decorations.

Jug...$55.00

No. 4156 jug with No. 693 Cloister cutting.

No. 4159 Classic tankard jug.

Classic, No. 4159
Dates: 1917 to 1939. Ice lip jug from 1948 to 1953.
Color: Crystal

Comments: Blown pitchers with applied handles. None are marked with the Diamond H. Some were made with wide optic. Similar to jugs made by many other companies. A No. 4159/1 9" vase was also made in a similar shape (without a handle) from 1929 to 1935. This was available in Moongleam, Flamingo, and Hawthorne (not Crystal) with diamond optic.

Jug, 8 oz. $20.00
Jug, 14 oz. 25.00
Jug, 21 oz. 35.00
Jug, 31 oz. 40.00
Jug, 42 oz. 60.00
Jug, 54 oz. 70.00
Jug, 65 oz. 75.00

Decorations Introduced in 1917

Cuttings: No. 604 Ornate Sprig, No. 605 Double Miter Band, No. 607 Periwinkle, No. 636 Clermont, No. 637 Polished Star, No. 639 Electro, and No. 640 Nassau.

Etchings: No. 33 Tatting needle etching, No. 35 Lacy Band needle etching, No. 36 Ric Rac needle etching, No. 305 Mollie plate etching, No. 342 Barberry plate etching, No. 343 Julie plate etching, No. 364 Vera plate etching, No. 378 Kilarney plate etching, No. 387 Augusta plate etching, No. 394 Zouave plate etching, No. 402 American Beauty plate etching, No. 403 Chartiers plate etching, No. 404 Muskingum plate etching, No. 405 Canterbury plate etching, No. 406 Duquesne plate etching, No. 407 Morning Glory plate etching, and No. 408 Lincoln plate etching.

1918:

In February 1918, the A. H. Heisey & Co. was incorporated in the state of Ohio. At this time A. H. Heisey was listed as president of the company. By December this incorporation was dissolved. The company was then designated as a joint stock company or joint trust and remained under this type of organization until the company closed.

Decorations Introduced in 1918

Cuttings: No. 638 Calais

Etchings: No. 160 Osage pantograph etching, No. 161 Somerset pantograph etching, No. 162 Raleigh pantograph etching, No. 410 Sabrina plate etching, No. 411 Landsdown plate etching, No. 412 Hermitage plate etching, and No. 413 Renaissance double plate etching.

1919:

Statuesque, No. 3331
Date: 1919 to 1921
Color: Crystal

Comments: A stemware line with blown bowl and pressed stem. Marked with the Diamond H on upper stem just below the bowl. Somewhat difficult to find.

Cocktail, 3 oz. $15.00	Parfait, 6 oz. 18.00
Finger bowl 8.00	Saucer champagne, 5½ or 6 oz...............15.00
Goblet, 9 or 10 oz. 20.00	Sherbet, footed, 4 oz..............................7.00
Grape juice, 4 oz. 20.00	Sundae, footed, 5 or 6 oz.........................7.00

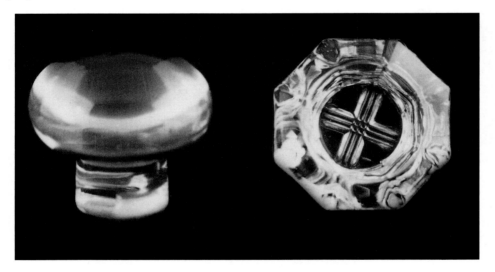

Heisey door knobs, 2 styles.
About 1919 the Heisey company began making a series of door knobs and drawer pulls. Many of these were to standards set by various companies, including Sargent, who made lock sets for doors. The following numbers are known for Heisey door knobs, but most of them are not identifiable today: 1, 2, 3, 4, 5, 6, 10, 11, 13, 14, 15, 16, 42, 43, 50, 59, 252, 253, 352, 353, 502, 508, 510, 511, 512, 513, 514, 602, 612, 642, 2002, 2010, 2011, 2012, 2013, 2014, 2018, 2033, 2042, 2046, and 2052. It is likely more were made, but information at this point is sketchy. Suffice it to say, door knobs were a substantial product of the company for many years.

No. 3331 Statuesque goblet with No. 415 Classic double plate etching.

Old Glory, No. 3333 — original name
Date: 1919 to 1941
Colors: Crystal, Hawthorne
Patent: Joseph O. Balda patented the Old Glory goblet with Renaissance
etching on 10-25-1921, given patent No. 59451. He assigned the
patent to the Heisey company.

Comments: A stem line with blown bowl, pressed stem. When marked, the Diamond H will be just below the bowl on the upper stem. Other companies made stemware similar to Old Glory. Prices given are for crystal. Add 150% for Hawthorne items.

Burgundy, 3 oz. $20.00	Ice tea, footed, handled, 12 oz. (#3476)..........28.00
Claret, 4½ oz...20.00	Oyster cocktail, 4½ oz. (#3542)........................7.00
Cocktail, 3 oz.or 2½ oz. 20.00	Parfait, 4½ oz. 20.00
Comport, high footed, 6"................................60.00	Pousse café, ¾ oz. 40.00
Cordial, 1 oz. 45.00	Saucer champagne, 5½ oz. 15.00
Finger bowl (#3309)...8.00	Sherry, 2 oz..25.00
Goblet, 8 oz. or 9 oz. 22.00	Soda, footed 12 oz. (#3476)..........................20.00
Grapefruit, footed..20.00	Sundae or sherbet, 5½ oz. 7.00
Grape juice, 6 oz. 22.00	Wine, 2 oz..22.00

No. 3333 Old Glory goblet with No. 413 Renaissance double plate etching.

Detail of No. 413 Renaissance double plate etching.

Saucer Champagne   Goblet   Footed Sherbet

The lure of gleaming glassware on your table

Like fairy etchings of frost on a window, like lacy network of summer leaves is the tracery on sparkling Heisey glassware. It lends an extra lure to the charms of a dainty table.

Delicate as these patterns are, their use is a pleasure you may enjoy daily, as they can always be quickly replaced and so inexpensively! You need not grieve for "broken sets" or too costly completing, with Heisey's lovely pieces.

We will supply you direct, if your dealer refuses to do so. A. H. Heisey Co., Dept. 91, Newark, O.

HEISEY'S *TRADE* H *MARK* **GLASSWARE**
FOR THE TABLE
On every piece   On every piece

Lady Leg, No. 3335
Date: 1919 to 1924
Color: Crystal
Patents: The goblet with No. 431 Victory etching was given patent No. 59474 on 10-25-1921 with T. C. Heisey listed as designer. The No. 674 Adams cutting was patented on 2-17-1925 and given No. 66599 with Joseph O. Balda given as designer. He also patented No. 680 Crusader cutting on 11-24-1925. The number given was 68844.

Comments: A stemware line with blown bowl and pressed stem. Marked with the Diamond H at the top of the stem just below the bowl.

Claret or grape juice, 4 oz.	$18.00
Cocktail, 3½ oz.	18.00
Finger bowl	8.00
Fruit cocktail, 5 oz.	7.00
Goblet, 8 oz.	18.00
Parfait, 4½ oz.	18.00
Saucer champagne, 5 oz.	12.00
Sherbet, footed, 5 oz.	7.00
Wine, 2½ oz.	18.00

No. 3335 Lady Leg saucer champagne, goblet, sherbet with No. 431 Victory etching.

Lady Leg, No. 3336
Date: 1919 to 1924
Color: Crystal

Comments: A stemware line with blown bowl and pressed stem. Marked with the Diamond H at the upper stem just below the bowl. Similar to No. 3335 Lady Leg but taller and with a flared bowl.

Burgundy, 3 oz.	$18.00
Claret	20.00
Cocktail, 3 oz.	18.00
Cordial, 1 oz.	40.00
Fruit cocktail	7.00
Goblet, 10 oz.	18.00
Grape juice, 4 oz.	18.00
Ice cream, footed	7.00
Saucer champagne	15.00
Sherbet, 4 oz.	7.00
Wine, 2 oz.	20.00

No. 3336 Lady Leg goblet with No. 422 Cumberland double plate etching.

Whaley, No. 4163
Dates: Jugs from 1919 to 1953. Pretzel jar from 1933 to 1938.
Beer mugs from 1933 to 1945.
Colors: Jugs were made only in crystal. Pretzel jar in crystal and Sahara.
Beer mugs made in crystal with handles of Moongleam,
Flamingo, Sahara, Stiegel Blue, Tangerine, and Red.

Comments: Jugs were made in plain or wide optic, and the 108 ounce size was made in saturn optic. The pretzel jar and beer mugs are marked with the Diamond H — the jugs are not. The pretzel jar was a design winner from a Heisey contest for employees in 1933.

Jug, 54 oz..$75.00
Jug, 108 oz..90.00
Jug, ice lip, 54 oz. 75.00
Mug, beer, 12 oz. 90.00
Mug, beer, 16 oz. 100.00
Pretzel jar & cover ....500.00+

No. 4163 Whaley pretzel jar.

No. 4163 Whaley jug with No. 679 Windsor cutting.

Gallagher, No. 4164
Date: 1919 to 1957
Colors: Crystal, Moongleam, Flamingo, Marigold, Sahara, Hawthorne, Alexandrite

Comments: A blown jug not marked with the Diamond H. Made plain, wide optic, or with diamond optic. May have cut and polished flutes about neck. Later jugs were made with ice lips. For Flamingo, add 100%. For Moongleam or Sahara, add 150%. For other colors, add 500%.

Jug, 73 oz. $95.00

No. 4164 Gallagher jug.

Olympia, No. 4191
Date: 1919 to 1944
Color: Crystal

Comments: Blown vases. Pressed, applied foot. The vase with no foot was probably for an automobile vase.

Vase, footed...$35.00
Vase, no foot....35.00

No. 4191 Olympia footed vase with No. 672 Bachelor's Button cutting.

No. 4192 Vase
Date: 1919 to 1929
Color: Crystal

Comments: A blown vase with applied pressed foot.

Vase $35.00

No. 4192 vase.

Cynthia, No. 4198
Date: 1919 to 1950s
Color: Crystal

Comments: Blown vases not marked with the Diamond H. These would be practically impossible to attribute to Heisey without a known Heisey decoration.

Vase, 8"...........................$35.00
Vase, 10"...........................45.00

No. 4198 Cynthia vases with No. 507 Orchid etching.

Marlene, No. 4291
Date: 1919 to 1929
Color: Crystal

Comments: A blown candy jar and cover with pressed stem. Marked on the pressed stem.

Candy jar & cover $50.00

No. 4291 Marlene covered candy jar with No. 431 Victory etching.

Decorations Introduced in 1919

Cuttings: No. 657 Liberty, No. 661 Constellation, No. 667 Sir George, No. 671 Entente, No. 672 Bachelor's Button, No. 674 Adams, No. 679 Windsor, No. 680 Crusader, No. 682 Greenbriar, No. 688 Cassaba, No. 693 Cloister, No. 694 Balboa, and No. 697 Trellis.

Etchings: No. 27 Crochet needle etching, No. 31 Roman Key needle etching, No. 9001 Trefoil needle etching, No. 38 Tallahassee needle etching, No. 41 Braided Loop needle etching, No. 163 Monticello pantograph etching, No. 164 Salem pantograph etching, No. 165 Dundee pantograph etching, No. 414 Oxford etching/cutting, No. 415 Classic plate etching, No. 416 Vintage plate etching, No. 418 Aceropolis plate etching, No. 421 Rose plate etching, No. 422 Cumberland plate etching, No. 423 Violets plate etching, No. 424 Cherries plate etching, No. 425 Dogwood plate etching, No. 426 Mt. Vernon plate etching, No. 428 Simplex plate etching, No. 429 Zodiac plate etching, No. 430 Highlander plate etching, No. 431 Victory plate etching, No. 432 Londonderry plate etching, and No. 433 Duchess plate etching.

1920:

Hexagon Stem, No. 485, No. 487
Date: No. 485, 1920 to 1935; No. 487, 1920 to 1933.
Colors: Crystal, Moongleam, Flamingo

Comments: Marked with the Diamond H on the bottom of the foot. No. 485 has a No. 64 pointed stopper. No. 487 has a No. 63 flat topped stopper. No. 485 was also made with a No. 71 peg stopper. The powder box is footed similar to the colognes, and very heavy. The top is the same as the No. 1186 powder box lid.

Cologne & stopper, ½ oz. $125.00
Cologne & stopper, 1 oz..95.00
Cologne & stopper, 1¾ oz. 95.00
Cologne & stopper, 3½ oz. 175.00
Powder box & cover 150.00

No. 485 Hexagon Stem cologne with No. 730 Cornflower cutting.

No. 490 Karen colognes with No. 4301 puff box, all with special engraving.

Karen, No. 490 or No. 491
Date: 1920
Color: Crystal

Comments: These colognes are marked with the Diamond H, but the blown puff box is not. No. 490 colognes have the pointed stopper while No. 491 colognes have a flat top stopper.

Cologne, 2 oz..............$95.00

Phyllis, No. 1020
Date: 1920 to 1933
Colors: Crystal, Moongleam, Flamingo, Canary
Patent: No. 58832 granted on 8-30-1921. Andrew J. Sanford was the designer.

Comments: A pressed cream and sugar marked with the Diamond H. Sometimes these are also found with the patent date in the bottoms. Made in plain or wide optic. For Moongleam or Flamingo, add 300%. For Canary, add 1,000%+.

No. 1020 Phyllis cream and sugar with No. 724 Daffodil cutting

Cream or sugar $25.00

Etchings Introduced in 1920:
166 Mayflower pantograph etching.

1921:

Carolina, No. 3344
Date: 1921 to 1924
Color: Crystal

Comments: A stemware line with blown bowl and pressed stem. Marked with the Diamond H on upper stem just below the bowl. There are two other stem lines by Heisey which are very similar to Carolina.

No. 3344 Carolina goblet with No. 160 Osage pantograph etching.

Cocktail, 3 oz. $18.00
Cordial, 1 oz.....................................35.00
Finger bowl......................................7.00
Goblet, 9 oz. 18.00
Saucer champagne, 5½ oz................15.00
Sundae, footed, 6 oz. 7.00
Wine, 2 oz. 18.00

Decorations Introduced in 1921

Cuttings: No. 704 Magnolia, No. 706 Warrick, No. 711 Dante, No. 717 Ulysses, No. 720 Cristobal, No. 723 Azalea, No. 724 Daffodil, No. 729 Fairfield, No. 730 Cornflower, and No. 732 Palisade.

Etchings: No. 151 Zeus pantograph etching, No. 152 Apollo pantograph etching, No. 154 Brunswick pantograph etching, No. 155 Neptune pantograph etching, No. 156 Fantan pantograph etching, and No. 158 Barcelona pantograph etching.

Mary 'n' Virg, No. 3345
Date: 1921 to 1928
Colors: Crystal, rare in Canary
Patent: No. 59651 assigned to T. C. Heisey. Applied for on 11-15-1921.

Comments: A stemware line with blown bowl and pressed stem. Marked with the Diamond H on the upper stem just below the bowl. Canary items are valued at $150.00+.

Cocktail, 3 oz. $18.00
Goblet, 9 oz. 20.00
Saucer champagne, 6 oz. 12.00
Sherbet, footed, 6 oz. 7.00
Wine, 2 oz. 18.00

No. 3345 Mary 'n' Virg goblet, unknown cutting.

Balda, No. 4166
Date: 1921 to 1937
Color: Crystal

Comments: A blown jug with applied foot. Not marked with the Diamond H. Named for Joseph Balda, the designer.

No. 4166 Balda footed jug.

Jug, footed, 40 oz. $55.00

173

1922:

Wabash, No. 3350 — original name
Date: 1922 to 1947
Colors: Crystal, Flamingo, Hawthorne, Crystal stem and foot with Marigold bowl, Moongleam stem and foot with Crystal bowl
Patent: Joseph O. Balda patented the goblet on 2-16-1926 with No. 69434 assigned. Interestingly, the No. 440 Frontenac etching was patented earlier on 2-26-1924 and given No. 64040, and No. 439 Pied Piper etching was patented on 2-10-1925 and given No. 66547. Balda applied for all of these in 1922.

Comments: A stemware line with blown bowl, pressed stem. Added items include ice teas, comport, and two types of jugs. Fenton made an all-pressed stem line very similar to Wabash. Prices are for pieces in crystal. Add 100% for Moongleam or Flamingo. Add 400% for Hawthorne or Marigold.

Claret, 4 oz.	$22.00
Cocktail, 3 oz.	15.00
Comport & cover, 6"	65.00
Cordial, 1 oz.	50.00
Finger bowl (2 styles)	8.00
Goblet, 10 oz.	22.00
Grapefruit, footed	20.00
Ice tea, footed & handled, 12 oz.	22.00
Ice tea, footed, 12 oz.	18.00
Jug, squat, 3 pint	145.00
Oyster cocktail, 4 oz.	10.00
Parfait, 5 oz.	20.00
Saucer champagne, 6 oz.	15.00
Sherbet, 6 oz.	10.00
Tankard, 3 pint	145.00
Tumbler, footed, 10 oz.	15.00
Vase, bud	95.00
Wine, 2½ oz.	22.00

No. 3350 Wabash grapefruit with No. 439 Pied Piper double plate etching.

No. 3350 Wabash goblet with unknown Heisey cutting (from former employee's estate).

Bud Vase
Date: Ca. 1922 due to its similarity to the Wabash bud vase
Color: Crystal

Comments: This bud vase is very similar to the bud vase in the No. 3350 Wabash line except that it lacks the typical Wabash rings at the top of the stem and is slightly flared at the top rim. The vase is marked with the Diamond H on one of the panels of the stem. It is not shown in Heisey catalogs and was previously unknown.

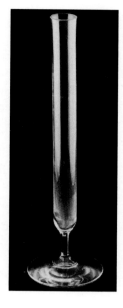

Unknown number Heisey blown bud vase.

Bud vase......................................$95.00

Decorations Introduced in 1922
Cuttings: No. 625 El Dorado.

Etchings: 439 Pied Piper double plate etching and No. 440 Frontenac plate etching.

1923:

No. 10 Gibson Girl floral plateau with No. 730 Cornflower cutting.

Gibson Girl, No. 10
Date: 1923 to 1933
Colors: Crystal, Moongleam, Flamingo, Hawthorne
Patent: Patent No. 75653 granted 6-26-1928. Designed by Andrew J. Sanford.

Comments: This floral plateau is pressed and marked with the Diamond H. It came in three sizes: No. 9 is 8", No. 10 is 10", No. 11 is 11½". For Moongleam or Flamingo, add 25%. For Hawthorne, add 100%.

Floral plateau (any size) $40.00

Coarse Rib, Nos. 406, 407
Dates: 1923 to 1937
Colors: Crystal, Moongleam, and Flamingo.
A limited number of items
in Hawthorne.
Patents: Patent No. 72064 was granted on 2-22-1927 to E. W. Heisey for the high
footed jelly. The No. 407 plate was patented on 2-17-1925 and given
No. 66630, while the nappy was patented on 3-24-1925 and assigned
No. 66853 with E. W. Heisey listed as designer for both.

Comments: Heisey used both No. 406 and 407 for Coarse Rib. Items with no pattern
number following the entry are No. 407. Prices are for crystal pieces. For Moongleam
and Flamingo, add 120%. For Hawthorne, add 400%.

Reproductions: Imperial Glass Corp. made a large one-piece chip and dip in crystal
and cobalt, marked with the Diamond H. This piece was never made by Heisey.

Celery tray, 9" $14.00
Celery tray, 12" 18.00
Cream, hotel 25.00
Cream, hotel (#406) 20.00
Cream, individual 27.00
Custard 10.00
Dish, lemon and cover, 5" 35.00
Finger bowl 9.00
Goblet, 8 oz. 18.00
Ice tea or soda, 12 oz. (#406) 18.00
Ice tub 80.00
Jelly, 2 handled, 5" 20.00
Jelly, high foot, 5" 25.00
Jelly, low foot, 5" 18.00
Jug, pint 35.00
Jug, quart 65.00
Jug, 3 pint 80.00
Jug, ½ gallon 90.00
Mustard & cover 60.00
Nappy, 4", 4½", 5", or 6" (#406) 7.00
Nappy, 4½" 7.00
Nappy, 7", 8", or 9" (#406) 20.00
Nappy, 9" 20.00
Oil & stopper, 6 oz. 55.00
Pickle jar & cover 60.00
Pickle tray, 6" 14.00
Plate, 4½", 5½", or 6" 8.00
Plate, 7", 8", or 9½" 9.00
Plate, 11" 45.00
Plate, 15" 65.00
Preserve, 6" 15.00
Saucer champagne, 5½ oz. 15.00
Sherbet, 6½ oz. 8.00
Soda, 8 oz. (#406) 15.00
Sugar & cover, hotel 40.00
Sugar & cover, hotel (#406) 40.00
Sugar, individual 35.00

Tankard, 3 pint 100.00
Tumbler, 8 oz. (#406) 20.00
Tumbler, straight, 8 oz. 20.00

No. 407 Coarse Rib tankard and jug.

No. 407 Coarse Rib. Top: preserve, hotel sugar and cream.
Bottom: ice tub, two-handled jelly, pickle jar.

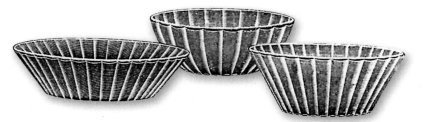

No. 406 Coarse Rib nappy, No. 407 Coarse Rib nappy, finger bowl.

Tudor, Nos. 411, 412, 413 — original name
Date: 1923 to 1939. Some items until 1944.
Colors: Crystal, Moongleam, Flamingo. Limited number of items made in Hawthorne.
Patents: The No. 411 Tudor goblet was patented on 9-14-1926 and given 71064; the plate was patented on 2-12-1924 and given No. 63947; and the floral compotier was patented on 11-24-1925 and given No. 68857. All patents were applied for in March 1923. The No. 411 two-handled mint was patented on 12-23-1924, and assigned No. 66288. The No. 411 soda was patented on 3-11-1924 and assigned No. 64183; the No. 411 nappy was patented on 5-25-1926 and given No. 70224 while the No. 411 flared tumbler was patented on 12-16-1924 and assigned No. 66233. All of these patents listed T. C. Heisey as designer.

Comments: A pressed tableware pattern, usually marked with the Diamond H. All items are No. 411 unless otherwise noted. McKee made a similar pattern named Lenox. Some Tudor items have only handles in color. Not all pieces were made in all colors. Prices are for crystal. For Moongleam or Flamingo, add 100%. For Hawthorne, add 200%.

Almond, individual $45.00
Banana split, footed, 8" (#412) 30.00
Bar tumbler, 2½ oz. 25.00
Bonbon, 2 handled 18.00
Bowl, floral, footed, 12½" 42.00
Bowl, nut, 4½" 32.00
Celery tray, 12" 27.00
Cheese, 2 handled, 6" 18.00
Cigarette box & cover (#412) 65.00
Cigarette jar & ashtray 80.00
Cream, hotel 30.00
Custard, 4½ oz. (punch cup) 15.00
Dish, fruit, 10" (deep nappy) 40.00
Dish, lemon & cover, 5" 38.00
Finger bowl (#411 or #412) 10.00
Goblet, 7½ oz. (#412) 24.00
Goblet, 8 oz. (#411, #412 or #413) 24.00
Goblet, heavy, 10 oz. (#413) 30.00
Goblet, luncheon, 7 oz. 22.00
Grapefruit, 6½" 18.00
Grapefruit, footed, 5" 25.00
Ice tea, handled & footed, 12 oz. (#412) 32.00
Jelly, 2 handled, 5" 18.00

No. 411 Tudor jug.

Jelly, high footed, 5" 35.00
Jug cover 27.00

Jug, pint	45.00	Preserve & cover, footed, 5"	50.00
Jug, quart	60.00	Preserve, 6½"	27.00
Jug, 3 pint	75.00	Punch bowl & foot, 20"	285.00
Jug, ½ gallon.	90.00	Salt & pepper, pr.	45.00
Marmalade, 7"	27.00	Saucer champagne, 5½ oz.	18.00
Mayonnaise	50.00	Saucer champagne, 6 oz. (#412 or #413)	18.00
Mint, 2 handled, 6"	17.00	Sherbet, 5 oz.	10.00
Mug (#412)	75.00	Sherbet, 5½ oz. (#412)	12.00
Mustard & cover	52.00	Sherbet, low footed, 3½ oz. or 5½ oz. (#413)	12.00
Nappy, 4½" or 5"	12.00	Soda, 12 oz.	17.00
Nappy, 7", 8", or 9"	32.00	Soda, footed, 10½ oz. (#413)	18.00
Oil & stopper, 4 oz.	60.00	Soda, footed, heavy, 10 oz.	17.00
Oil & stopper, 6 oz.	55.00	Sugar & cover, hotel (#411 or #412)	50.00
Orange juice glass, 4½ oz.	22.00	Sugar dispenser	55.00
Oyster cocktail, 4 oz.	10.00	Tankard, footed (#412)	115.00
Parfait, 4 oz.	25.00	Tumbler, 8 oz. (#411 or #412)	18.00
Parfait, 4½ oz. (#412)	25.00	Vase, 8"	48.00
Pickle or olive tray, 7"	18.00	Vase, 10"	55.00
Plate, 4½", 5", 5½", or 6"	10.00	Water bottle	65.00
Plate, 7" or 8"	12.00	Wine, 3 oz.	25.00
Plate, 11"	65.00		

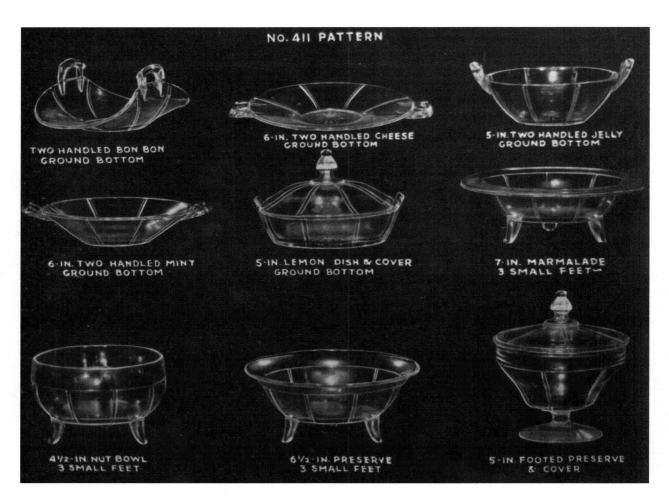

No. 411 Tudor assortment.

Double Rib & Panel, Nos. 417, 418
Date: 1923 to 1937
Colors: Crystal, Moongleam, Flamingo, Hawthorne
Patents: The tumbler was patented on 2-19-1924 and assigned No. 64011;
the bowl was patented on 6-10-1924 and given No. 64850 while the
goblet was patented the same day and given No. 64851 with
E. W. Heisey listed as designer for all three items.

Comments: Not all items were made in all colors. Most pieces will be marked with
the Diamond H. The basket mold was redesigned later into the No. 1503 Crystolite
basket. For Moongleam and Flamingo pieces, add 100%. For Hawthorne, add 150%.

Bar, 1 oz. $25.00
Bar, 2 oz. 20.00
Basket, 6" 165.00
Bowl, floral, 10" 55.00
Carafe, cocktail 150.00
Cream..30.00
Goblet..25.00
Mustard & cover...60.00
Nappy 4½" 10.00
Nappy, 8" 35.00
Oil & stopper, 3 oz. 75.00
Oyster cocktail, 2½ oz. 12.00
Pitcher, ½ gallon 75.00
Plate, 6" 12.00
Plate, 11" 55.00
Salt & pepper, pr. 55.00
Saucer champagne, 6 oz. 18.00
Sherbet..12.00
Sugar & cover 45.00
Tumbler, 8 oz...35.00

No. 417 Double Rib & Panel oil.

Inside Scallop, Nos. 1192, 1193
Date: 1923
Colors: Crystal, Flamingo, Moongleam, Hawthorne, Canary

Comments: A small pressed ware line marked with the Diamond H. The pattern is
basically a large melon ribbed design. For Flamingo and Moongleam items, add 100%.
For Hawthorne, add 200%. As a guide, the Canary 9" fruit is valued at $650.00+.

Cucumber dish..$22.00
Fruit, 5" 15.00
Fruit, 9" 50.00
Jelly, high footed, 6½" 45.00
Nappy, shallow, 5" (#1192) 15.00
Nappy, shallow, 8" (#1192) 40.00

No. 1193 Inside
Scallop high footed
jelly.

No. 1193 Inside Scallop cucumber dish.

1924:

Elegance, No. 42
Date: 1924 to 1953
Colors: Crystal, Moongleam foot, Flamingo, Marigold, Sahara

Comments: A blown salt, not marked with the Diamond H. Made in plain or diamond optic. Used for many Heisey decorations. For Moongleam or Flamingo, add 100%. For Marigold, add 250%. For Sahara, add 125%. See color plate for illustration.

Salt & pepper, pr. $40.00

No. 201 Photo candle-stick.

Photo, No. 201
Date: 1924. Made for less than a year.
Color: Crystal

Comments: A very unusual candlestick made to hold a photograph which is covered by the glass of the oval. Very hard to find. Marked with the Diamond H on the short column just above the base.

Candlestick, 10", ea. ....$2,500.00+

Circle Pair, No. 2516
Date: 1924 to 1937
Colors: Crystal, Flamingo, Moongleam, Marigold, Sahara
Patent: The tumbler was patented on 6-29-1926 and given No. 70476 with T. C. Heisey signing the patent as designer.

Comments: A blown stemware and soda line. Not marked with the Diamond H. Made in diamond optic. For Moongleam or Flamingo, add 125%. For Marigold, add 150%. For Sahara, add 100%.

Goblet	$22.00
Jug, ½ gallon	75.00
Soda, 5 oz. (juice)	12.00
Soda, 8 oz.	15.00
Soda, 12 oz. (ice tea)	15.00
Soda, footed, 12 oz.	20.00
Tumbler, 10 oz.	20.00

No. 2516 Circle Pair 5 oz., 8 oz., 12 oz. sodas.

Portsmouth, No. 3440 — original name
Date: 1924 to 1935
Colors: Crystal, Flamingo, Moongleam bowl with Crystal foot. A rare goblet is known with a Tangerine bowl and stem, Crystal foot.

Comments: A short stemware line with blown bowl and pulled stem. Not marked with the Diamond H. Made with diamond optic. According to old factory records, a very limited number of goblets were listed with Flamingo bowls and Moongleam feet. At this time none of these are known. For Flamingo or Moongleam, add 100%.

Cocktail, 3½ oz.	$10.00	Saucer champagne, 7 oz.	12.00
Goblet, 9 oz.	15.00	Sherbet, 7 oz.	8.00

No. 3440 Portsmouth items.

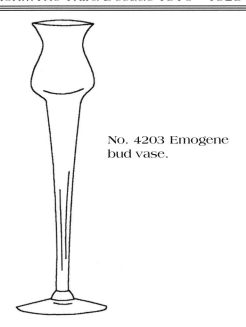

No. 4203 Emogene
bud vase.

Emogene, No. 4203
Date: 1924 to 1937
Colors: Crystal, Moongleam, Flamingo,
Hawthorne

Comments: A blown vase, not marked with
the Diamond H. Made in diamond optic. For
Moongleam or Flamingo, add 100%. For
Hawthorne, add 150%.

Vase, bud, 9" $45.00

Decorations Introduced in 1924

Cuttings: No. 740 Hermitage, No. 741 Chantilly, No. 745 Media, No. 746 Mt. Vernon, No. 748 Euridice, No. 751 Avalon, No. 752 Camelot, No. 753 Trieste, and No. 754 Seville.

Etchings: No. 46 Weaver's Stripe needle etching, No. 168 Adam pantograph etching, and No. 169 Biltmore pantograph etching.

1925:

Sussex, No. 419 — original name
Date: 1925 to 1946
Colors: Crystal; Moongleam, Flamingo, and Stiegel Blue bowls with Crystal stems. Tumblers and the finger bowl are solid colors.

Comments: Primarily a pressed stemware and tumbler line. Marked with the Diamond H. Heisey copied a Steuben pattern which was all handmade. Marked pieces of Steuben include the goblets with green bowls and a soda with a color similar to Marigold. This pattern is moderately available for collectors. Prices are for crystal items. For Moongleam or Flamingo, add 100%. For Stiegel Blue, add 500%.

No. 419 Sussex soda (l) and Steuben soda (r).

Cocktail, 2½ oz...$18.00
Finger bowl..20.00
Goblet, 8 oz. 25.00
Goblet, 10 oz. 25.00
Saucer champagne, 5½ oz................................22.00
Sherbet, 5½ oz. 15.00
Soda, 5 oz. (juice)..15.00
Soda, 8 oz. (water) 18.00
Soda, 12 oz. (ice tea).......................................22.00

Pleat & Panel, No. 1170
Date: 1925 to 1937
Colors: Crystal, Moongleam, Flamingo. A few pieces in Hawthorne or Sahara.
Rare oils are known in amber.

Comments: Prices are for pieces in crystal. For Moongleam and Flamingo, add 50%
to 100%. For Hawthorne or Sahara, add 100% to 125%.

Bouillon cup...$18.00
Cheese & cracker, 10½" 32.00
Chow chow, 4"...17.00
Comport & cover, low footed, 6" 50.00
Compotier & cover, high footed, 5" 70.00
Cream, hotel 25.00
Cup & saucer 35.00
Dish, lemon & cover, 5"..................................35.00
Dish, vegetable, 9" 32.00
Goblet, 8 oz. 25.00
Goblet, luncheon, 7½ oz. 20.00
Grapefruit or cereal, 6½"................................15.00
Ice tea, 12 oz. 18.00
Jelly, 2 handled, 5" 18.00
Jug, 3 pint 75.00
Jug, ice, 3 pint...75.00
Marmalade, 4¼"...17.00
Nappy, 4½" 10.00
Nappy, 8"...25.00
Oil & stopper, 3 oz..45.00
Plate, 6", 7" or 8"..15.00
Plate, 10¾"...85.00
Plate, 14"...75.00
Platter, oval, 12" 35.00
Saucer champagne, 5 oz. 17.00
Sherbet, 5 oz. 12.00
Sugar & cover, hotel.......................................28.00
Tray, spice, 5 compartment, 10"......................40.00
Tumbler, 8 oz. 20.00
Vase, 8"...32.00

No. 1170 Pleat &
Panel luncheon
goblet, Moon-
gleam with floral
cut panels.

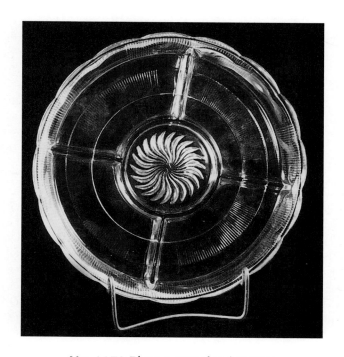

No. 1170 Pleat & Panel spice tray.

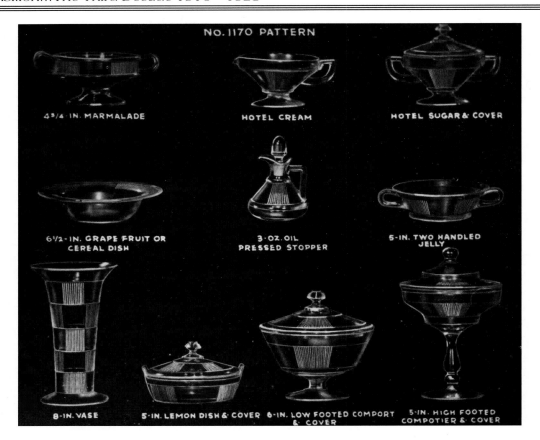

NO. 1170 PATTERN

4³/4-IN. MARMALADE

HOTEL CREAM

HOTEL SUGAR & COVER

6½-IN. GRAPE FRUIT OR CEREAL DISH

3-OZ. OIL PRESSED STOPPER

5-IN. TWO HANDLED JELLY

8-IN. VASE

5-IN. LEMON DISH & COVER

6-IN. LOW FOOTED COMPORT & COVER

5-IN. HIGH FOOTED COMPOTIER & COVER

No. 1170 Pleat and Panel assortment.

Octagon, No. 1229
Date: 1925 to 1937
Colors: Crystal, Flamingo, Moongleam, Hawthorne
Patent: The sandwich plate was patented on 12-22-1925 and assigned
No. 69081 with T. C. Heisey listed as designer. Ray Cobel, head of
Heisey's mold shop, was granted patent No. 1774871 for the pressed
handles of the pattern in 1930.

Comments: A short, plain pressed pattern. Most pieces are not marked with the Diamond H, but some larger pieces may be marked on the handles. Items were available plain or with diamond optic. Prices are for items in crystal. For Moongleam and
Flamingo, add 50%. For Hawthorne, add 125%.

Bonbon, 6"	$15.00
Bowl, footed, 8"	25.00
Cheese dish, 6"	15.00
Dish, oval dessert, 8"	25.00
Hors d' oeuvre, 13"	20.00
Jelly, 5¼"	15.00
Mayonnaise, footed, 5½"	15.00
Mint, 6"	15.00
Nut, individual	15.00
Plate, muffin, 10"	20.00
Plate, muffin, 12"	25.00
Plate, sandwich, 10"	20.00
Plate, sandwich, 12"	25.00

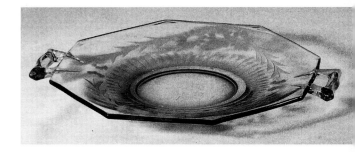

No. 1229 Octagon cheese plate, Hawthorne, cut.

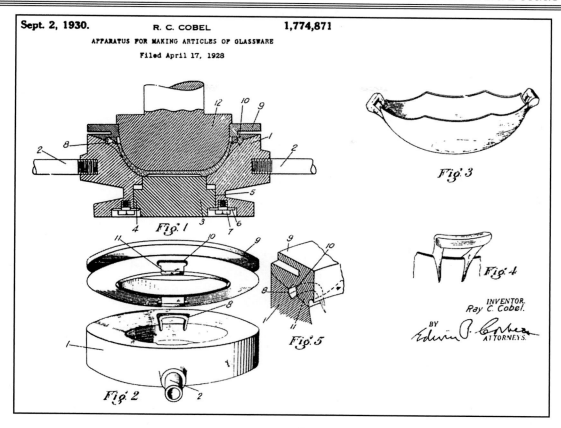

No. 1229 Octagon pattern patent drawing.

No. 1229 Octagon hors d' oeuvre, mayonnaise, individual nut, 8" footed bowl, and 8" oval dessert.

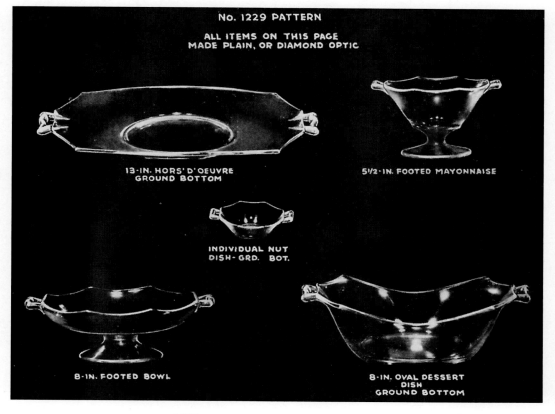

Ribbed Octagon, No. 1231
Date: 1925 to 1936
Colors: Crystal, Flamingo, Moongleam, Hawthorne

Comments: Most pieces are marked with the Diamond H. The rare rum pot was made in crystal, Moongleam, Flamingo, Sahara ($1,700.00+), and cobalt ($1,900.00+). If these rum pots are complete with stoppers, values are greater. Heisey made patterns called No. 500 and No. 1229, also known to collectors as Octagon, but these are separate patterns. Do not confuse this with McKee's Octagon Edge pattern. Prices are for crystal. For Moongleam and Flamingo, add 50%. For Hawthorne, add 125%.

Bowl, salad, 12½"	$28.00
Candlesticks, 3", pr.	45.00
Celery tray, 9"	17.00
Celery tray, 12"	18.00
Cream soup, 2 handled	18.00
Cream, hotel	18.00
Cup & saucer	20.00
Cup & saucer, after dinner coffee	25.00
Dish, vegetable, 9"	18.00
Grapefruit, 6½"	14.00
Plate, 6" or 7"	10.00
Plate, 8"	12.00
Plate, 10½"	50.00
Plate, 14"	42.00
Plate, soup, 9" (bowl)	20.00
Platter, oval, 12¾"	25.00
Rum pot	600.00+
Sandwich plate, center handled, 10½"	30.00
Sugar, hotel	18.00

No. 1231 Ribbed Octagon cream, sugar, grapefruit, after dinner cup and saucer, cup and saucer, cream soup, vegetable dish, candlestick, soup plate.

Eagle, No. 1236
Dates: 1925 to 1933; 1937 to 1941
Colors: Crystal, Moongleam

Comments: This pressed plate is a copy of a Sandwich design. It is not marked with the Diamond H.

Plate, 8".......................................$55.00

No. 1236 Eagle plate.

No. 1238 Beehive plate, Flamingo.

Beehive, No. 1238
Date: 1925 to 1944+
Colors: Crystal, Moongleam, Flamingo, Hawthorne, Sahara, Zircon

Comments: This pressed plate is a copy of a Sandwich design. It is not marked with the Diamond H. For Moongleam or Flamingo, add 100%. For Hawthorne or Sahara, add 300%. For Zircon, add 350%.

Plate, 5"...$15.00
Plate, 8"...25.00
Plate, 14"...65.00

Teardrop, No. 2517
Date: 1925 to 1930
Colors: Crystal, Moongleam, Flamingo. Some pieces in Hawthorne. Vase and floral bowl not listed in Crystal. Jug made in Crystal with Moongleam handle.

Comments: Blown items, not marked with the Diamond H with an interesting teardrop shaped optic. The vase was made into the floral bowl having a broad, turned down rim. For Moongleam or Flamingo, add 250%. For Hawthorne, add 350%.

Bowl, floral, 12" hat shape
(Moongleam or
Flamingo) $90.00
Jug, ½ gallon 95.00
Soda, 12 oz. 22.00
Vase, 9½" (Moongleam
or Flamingo) 100.00

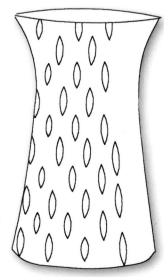

No. 2517 Teardrop vase.

Fairacre, No. 3355 — original name
Date: 1925 to 1937
Colors: Crystal. Moongleam stem and foot, Crystal bowl. Flamingo stem and foot, Crystal bowl. The jug was listed in company price lists as available in all Moongleam or Flamingo and with Moongleam foot and handle or Flamingo foot and handle. This jug was also used with the No. 3357 King Arthur stem line. King Arthur utilizes the same stem but has a cupped bowl. The vase was made in Flamingo and Moongleam foot with Crystal bowl, plus all Flamingo.

Comments: A stemware line with blown bowl, pressed stem. Optics include wide optic or diamond optic. This line has average availability. There are no reproductions of this line. For Flamingo or Moongleam, add 75%.

Claret, 4½ oz.	$20.00
Cocktail, 3½ oz.	20.00
Cordial, 1 oz.	55.00
Finger bowl (#4074)	7.00
Goblet, 10 oz.	22.00
Goblet, luncheon, 10 oz.	20.00
Ice tea, footed & handled, 12 oz.	22.00
Ice tea, footed, 12 oz.	22.00
Jug, footed, 54 oz.	140.00
Oyster cocktail, 3¼ oz.	8.00
Parfait, 5 oz.	20.00
Saucer champagne, 6½ oz.	18.00
Sherbet, 6½ oz.	12.00
Vase, 12" (in colors)	200.00+
Wine, 2½ oz.	25.00

No. 3355 Fairacre goblet, No. 170 Cleopatra pantograph etching.

King Arthur, No. 3357 — original name
Date: 1925 to 1937
Colors: Crystal, Flamingo. Crystal bowl with Moongleam or Flamingo stem and foot.
Patent: The goblet was patented on 6-23-1925 and was assigned No. 67658. T. C. Heisey signed the patent as designer.

Comments: Blown bowl, pressed stem. Made with diamond optic or plain. No. 3335 Fairacre has the same stem as King Arthur but has a flared rim bowl. For colors, add 75%.

Cocktail, 4 oz.	$20.00	Goblet, luncheon, 10 oz.	20.00
Cordial, 1 oz.	35.00	Ice tea, footed, 12 oz.	20.00
Finger bowl	7.00	Jug, 54 oz. (#3355)	140.00
Goblet, 10 oz.	22.00	Oyster cocktail, 33/4 oz.	8.00

Parfait, 5 oz. 25.00
Saucer champagne, 6½ oz. 20.00

Sherbet, 6½ oz. 18.00
Wine, 2½ oz. 35.00

No. 3357 King Arthur stems and jug.

Koors, No. 3480
Date: 1925 to 1937
Colors: Sodas made in Crystal, Flamingo, Hawthorne, or with Crystal body and Moongleam foot. Salt made in Crystal, Moongleam, Flamingo. Also with Crystal body and either Moongleam or Flamingo feet. Rare in Alexandrite.

Comments: A blown soda line, not marked with the Diamond H. It is difficult to find with a swirl optic, but relatively common in diamond optic. A similar salt shaker was made and given No. 48. For Moongleam or Flamingo, add 50%. For Hawthorne, add 300%.

Bar, footed, 1½ oz. $15.00
Bowl, floral, 7" (made in colors only) 85.00
Cocktail, footed, 3 oz. 12.00
Salt & pepper, pr. (#48) 45.00
Soda, footed, 5 oz. (juice)............................12.00
Soda, footed, 8½ oz. (water).........................15.00
Soda, footed, 12 oz. (ice tea)........................15.00

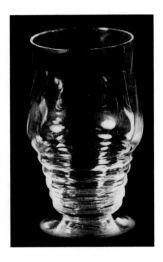

No. 3480 Koors soda with rare swirl optic.

No. 3481 Glenford 5 oz., 8½ oz., 12 oz. sodas.

Glenford, No. 3481
Date: 1925 to 1937
Colors: Crystal, Moongleam foot with Crystal bowl, Flamingo, Flamingo foot with Crystal bowl, Hawthorne, Flamingo bowl with Moongleam foot (rare).

Comments: A blown soda and tumbler line not marked with the Diamond H. Made in diamond optic and occasionally wide optic. Hawthorne items usually have checker optic — an optic similar to a checkerboard made of fine ribs. For Moongleam or Flamingo, add 50%. For Hawthorne, add 300%.

Bar, footed, 1 oz. $15.00
Cocktail, 3 oz...12.00
Soda, footed, 5 oz. (juice) 12.00
Soda, footed, 8 oz. (water).........................15.00
Soda, footed, 12 oz. (ice tea) 15.00

Christos, No. 4027
Date: 1925 to 1944
Colors: Crystal, Crystal with Moongleam foot and stopper, Flamingo, Crystal with Flamingo foot and stopper, Sahara, Alexandrite, Stiegel Blue with Crystal foot and stopper.

Comments: A blown decanter with applied foot. Not marked with the Diamond H. The steeple shaped stopper is often fully ground and polished. Usually found in diamond optic, but occasionally plain (no optic). For Moongleam and Flamingo, add 200%. For Sahara, add 275%. For Alexandrite, add 1,500%. For Stiegel Blue, add 500%+.

Decanter, 32 oz. $125.00

No. 4027 Christos decanter with No. 467 Tally Ho deep plate etching.

No. 4157 Steele rose bowl with Arctic etching.

Steele, No. 4157
Date: 1925 to 1939
Colors: Crystal. Rose bowl also made in Moongleam, Flamingo, Hawthorne, Sahara.

Comments: Blown pieces, not marked with the Diamond H. Usually items have ground and polished pontils. For Moongleam, Flamingo, or Sahara, add 70 to 100%. For Hawthorne, add 300%.

Jug, 1 pint $45.00
Jug, 1 quart 60.00
Jug, 3 pint 80.00
Jug, ½ gallon 95.00
Rose bowl.......................35.00

No. 4157 Steele jug.

Optic Tooth, No. 4206
Date: 1925 to 1937
Colors: Crystal, Moongleam foot with Crystal bowl, Flamingo, Flamingo foot with Crystal bowl, Hawthorne.

Comments: A blown line and not marked with the Diamond H. Made in diamond optic. Later the "claw foot" was left off and the vase modified into the No. 4057 Cecelia as redesigned by Walter von Nessen. For Moongleam and Flamingo, add 100%. For Hawthorne, add 300%.

No. 4206 Optic Tooth soda, Flamingo.

Jug, 3 pint	$150.00
Lamp, water, 8"	800.00+
Lamp, water, 10"	1,500.00+
Lamp, water, 12"	2,000.00+
Soda	25.00

Vase, 8"	45.00
Vase, 10"	60.00
Vase, 12"	80.00

No. 4209 Oval vase, Moongleam with La Furiste etching by Lotus Glass Co.

Oval, No. 4209
Dates: 1925 to 1937
Colors: Crystal, Moongleam, Flamingo, Marigold, Sahara

Comments: A blown vase and not marked with the Diamond H. Most often with Diamond optic. It has a fully ground and polished bottom. For Moongleam or Flamingo, add 100%. For Marigold, add 200% to 250%. For Sahara, add 125%.

Vase, 7"	$45.00
Vase, 9"	55.00

Decorations Introduced in 1925
Etchings: No. 170 Cleopatra pantograph etching and No. 442 Diana double plate etching.

Susan Duncan Heisey, A. H. Heisey's widow who had been ill for some time, died in early 1927.

The new color introduced in 1928 was Hawthorne, a pale lavender color with some tints of brown. It did not prove a success and remained in the line for only a year, to be replaced in 1930 by Alexandrite. One of Heisey's most collectible patterns, No. 1252 Twist was introduced.

Also in 1928, E. Wilson Heisey ran for director of the United States Chamber of Commerce as a representative of the Department of Manufacture. Unfortunately he was defeated in this race. However, of interest to Heisey collectors is that some of the No. 1186 Yeoman ashtrays are etched with the phrase "Heisey for Director." These are scarce today.

The Marigold color was introduced in 1929 — a bright, strong yellow, typical of the color of marigolds. Like its predecessor, Hawthorne, the color was made for only about a year, being replaced in 1930 by Sahara. The color seems to have been popular at the time, as it is found in fair quantity now, but the years have not been kind to Marigold. Some of the glass has proved to be unstable, and often disintegrates, showing a "sugary" or crizzled effect to actual flaking and splintering. Be assured that all Marigold does not suffer from this disease, and it is likely that most pieces have reached the maximum disintegration by this time.

During 1929, Heisey lost an important person from the early years of the company. Andrew Sanford, who had come with A. H. Heisey from Pittsburgh to work at the new company, died. He was Heisey's first designer, producing many of the early Heisey patterns, including most of the Colonial lines plus early glass shades, both electric and gas.

The new yellow color, Sahara, was introduced in 1930 and received much attention from the glass industry. It was reported that this was the first true yellow lead glass made. Another color which was an immediate hit was Alexandrite, a dichromatic glass (changes color in different light) with a beautiful orchid hue with ruby highlights.

The Heiseys were always interested in local and national politics, and E. Wilson Heisey was elected treasurer of the Ohio State Executive Committee of the Republican Party in 1929.

By 1935 most of Heisey's colors were discontinued including Moongleam, Flamingo, Alexandrite, and Tangerine. Stiegel Blue (cobalt), Zircon, and Sahara remained in production.

1926:

Mercury, No. 112
Date: 1926 to 1957
Colors: Crystal, Moongleam, Flamingo, Sahara, Hawthorne

Comments: These candlesticks were made in two sizes. A similar patterned insert for a candle-block is No. 123 made to fit the No. 15 floral block. Heisey also made a figural duck which fit into this floral block. Another figural floral block was the No. 14 Kingfisher which had the block attached to the base of the Kingfisher. The 3" size is marked with the Diamond H on the stem just below the candle cup, the 9" size at the top of the column, and the No. 123 on the underside of the base. The 3" size is common, but the others are difficult to find. For Moongleam and Flamingo, add 100%. For Sahara, add 150%. For Hawthorne, add 350%.

Candlesticks, 1 light, 3", pr. $40.00
Candlesticks, 1 light, 9", pr. 200.00
Candle insert, 1 light, 1 only.......100.00

No. 112 Mercury one-light candlestick, Moongleam.

Patent drawing for the Duck insert in the No. 15 floral block.

Delaware, No. 3324 — original name
Date: 1926 to 1935+
Colors: Crystal, Flamingo

Comments: A stemware line with blown bowl, pulled stem, and not marked with the Diamond H. Made in diamond optic. Hawthorne was made in checker optic, which is a delicate checkerboard effect. Delaware has not been reproduced. The most available color is Flamingo which is moderately available. It is difficult to find in Hawthorne or crystal. For Flamingo, add 100%; for Hawthorne, add 200%.

Cocktail, 3½ oz. $12.00
Finger bowl 8.00
Goblet, 9 oz. 15.00
Goblet, luncheon, 9 oz. 15.00
Oyster cocktail, 4 oz. 8.00
Parfait, 4½ oz. 15.00
Saucer champagne, 6½ oz. 12.00
Sherbet, 6½ oz. 8.00

No. 3324 Delaware saucer champagne, Flamingo, with No. 172 Dover pantograph etching.

194

Plateau, No. 3359
Date: 1926 to 1937
Colors: Crystal, Flamingo, Marigold. Limited pieces in Moongleam,
Hawthorne, and Stiegel Blue.
Patent: The soda was patented on 7-12-1927 and assigned No. 73031
with T. C Heisey signing as designer.

Comments: A stemware line with blown bowl, pulled stem, and not marked. Made in plain or diamond optic. Plateau is moderately available, especially in Flamingo. For Flamingo, add 100%; for Marigold, add 200%.

Cocktail, 3 oz.	$12.00
Finger bowl	8.00
Goblet, 8½ oz.	12.00
Goblet, luncheon, 8 oz.	12.00
Jug, ½ gallon	85.00
Oyster cocktail, 4 oz.	8.00
Rose bowl, 6"	35.00
Saucer champagne, 6½ oz.	10.00
Sherbet, 6½ oz.	8.00
Soda or ice tea, 12 oz.	15.00
Soda, 5 oz. or 5½ oz. (juice)	12.00
Soda, 8 oz. (water)	12.00
Tumbler, 9 oz.	12.00

No. 3359 Plateau saucer champagne, 5 ounce soda, goblet, Flamingo.

Penn Charter, No. 3360 — original name
Date: 1926 to 1937
Colors: Crystal, Flamingo, Hawthorne

Comments: A stemware line with blown bowl, pressed stem. May be marked with the Diamond H on the upper stem just below the swirled knop. This line is very similar to No. 3408 Jamestown and No. 3409 Plymouth. All three use the same stem portion but have differently shaped bowls. The footed bar is taken from the No. 3381 Creole stem line. A few pieces (sherry, claret, and footed sodas) were listed only in crystal. Crystal items were made with wide optic. Flamingo items were made in diamond optic or checker optic. Hawthorne pieces were made in checker optic. The line has not been reproduced. Prices are for crystal items. For Flamingo, add 150%. For Hawthorne, add 175%.

Bar, footed, 2½ oz. (#3381)	$30.00	Finger bowl (#3309)	8.00
Claret, 4½ oz.	22.00	Goblet, 10 oz. or 8½ oz.	22.00
Cocktail, 3 oz.	15.00	Oyster cocktail, 4 oz.	8.00

Parfait, 5 oz. 20.00
Saucer champagne, 6 oz..............15.00
Sherbet, 6 oz. 9.00
Sherry, 1½ oz................................25.00
Soda, 5 oz. (juice) 10.00
Soda, 8 oz. (water).......................10.00
Soda, 12 oz. (ice tea) 15.00

Penn Charter, No. 3360 parfait, Hawthorne; and goblet, Flamingo.

Charter Oak, No. 3362 — original name
Date: 1926 to 1935
Colors: Crystal; Moongleam; Flamingo; Marigold; Marigold bowl, Crystal stem & foot. Hawthorne is rare and made only in a few items.
Patent: Patent No. 70754 granted for a goblet on 8-3-26 with E. Wilson Heisey listed as designer.

Comments: A stemware line with blown bowl, pressed stem. May be marked with the Diamond H on the stem just below the bowl. Made in diamond optic. This pattern is moderately available. Prices are for crystal. For Moongleam and Flamingo, add 80% to 100%. For Marigold and Hawthorne, add 150%. A water lamp matches Charter Oak, but is listed as No. 4262.

Cocktail, 3 oz. $12.00
Comport, high footed, 7" 65.00
Comport, low footed, 6" 55.00
Finger bowl 8.00
Goblet, 8 oz.....................................22.00
Goblet, luncheon, 8 oz. 20.00
Ice tea, 12 oz..................................15.00
Jug, ½ gallon 95.00
Lamp, water, 10" (#4262) ....1,600.00+
Oyster cocktail, 3½ oz. 8.00
Parfait, 4½ oz.................................15.00
Saucer champagne, 6 oz. 15.00
Sherbet, 6 oz...................................8.00
Tumbler, 10 oz. 15.00

No. 3362 Charter Oak half-gallon jug, Flamingo.

No. 3362 Charter Oak goblet, Flamingo.

Trojan, No. 3366 — original name
Date: 1926 to 1931
Colors: Crystal; Crystal bowl, Moongleam stem; Flamingo; Hawthorne

Comments: A stemware line with blown bowl, pressed stem. May be marked with the Diamond H on the upper stem below the wafer. Made in diamond optic. This line is very similar to No. 3365 Ramshorn. Trojan is moderately available. Prices are for crystal. For Moongleam and Flamingo, add 120%; for Hawthorne, add 400%. A water lamp matches Trojan stemware but bears No. 4366.

Bar, 1½ oz.	$14.00	Parfait, 4½ oz.	15.00
Claret, 4 oz.	15.00	Saucer champagne, 5 oz.	15.00
Cocktail, 3 oz.	12.00	Sherbet, 5 oz.	8.00
Comport, high footed, 7"	55.00	Soda or ice tea, 12 oz.	12.00
Cordial, 1 oz.	50.00	Soda, 5 oz. (juice)	10.00
Goblet, 8 oz.	15.00	Soda, 8 oz. (water)	10.00
Lamp, water, 9" (#4366)	1,800.00+	Tumbler, footed, 10 oz. (water)	12.00
Oyster cocktail, 3 oz.	8.00	Wine, 2½ oz.	15.00

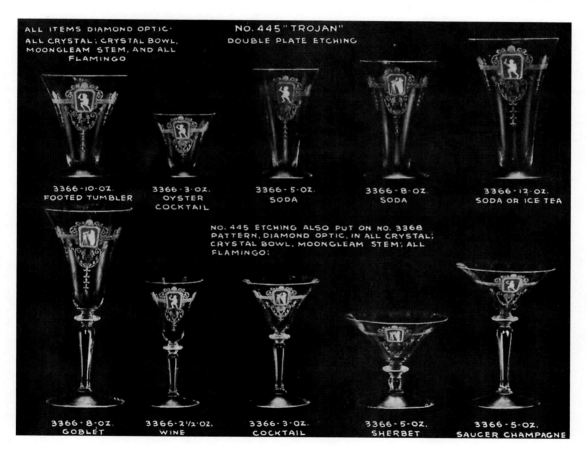

No. 3366 Trojan stemware with No. 445 Trojan double plate etching.

Decorations Introduced in 1926
Cuttings: No. 658 Tripoli.

Etchings: 172 Dover pantograph etching.

No. 479 Petal marmalade and cover.

Petal, No. 479
Dates: Ca. 1927 to 1935. Jelly in 1919.
Colors: Crystal, Moongleam, Flamingo, Sahara, Hawthorne

Comments: A very short line, with only the cream and sugar easily found. These are marked on the stems with the Diamond H. The jelly and marmalade are known only in crystal at this time. For Moongleam and Flamingo, add 350%; for Sahara add 400%; and for Hawthorne, add 500%+.

Cream $28.00
Jelly, handled 75.00
Marmalade & cover 145.00
Sugar...28.00

Grape Leaf Square, No. 441
Date: 1927
Colors: Crystal, Moongleam, Flamingo, Hawthorne. Very rare in Tangerine.

Comments: A pressed ashtray, not marked with the Diamond H. This is a copy of a Lalique design, and Heisey marketed it with the description of "Lalique style" as it has satinized highlights. Add 250% for Moongleam or Flamingo. Add 325% for Hawthorne.

Ashtray $65.00

No. 441 Grape Leaf Square ashtray.

No. 1191 Lobe pickle & olive, Flamingo.

Lobe, No. 1191
Dates: 1927 to 1933. Pickle & olive only from 1933 to 1937
Colors: Crystal, Moongleam, Flamingo, Hawthorne

Comments: Pressed items. The pickle & olive is not marked with the Diamond H. The handled spice may be marked with the Diamond H on the handle.

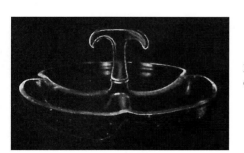

No. 1191 Lobe handled spice dish.

Dish, handled spice, 3
    compartment, 9" $50.00
Dish, spice, 3 compartment, 9"
    (no handle) 35.00
Pickle & olive...............................20.00

Ramshorn, No. 3365 — original description of optic
Dates: 1927 to 1931. Made in crystal in 1937
Colors: Crystal, Flamingo. Fruit salad with Crystal bowl, Moongleam foot.
Patent: Patent No. 77673 was granted on 2-12-1929 to Ramshorn with Ray C. Cobel listed as designer. Mr. Cobel was in charge of Heisey's mold making shop.

Comments: A stemware line with blown bowl, pressed stem. May be marked with the Diamond H on upper stem below the wafer. The name derives from the ram's horn optic of the bowls. When decorated, the stems are usually plain without optic. Compare this with the similar No. 3366 Trojan. This line is scarce and difficult to find. Prices are for crystal. For Flamingo, add 50%.

Bar, footed, 1½ oz. $20.00
Cocktail, 3 oz...15.00
Fruit salad, 5" 10.00
Goblet, 9 oz...25.00
Parfait, 4½ oz..22.00
Saucer champagne, 6 oz...............................15.00

Sherbet, 6 oz...8.00
Soda, footed, 5 oz. (juice)............................12.00
Soda, footed, 8 oz. (water)...........................12.00
Soda, footed, 12 oz. (ice tea).......................12.00
Wine, 2½ oz...20.00

No. 3365 Ramshorn goblet with Sea Nymph etching.

Detail of Sea Nymph double plate etching.

Decoration Introduced in 1927
Etching: No. 9008 Sea Nymph double plate etching.

1928:

No. 358 Solitaire ashtray, Flamingo.

Solitaire, No. 358
Date: 1928 to 1938
Colors: Crystal, Moongleam, Flamingo, Marigold, Sahara. Rare in Experimental Gold.

Comments: Ashtray only. Not usually marked with the Diamond H. Pressed. For Moongleam, add 300%. For Flamingo or Sahara, add 50%. For Marigold, add 350%.

Ashtray, individual $25.00

Octagon, No. 500
Dates: 1928 to 1935; 1955 to 1957
Colors: Crystal, Moongleam, Flamingo. Sugar and cream also made in Sahara and Crystal with Moongleam handles. Ice tub is available in Moongleam, Flamingo, Sahara, and Marigold. The variety tray was made in Moongleam, Flamingo, Sahara, and Dawn.
Patent: E. W. Heisey was granted patent No. 78024 on 3-19-1929 for the ice tub.

Comments: Most items are marked with the Diamond H and have ground and polished bottom rims. The frozen dessert has a small oblong recess in the base; it is not marked with the Diamond H. The variety tray was added to the Revere line in later years. For Moongleam & Flamingo, add 100%. For Sahara, add 125%. For Marigold, add 300%.

Cream	$18.00
Basket, 5"	95.00
Frozen dessert	18.00
Ice tub	50.00
Nappy, 6"	20.00
Sugar	18.00
Tray, oblong, 6"	18.00
Variety tray, oblong, 12"	65.00

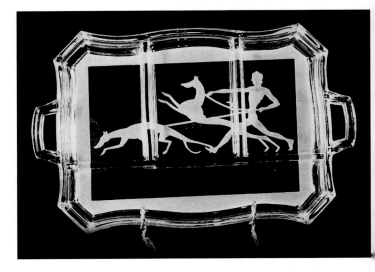

No. 500 Octagon variety tray with No. 5003 Nimrod carving.

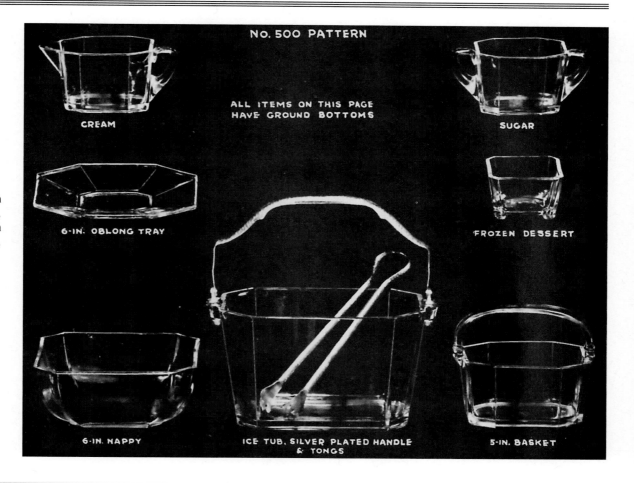

NO. 500 PATTERN

ALL ITEMS ON THIS PAGE HAVE GROUND BOTTOMS

CREAM

SUGAR

6-IN. OBLONG TRAY

FROZEN DESSERT

6-IN. NAPPY

ICE TUB, SILVER PLATED HANDLE & TONGS

5-IN. BASKET

No. 500 Octagon cream, sugar, tray, frozen dessert, nappy, ice tub, basket.

Twist, No. 1252

Dates: 1928 to 1937. A small 4" nappy was continued until 1957 and then continued by Imperial Glass.

Colors: Crystal, Moongleam, Flamingo, Marigold. Limited production in Sahara.

Patents: T. C. Heisey was granted patent No. 79885 on 11-12-1929 for the Twist plate. The bowl was granted No. 79716 on 10-29-1929 with T. C. Heisey listed as designer.

Comments: The original item in this pattern was a plate and the entire line developed from its design. Twist is Art Deco in design with lightning handles and square stems and feet. Twist is a name given by researchers and not original. Most pieces in this pattern are marked with the Diamond H. In 1952, to celebrate the Ohio Sesquicentennial, Heisey made a figured bottom featuring a pioneer and cabin in the base of the 12" platter. Oil bottles and French dressing bottles sometimes have Moongleam stoppers. Two styles of salt and pepper shakers are known, a footed type and a flat type also known as No. 54. Prices given are for crystal pieces. For Moongleam, Flamingo, and Sahara, add 100%. For Marigold, add 150%. Imperial Glass Corp. made the small nappy in crystal.

Almond, footed (same as individual sugar)...$35.00	Bowl, floral, flared, 9".....................................35.00
Baker, oval, 9"..25.00	Bowl, floral, oval, 12".....................................40.00
Bonbon, 2 handled, 6"...................................20.00	Bowl, floral, rolled edge, 9"............................35.00
Bonbon, individual..28.00	Bowl, floral, round, 12"..................................40.00
Bottle, French dressing & stopper..................50.00	Bowl, low foot, 8"...30.00

No. 1252 Twist jug, mustard and 4½" plate, pair of candlesticks.

Bowl, nasturtium, 8"	45.00
Bowl, nasturtium, oval, 8"	55.00
Candlesticks, 2", pr.	50.00
Celery, 10"	25.00
Celery, 13"	30.00
Cheese, 2 handled, 6"	15.00
Claret, 4 oz.	30.00
Cocktail, 3 oz.	20.00
Cocktail shaker, 1 quart (has threaded top)	.500.00+
Comport, high foot, 7"	40.00
Cream soup or bouillon	25.00
Cream	30.00
Cream, footed	40.00
Cream, individual	30.00
Cream, oval hotel	40.00
Cup & saucer	30.00
Goblet, 9 oz.	40.00
Goblet, luncheon, 9 oz.	35.00
Grapefruit, footed	20.00
Ice tea or soda, 12 oz.	30.00
Ice tea or soda, footed, 12 oz.	30.00
Ice tub	62.00
Jelly, 2 handled, 6"	15.00
Jug, 3 pint	90.00
Mayonnaise	30.00
Mayonnaise, footed (#1252½)	30.00

Mint & cover, 3 cornered (#1253)	40.00
Mint, 2 handled, 6"	15.00
Mustard & cover	50.00
Nappy, 4"	8.00
Nappy, 8"	28.00
Nut, individual	15.00
Oil bottle & stopper, 2½ oz.	70.00
Oil bottle & stopper, 4 oz.	55.00
Oyster cocktail, 3 oz.	15.00
Pickle tray, 7"	15.00
Plate, 4½"	10.00
Plate, 6" or 7"	11.00
Plate, 8" or 9"	12.00
Plate, 10½"	60.00
Plate, 12"	50.00
Plate, Kraft cheese, 8"	50.00
Plate, muffin, 2 handled, 12"	28.00
Plate, sandwich, 2 handled, 12"	28.00
Plate, utility, 3 feet, 10"	28.00
Platter, 12"	28.00
Platter, Ohio Sesquicentennial, 12"	125.00
Relish, 2 compartment	50.00
Relish, 3 compartment, 13"	22.00
Salt & pepper (#54), pair	50.00
Salt & pepper, footed, pair	75.00
Saucer champagne, 5 oz.	25.00
Sherbet, 5 oz.	15.00
Soda, 5 oz.	12.00
Soda, 8 oz.	20.00
Soda, footed, 6 oz.	17.00
Soda, footed, 9 oz.	24.00
Sugar & cover	40.00
Sugar, footed	40.00
Sugar, individual	45.00
Sugar, oval hotel	40.00
Tumbler, 8 oz.	25.00
Wine, 2½ oz.	30.00

No. 1252 Twist individual cream and sugar.

No. 1252 Twist Kraft cheese plate with original Heisey sticker.

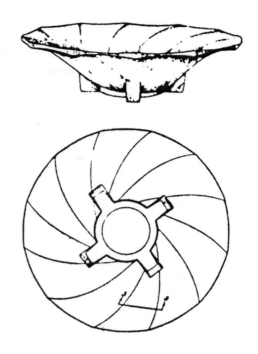

Patent drawing for No. 1252 Twist floral bowl.

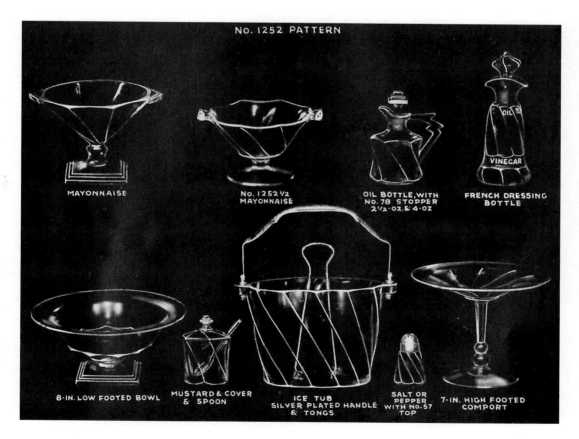

No. 1252 Twist mayonnaise, No. 1252½ mayonnaise, No. 1252 oil, French dressing, low footed bowl, mustard, ice tub, salt, high footed comport.

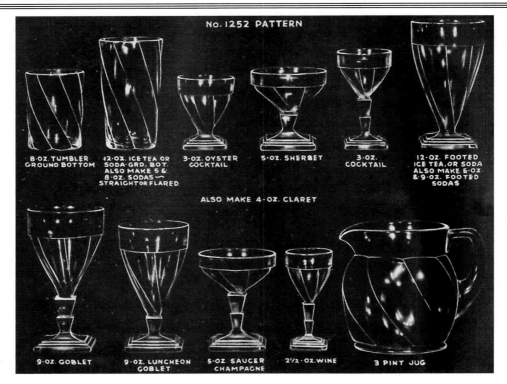

No. 1252 Twist stemware and jug.

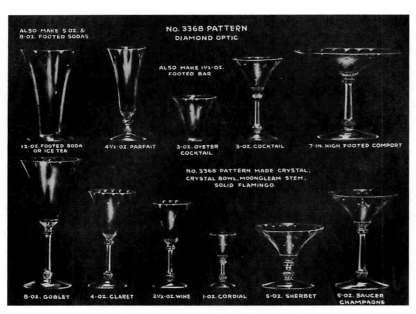

No. 3368 Albemarle stemware.

Albemarle, No. 3368 — original name
Date: 1928 to 1951
Colors: Crystal, Flamingo, Crystal with Moongleam stem and foot, Marigold with Crystal stem and foot.

Comments: A long-lived stemware line with blown bowl, pressed stem. Often made with diamond optic bowls. Marked with the Diamond H on the stem below the knop. Compare with No. 3380 Old Dominion which has a cupped bowl but the same stem portion. Add 50% for Flamingo and Moongleam. Add 125% for Marigold.

Bar, footed, 1½ oz.	$18.00
Claret, 4 oz.	15.00
Cocktail, 3 oz.	12.00
Comport, high footed, 7"	55.00
Cordial, 1 oz.	55.00
Finger bowl (#3309)	8.00
Goblet, 8 oz.	20.00
Oyster cocktail, 3 oz.	8.00
Parfait, 4½ oz.	20.00
Saucer champagne, 5 oz.	15.00
Sherbet, 5 oz.	12.00
Soda or ice tea, 12 oz.	12.00
Soda, 5 oz. (juice)	10.00
Soda, 8 oz. (water)	12.00
Tumbler, footed, 10 oz.	12.00
Wine, 2½ oz.	18.00

African, No. 3370
Date: 1928 to 1933
Colors: Crystal; Crystal bowl, Moongleam stem; Flamingo

Comments: Stemware line with blown bowl, pressed stem. Made in diamond optic. African is not marked with the Diamond H. Heisey indicated that the footed sodas from No. 3365 Ramshorn or No. 3366 Trojan were to be used with African. This stemware has not been reproduced. It is scarce. Prices are for crystal. For colors add 80%.

No. 3370 African goblet, Moongleam stem and foot.

Cocktail, 4 oz.	$18.00
Goblet, 8 oz.	35.00
Saucer champagne, 6 oz.	22.00
Sherbet, 6 oz.	12.00
Wine, 3 oz.	30.00

Decorations Introduced in 1928
Etchings: No. 445 Trojan double plate etching, No. 1 Sport plate etching, and No. 447 Empress plate etching.

1929:

"One of the distinctive new colors put on the market this season is unquestionably the 'marigold' which A. H. Heisey & Co., Newark, Ohio, has just produced. The Heisey concern has been working on this marigold for many months, and has certainly produced a tone that is well worth while. It is a distinct though lightish yellow, with a touch of green about it. As a matter of fact, it is somewhat suggestive of the plumage of the canary that shows a bit of the green in its feathers. This green suggestion, however, is so slight that it can only be seen when the items are studied carefully and held in just the proper light. Under ordinary illumination the color is true yellow. The green touch, incidentally, was no mistake, but was put in with deliberation and adds much to the tone. Here is a color, by the way, that is absolutely up to date and novel, and is a real addition to the Heisey color range." *Pottery, Glass & Brass Salesman,* January 1929.

Sunburst, No. 132
Date: Ca. 1929 to 1936
Colors: Crystal, Moongleam, Flamingo, Marigold

Comments: During this period, Heisey made a number of console sets (candlesticks and floral bowl), including this set. The floral bowl is rare and has only been seen in crystal. The candlesticks are found more easily. Both are marked with the Diamond H. For Moongleam or Flamingo, add 75% to 100%. For Marigold, add 300%.

Bowl, oval floral	$175.00
Candlesticks, 2", pr.	55.00

No. 132 Sunburst floral bowl.

No. 372 McGrady
syrup, Flamingo.

McGrady, No. 372
Date: 1929 to 1948
Colors: Crystal, Moongleam, Flamingo, Sahara

Comments: Pressed syrups marked with the Diamond H on the side of the spout. For Moongleam, Flamingo, or Sahara add 200%.

Syrup, 5 oz...$50.00
Syrup, 7 oz...60.00
Syrup, 12 oz...75.00

Fogg, No. 501
Date: 1929 to 1933
Colors: Crystal, Moongleam, Flamingo, Marigold

Comments: A pressed window box type flower box. Special flower blocks were made to fit the box, but these are rarely found today. Marked in the bottom with the Diamond H. For Moongleam and Flamingo, add 250%. For Marigold, add 500%.

Flower box $85.00

No. 501 Fogg flower box, Moongleam.

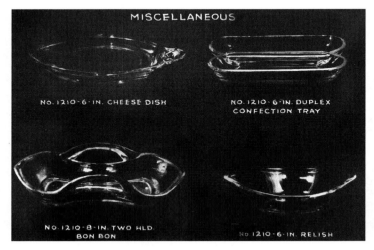

No. 1210

No. 1210 8" two-handled
bonbon, Flamingo.

No. 1210
Date: 1929 to 1933
Colors: Crystal, Moongleam, Flamingo, Marigold

Comments: Pressed items. None marked with the Diamond H. For moongleam and Flamingo, add 50%. For Marigold, add 200 to 300%

Bonbon, 2 handled, 8"............................$20.00
Dish, cheese, 6" (frog handle) 150.00
Relish, 6"..15.00
Tray, duplex confection, 6"......................20.00

Adam, No. 3376 — original name
Date: 1929 to 1933
Colors: Crystal, Flamingo

Comments: A stemware line with blown bowl, pressed stem. Adam is not marked with the Diamond H and not reproduced. Made in diamond optic. Adam is an industry term for this shape of bowl.

Claret, 4 oz. $20.00	Sherbet, 6 oz. 8.00
Cocktail, 3½ oz. 15.00	Soda or ice tea, footed, 12 oz............10.00
Finger bowl 8.00	Soda, footed, 5 oz. (juice) 10.00
Goblet, 11 oz. 25.00	Soda, footed, 8 oz. (water)................10.00
Oyster cocktail, 4 oz. 8.00	Tumbler, footed, 10 oz......................10.00
Saucer champagne, 6 oz. 15.00	Wine, 3 oz.......................................22.00

No. 3376 Adam with No. 168 Adam pantograph etching.

1930:

In 1930 an interesting comment on color was published in *China, Glass & Lamps:* "While Fostoria finds that their topaz and green are followed in order of popularity by rose and then amber, A. H. Heisey & Co. place crystal between their Sahara and their green. In stemware, particularly, crystal is selling especially well this fall, they find, and in tableware it is much wanted. On the other hand, in such decorative pieces as vases and center-pieces, colors are more in demand than crystal."

"One of these new colors is known as the 'Alexandrite,' it is not going too far to say that this is as striking a color as has ever made its appearance in glassware, and the more it is studied the more its richness becomes apparent and the difficulties that surround its manu-facture are appreciated. It is a foreign invention brought to this country with rare progres-siveness by the Heisey organization. It is a combination of powder blue, ruby, and amethyst. The complexity of its nature is best seen under artificial light. When viewed from one angle the powder blue is most in evidence. A little twist and the ruby becomes promi-nent. Again a turn and it is the amethyst that is outstanding. By its very nature the color will appeal most to the high-class, exclusive trade, and has already found a considerable mar-ket in this field. Then, there is a 'Sahara.' This is a golden yellow, and, as the name would indicate, it suggests the golden sands of the desert. It is a rich and attractive tone." *Pottery Glass & Brass Salesman,* February 1930.

When introducing the new Empress pattern, Heisey described the colors in which it was made as follows: "It is especially distinctive in the amethyst glow of the new Alexan-drite color (the only amethyst tint which is brilliant under artificial light) and it is a beau-tiful line in the new Sahara golden yellow, as well as in the popular Flamingo and Moon Gleam tints." *China, Glass & Lamps,* May 1930.

Trident, No. 134
Date: 1930 to 1957
Colors: Crystal, Moongleam, Flamingo, Sahara, Alexandrite. Candlesticks with Moongleam foot and Crystal top. Rare in Tangerine with Crystal foot and light blue.

Comments: Pressed console set. The candlesticks are sometimes marked with the Diamond H in the column above the base. For Moongleam, Flamingo, or Sahara, add 250% – 300%. For Alexandrite, add 500%.

Bowl, floral, oval 14" $55.00
Candlestick, 2 light, pr. 75.00

No. 134 Trident candlestick.

Empress, No. 1401 — original name
Date: 1930 to 1938
Colors: Crystal, Flamingo, Moongleam, Sahara. Many pieces in Alexandrite. Limited production in Tangerine and Cobalt.
Patents: The Empress plate was granted No. 82887 on 12-23-1930 and the bowl with ring handle and stub feet was given No. 82888 on 12-23-1930 with T. C. Heisey listed as designer for both.

Comments: Empress is the original company name. A few early Heisey ads refer to this pattern as Fleur de Lis or Lilies of France pattern. "...a new glass dinner service made in colors of green, rose or crystal. The shape of this which is particularly noticeable and attractive on the tea cups had found its origin in the iris." *China, Glass & Lamps*, February 1930.

Most items are marked with the Diamond H. Plates and several serving pieces were made in round and square styles. Several pieces have three dolphin feet — designated d. f. in the following list. When marked, the Diamond H is located on the back of one of the dolphin feet. The cover of the lemon dish has a dolphin finial. "Two of the latest of these to be received...are a unique bowl and a three — ply candlestick that is quite unusual in its construction. The bowl...is set on four lion's claw feet. Directly above each claw and near the top is a lion's head pressed in the mold." October 1931. The previous quote refers to the lion's head floral bowl in Empress and the No. 136 candlestick. The No. 1401½ square plate has the fans on the corners rather than in the centers of the sides. Many pieces of the pattern were reworked with an internal optic and became pattern No. 1509 Queen Ann. Add 50% for Moongleam, Flamingo, or Sahara. Unusual colors such as Alexandrite, Tangerine, and cobalt are valued at 100% more. Rare pieces command up to 500%+. Imperial Glass Corp. made the dolphin footed three-toed candlestick in sunshine yellow in 1981. These can cause confusion with authentic Heisey items.

Ashtray $110.00
Bonbon, 6"...20.00
Bouillon, 2 handled.....................................30.00
Bowl, floral, 10" (lion) 450.00
Bowl, floral, 2 handled, footed, 8½" 50.00
Bowl, floral, d. f., 11" 75.00
Bowl, floral, flared, 9" (leaf design on bowl).110.00
Bowl, floral, rolled edge, 9"...........................35.00
Bowl, frappe and center 55.00
Bowl, nasturtium, d. f., 7½"..........................115.00
Bowl, salad, 2 handled, 10".........................50.00
Bowl, salad, square, 2 handled, 10"............50.00
Candlestick, d. f., 6", 3 toed, pr..................275.00
Candlestick, 2 handled, footed, 2", pr..........75.00
Candy box & cover, d. f., 6" 100.00
Celery, 13" 28.00
Comport, footed, round, 6" 55.00
Comport, oval, 7"..60.00
Comport, square, 6".....................................65.00
Compotier, d. f., 6" 150.00
Cream soup, 2 handled 25.00
Cream, d. f..30.00
Cream, individual...32.00

No. 1401 Empress 7" triplex relish with No. 842 Singapore cutting.

No. 1401 Empress cheese & cracker, cut at Krall Studios.

Cup & saucer 32.00
Cup & saucer, after dinner coffee...................52.00
Cup & saucer, plain rim (#1401½) 40.00
Custard, 4 oz. 32.00
Dessert, oval, 2 handled, 10".........................52.00
Dish, vegetable, oval, 10".................................32.00
Goblet, 9 oz. 60.00
Grapefruit, square, 6"......................................20.00
Hors d' oeuvre, 2 handled, 13" 45.00
Hors d' oeuvre, 7 compartment, 10" 75.00
Ice tub, d. f. 110.00
Jelly, footed, 2 handled, 6".............................20.00
Jug, d. f., 3 pint..150.00
Lemon & cover, oval, 6½".................................72.00
Marmalade & cover, d. f. 100.00
Mayonnaise, d. f., 5½".......................................30.00
Mint, d. f., 6"...35.00
Mint, footed, 8"...40.00
Mustard & cover...70.00
Nappy, 4½"...12.00
Nappy, 8"...30.00
Nappy, d. f., 7½"...32.00
Nut, individual, d. f...25.00
Oil & stopper, 4 oz. 110.00
Oyster cocktail, 2½ oz......................................15.00
Pickle & olive, 2 compartment, handled, 12" 25.00
Plate, muffin, 2 handled, 12".........................42.00
Plate, round, 4½"..10.00
Plate, round or square, 6" or 7"....................12.00
Plate, round or square, 8" 15.00
Plate, round, 9"..18.00
Plate, round or square, 10½".....................130.00
Plate, round, 12" 55.00

Plate, round, 15" 70.00
Plate, sandwich, 2 handled, 12" 55.00
Plate, sandwich, 2 handled, 13" 40.00
Plate, sandwich, 2 handled, square, 12".....40.00
Plate, square, 8" (#1401½) 48.00
Platter, 14" 45.00
Preserve, footed, 2 handled, 5" 20.00
Punch bowl, d. f., 15" 1,000.00
Relish buffet, 4 compartment, 16"..............110.00
Relish, combination, 3 compartment, 10".....60.00
Relish, triplex, 7"...35.00
Relish, triplex, 10"...52.00
Relish, triplex, center handled, 7" 65.00
Salt & pepper, pr 100.00
Saucer champagne, 4 oz................................45.00
Sherbet, 4 oz. 20.00
Soda, 5 oz. 20.00
Soda, 12 oz. 35.00
Sugar, d. f. 30.00
Sugar, individual 32.00
Tray, condiment (for individual cream and
    sugar)..32.00
Tray, sandwich, center handled, 12"............60.00
Tumbler, 8 oz..40.00
Tumbler, d. f., 8 oz..110.00
Vase, d. f., 9" 140.00
Vase, flared, 8"..70.00

No. 1401 Empress mayonnaise, Antarctic etch,
note dolphin feet.

No. 1401 Empress salt & pepper, individual cream and sugar, footed cream and sugar, footed oil, ice tub, mustard and cover.

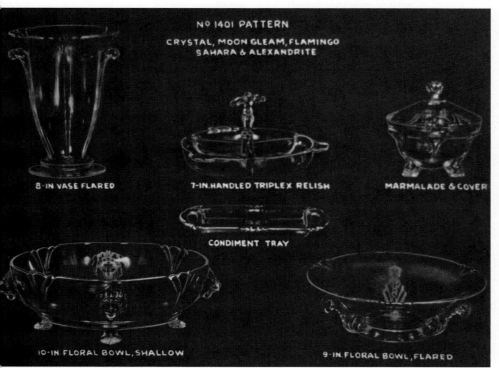

No. 1401 Empress vase; triplex relish, handled; marmalade; condiment tray; Lion's head floral bowl; 9" floral bowl.

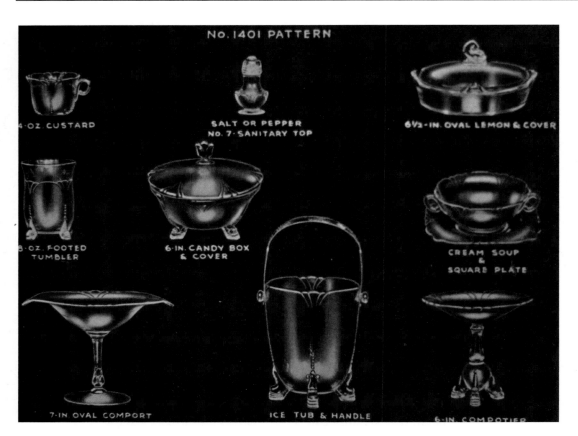

NO. 1401 PATTERN

4-OZ. CUSTARD

SALT OR PEPPER
NO. 7-SANITARY TOP

6½-IN. OVAL LEMON & COVER

8-OZ. FOOTED TUMBLER

6-IN. CANDY BOX & COVER

CREAM SOUP & SQUARE PLATE

7-IN OVAL COMPORT

ICE TUB & HANDLE

6-IN. COMPOTIER

No. 1401 Empress custard, salt, oval lemon & cover, footed tumbler, candy box & cover, cream soup & plate, oval comport, ice tub, compotier.

No. 3380 Old Dominion goblet, Moongleam stem and foot.

Old Dominion, No. 3380 — original name

Date: 1930 to 1939

Colors: Crystal, Flamingo, Sahara (discontinued in 1937). Crystal stem and foot with Marigold or Moongleam bowl. Crystal bowl with Alexandrite or Moongleam stem and foot. Rare in all Alexandrite.

Comments: A long-lived stemware line with blown bowl, pressed stem. Pieces are often marked with the Diamond H on the upper stem below the knop. Pieces are relatively easy to find. Compare this with No. 3368 Albemarle which has the same stem portion but a flared bowl. For Flamingo, Moongleam, and Sahara, add 100%. For Marigold, add 125% to 150%. For Alexandrite, add 500%.

Bar, 1 oz. $20.00	Parfait, 5 oz. 20.00
Bar, 2 oz. 18.00	Saucer champagne, short
Claret, 4 oz. 15.00	stem or tall stem, 6 oz. 18.00
Cocktail, 3 oz. 15.00	Sherbet, 6 oz. 10.00
Cordial, 1 oz. 45.00	Soda, 5 oz. (juice)...........10.00
Finger bowl (#4075) 8.00	Soda, 8 oz. (water) 12.00
Goblet, short stem or tall	Soda or ice tea, 12 oz. ...12.00
stem, 10 oz. 22.00	Soda, 16 oz. 15.00
Grapefruit, footed 22.00	Tumbler, footed, 10 oz. ..12.00
Oyster cocktail 8.00	Wine, 2½ oz. 18.00

Creole, No. 3381 — original name
Date: 1930 to 1939
Colors: Alexandrite; Alexandrite bowl, Crystal stem; Sahara bowl, Crystal stem
Patent: The goblet was granted No. 82151 on 9-3-1930 with
T. C. Heisey listed as designer.

Comments: A stemware line with blown bowl, pressed stem, not marked or reproduced. Made in diamond optic. One of the few Heisey patterns not made in crystal. It is moderately available, but highly sought. Alexandrite commands high prices in any piece. Prices are for Alexandrite or Alexandrite/crystal combination. While Sahara is more difficult to find, it is valued less. For Sahara, deduct 25%.

Bar, footed, 2½ oz. $200.00
Cocktail, 4 oz. 110.00
Cordial, 1 oz. 350.00
Finger bowl 80.00
Goblet, 11 oz., tall or short 190.00
Grapefruit, footed 110.00
Oyster cocktail, 5 oz.................................90.00
Parfait, 5 oz. 130.00
Saucer champagne, 7 oz., short...............115.00
Saucer champagne, 7 oz., tall 130.00
Sherbet, 7 oz..90.00
Soda or ice tea, footed, 13 oz. 100.00
Soda, footed, 5 oz. (juice).........................90.00
Soda, footed, 8½ oz. (water).....................90.00
Tumbler, footed, 10 oz. 100.00
Wine, 2½ oz...190.00

No. 3381 Creole oyster cocktail, soda, juice, Sahara bowl, crystal foot.

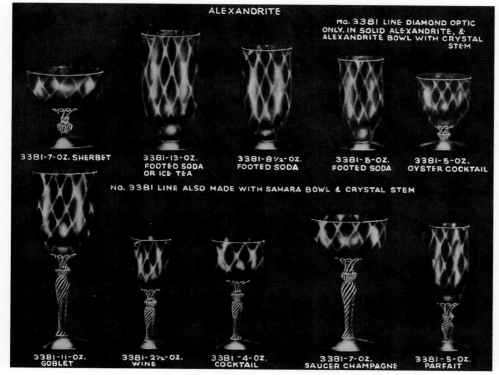

No. 3381 Creole stemware.

No. 3386 Diamond Rose
goblet, Moongleam bowl.

Diamond Rose, No. 3386
Dates: 1930 to 1933. Pilsners from 1933 to 1944
Colors: Crystal; Crystal bowl, Moongleam stem; Moongleam bowl, Crystal stem; Flamingo; Marigold bowl, Crystal stem. Sahara or Stiegel Blue on pilsners only.

Comments: A short stemware line but highly desirable. Blown bowl, pressed stem. Made in diamond optic. May be marked on one of the flower petals below the bowl. The flower motif is very similar to the motif of No. 3389 Duquesne stemware. Not reproduced and hard to find. For Flamingo or Moongleam bowl, crystal stem, add 100%. For crystal bowl, Moongleam stem, Sahara, or Stiegel Blue, add 400%.

Cocktail	$35.00
Goblet, 12 oz.	65.00
Pilsner, 8 oz.	60.00
Pilsner, 10 oz.	70.00
Pilsner, 12 oz.	80.00
Saucer champagne	55.00
Sherbet	35.00

Duquesne, No. 3389 — original name
Date: 1930 to 1952
Colors: Crystal, Sahara. Crystal stem and foot, Sahara bowl. Crystal stem and foot, Tangerine bowl.

Comments: A stemware line with a blown bowl, pressed stem. Made either plain or in wide optic. It has not been reproduced. It is relatively common to moderately available. Prices are for pieces in crystal. For Sahara, add 75%. For Tangerine, add 1,000%.

No. 3389 Duquesne goblet,
unknown cutting.

Claret, 4 oz.	$15.00
Cocktail, 3 oz.	12.00
Cordial, 1 oz.	45.00
Finger bowl (#4071)	8.00
Goblet, 9 oz.	22.00
Grapefruit, footed	22.00
Oyster cocktail, 4 oz.	8.00
Parfait, 5 oz.	20.00
Saucer champagne, 5 oz.	15.00
Sherbet, 5 oz.	8.00
Soda, footed, 5 oz. (juice)	8.00
Soda, footed, 8 oz. (water)	8.00
Tumbler, footed, 10 oz.	8.00
Wine, 2½ oz.	18.00

No. 3389 Duquesne items with No. 450 Chintz etching.

Decorations Introduced in 1930 Etchings: No. 448 Old Colony plate etching and No. 451 Lafayette plate etching.

Carcassonne, No. 3390 — original name
Date: 1930 to 1941
Colors: Crystal, Crystal bowl with Moongleam stem and foot, Flamingo, Sahara, Stiegel Blue bowl with Crystal stem and foot, Alexandrite bowl with Crystal stem and foot

Comments: A stemware line with a blown bowl, pressed stem. The Diamond H may be found on the upper stem just below the bowl. Made with wide optic. Moongleam and Flamingo were special order only. For Moongleam, Flamingo, and Sahara, add 100%. For Stiegel Blue (cobalt) and Alexandrite, add 600%.

Bar, footed, 2 oz.	$22.00
Cigarette holder	25.00
Claret, 4 oz.	20.00
Cocktail, 3 oz.	15.00
Cordial, 1 oz.	55.00
Decanter, footed, 1 pt.	120.00
Finger bowl, footed	8.00
Flagon, 12 oz.	50.00
Goblet, short stem, 11 oz.	22.00
Goblet, tall stem, 11 oz.	24.00
Jug, footed, 3 pt.	165.00
Morning after, 10½ oz.	30.00
Oyster cocktail, 3 oz.	10.00
Saucer champagne, 6 oz.	15.00
Sherbet, 6 oz.	10.00
Soda or ice tea, 12 oz.	17.00
Soda, footed, 5 oz. (juice)	15.00
Soda, footed, 8 oz. (water)	17.00
Vase, footed, 8"	50.00
Wine, 2½ oz.	22.00

No. 3390 Carcassonne items with No. 448 Old Colony etching.

1931:

In 1931 the Heisey company advertised their new etched patterns extensively. In keeping with the revival of early American styles, the company introduced two patterns based on early Sandwich glass — Old Sandwich and Ipswich. In addition, the company began producing several other occasional pieces inspired by Sandwich designs. This trend was initiated by Heisey's access to several of the original Sandwich mahogany models for pieces. One of the Heisey salesmen had formerly worked at Sandwich and had several dozen of these models and brought these to Heisey.

Old Sandwich, No. 1404 — original name
Date: 1931 to 1956
Colors: Crystal, Sahara. Some pieces in Flamingo, Moongleam, Stiegel Blue, and Amber. Rare pieces are known in Tangerine and Zircon.

Comments: This is a pressed tableware and stemware pattern created as a copy of early Sandwich glass (Pillar) but in contemporary shapes. Usually pieces are marked with the Diamond H. First ads called this pattern Early American Thumbprint, but the name was changed to Old Sandwich within weeks. Beer mugs were also made into creams. The round cream and sugar molds were made into No. 1503 Crystolite. The basket with applied handle was handwritten into one Heisey price list. It probably never was truly in the line and was discontinued before the next price list was issued. Imperial reissued most of the stemware and sodas in crystal only, but using the Heisey mark. Prices are for pieces in crystal. For pieces in Sahara, add 100%. For Moongleam and Flamingo, add 125% to 175%. For Stiegel Blue, add 450%.

Ashtray, individual......................................$12.00
Bar, 1½ oz. 25.00
Basket, applied handle (made from soda)..325.00+
Beer mug, 12 oz. 50.00
Beer mug, 16 oz. 65.00

No. 1404 Old Sandwich cream made from beer mug.

Beer mug, 18 oz. 75.00
Beer mug, sham, 10 oz. 140.00
Bowl, floral, oval, footed, 12"......................45.00
Bowl, floral, round, footed, 11" 55.00
Candlesticks, 6", one light, pr....................95.00
Catsup bottle & stopper 55.00
Cigarette holder (square) 110.00
Claret, 4 oz. 20.00
Cocktail, 3 oz. 15.00
Comport, 6"..45.00
Cream, 12 oz., made from beer mug..........80.00
Cream, 14 oz., made from beer mug........110.00
Cream, 18 oz., made from beer mug........140.00
Cream, oval 20.00
Cream, round...45.00
Cup & saucer 30.00
Decanter & stopper, 1 pint (oval) 135.00
Finger bowl or nappy, 4½" 15.00
Goblet, low footed, 10 oz. 20.00
Hi-ball, straight or cupped, 8 oz. 18.00
Ice tea, footed 12 oz. 20.00
Jug, ½ gallon...75.00
Jug, ice, ½ gallon. 75.00
Juice, straight or cupped, 5 oz. 12.00

Oil & stopper, 2½ oz. 75.00
Oyster cocktail, 4 oz. 12.00
Parfait, 4½ oz. 20.00
Pilsner, 8 oz. 75.00
Plate, square, 6" 15.00
Plate, square, 7" or 8" 18.00
Popcorn bowl, cupped, footed 120.00
Salt & pepper, pr. 55.00
Saucer champagne, 5 oz. 18.00
Sherbet, 4 oz. 10.00
Soda or ice tea, cupped or straight, 8 oz. 20.00
Soda or ice tea, footed, 12 oz. 20.00
Soda, cupped or straight, 5 oz. (juice) 20.00
Soda, cupped or straight, 10 oz. (water) 20.00
Soda, cupped or straight, 12 oz. (ice tea) 20.00
Sugar, oval 20.00
Sugar, round 45.00
Sundae, 4 oz. or 6 oz. 12.00
Toddy, 6½ oz. 18.00
Tumbler, straight or cupped, 8 oz. 18.00
Tumbler, low footed, 10 oz. 18.00
Wine, 2½ oz. 25.00

No. 1404 Old Sandwich stemware and other items.

No. 1404 Old Sandwich items.

Ipswich, No. 1405 — original name
Dates: 1931 to 1946. Crystal only from 1952 to 1953.
Colors: Crystal, Sahara, Flamingo, Moongleam. Limited number of items in Stiegel Blue. Rare in Alexandrite.

Comments: This is a pressed tableware and stemware line available in a moderate number of pieces, some of which are quite scarce. The jug, cologne, and cocktail shaker are all difficult to find. Pieces are usually marked. The Sandwich Glass pattern Comet was the inspiration for Ipswich. Heisey used the same motif but made pieces in modern shapes. Heisey's earliest ads called this Early American Sandwich, but within weeks the name Ipswich was used. The covered candy jar was reproduced by Imperial Glass and also a bowl with a wide, crimped edge was made. The bowl was not originally made by Heisey. Both these items are marked with the Diamond H and were made in several Imperial colors. The Heisey museum had a basket made by Fenton in Dusty Rose — an item not made by Heisey. Goblets in Alexandrite are $800.00+. In Stiegel Blue, the floral bowl is worth $400.00, the cocktail shaker $1,200.00, the complete centerpiece with vase and prisms, a pair, is worth $1,200.00. Not all items are available in all colors, but Sahara is the most common color found. Prices are for items in crystal. For Sahara, add 200%, for Flamingo or Moongleam, add 225%.

Bowl, floral, 11" $70.00
Candlesticks, 6" (one light), pr....................300.00
Candy jar and cover, ¼ lb. 110.00
Candy jar and cover, ½ lb. 125.00
Centerpiece with vase and prisms, footed,
    pr 550.00
Cocktail shaker, 1 quart ....325.00+
Cologne & stopper....................................400.00
Cream..40.00
Finger bowl...20.00
Goblet, 10 oz..20.00
Jug, ½ gallon, stuck handle.......................320.00+
Oil & stopper, 2 oz. 145.00
Oyster cocktail, 4 oz. 9.00

No. 1405 Ipswich floral bowl

No. 1405 Ipswich candlevase with insert and prisms.

Plate, finger bowl, 6" (round).........................24.00
Plate, square, 7" or 8" 20.00
Saucer champagne, 4 oz. 15.00
Schoeppen, 12 oz. 20.00
Sherbet, 4 oz. 10.00
Soda, footed, 5 oz. (juice) 22.00
Soda, footed, 8 oz. (water)............................20.00
Soda, footed, 12 oz. (ice tea) 20.00
Sugar 40.00
Tumbler, 10 oz..60.00

No. 1405 Ipswich items.

Twentieth Century, No. 1415 — original name
Dates: 1931 to 1937. 1956 to 1957 in Dawn
Colors: Crystal, Flamingo, Moongleam, Sahara, Stiegel Blue, and Dawn

Comments: Twentieth Century is a short pressed pattern, usually marked. Note that the cereal bowl and plate were originally numbered 1410. This pattern was made in two time periods. The first was in 1931 when all pieces were made in Crystal, Moongleam, Flamingo, and Sahara. The cereal bowl is difficult to find. In 1955 some of the pieces were brought back in Dawn. Most pieces in this short pattern are marked with the Diamond H. Cobalt sodas are valued at $135.00+. Heisey Collectors of America has produced several styles of baskets (never originally made) in several colors from the sodas. Prices are for pieces in crystal. For Moongleam, Flamingo, and Sahara, add 80% to 100%. For Dawn, add 100%.

Bowl, cereal	$40.00
Pitcher, milk, 1 pint	65.00
Plate, 7"	10.00
Sherbet, footed, 4 oz.	15.00
Soda, footed, 5 oz. (juice)	20.00
Soda, footed, 12 oz. (ice tea)	20.00
Tumbler, footed, 9 oz.	20.00

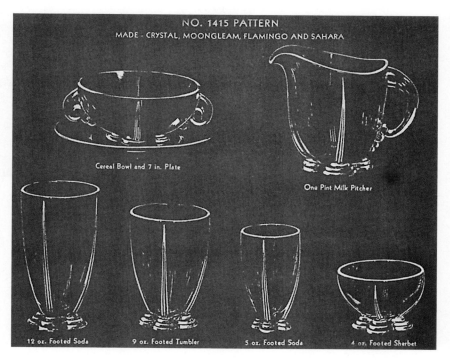

No. 1415 Twentieth Century items.

No. 4222 Horseshoe cream & sugar.

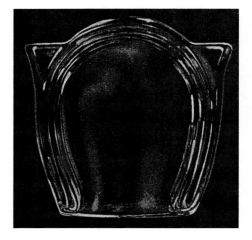

No. 4222 Horse-
shoe vase.

Horseshoe, No. 4222
Date: 1931 to 1937
Colors: Crystal, Moongleam,
Flamingo, Sahara, Crystal with
Moongleam handles

Comments: Blown items, not
marked with the Diamond H. Full
ground and polished bottoms and
about the tops of pieces. For Moongleam, add 100%. For Flamingo or
Sahara, add 75%.

Cream $50.00
Sugar 50.00
Vase, 6"...............................75.00

Decorations Introduced in 1931
Etchings: No. 449 Pompeii plate etching
and No. 450, 450½ Chintz plate etching.

No. 4224 Steeplechase
cocktail.

No. 4224-3 in.
Cocktail

No. 4224-9 in.
Cocktail Mixer

No. 4224 Steeplechase cocktail and cocktail
shaker.

Steeplechase, No. 4224
Date: 1931 to 1935
Colors: Crystal, Crystal bowl Moongleam
foot, Crystal bowl Sahara foot

Comments: "Something rather out of the
ordinary in the way of cocktail sets has just
been developed by A. H. Heisey & Co., of
Newark, Ohio. This set consists of a 16
ounce shaker and six 3 ounce cocktail glasses. The distinguishing feature is the base
portion, which is constructed along the lines
of an inverted cup. As a matter of fact, the
cocktail itself, when inverted, would serve
as an English egg cup. This base part is
treated with a matt finish in the Lalique style
and is quite effective. The bowl portion is in
conformance and can be had in 'Sahara,' a
golden tone, or else in green." *Pottery, Glass
& Brass Salesman*, August 1931.
  A cocktail set with pressed base and
blown bowl. Not marked with the Diamond
  H. Add 100%+ for colors.

Cocktail, 3 oz. $85.00
Cocktail mixer 200.00

1932:

"In the 1932 Heisey line a step forward has been made that cannot be stressed too strongly. This is the feat of producing the sparkling gold Sahara color in ringing, resonant lead glass. Until achieved by Heisey the production of golden yellow glass commonly called topaz in the lead glass was considered an impossibility." *China, Glass & Lamps,* March 1932.

In August of 1932, Heisey announced its new color of Tangerine with the comment that the company was the first to produce this color.

Fleur de Lis, No. 1406
Date: 1932
Colors: Crystal, Moongleam, Flamingo, Sahara

Comments: Only two styles of pressed salad plates, usually marked with the Diamond H. The square version has small teardrops extending from the fleur de lis to the center of the plate. The round version is plain, without the teardrops. Imperial Glass reproduced a small bowl in pink satin in 1981, marked LIG. Prices are for crystal. For colors, add 100%.

Plate, round or square, 8" $55.00

No. 1406 Fleur de Lis plate, No. 3397 Gascony Sherbet, No. 1410 cream soup (became No. 1415 Twentieth Century), and No. 1409 plate.

No. 1409
Date: 1932
Colors: Crystal. Others possible but unknown.

Comments: A pressed salad plate only. Other details are unknown.

Plate, 8"....................................$30.00

Cathedral, No. 1413
Date: 1932 to 1944. The flared version was made after 1939.
Colors: Crystal, Moongleam, Flamingo, Sahara, Stiegel Blue, Alexandrite

Comments: Only made in several styles of vases. May be marked with the Diamond H on the base, but often it is not. The flared version is the most common, while the handled version is difficult to find. Imperial Glass reproduced the flared vase in rose pink for Collectors Guild and marked with a CG in a circle. Rose pink could easily be confused for Flamingo. Prices are for vases in crystal. For Moongleam, Flamingo, or Sahara, add 250%. For Stiegel Blue or Alexandrite, add 500%+.

Vase, flared $65.00
Vase, straight 75.00
Vase, straight, stuck handles.........100.00

No. 1413 Cathedral handled vase.

No. 1413 Cathedral flared vase with No. 855 Fuchsia cutting.

Saxony, No. 3394 — original name
Date: 1932 to 1935
Colors: Crystal, Sahara

Comments: A short — lived stemware line with blown bowl, pressed stem that is not marked with the Diamond H. It has not been reproduced. Compare this with No. 3390 Carcassonne stemware which uses the same squarish foot as Saxony. The most remarkable difference is in the bowl shapes. "A low footed goblet with a bowl in step effect should draw many admirers. With a dainty needle etching it is most enticing. It can be had in both crystal and Sahara." *China, Glass & Lamps*, March 1932.

While there is a tall stemmed goblet known in this pattern, the low — footed examples are the most often found. Examples are difficult to find. Prices are for crystal items; for Sahara, add 100%.

Cocktail, 3 oz.	$15.00
Cordial, 1 oz.	120.00
Finger bowl	8.00
Goblet, 12 oz., short stem	30.00
Goblet, 12 oz., tall stem	55.00
Oyster cocktail, 4 oz.	10.00
Saucer champagne, 5½ oz.	15.00
Sherbet, 5½ oz.	10.00
Soda, footed, 5 oz. (juice)	20.00
Soda, footed, 8 oz (water)	20.00
Soda, footed, 12 oz. (ice tea)	22.00
Vase, footed	70.00
Wine, 2½ oz.	18.00

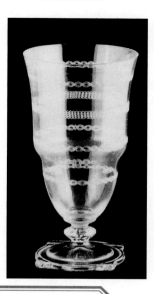

No. 3394 Saxony ice tea with No. 50 Dresden needle etching.

Gascony, No. 3397 — original name
Date: 1932 to 1938
Colors: Crystal, Sahara. Crystal foot with Tangerine bowl. Some with Crystal foot and Stiegel Blue (cobalt) bowl. The candlesticks were also made in Moongleam and Flamingo.
Patent: T. C. Heisey was granted patent No. 87576 on 8-16-1932 for the soda.

Comments: A low footed stem line with blown bowl, pressed foot. Pieces are usually marked on the base. The vase listed is known in Tangerine and may be a whimsy rather than a production piece. "Standing out in the new offerings is a line of low hexagon-footed stemware. The footed sodas, which come in 12 sizes, should prove especially popular. In the same group is a tomato juice server and six accompanying glasses. The line can be had in crystal and 'Sahara' either etched or plain. The new etchings, the 448 and 451, are used to decorate this grouping." *China, Glass & Lamps*, March 1932.

By this time, it was apparent that Prohibition would be repealed, and Heisey was preparing for the need for drinking items. The "tomato juice pitcher" was in fact a martini mixer. For Sahara, add 100%. For Tangerine, add 600 – 700%.

Bowl, floral, 10"	$85.00	Bowl, floral, oval, footed (pressed)	65.00
Bowl, floral, footed, 10"	120.00	Candlesticks, 5", pr. (pressed #138)	160.00

No. 3397 Gascony ice tea with No. 458 Olympiad etching.

Cocktail, 3 oz.	15.00
Cream (pressed)	50.00
Decanter & stopper, footed, 1 pint.	145.00
Goblet, low footed, 11 oz.	35.00
Mayonnaise, 2 compartment (pressed)	65.00
Oyster cocktail, 4 oz.	15.00
Pitcher, tomato juice	95.00
Saucer champagne, 6 oz.	15.00
Sherbet, 6 oz.	12.00
Soda, footed, 5 oz. (juice)	12.00
Soda, footed, 10 oz.	20.00
Soda, footed, 12 oz.	22.00
Soda, footed, 14 oz.	30.00
Soda, footed, 18 oz.	40.00
Sugar (pressed)	50.00
Tumbler, footed, 10 oz.	30.00
Vase, 8"	800.00+
Wine, 2½ oz.	32.00

No. 3397 Gascony decanter with No. 456 Titania etching.

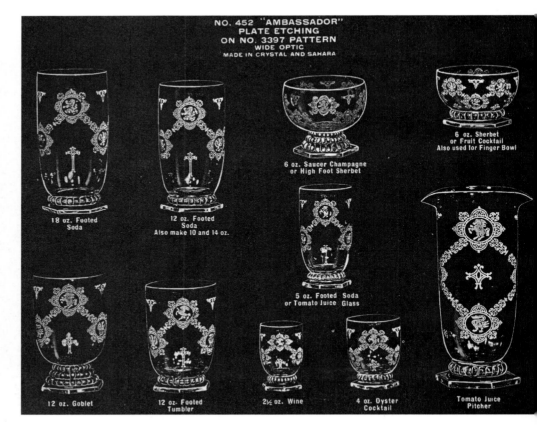

No. 3397 Gascony items with No. 452 Ambassador etching.

Cobel, No. 4225
Date: 1932 to 1957
Colors: One quart: Crystal, Moongleam, Sahara, Stiegel Blue. Rare in experimental red. One pint and Rock & Rye: Crystal. Two quart might be found in colors.
Patent: Carl Cobel patented this shaker for the company. Patent No. 1966611 was given to the Cobel cocktail shaker on 7/17/1934.

Comments: Heisey introduced a completely new design for cocktail shakers with this design. "It is the No. 4225 and is made in quart size in crystal and Heisey's Sahara color. The stopper and strainer are in two separate pieces each of which is ground in and seal proof. This is a very original number and a splendid one for the decorative trade." *China, Glass & Lamps*, February 1932.

In the 1940s the company had several novelty stoppers designed that were used in these shakers. Included were the Rooster Head, large and small Horse Heads, Girl's Head, and Ram's Head. Heisey made cocktails to match all the stoppers except the Ram's Head. A Dancer's Leg cocktail matches the Girl's Head stopper. The Rock & Rye bottle is the same shape as the one quart cocktail shaker, but lacks the glass strainer and is fitted only with a stopper. Imperial Glass made the one quart until 1968 and the one pint and two quart until 1961. Add 700% for Moongleam or Flamingo. Add 500% for Sahara. Add 800% for Stiegel Blue.

No. 4225 Cobel cocktail shakers: two quart, one quart, one pint — engraved Us.

Cocktail shaker, 1 pint $80.00
Cocktail shaker, 1 quart..............65.00
Cocktail shaker, 2 quart..............80.00
Rock & Rye, 1 quart 150.00

Cocktail shaker stoppers: Rooster Head, Girl's Head, large Horse Head, Ram's Head — these were used in the Cobel and No. 4026 Marshall cocktail shakers.

Decorations introduced in 1932
Cuttings: No. 781 St. Anne cutting, No. 785 Coral Gables cutting.

Etchings: No. 452 Ambassador plate etching, No. 453 Inca plate etching, No. 454 Antarctic etching, and No. 455 Sportsman plate etching.

1933:

"Mr. Nock has also received from the factory a new complete range of table and stemware in a blue color which is a new Heisey product. Strangely enough, while Heisey has always pioneered in colors, the concern has never before brought out a deep blue. This is a real royal blue. It might even be referred to as a cobalt. Certain it is that it would tie up well with a dinnerware service carrying a rich cobalt band. Possibly the concern had that in mind when the color was produced." *Pottery, Glass & Brass Salesman*, January 1933.

In 1933, the Heisey company was ready for the repeal of Prohibition with a wide variety of drinking items. A series of beer mugs were added to the line and various types of wines or other forms were added to new stemware lines.

No. 141 Edna candlestick.

Edna, No. 141
Date: 1933 to 1936
Colors: Crystal, Moongleam, Flamingo, Sahara, Stiegel Blue

Comments: An unusual candlestick which holds a U-shaped candle — "burning a candle on both ends." The candlesticks are marked with the Diamond H on the narrow portion just below the candleholder. "Pat. Applied For" appears in the candleholder portion, although the patent was not granted to Heisey. Very difficult to find. Prices on colors are at the discretion of the seller.

Candlesticks, 6", pr. ....$700.00+

Cascade, No. 142
Date: 1933 to 1957
Colors: Crystal, Sahara, Stiegel Blue

Comments: A pressed candlestick, not often marked with the Diamond H. Add 300% for Sahara; 1000% for Stiegel Blue.

Candlestick, 3 light, pr. $100.00

No. 142 Cascade candlestick with special Heisey engraving.

Arch, No. 1417
Date: 1933 to 1937
Colors: With toes: Crystal. Very rare in Tangerine. Round foot: Crystal, Moongleam, Flamingo, Sahara, Stiegel Blue, Amber

Comments: The earlier version of this tumbler had the tiny toes as shown in the photo. Shortly after being introduced, the mold was reworked to have a round foot lacking the toes. Most tumblers have the round foot and are found in colors. Add 400% for Moongleam; 300% for Flamingo or Sahara; add 500% for Stiegel Blue or Amber.

Tumbler, round foot $30.00
Tumbler, with toes 90.00

No. 1417 Arch tumbler with toes.

No. 1420 Tulip vase.

No. 1420
9 in. Footed Vase

Tulip, No. 1420
Date: 1933 to 1937
Colors: Crystal, Moongleam, Flamingo, Sahara, Stiegel Blue

Comments: A pressed vase, marked with the Diamond H on the underside. It is most often seen in Stiegel Blue and hard to find in crystal. Interestingly, in 1957 the company must have been trying to sell some old stock as it advertised the vases in Stiegel Blue at that time! Add 300% for colors.

Vase, footed, 9" $175.00

Hi Lo, No. 1421
Date: 1933 to 1937
Colors: Crystal, Moongleam, Flamingo, Sahara, Stiegel Blue

Comments: A pressed vase, which may or may not be marked with the Diamond H. Somewhat scarce. Add 400% for colors.

Vase, footed & handled, 8" $120.00

No. 1421 Hi Lo vase.

Sweet Ad-o-line, No. 1423 — original name
Date: 1933 to 1935
Colors: Crystal, Moongleam, Flamingo, Sahara,
Stiegel Blue

Comments: A large pressed beer goblet. Marked with the Diamond H on the interior of the bowl. Very hard to find. For colors add 250% to 500%.

Goblet, 14 oz. ....$250.00+

No. 1423 Sweet Ad-o-line goblet.

Victorian, No. 1425 — original name
Dates: 1933. Discontinued during World War II. Reintroduced in 1951 to 1953.
Colors: Crystal, Sahara, Stiegel Blue (cobalt). Goblets and sherbets in Moongleam and Flamingo.

Comments: When A. H. Heisey was involved in the Geo. Duncan & Sons Glass Co., they produced a pressed glass tableware pattern very similar to Victorian. In 1933 the A. H. Heisey & Co. reintroduced this familiar pattern of small squares in new shapes as its Victorian line. Note the handles of cruets and details of tiny "thousand eye" feet to avoid buying look-alike pieces. Most Victorian is marked with the Diamond H. Imperial Glass Corp. continued to make stemware, a nappy, plate, and a small compote (which was never made by Heisey) in crystal, amber, azalea, and verde. All Imperial pieces are marked with the Diamond H. Prices are for crystal pieces. For Sahara, add 200%. For Stiegel Blue, add 550%.

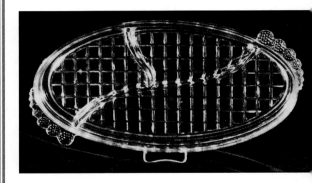

No. 1425 Victorian divided relish.

Bar, 2 oz.	$25.00
Bottle, French dressing & stopper	60.00
Bottle, rye & stopper, 27 oz.	120.00
Bowl, floral, 10½"..................................	52.00
Bowl, triplex	65.00
Butter dish & cover, ¼ lb............................	60.00
Candlesticks, 2 light, pr.	200.00
Celery tray, 12"	25.00
Cheese & cracker, 2 piece..........................	90.00
Cigarette box & cover, 4"	55.00
Cigarette box & cover, 6"	60.00
Cigarette holder/ashtray, individual ..	40.00
Claret, 4 oz.	20.00
Cocktail, 3 oz...................................	15.00
Comport, 5"	40.00
Condiment set: tray, salt, pepper, mustard & cover......................	160.00
Cream	28.00
Custard, 5 oz. (punch cup)	15.00
Finger bowl	12.00
Goblet, 9 oz....................................	25.00
Goblet, high footed, 9 oz...........................	25.00
Jug, ½ gallon....................................	225.00
Nappy, 8"....................................	32.00
Oil & stopper, 3 oz.	75.00
Old fashion cocktail, 8 oz.	17.00
Oyster cocktail, 5 oz.	12.00
Plate, 7" or 8".................................	18.00

Plate, buffet, 21" 110.00
Plate, sandwich, 13" 38.00
Punch bowl 265.00
Relish, 3 compartment, 11" 45.00
Rose bowl 260.00
Salt & pepper, pr. 55.00
Saucer champagne, 5 oz. 18.00
Sherbet, 5 oz. 15.00
Soda, 5 oz. (juice) 12.00
Soda, 12 oz. (ice tea) 15.00
Soda, footed, 12 oz. (ice tea) 15.00
Sugar 28.00
Tumbler, footed, 10 oz. 22.00
Vase, 4" 28.00
Vase, 5½" 30.00
Vase, footed, 6" 45.00
Vase, footed, 9" 75.00
Wine, 2½ oz. 25.00

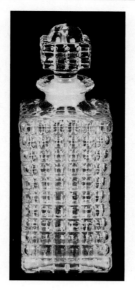

No. 1425 Victorian rye bottle.

No. 1425 Victorian goblet.

No. 1426 Clover Rope beer
mug.

Clover Rope, No. 1426
Date: 1933 to 1935
Colors: Crystal, Sahara, Stiegel Blue

Comments: A pressed beer mug marked with the Diamond H. Reproductions in odd colors were made by the Heisey museum. Add 50% to 100% for Sahara or Stiegel.

Beer mug, 12 oz. $300.00

Warwick, No. 1428 — original name
Date: 1933 to 1957
Colors: Crystal, Moongleam, Flamingo, Sahara, Stiegel Blue. Very rare in Alexandrite.

Comments "A horn-of-plenty vase setting on a shell-shaped base is another attractive new item, shown either in crystal or Sahara." *China, Glass & Lamps,* August 1933.

Basically console sets with a variety of vases and candlesticks. The individual vase is most often found, and in later years it was listed also as a candleholder. The true candlestick has a much narrower opening more like other candlesticks. Items are marked on the bases. Imperial Glass reproduced the two-light candlestick and 7" vase in heather and verde. There is also a 7" vase reproduction in poor quality yellowish glass. Items are easily found. Prices are for crystal. For Moongleam and Flamingo, add 1,000% or more. For Sahara, add 400%. For Stiegel Blue, add 600%.

No. 1428 Warwick individual vase
with frosted base.

Bowl, floral, horn of plenty, 11"..$120.00
Candlestick, horn of plenty, individual,
    pr. 45.00

Candlesticks, horn of plenty, 2 light,
    pr. 60.00
Cigarette holder, horn of plenty......50.00
Vase, horn of plenty, 5".................55.00
Vase, horn of plenty, 7".................60.00
Vase, horn of plenty, 9".................65.00
Vase, horn of plenty, individual......40.00

No. 1428 Warwick
cornucopia vase.

Aristocrat, No. 1430
Date: 1933 to 1937
Colors: Crystal, Moongleam, Sahara, Cobalt.
Very rare in Tangerine

Comments: Only made in two styles of candy jars with lids. There are two styles of lids, one with a beaded top and the other plain. Notice that the ball in the stem is very like the one in No. 3404 Spanish stemware. Pieces are usually marked on the base. These have not been reproduced. Prices are for crystal jars complete with lids. Jars in colors are commanding very high prices due to their scarcity.

Candy jar & cover, ½ lb. ....$255.00   Candy jar & cover, high footed, ½ lb. 275.00

No. 1430 Aristocrat
tall candy jar.

No. 1430 Aristocrat
short candy jar.

Spanish, No. 3404 — original name
Date: 1933
Colors: Crystal, Stiegel Blue with Crystal stem and foot, Tangerine
with Crystal stem and foot, Sahara with Crystal stem and foot.

Comments: A stemware line with blown bowl, pressed stem. May be marked with
the Diamond H on the stem near the base just above the rings. Made in wide optic. It
is very similar to Duncan's Granada except that the knops on Duncan's Granada are
formed with flat facets while the Heisey Spanish has a larger knop with round inden-
tations deeply into the knop. Both are modern interpretations of an ancient glass
form. "It is very smart and can be had in all crystal or a number of combinations such
as Sahara bowl and crystal stem or a crystal stem with the bowl in dark blue. In plain
crystal it is featured in three new etchings." *China, Glass & Lamps*, February 1933.
Prices are for crystal. For Sahara, add 350%. For Stiegel Blue (cobalt), add 300%. For
Tangerine, add 800%.

No. 3404 Spanish goblet with No. 797 Killarney cutting.

Claret, 4 oz. $40.00
Cocktail, 3½ oz. 40.00
Comport, 6" 110.00
Cordial, 1 oz. 135.00
Finger bowl (#3335) 10.00
Goblet, 10 oz. 50.00
Oyster cocktail, 3½ oz......................................30.00
Saucer champagne, 5½ oz. 38.00
Sherbet 5½ oz...18.00
Soda, footed, 5 oz. (juice) 24.00
Soda, footed, 12 oz. (ice tea) 27.00
Tumbler, footed, 10 oz....................................24.00
Wine, 2½ oz. 75.00

No. 3405 Coyle beer mug.

Coyle, No. 3405
Date: 1933 to 1937
Colors: Crystal, Moongleam, Flamingo,
Sahara, Alexandrite, Tangerine

Comments: A blown beer mug, not
marked with the Diamond H. Very difficult to find. Colors are usually in combination with crystal. For colors, add 300%
or more.

Beer mug, 12 oz. $125.00

No. 3406 Thran beer mug.

Thran, No. 3406
Date: 1933 to 1937
Colors: Crystal, Moongleam, Flamingo, Sahara, Tangerine, Stiegel Blue

Comments: A blown beer mug, not marked with the Diamond H. Very difficult to find. Colors are usually in combination with crystal. For colors, add 300% or more.

Beer mug, 12 oz. $125.00

Overdorf, No. 3407
Date: 1933 to 1937
Colors: Crystal, Moongleam, Flamingo, Sahara, Tangerine, Stiegel Blue

Comments: A blown beer mug, not marked with the Diamond H. Very difficult to find. Colors are usually in combination with crystal. For colors, add 300% or more.

Beer mug, 12 oz. $125.00

No. 3407 Overdorf beer mug.

No. 3408 Jamestown goblet with No. 866 Kent cutting, wine with special Heisey cutting.

Jamestown, No. 3408 — original name
Date: 1933 to 1957
Colors: Crystal, Sahara (rare)

Comments: A stem line with blown bowl, pressed stem. Marked with the Diamond H at the top of the stem below the swirl. Made in wide optic. Very similar to No. 3360 Penn Charter and No. 3409 Plymouth which have differently shaped bowls. Beer mugs have colored handles in Moongleam, Flamingo, Sahara, Tangerine, Stiegel Blue, and amber. For these colored handled pieces, add 300% or more. For Sahara stemware, add 500% or more.

Claret, 4½ oz. $20.00	Goblet, 9 oz. 24.00
Cocktail, 3 oz. 15.00	Mug, beer...55.00
Cordial, 1 oz..................................55.00	Saucer champagne, 6 oz. 15.00
Finger bowl....................................8.00	Sherbet, 6 oz. 10.00
	Sherry, 1½ oz. 45.00
	Soda, footed, 13 oz. (ice tea).......................17.00
	Tumbler, footed, 9 oz. 20.00
	Vase, 9"..70.00
	Wine, 2 oz...25.00

Plymouth, No. 3409 — original name
Date: 1933 to 1937
Colors: Crystal, Sahara; goblet known in Stiegel Blue

Comments: A stemware line with blown bowl, pressed stem. Items may be marked with the Diamond H on the upper stem below the swirl. It has not been reproduced. Made with wide optic. One of the three stem lines to use the same stem portion. See also No. 3408 Jamestown and No. 3360 Penn Charter. Pieces are hard to find, especially in color. Prices are for crystal pieces; for Sahara, add 50%. The Stiegel Blue goblet would be $400.00+.

Cocktail, 3 oz...$27.00
Finger bowl (#3335)..8.00
Goblet, 10 oz...45.00
Goblet, banquet, 12 oz. 85.00
Oyster cocktail, 3 oz. 15.00
Parfait, 5 oz. 30.00
Saucer champagne, 6 oz. 20.00
Sherbet, 6 oz. 15.00
Soda, footed, 5 oz. (juice) 15.00
Soda, footed, 12 oz. (ice tea) ..22.00

No. 3409 Plymouth stemware.

233

No. 3411 Monte Cristo goblet with No. 456 Titania plate etching.

Monte Cristo, No. 3411 — original name
Date: 1933 to 1941
Color: Crystal

Comments: A stem line with blown bowl, pressed stem. Pieces are not marked with the Diamond H and have not been reproduced. Made with wide optic. Sahara was listed in a Heisey price list, but to date we have not seen an example. The upper large ball in the stem has many raised dots, giving a thousand eye appearance to this portion. The same stem portion was used in No. 3414 Marriette with a tapered bowl. Monte Cristo is relatively easy to find.

Cocktail, 3½ oz.	$24.00
Comport, 7"	70.00
Cordial, 1 oz.	90.00
Finger bowl	8.00
Goblet, 9 oz.	30.00
Oyster cocktail, 4½ oz.	8.00
Saucer champagne, 6 oz.	18.00
Sherbet, 6 oz.	10.00
Sherry, 1½ oz.	65.00
Soda, footed, 5 oz. (juice)	15.00
Soda, footed, 12 oz. (ice tea)	20.00
Tumbler, footed, 9 oz.	18.00
Wine, 2½ oz.	50.00

Marriette, No. 3414 — original name
Date: 1933 to 1937
Color: Crystal only

Comments: A stemware line with blown bowl, pressed stem and not marked with the Diamond H or reproduced. Made with wide optic bowls. This is more difficult to find than Monte Cristo, but uses the same stem portion. Monte Cristo bowls are flared, while Marriette's are tapered. The sherries are common to both patterns, while the oyster cocktail is borrowed from the No. 3409 Plymouth pattern.

Claret, 3½ oz.	$32.00
Cocktail, 3½ oz.	22.00
Cordial, 1 oz.	110.00
Finger bowl (#3335)	8.00
Goblet, 10 oz.	50.00
Oyster cocktail, 3 oz. (#3409)	8.00
Saucer champagne, 6 oz.	20.00
Sherbet, 6 oz.	15.00
Sherry, 1½ oz.	45.00
Soda, footed, 12 oz. (ice tea)	20.00
Tumbler, footed, 10 oz.	18.00
Wine, 2½ oz.	45.00

No. 3414 Marriette stemware.

Barbara Fritchie, No. 3416 — original name
Date: 1933 to 1939
Colors: Crystal; brandy/cordial in Sahara, Alexandrite, Stiegel Blue

Comments: A difficult to find stemware line with blown bowl, pressed stem. It is not marked with the Diamond H, and has not been reproduced. The oyster cocktail and footed sodas are taken from the No. 3409 Plymouth pattern. Compare this line with No. 4092 Kenilworth which has a flared bowl but the same stem portion. Note should be made of the ¾ ounce brandies and the one ounce cordial. When first made, the cordial had a slightly taller bowl than the brandy. In later years, the tall bowled cordial was dropped, and the shorter brandy was called a cordial. This piece was made with several different colored bowls: Sahara, add 425%; Alexandrite, add 300%; and Stiegel Blue, add 150%. Note the brandy snifter and Rhine wine — both pieces not usually found in Heisey stemware lines.

Brandy snifter, 18 oz. $200.00
Brandy, tall stem, ¾ oz. 95.00
Claret, 3¾ oz. 35.00
Cocktail, 3½ oz. 20.00
Cordial, tall stem, 1 oz. 95.00
Finger bowl (#3335)..8.00
Goblet, 10 oz. 35.00
Goblet, low footed, 10 oz. 30.00
Oyster cocktail, 3 oz. (#3409) 10.00
Rhine wine, 6 oz. 170.00
Saucer champagne, 6 oz...............................17.00

Sherbet, 6 oz. 10.00
Sherry, tall stem, 1½ oz. 85.00
Soda, footed, 12 oz. (#3409) 20.00
Tumbler, footed, 10 oz. 18.00
Wine, 2½ oz. 35.00

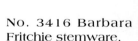

No. 3416 Barbara Fritchie stemware.

No. 4002 Aqua Caliente cocktail with No. 448 Old Colony plate etching.

> **Aqua Caliente, No. 4002**
> Dates: 1933 to 1944. 1948 to 1953 only in Crystal.
> Colors: Crystal, Moongleam, Flamingo, Sahara, Stiegel Blue
>
> Comments: A blown cocktail with pressed stem. Signed with the Diamond H on the stem. Very similar to No. 5024 Oxford stems.

Cocktail or Aqua Caliente.................$20.00

Decorations Introduced in 1933

Cuttings: No. 789 Aberdeen, No. 790 Fleur, No. 793 Monterrey, No. 794 Riviere, No. 795 Will o'the Wisp, No. 796 Suffolk, No. 797 Killarney, No. 798 Malta, No. 799 Manhattan, No. 800 Graystone, No. 801 Wakiki, No. 802 Manchester, No. 803 Hialeah, No. 804 Biscayne, No. 805 Baton Rouge, No. 807 Lorain, No. 808 Gateway, No. 809 Calcutta, No. 810 Dotted Swiss, No. 812 Sweet Briar, No. 813 Pyramids, No. 814 Laredo, No. 815 Japanese Boat Scene, and No. 816 Palmetto.

Etchings: No. 456 Titania plate etching, No. 457 Springtime plate etching, No. 458 Olympiad plate etching, No. 459 Fisherman silhouette etching, No. 460 Club Drinking Scene silhouette etching, No. 461 Concord plate etching, No. 462 Fox Chase silhouette etching, No. 463 Equestrian silhouette etching, No. 464 Harlequin etching, No. 465 Golf Scene silhouette etching, No. 466 Athletic Scenes in Border silhouette etching, No. 467 Tally Ho silhouette etching, No. 468 Chateau plate etching, No. 469 Mermaids silhouette etching, Nos. 471-465 Circus silhouette etchings, No. 605 Frosted (satin), and No. 9010 Pan plate etching.

1934:

During this year, Heisey promoted its new line of sand carved glassware quite heavily, featuring various patterns in several ads during the year. In March, an interesting comment from the company was printed in *China, Glass & Lamps*: "A. H. Heisey & Co. finds that colors are continuing to lose ground to crystal. In crystal, deep-cut and etched ware is selling very well."

In September, arrangements were made with designer, Walter von Nessen, to revamp some of Heisey's existing pieces into entirely new designs to be exhibited at the Metropolitan Museum of Art in November. Von Nessen reworked the early Optic Tooth vase into one with a plain foot — probably the forerunner of the popular No. 4057 Cecelia which remained in the Heisey line for many years. He requested a plain Gascony bowl without foot, a Yeoman buffet plate, and other articles. He also reworked stoppers and shapes of decanters. This display gave rise to several "Museum Cuttings" which were available from Heisey on special orders. These are usually very modern and are hard to find today.

In November an announcement was made that Macy's had purchased a huge amount of Heisey glass and was having a monumental sale. "There were six carloads of glass on display, or to particularize, 301,578 pieces, including stemware, tumblers, plates, and fancy items of all sorts in crystal, rose, and green. Hand-blown, pressed, fire-polished, etched and optic ware was there, laid out in long unpainted wooden bins placed across the counters. The glass was displayed according to price ranges, which ran the gamut from 5 cents to $1.99 per piece. This glass represented stock valued at $127,000 and it was sold at 25 cents on the dollar." *China, Glass & Lamps*, November 1934.

No. 1433 Thumbprint
& Panel vase.

Thumbprint & Panel, No. 1433
Date: 1934 to 1937
Colors: Crystal, Moongleam, Flamingo, Sahara, Stiegel Blue. The cheese & cracker plate was made only in Crystal and Sahara.

Comments: A very short pressed ware line, sometimes marked with the Diamond H, but often not. The crystal is of excellent quality and the pieces are heavy and sturdy. These have not been reproduced. Prices are for crystal pieces. For Moongleam, Flamingo, and Sahara, add 125%. For Stiegel Blue, add 225%.

Bowl, floral, 11".....................................$65.00
Candlesticks, 2 light, pr. 110.00
Cheese & cracker...................................75.00
Vase, 8½" 90.00

No. 1433 Thumbprint & Panel cheese & cracker.

Rococo, No. 1447 — original name
Date: 1934 to 1938
Colors: Crystal, Sahara. Combination mayonnaise and relish in Limelight.

Comments: A short pressed tableware line. Most items are marked with the Diamond H. Most items today are difficult to find. The tiny feet on several pieces are very prone to chipping. "The Rococo pattern has been designed from the Louis XV period and is distinctly feminine in feeling." *China, Glass & Lamps*, February 1934.

The footed cheese was later used with No. 1509 Queen Ann with a cracker plate. A plate with a stippled background was made in 1939 and given No. 1512 and called Stippled Rococo. The Heisey Collectors of America used the Rococo plate as a money-making convention souvenir from 1971 to 1976 in amberglo, blue haze, verde, nut brown, ultra blue, and crystal. These plates bear both the Diamond H and the Imperial IG marks. The Heisey museum had a basket made by Fenton in blue and green — a piece not originally made by Heisey. Prices are for crystal. For Sahara, add 200 to 300%. The relish in Limelight is 500+% of crystal.

Bonbon	$50.00
Bowl, floral, oval, 12"	90.00
Candlestick, 2 light, pr.	450.00
Celery, 12"	50.00
Cheese & cracker, 2 piece	95.00
Cigarette box & cover	145.00
Comport, 6"	95.00
Cream	60.00
Jelly	50.00
Mayonnaise & relish & cover, combination	200.00
Nappy, 4½"	25.00
Nappy, handled, 8"	50.00
Nappy, shallow, handled, 9½"	50.00
Plate, 7" or 8"	28.00
Salt & pepper, pr.	225.00
Soda, footed, 12 oz.	150.00
Sugar	60.00
Tray, roll	70.00

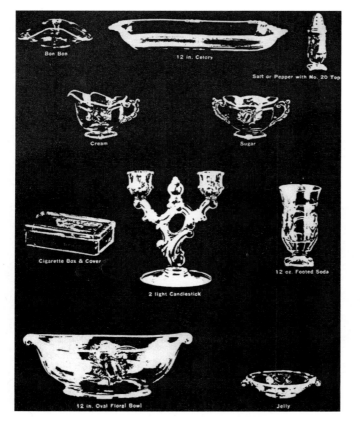

No. 1447 Rococo items.

New Era, No. 4044 — original name
Dates: 1934 to 1941. Candlesticks, celery, and stemware
again made from 1944 to 1957.
Colors: Crystal; Stiegel Blue in 1934 only, so it is very difficult to find.
Patents: R. C. Irwin was granted patent on 92247 for the goblet and
No. 92248 for the plate on 5-15-1934.

Comments: A pressed tableware pattern with matching stemware with blown bowls and pressed stems. Many pieces are not marked with the Diamond H, but some stemware is marked on the bottom of the foot. Art Deco styling sets this pattern apart from many more conservative Heisey patterns. The inspiration for its design came from a French china pattern. Heisey first referred to this as Modern, but changed the name to New Era shortly after its introduction. "Acclaim greets Heisey's new Modern Line wherever it is shown, as a glassware achievement dominating in 1934. In beautiful bold simplicity and twentieth century spirit, it is dynamic, breath-taking, thoroughly Heisey in artistry and execution!... Comes in all crystal or with blue bowls and crystal stems. Available also with satin finished feet and superb rock crystal cuttings." *China, Glass & Lamps*, March 1934.

Imperial Glass Corporation reproduced the candelabrum in crystal for about 14 years. Prices are for crystal pieces. For pieces in Stiegel Blue (cobalt) add as much as 500%.

Ashtray or individual nut $40.00	Oyster cocktail, 3½ oz. 16.00
Bowl, floral, 11"...70.00	Pilsner, 12 oz. 60.00
Candlestick with bobeches & prisms, 2 light,	Plate, 9" x 7", luncheon 40.00
pr...170.00	Plate, 10" x 8½", dinner 115.00
Celery tray, 13"...40.00	Plate, bread & butter, 5½" x 4½"......................27.00
Claret, 4 oz..25.00	Relish, 3 compartment, 13"............................38.00
Cocktail, 3½ oz...20.00	Rye bottle & stopper 155.00
Cordial, 1 oz..65.00	Saucer champagne, 6 oz. 22.00
Cream..38.00	Sherbet, 6 oz...14.00
Cup & saucer 55.00	Soda, footed, 12 oz..25.00
Cup & saucer, after dinner.............................75.00	Sugar 38.00
Finger bowl..10.00	Tumbler, footed, 10 oz. 22.00
Goblet, 10 oz. 28.00	Wine, 3 oz. 32.00

No. 4044 New Era ice tea, oyster cocktail, and wine with Pairpoint Greek Key cutting.

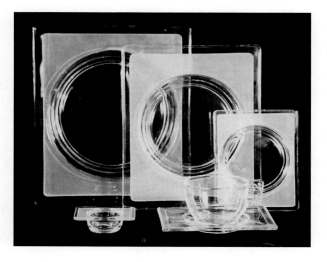

No. 4044 New Era. Back: dinner plate, luncheon plate, bread & butter plate with frosted areas. Front: individual nut, cup & saucer.

No. 4044 New Era rye bottle and wines with No. 831 Valencia cutting.

Decorations Introduced in 1934

Carvings: No. 5000 Bacchus, No. 5002 Sweet Adeline, No. 5003 Nimrod, No. 5004 Scotch, No. 5005 Bourbon, No. 5006 Gin, No. 5007 Rye, No. 5008 Castle Harbor, and No. 5009 Diana.

Cuttings: No. 821 Sky Scene, No. 825 Sea Glade, No. 826 Venus, No. 827 Star Secession, No. 828 Stardust, No. 829 Roxy, No. 830 California, and No. 831 Valencia.

1935:

Grape Cluster, No. 1445
Date: 1935 to 1944
Colors: One light: Crystal, Stiegel Blue. Two light: Crystal, Alexandrite, Sahara, Stiegel Blue. Bowl: Crystal, Moongleam, Sahara, Stiegel Blue, and an off shade of Zircon.

Comments: Pressed console set, usually marked with the Diamond H. Heisey sometimes added bobeches and prisms to the candlesticks, making them into candelabra. Another company also used the one light candlestick as a lamp base. A mold drawing was found of a three light candlestick, but there is no evidence it was ever made.

Bowl, oval floral $95.00
Candlesticks, 1 light, pr. 300.00
Candlesticks, 2 light, pr. 400.00

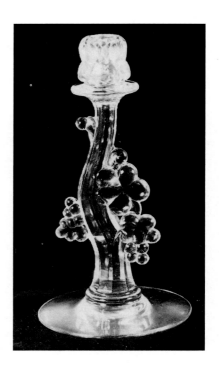

No. 1445 Grape Cluster one light candlestick.

No. 1454 Diamond Point individual jelly.

Diamond Point, No. 1454
Date: 1935 to 1944
Color: Crystal only

Comments: A three item pattern, marked with the Diamond H. The jelly and ashtray are made from the same mold and common. Imperial Glass reproduced the top hat match holder in their carnival, Aurora Jewels. Heisey made it only in crystal and hand tooled the brim into a pleasing shape. Imperial's hat has a plain, flat brim.

No. 1454 Diamond Point individual ashtray.

Ashtray, individual $10.00
Jelly, individual, 2½" 10.00
Match holder, top hat .... 250.00+

No. 1460 Flame tumbler.

Flame, No. 1460
Date: 1935 to 1944, possibly later
Colors: Crystal, Stiegel Blue

Comments: A pressed tumbler, marked with the Diamond H on the bottom.

Tumbler, footed $50.00

Quaker, No. 1462 — original name
Date: 1935 to 1937
Color: Crystal only

Comments: Pressed berry sets and plates, marked with the Diamond H and not reproduced. For illustration see No. 355 Quator, page 128 – 129.

Nappy, 4½" $9.00
Nappy, 7" 25.00
Nappy, 8" or 9" 35.00
Plate, 5" 9.00
Plate, 9" 25.00
Plate, 10" or 11" 32.00

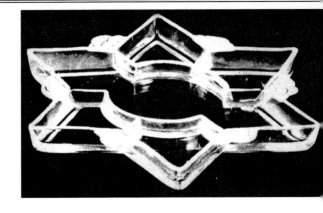

Star, No. 1466
Date: 1935 to 1953
Color: Crystal

Comments: A pressed relish dish, not marked with the Diamond H.

No. 1466 Star relish.

Relish, 5 compartment $55.00

Ridgeleigh, Nos. 1469, 1469¼, 1469½ — original name
Dates: 1935 to 1944. A small number of pieces were still listed in 1957.
Colors: Crystal. Limited items in Zircon and Sahara.
Patent: T. C. Heisey was listed as designer on all patents. The oval cigarette box was granted No. 99085 on 3-24-1936; the vase was granted No. 99798 on 6-26-1936; the diamond ashtray was granted No. 101630 on 10-20-1936 and the bowl without swan handles was granted No. 99799 on 5-26-1936.

Comments: "Vertical flutings, reflecting finely in mirrors, also reflect a trend in glassware design. This is the 'Ridgeleigh' design of A. H. Heisey & Co." *China, Glass & Lamps.* A small number of items were made in Zircon and Sahara and are marked with an asterisk (*). Both Fenton and Imperial made similar ribbed patterns. Many of the Ridgeleigh pieces are marked with the Diamond H. Imperial Glass Corp. reproduced the cigarette holder and ashtrays in heather and charcoal and the coaster in crystal. Imperial also modified the coaster into a ring tree which was never made by Heisey.

No. 1469 Ridgeleigh roly-poly cocktail and rest.

Ashtray, 4" (#1469½)	$28.00
Ashtray, bridge	20.00
Ashtray, club, diamond, heart, or spade.......	25.00
Ashtray, round..	20.00
Ashtray, square *	8.00
Ashtray, square, 6"	35.00
Bar, 2½ oz.	45.00
Bonbon, 6" (#1469½)	25.00
Bottle, bitters, 5 oz.	70.00
Bottle, French dressing & stopper	90.00
Bottle, rock & rye with stopper	185.00
Bowl, berry, cupped, 8½".............................	45.00
Bowl, cone beverage, 11"	110.00
Bowl, cone floral, 13"	70.00
Bowl, floral, 11½"..	65.00
Bowl, floral, oblong (swan handled), 14" 325.00	
Bowl, floral, oblong, 14" (without swan handles)...	85.00
Bowl, fruit, 12"	65.00
Bowl, orange	75.00

Bowl, oval floral, 12" * 55.00
Bowl, salad, 9" 45.00
Bowl, salad, 11" 50.00
Candelabra with bobeche, 7", pr. (bell
    shaped foot) 235.00
Candelabra with prisms, 1 light, pr.
    (#1469½)..190.00
Candelabra with prisms, 2 light, pr. ....400.00+
Candle vase, 6", pr. * 75.00
Candlestick with center bobeche, 2 light,
    pr. 230.00
Candlestick, 5" (cylinder) (#1469½), pr..........70.00
Candlestick, square, 2", pr. 60.00
Celery & olive tray, 12" 40.00
Celery tray, 12" 35.00
Centerpiece, 8" (#1469½) 65.00
Cheese, 6" (#1469½) 22.00
Cigarette box & cover, 4" 50.00
Cigarette box & cover, oval...........................100.00
Cigarette holder & cover 80.00
Cigarette holder, round or square 18.00
Cigarette holder/ashtray, oval, 2 comp.
    (#1469¼)...90.00
Claret...25.00
Coaster or cocktail rest................................25.00
Coaster, 3½" (#1469½) * 12.00
Cocktail...25.00
Cocktail shaker, 1 quart. 200.00
Cologne & stopper, 4 oz. 150.00
Comport & cover, low footed, 6"...................75.00
Comport, low footed, flared, 6"....................40.00
Cream, oval..30.00
Cream, oval, individual................................32.00
Cup & saucer..45.00
Cup, beverage...22.00
Custard or punch cup..................................15.00

No. 1469 Ridgeleigh old fashion, goblet.

Decanter & stopper, 1 pint (icicle shape).....195.00
Dessert, 2 handled, 10" 45.00
Dish, lemon & cover, 5" 60.00
Floral box, 8" 65.00
Goblet..45.00
Hors d'oeuvre, oval 50.00
Ice tub, 2 handled.......................................80.00
Jelly, 2 compartment, 6" (#1469½) 27.00
Jelly, 3 handled...27.00
Jelly, 6" (#1469½) 27.00
Jelly, individual oval....................................22.00
Jug, regular or ice, ½ gallon 180.00
Marmalade & cover......................................80.00
Mayonnaise 35.00
Mustard & cover 80.00
Nappy, 4½" 10.00
Nappy, 5" 12.00
Nappy, scalloped, 5½" 12.00
Nappy, square, 5" 12.00
Nut, individual (#1469½) 15.00
Nut, individual, 2 compartment (#1469½) 20.00
Oil & stopper, 3 oz. 60.00
Old fashion, 8 oz. 25.00
Oyster cocktail..12.00
Perfume & stopper, 5 oz. 200.00
Plate, 6" 15.00
Plate, ice tub, 2 handled..............................45.00
Plate, round, 8" 20.00
Plate, round, 8" (plain edge)........................25.00
Plate, round, 14" 50.00
Plate, sandwich, 13½" 50.00
Plate, square, 8" 55.00
Plate, torte, 13" or 14"................................50.00
Plate, torte, footed, 13½" (#1469½) 60.00

No. 1469 Ridgeleigh oil.

Puff box & cover, 5" 95.00
Punch bowl, 11" 170.00
Relish, 2 compartment, 7" (#1469½) 40.00
Relish, 3 compartment, 11" 55.00
Relish, 5 compartment (star), 10" 65.00
Roly poly with rest..125.00
Salt & pepper, pr. 50.00
Salt & pepper, pr. (#1469½) 45.00
Salt, individual 15.00
Salver, footed, 14" 60.00
Saucer champagne 16.00
Sherbet 12.00
Soda, 5 oz. (#1469½)....................................25.00
Soda, cupped or flared, 12 oz. (#1469½). 25.00
Soda, footed, 12 oz. 35.00
Sugar, oval..30.00
Sugar, oval, individual 32.00
Tray, 3 compartment, oblong, 10½" 50.00
Tray, for individual cream and sugar............50.00
Tray, oblong, 10½" 50.00
Tumbler, 10 oz. (#1469½) 30.00
Vase, 3½" 32.00
Vase, 6" 35.00
Vase, 8" (#1469½) 75.00
Vase, 8" (triangular) (#1469¼) 65.00
Vase, 9" 80.00
Vase, 10" 85.00
Vase, ball..110.00
Vase, ball, flared top, 7" 125.00

Vase, flared, 9" 80.00
Vase, individual, (5 shapes) 35.00
Wine 40.00

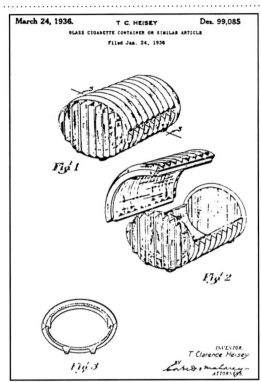

Patent drawing for No. 1469 Ridgeleigh oval cigarette box.

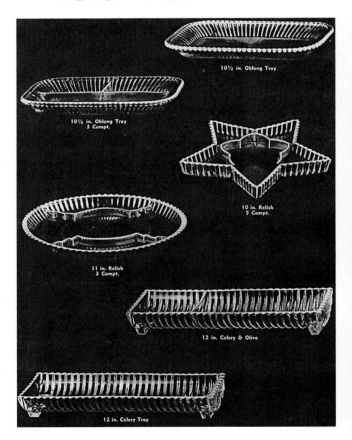

No. 1469 Ridgeleigh items.

244

No. 1469 Ridgeleigh items.

No. 4069 Ridgeleigh stemware
Blown bowl, pressed stem. Not marked with the Diamond H. An early name for this stem was Reis-Ridgeleigh.

Claret, 4 oz..............................$32.00
Cocktail, 3½ oz. 28.00
Cordial, 1 oz...........................125.00
Goblet, 8 oz..............................65.00
Goblet, luncheon, 8 oz. 45.00
Oyster cocktail, 4 oz.................18.00
Saucer champagne, 5 oz. 22.00
Sherbet, 5 oz............................18.00
Sherry, 2 oz. 75.00
Soda, 5 oz. (juice).....................20.00
Wine, 2½ oz..............................45.00

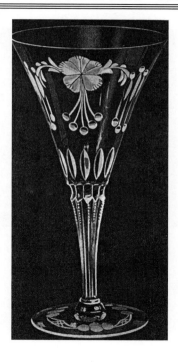

No. 4069 Ridgeleigh goblet with No. 874 Exotique cutting.

No. 1472 Parallel Quarter candlestick.

Parallel Quarter, No. 1472
Date: 1935 to 1942
Color: Crystal only

Comments: Made only as a console set. Usually marked and not reproduced. Easy to find to moderately available.

Bowl, floral $55.00
Candlesticks, pr. 65.00

No. 1472 Parallel Quarter floral bowl.

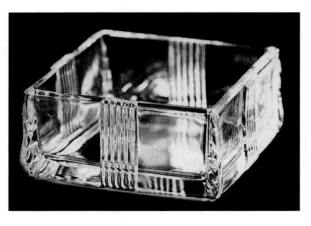

No. 1473 Buttress center piece, medium.

Buttress, No. 1473
Date: 1935 to 1938
Color: Crystal only

Comments: This is a small special pattern consisting of variously shaped floral arrangers, meant to be combined in various manners to form center-piece displays for flowers. Pieces are marked with the Diamond H.

Center piece, corner $35.00
Center piece, large..55.00
Center piece, medium 50.00
Center piece, small...40.00

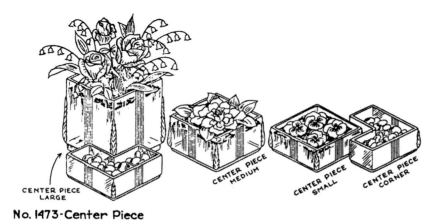

No. 1473-Center Piece

No. 1473 Buttress center piece grouping, from original ad.

Morse, No. 1476
Date: 1935 to 1937
Colors: Crystal, Stiegel Blue reported

Comments: This large pressed torte plate is sometimes used with the Pumpkin punch bowl. The base design is a series of dots and dashes. For Stiegel Blue, add 500%+.

Plate, torque, 18" $60.00

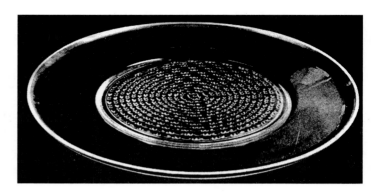

No. 1476 Morse torque plate.

Cable, No. 1478
Date: Ca. 1935
Color: Crystal

Comments: A one-item pattern, pressed, marked with the Diamond H. Very hard to find.

No. 1478 Cable footed soda.

Soda, footed $165.00

No. 3418 Savoy Plaza goblet with satin finish stem and foot.

Savoy Plaza, No. 3418 — original name
Date: 1935 to 1937
Color: Crystal only

Comments: A very hard to find stemware line with blown bowl, pressed stem. This has not been reproduced. It is marked with the Diamond H on the upper stem just below the bowl. It is very Art Deco in design, having a square stem and square foot. Compare with No. 3424 Admiralty which has a flared bowl.

Claret, 4 oz. $40.00
Cocktail, 3½ oz. 22.00
Cordial, 1 oz. 95.00
Finger bowl (#4080) 10.00
Goblet, 10 oz. 40.00
Oyster cocktail, 3½ oz. 18.00

Saucer champagne, 6 oz. 30.00
Sherry, 1½ oz. 60.00
Soda, footed, 5 oz. (juice).....18.00
Soda, footed, 12 oz. (ice tea).22.00
Wine, 3 oz. 40.00

Bethel, No. 4035
Date: 1935 to 1953
Color: Crystal

Comments: Not marked with the Diamond H. A blown decanter.

Decanter & stopper, 32 oz. ..$110.00

No. 4035 Bethel decanter with No. 815 Sweet Briar cutting with bar glasses.

No. 3422 Loren goblet, special engraving.

Loren, No. 3422
Date: 1935
Color: Crystal

Comments: A goblet which is not marked with the Diamond H. Very hard to find. It is unknown if other pieces were made in this pattern.

Goblet $100.00

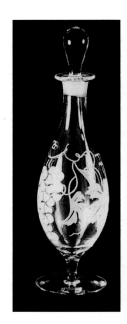

No. 4036 Marshall decanter with No. 5000 Bacchus carving.

Marshall, No. 4036
Dates: 1935 to 1946 for decanter. 1941 to 1957 for cocktail shaker.
Color: Crystal

Comments: A blown decanter and cocktail shaker, not marked with the Diamond H. The cocktail shakers also used the figural stoppers sometimes used with the Cobel cocktail shakers.

Cocktail shaker, 1 quart............................$80.00
Decanter & stopper, 1 pint 100.00

No. 4036 Marshall cocktail shaker with Rooster Head stopper with No. 941 Barcelona cutting.

Coronation, No. 4054 — original name
Date: 1935 to 1957
Colors: Crystal; listed in Zircon in 1937
Patent: The soda was patented on 2/7/1940 and given No. 119856.
T. Clarence Heisey listed as designer.

Comments: Basically a blown barware line which is not marked with the Diamond H. Usually made plain, but rarely found in saturn optic. A few sodas are known in Zircon and Dawn in an experimental screen optic which used window screening to produce the optic. Any example of these would be valued at $250.00+. Easy to find. Reproductions done by Imperial Glass include an ice tub (in spike optic) and 7" vase (in three swirl optic) made from the cocktail shaker mold, both of which were made in crystal, plum, sunshine yellow, and ultra blue.

Bar, 1 oz. $25.00	Martini mixer, 30 oz. 65.00
Bar, 2½ oz. 18.00	Old fashioned, 8 oz. 18.00
Cocktail shaker 75.00	Slim Jim, 14 oz. 45.00
Cocktail, 3 oz. 15.00	Soda, 5 oz. 15.00
Cocktail, footed, 4 oz. 22.00	Soda, 8 oz. or 10 oz. 18.00
Hot toddy, 11 oz. 18.00	Soda, 13 oz. 30.00
Ice tub.. 65.00	Tankard, ice, ½ gallon 135.00
Jug, ½ gallon 110.00	

No. 4054 Coronation old fashion, tall soda, slim jim, bar.

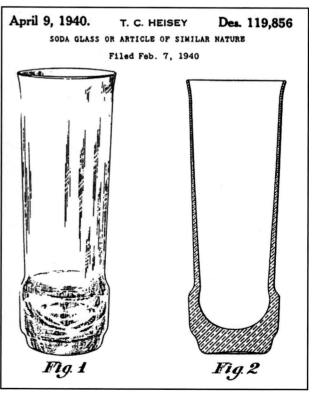

April 9, 1940.   T. C. HEISEY   Des. 119,856
SODA GLASS OR ARTICLE OF SIMILAR NATURE
Filed Feb. 7, 1940

Fig. 1   *Fig. 2*

Patent drawing of No. 4054 Coronation soda.

No. 4055 Park Lane goblet
with unknown cutting.

Park Lane, No. 4055 — original name
Date: 1935 to 1941
Color: Crystal only

Comments: A stemware line with blown bowl, pressed stem. Not marked with the Diamond H and not reproduced. Moderately available.

Claret, 4 oz.	$24.00	Sherbet, 6 oz.	10.00
Cocktail, 3 oz.	18.00	Sherry, 1½ oz.	35.00
Cordial, 1 oz.	75.00	Soda, footed, 5 oz. (juice)	15.00
Finger bowl	8.00	Soda, footed, 9 oz. (water)	18.00
Goblet, 10 oz.	25.00	Soda, footed, 13 oz.	
Oyster cocktail, 3 oz.	10.00	(ice tea)	18.00
Saucer champagne, 6 oz.	12.00	Wine, 2½ oz.	35.00

Caesar, No. 4056
Date: 1935 to 1956
Color: Crystal

Comments: Designed by Walter von Nessen for inclusion in a special exhibit at the Metropolitan Museum of Art. This is a blown bowl and so not marked with the Diamond H.

Bowl, salad, 9"	$35.00
Bowl, salad, 11"	45.00

No. 4056 Caesar salad bowl with No. 859 Cohassett cutting.

Pumpkin, No. 4058 — original name
Date: 1935 to 1944
Color: Crystal

Comments: A blown punch bowl with a lid; not marked with the Diamond H. The custards also are not marked since they are blown.

Custard (#4266 or #4058) ....$20.00   Punch bowl and cover.............850.00+

No. 4266 custard, No. 4058 custard, and No. 4058 Pumpkin punch bowl.

Decorations Introduced in 1935

Carvings: No. 5010 Vanity Fair, No. 5011 Chevy Chase, No. 5012 Amfulula Tree, No. 5013 Nymph and Satyr, No. 5014 Swan Dive, No. 5015 Stripes, and No. 5016 Stars and Stripes.

Cuttings: No. 832 Continental, No. 833 Bavaria, No. 834 Moulin Rouge, No. 835 Larkspur, No. 837 Cristobal, No. 838 St. Moritz, No. 839 Bonnie Briar, No. 840 Briar Cliff, No. 841 Wyandotte, No. 842 Singapore, No. 843 Tahiti, No. 844 Piccadilly, No. 845 Fontaine, No. 846 Neo Classic, No. 847 Streamline, No. 848 Botticelli, No. 849 Nomad, No. 850 Del Monte, No. 851 Kalarama, No. 852 Navarro, No. 853 Pinehurst, No. 854 Lombardy, No. 859 Cohassett, No. 860 Vienna, No. 861 Neapolitan, No. 862 Monaco, No. 863 Contessa, No. 864 Blue Willow, No. 865 Florentine, No. 866 Kent, and No. 867 Chateau.

Etchings: No. 477 Japanese Scene plate etching, No. 480 Normandie plate etching, No. 600 Satin Finish, No. 602 Simplex (satin), No. 603 Bandelino (satin), and No. 9022 Jack Frost (satin).

E. Wilson Heisey

E. Wilson Heisey, 66, president and general manager of the A. H. Heisey Glass Company, died Wednesday, January 21, 1942, at 2:40 A.M., in the Newark City Hospital.

Mr. Heisey had been in failing health for several months and on January 6 was admitted to the hospital for treatment preparatory to an operation. His condition had been serious since the operation which he underwent January 17.

The son of the late Augustus H. Heisey, founder of the table glass industry here almost 50 years ago, Mr. Heisey became president of the company following the death of his father in 1922, and with his brother, T. Clarence Heisey, vice president and treasurer, successfully directed the business of the company, which is one of the outstanding glass manufacturing plants in the United States.

Mr. Heisey was born in Pittsburgh, Pennsylvania, October 9, 1875, the son of Major A. H. Heisey and Mrs. Susan N. (Duncan) Heisey.

In 1936 the Heisey company was one of several companies featured at an American glass exhibit at the Metropolitan Museum of Art in New York City. All exhibits were required to be new items, never before in production. Due to the short period of time involved in preparing items for exhibition, Heisey designers revamped existing pieces, especially creating new cuttings which later became known as "museum cuttings" and were offered by the company to regular customers.

The Heisey mare, Goodness Gracious, won first prize at the Atlantic City Horse Show for a walk-trot mare. This was the highest prize ever won by the Heisey stables and was commemorated in a No. 1489 Puritan ashtray with a likeness of Goodness Gracious with Tim Heisey riding etched into the base. It is also generally agreed that Heisey's Show Horse figurine is a likeness of Goodness Gracious.

Another award given to the Heiseys, this time for glassware, was for the use of the plastic insert knops and handles used in the Stanhope pattern. They were awarded a plaque from the Modern Plastic Competition in 1936.

E. Wilson Heisey continued his active participation in the Republican Party, serving as state manager for the National Convention of the Republican Party held in Cleveland, Ohio, for Alf Landon's nomination for the presidency. Favors at this banquet were No. 4044 New Era demitasse cups and saucers and a plain plate etched with the likeness of Alf Landon. At the convention, the famous picture frame engraved by Emil Krall with sunflowers was used to frame a picture of Alf Landon. Later this frame was partially broken, but Krall engraved other panels and it was incorporated into a display cabinet which traveled with Krall when he made personal appearances at various department stores and display rooms. The cabinet held exquisite examples of Krall's engraved glassware. All carried price tags, but they were extremely expensive and it is doubtful that many more than the actual samples were ever made.

In 1937 Heisey introduced a new color, Zircon — a turquoise blue green.

The Heisey Co. began a new, successful venture when they introduced the Fighting Rooster figurine in 1940. This led to more solid animal figurines in the coming years, many of them designed by the famous designer, Royal Hickman, who had a knack for portraying the animals in a whimsical way.

In 1940 Stiegel Blue (cobalt) was discontinued from the Heisey line. This was the last color during this period and after this Heisey made only crystal glass for many years.

In 1942, E. Wilson Heisey died after having surgery. T. Clarence Heisey, his brother, succeeded to the presidency of A. H. Heisey & Co. About this time, Emil Krall also terminated his association with the Heisey company and opened his own cutting shop on Cedar Street in Newark. Eventually, several of the other Kralls joined him, including his son and several nephews. His brother, Willibald Krall, remained in the Heisey company's employ.

With the difficulties and travel restrictions imposed because of World War II, the Heisey company sought other ways to sell

Mr. Heisey attended private schools in Pittsburgh and spent a year in the preparatory department of the Colorado Agricultural College. Following a year's training as a cadet at Kenyon Military Academy at Gambier, he entered Park Institute of Allegheny, Pennsylvania, for a two-year course. For three years Mr. Heisey was a student at Washington and Jefferson College in Washington, Pennsylvania, and while there was a recognized athlete. Leaving college he entered the glass company of which his father was head, mastered the details of the business and became factory manager. In time he was made vice president of the company and at the death of his father succeeded him to the office of president.

E. Wilson Heisey was keenly interested in sports and also kept a number of pure bred setter dogs at the plant property. From boyhood Mr. Heisey was an enthusiastic devotee of baseball. He gained prominence as a player at Washington and Jefferson College and attracted the attention of major league scouts. He turned down numerous offers to enter professional baseball. Though passing up baseball as a profession, he found an outlet for his interest in the sport through the backing and managing of the Heisey baseball team.

For several years Mr. Heisey was a power in Republican politics but never held any public office himself. He served as a delegate to the national convention in 1936 and was a former member of the State Executive Committee and treasurer of the committee in 1930.

its product. The Wartime Salesmen were developed in 1943. These were small brochures serving as catalog, order sheet, and envelope for ordering Heisey glassware. There were four Wartime Salesmen sheets developed: Orchid etching, Crystolite, Lariat, and Gift Items which included various small items plus the animals.

As part of the war effort, the Heisey company began making ring and plug gauges for industry. These measuring devices were formerly made of metal, but due to the critical need for war materiel, these were now changed to glass. Certainly there was a high mortality on these items, as they are very difficult to find today. "Mass production of the tools of war demands extreme accuracy in production of interchangeable parts. It is in this field that a new form of gauge has been developed for measuring the accuracy of interior and exterior diameters of rods, gun barrels, etc. The Heisey factory is busy turning out GLASS gauges. Formerly all gauges were made of high-quality steel, a very critical material. Over a year ago Heisey began to experiment in this field and, working closely with the Frankford Arsenal, developed these glass gauges, which not only release much high-quality steel for other uses, but have many advantages over the metal ones." *Crockery & Glass Journal*, September 1943.

T. Clarence Heisey now employed Horace King, an art professor at nearby Denison University, as a designer for Heisey. He produced many patterns such as Plantation, Waverly, and Zodiac. He also added to lines such as Crystolite and Lariat.

1936:

Stanhope, No. 1483 — original name
Date: 1936 to 1941
Color: Crystal
Patents: Walter von Nessen patented the plate on 9-29-1936 and was granted No. 101410 and the sugar on 11-10-1936 and granted No. 101900.

Comments: "The pressed motif is a grouping of deep swags and a highly unusual feature is the use of colored buttons or short rods made of Plascon and inserted in the circular handles and knops. These inserts are made in such colors as red, blue, black, yellow, and ivory. All of the plates are couped and rimless, and there are two types of stemware — all pressed or with a pressed stem and blown bowl. The line may be had plain, etched, cut or with frosted swags. Interesting is news that the General Electric Co. has adopted a 'Stanhope' set for use with its coffee maker, the colors of the inserts matching the trim of the coffee maker and the tray." *China, Glass & Lamps*, August 1936.

Stanhope was designed by Walter von Nessen. In the Modern Plastics Competition, Heisey's Stanhope won an award for the use of plastic handles and knops. The plastic inserts were either flat discs or a rod used as a handle. A lamp was made from the ball vase. Imperial Glass made the vase in Stiegel Green (a deep green) for the Smithsonian Institution in 1980.

Mr. Heisey was at all times interested in the betterment of the community which the Heisey business helped to make a progressive industrial center, and took an active part in civic affairs.

He served about 20 years as a member of various committees in the National Glass Manufacturers' Association and was a member of the Society of Glass Technology.

Surviving him are his widow, formerly Hazel Reese, whom he married in 1906; two sons, George Duncan Heisey and Augustus H. Heisey; four grandchildren; two sisters and two brothers, Mrs. O. H. Dockery, Mrs. Fred H. King, George D. Heisey, and T. Clarence Heisey all of Newark, Ohio.

Funeral services were held in Trinity Episcopal Church, the Reverend James E. Wolf officiating; and burial was made in Cedar Hill Cemetery.

Ashtray, individual	$28.00
Bowl, floral, 2 handled, 11"	75.00
Bowl, salad, 11"	55.00
Candelabra, 2 light with prisms, pr.	400.00
Candy box & cover, 6"	80.00
Celery, 12"	45.00
Cigarette box & cover	115.00
Cocktail, 3½ oz.	25.00
Cream	30.00
Cup & saucer	35.00
Goblet, 9 oz.	35.00
Ice tub, 2 handled	90.00
Jelly, 3 compartment, handled, 6"	35.00
Jelly, handled, 6"	30.00
Mayonnaise, 2 handled	40.00
Mint, 2 compartment, 2 handled, 6"	40.00
Mint, 2 handled, 6"	40.00
Nappy or porringer, 4½"	25.00
Nut, individual	40.00
Oil & stopper, 3 oz.	230.00
Plate, 7"	25.00
Plate, 15"	70.00
Plate, torte, 15"	75.00
Plate, torte, 2 handled, 12"	60.00
Relish, 4 compartment, 2 handled, 12"	50.00
Relish, 5 compartment, 2 handled, 12"	60.00
Relish, triplex, 2 handled, 11"	50.00
Salt & pepper, pr.	120.00
Saucer champagne, 5½ oz.	25.00
Soda, footed, 5 oz. (juice)	20.00
Soda, footed, 12 oz. (ice tea)	25.00
Sugar	30.00
Vase, 2 handled, 9"	70.00
Vase, ball, 7"	95.00
Wine, 2½ oz.	35.00

No. 1483 Stanhope plate, cup, and saucer.

No. 1483 Stanhope vase with No. 492 Frosty Dawn etching.

Patent drawing for No. 1483 Stanhope sugar.

101,900
DESIGN FOR A GLASS SUGAR BOWL OR SIMILAR ARTICLE
Walter von Nessen, New York, N. Y.
Application July 29, 1936, Serial No. 64,119
Term of patent 14 years

The ornamental design for a glass sugar bowl or similar article substantially as shown and described.

No. 4083 Stanhope blown stemware

Blown bowl, pressed stem. Not marked with the Diamond H. Made in crystal and crystal and Limelight combination. Add at least 200% for items in Limelight.

Claret, 4 oz. $25.00
Cocktail, 3½ oz. 12.00
Finger bowl (#4080) 8.00
Goblet, 10 oz. 25.00
Oyster cocktail, 4 oz. 10.00
Saucer champagne, 5½ oz. 15.00
Sherbet 10.00
Soda, footed, 5 oz. (juice) 12.00
Soda, footed, 8 oz. (water) 15.00
Soda, footed, 12 oz. (ice tea) 17.00
Wine, 2½ oz. 25.00

No. 4083 Stanhope ice tea, saucer champagne, Limelight bowls.

No. 3424 Admiralty goblet.

Admiralty, No. 3424 — original name
Dates: 1936 to 1939. Available for matching cuttings until 1943.
Color: Crystal only

Comments: A stemware line with blown bowl, pressed stem. This pattern has a square foot. Difficult to find. Marked with the Diamond H on the upper stem.

Claret, 4½ oz. $40.00	Saucer champagne 40.00
Cocktail, 3 oz. 30.00	Sherry, 2 oz. 55.00
Cordial, 1 oz. 95.00	Soda, footed, 5 oz. (juice) ...25.00
Finger bowl (#3309) 8.00	Soda, footed, 12 oz. (ice tea) .30.00
Goblet, 9 oz. 45.00	Wine, 2 oz. 45.00
Oyster cocktail, 4½ oz. 18.00	

Nos. 4045, 4085 Ball vase — original description
Date: 1936 to 1953
Colors: Crystal, Moongleam, Flamingo, Sahara, Stiegel Blue, Alexandrite,
Tangerine, Zircon (in saturn optic)

Comments: Blown ball shaped vases in several sizes. They are not marked with the Diamond H. In wide optic the number is 4045, but with saturn optic it becomes 4085. The Krall engravings are usually signed with his script signature. These engravings were available in crystal or Zircon. For Flamingo, add 1,500%. For Moongleam, add 2,000%. For Stiegel Blue, add 1,000%. For Zircon and Sahara, add 800%. For Tangerine, add 2,500%. As can be seen by these estimates, many of the colors are very elusive and prices will depend entirely on buyer and seller.

Ball vase, 3"	$55.00	Ball vase, 7"	60.00
Ball vase, 4"	45.00	Ball vase, 9"	70.00
Ball vase, 6"	50.00	Ball vase, 12"	120.00

No. 2508
Water Lily Engraving

No. 2509
Bird & Rose Engraving

No. 2510
Robin in the Tree Engraving

No. 2511
Light House & Boat Engraving

No. 4085 Ball vases with special Emil Krall engravings.

HEISEY PRESENTS distinction in clever vases...

Heisey's GLASSWARE for your table

No. 4045 Ball vases with No. 825 Sea Glade cutting.

256

Cecelia, No. 4057
Date: 1936 to 1957
Colors: Crystal; Zircon

Comments: A blown vase. Not marked with the Diamond H. Usually seen with a heavy saturn optic. When this vase was made for a short time with a Sultana (amber) base, it was given No. 5047. For Zircon, add 400%+.

Vase, 6" $32.00
Vase, 9" 50.00
Vase, 10½" 70.00

No. 4057 Cecelia vase with cupped rim, unusual.

No. 4057 Cecelia vase, saturn optic.

Decorations Introduced in 1936
Cuttings: No. 855 Fuchsia, No. 868 Minaret, No. 870 St. Albans, No. 871 Sophisto, No. 872 Mariemont, No. 873 Edwardian, No. 874 Exotique, No. 875 Sylvia, No. 876 Honolulu, No. 877 Pueblo, No. 878 Sea Glade, No. 879 Da Vinci, No. 880 Salem, No. 881 Kashmir, No. 882 Yorkshire, No. 883 Royal York, No. 885 Incognito, and No. 886 King's Ransom.

1937:

Horse Head, No. 1 — original name
Date: 1937 to 1956
Color: Crystal

Comments: Not marked with the Diamond H. Supposedly designed by T. Clarence Heisey, a great horse lover. Base of the figure is ground and polished.

Bookends, pr. $365.00

No. 1 Horse Head bookend.

Saturn, No. 1485 — original name
Dates: 1937 to 1953. A few pieces continued until 1957.
Colors: Crystal, Zircon, some pieces in Dawn.

Comments: "Saturn design is available either in crystal or in Heisey's newest color — the soft pale green of the sea on a cloudy day. This color has been named 'Zircon,' and it is being brought out in all of the many items in the 'Saturn' design — vases, bubble balls, plates, platters, both pressed and blown stemware, liquor glassware, and a full line of buffet plates." *China, Glass & Lamps*, March 1937.

Early pattern folders for Saturn show two pieces, a rose bowl and a floral bowl, in an optic called wavy line, which is the saturn optic in a wavy format. For Zircon, add 500%.

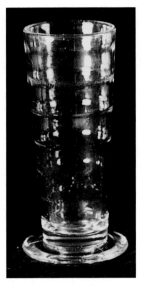

No. 1485 Saturn pressed vase with foot, difficult to find.

Hostess helper: 12" ice bowl, footed sauce, 3 toothpick holders, 3 chrome clips	85.00
Ice tea, 12 oz.	15.00
Jug, ice lip, 70 oz. (#4161 blown)	200.00
Juice, 5 oz.	12.00
Marmalade & cover	55.00
Mayonnaise	30.00
Mustard & cover	40.00
Mustard & paddle cover	140.00
Oil & stopper, 3 oz. (tall)	50.00
Oil & stopper (squat)	70.00
Old fashion, 7 oz.	20.00
Oyster or fruit cocktail, 4 oz.	10.00
Parfait, 5 oz.	15.00
Pickle, 7"	15.00
Plate, 6"	10.00
Plate, 7" or 8"	20.00
Plate, mayonnaise, 7"	20.00
Plate, party (torte), 14"	40.00
Plate, rolled edge, 6¼"	18.00
Plate, sandwich, 15"	50.00
Relish, 3 compartment, 9"	70.00
Rose bowl	65.00
Salt & pepper, pr.	40.00
Saucer champagne or tall sherbet, 6 oz.	15.00

Ashtray, 3½"	$15.00
Baked apple or grapefruit, 6¼ oz.	30.00
Beverage, 10 oz.	20.00
Bottle, bitters, 6 oz.	60.00
Bowl, flower, rolled edge, 12"	55.00
Bowl, gardenia, 12½"	55.00
Bowl, salad, 10"	50.00
Candelabra, 2 light, with bobeches & ball drops, pr.	450.00
Candleblock, 2 light, pr.	200.00
Candlesticks, footed, 3", pr.	70.00
Celery, 10"	25.00
Coaster, 3½"	15.00
Cocktail, 3 oz.	15.00
Cup & saucer	40.00
Cream	35.00
Dish, dessert or sauce (nappy), 4½" or 5"	20.00
Finger bowl	15.00
Fruit cocktail, 4 oz.	9.00
Goblet, 8 oz. or 10 oz.	20.00
Grapefruit or sauce, footed	20.00

No. 1485 Saturn Hostess helper, no clips.

Sherbet, low 3½ oz. or 4½ oz. 9.00
Sugar & cover, no handles 35.00
Sugar pourer, 5 oz. 45.00
Sugar, handled & cover 70.00
Tray, tidbit..30.00
Tumbler, 8 oz. 25.00

Vase, crimped, footed, 9" 50.00
Vase, flared or straight, 8¼" 50.00
Vase, violet..35.00
Whipped cream, 5" 35.00
Wine or cocktail, 3 oz. 18.00

No. 1485 Saturn cream and sugar, Zircon.

No. 1485 Saturn oil &
stopper (late style).

No. 1485 Saturn wine, cup, tumbler, Zircon.

No. 1487 Coleport soda, Dawn.

Coleport, No. 1486 — original name
Dates: 1937 to 1946; 1948 to 1957
Colors: Crystal. Tumbler and ice tea in Dawn from 1955 to 1957.
Patent: R. C. Cobel patented the soda on 7-27-1937 and was granted No. 105431.

Comments: A pressed tumbler line. Heisey's are marked with the Diamond H. Many other companies made similar tumblers, some in poor quality glass and others of exceptional quality, such as Moser who also made these in colors which could be confused with Heisey's earlier colors. Heisey planned a two light candleholder in an oval shape, but it is not known if these were commercially made. The mold exists today. When made in Dawn, the sodas and tumblers were given No. 1487. For pieces in Dawn, add 200%.

Bar, 2 oz.	$15.00
Beverage, 10 oz.	15.00
Bowl, oval, 14"	38.00
Candleblock, 2 light, pr.	500.00+
Cocktail, 3 oz.	15.00
Goblet, 8 oz.	28.00
Hi-ball, 8 oz.	20.00
Ice tea, 13 oz.	20.00
Ice tub	65.00
Juice, 5 oz.	15.00
Nappy, 4"	8.00
Nappy, 8"	20.00
Old fashion, 7 oz.	14.00
Oyster cocktail, 4 oz.	8.00
Saucer champagne, 5½ oz.	15.00

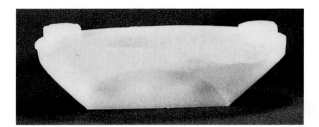

No. 1486 Coleport two-light candleblock, plastic model from mold.

Sherbet, 5½ oz.	8.00
Soda, 5 oz.	8.00
Soda, 8 oz. or 10 oz.	10.00
Soda, 13 oz.	15.00
Tumbler, 10 oz.	20.00
Wine, 2½ oz.	20.00

Kohinoor, No. 1488 — original name
Date: 1937 to 1939. Console set continued from 1941 to 1946.
Colors: Crystal, Zircon. Rare items known in Sahara.

Comments: "This console set is brand new. It is by A. H. Heisey from their Kohinoor line, and may be had in crystal or their new Zircon color." *China, Glass & Lamps,* April 1937.

Most items are marked with the Diamond H. The pattern was designed by Walter von Nessen. The name is taken from the diamond motif and refers to the famous Kohinoor diamond. Prices are for crystal, for Zircon add 300% to 600%.

No. 1488 Kohinoor cigarette holder.

The War Years...The Fifth Decade 1936 – 1945

Ashtray..$28.00
Ashtray, bridge (oval with match
   holder)...35.00
Bowl, floral, 13".................................90.00
Bowl, floral, 14".................................90.00
Bowl, fruit, 15"..................................90.00
Candelabra, 2 light with prisms, pr. .550.00
Cigarette holder.................................40.00
Hors d'oeuvres, 17".............................90.00

No. 1488 Kohinoor candelabrum.

No. 1488 Kohinoor ashtray and No. 4085½
soda, Zircon.

No. 4085 Kohinoor stemware
Blown bowl, pressed stem. The No. 4085 sodas
have a pressed foot similar in design to the round
ashtray. The No. 4085½ sodas have a cast on foot
and knop similar to the other stemware.

Bowl, salad, 11"..$40.00
Claret, 4½ oz. 30.00
Cocktail, 3 oz. 28.00
Cocktail, tall stem, 4½ oz. 38.00
Cordial, 1 oz..75.00
Finger bowl (#3335) 8.00
Goblet, 9 oz. 35.00
Goblet, low foot, 9 oz...35.00
Jug, ice lip, 32 oz. (#4161 blown)................120.00
Oyster cocktail, 4 oz...15.00
Rhine wine, 6 oz. 125.00
Saucer champagne, 5½ oz...............................25.00
Sherbet, 5½ oz. 15.00
Soda, footed, 5 oz. (pressed foot, juice).........25.00
Soda, footed, 5 oz. (#4085½, juice)................15.00
Soda, footed, 8 oz. (pressed foot, water) 30.00
Soda, footed, 8 oz. (#4085½, water)..............20.00
Soda, footed, 12 oz. (pressed foot, ice tea)....32.00
Soda, footed, 12 oz. (#4085½, ice tea)..........28.00
Wine, 2½ oz. 35.00

No. 4085½ Kohinoor ice tea and No. 4085
Kohinoor goblet, Zircon and crystal.

Puritan, No. 1489 — original name
Date: 1937 to 1957
Color: Crystal
Patents: T. C. Heisey was granted patents on the following: deep ashtray No. 127620 on 6-3-1941 and the bar bottle No. 129730 on 9-30-1941.

Comments: A moderately large line consisting of many smoking items, console set, and barware pieces. It is usually of excellent crystal and not marked. Most pieces are ground and polished on the bottoms. Many also may have ground tops (such as the floral bowls), and also some are found ground and polished all over — a very costly finishing process. Some French dressing bottles were also etched Oil and Vinegar by Heisey. "Clean-cut lines distinguish this new candy box from A. H. Heisey Co. priced to retail for about $3. The cigarette box with horses' head decoration is about $2 retail." *Crockery & Glass Journal*, August 1941.

    The candy box is difficult to find today. The card suit ashtrays and the square plates were made from the Ridgeleigh molds. The card suit ashtrays were reproduced by Imperial Glass in black.

No. 1489 Puritan card suit ashtrays — club and spade.

Ashtray, 2¾" (square)	$6.00
Ashtray, 4½" (square)	7.00
Ashtray, 6" (square)	8.00
Ashtray, 7" (square)	9.00
Ashtray, card suit, ea.	22.00
Ashtray, deep, 2½" (square)	6.00
Ashtray, deep, 4¾" (square)	7.00
Ashtray, horse head, 4½"	85.00
Ashtray, oblong, 6¾"	35.00
Bottle, bitters, 4 oz.	35.00
Bottle, cologne & stopper, 4 oz.	75.00
Bottle, French dressing & stopper, 6 oz.	35.00
Bottle, rye & stopper, 24 oz.	80.00
Bowl, camellia, 8" x 10"	50.00
Bowl, floral, hexagonal	265.00
Bowl, floral, oblong, 14"	50.00
Bowl, gardenia, 11" (square)	90.00
Candleblocks, 2½", pr.	60.00

Candleblocks, square, pr. (nappy)	150.00
Candleblocks, hexagonal, pr.	225.00
Candy box & cover	100.00
Cigarette box & colt cover, 6" (#1489¾)	1,000.00+
Cigarette box & cover, 4"	30.00
Cigarette box & cover, 6"	35.00
Cigarette box & horse head cover, 4" (#1489½)	125.00
Cigarette box & horse head cover, 6" (#1489½)	160.00
Hurricane block & No. 4061 10" globe	300.00
Plate, 6", 7", or 8" (square)	20.00
Plate, 10" (square)	75.00
Salt & pepper, pr.	70.00

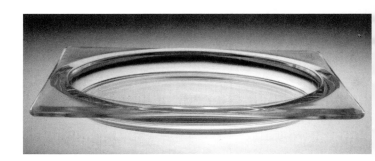

No. 1489 Puritan plate.

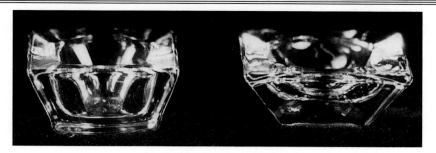

No. 1489 Puritan individual salt (l) and non-Heisey look-alike (r).

No. 1489 Puritan gardenia bowl and candleblocks.

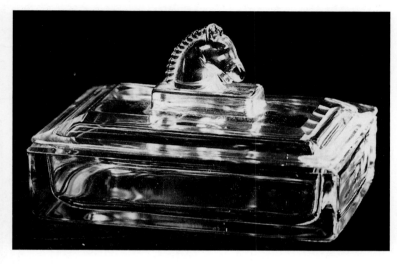

No. 1489½ Puritan king-size cigarette box, horse head cover.

No. 1489 Puritan hexagonal floral bowl and candleblocks.

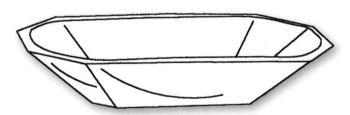

No. 1489 Puritan oblong floral bowl.

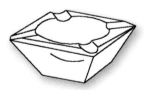

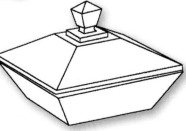

No. 1489 Puritan deep square ashtray and covered candy box.

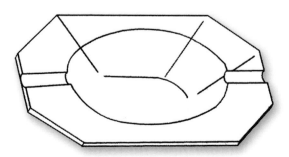

No. 1489 Puritan oblong ashtray.

263

Fern, No. 1495 — original name
Dates: 1937 to 1941+. The candlestick was continued until after 1953.
Colors: Crystal, Zircon. A few rare items in Dawn.

Comments: "Fern is the name of the new shape designed by Walter von Nessen and produced by A. H. Heisey & Co. A new idea is the single-handled motif.... They are decorated with a new etching, and the 'Fern' is available in crystal and Zircon." *China, Glass & Lamps*, July 1937.

Zircon items are very difficult to find. None of the items are marked with the Diamond H. Several pieces from this pattern were redesigned in later years as part of No. 1519 Waverly. The heavy, twisted Waverly optic and beaded edges were added to these pieces which were made only in crystal. For Zircon, add 250% to 500%. For Dawn pieces, add 600%.

Bonbon, handled, 6" $30.00
Bowl, fruit, handled, 13" 55.00
Bowl, oval floral, handled 55.00
Bowl, salad, handled, 11" 45.00
Bowl, sauce..25.00
Candlesticks, 2 light, pr.............................175.00
Cheese & cracker plate with cover, 15"........120.00
Cheese, handled, 6" 30.00
Cream..40.00
Cream, individual..55.00
Dish, jello, 2 handled & footed 55.00
Jelly, handled, 6"..35.00
Mayonnaise or whipped cream, handled 55.00
Mayonnaise, twin, handled...........................55.00
Mint, handled, 6" 30.00
Nappy, 4½"...30.00
Plate, handled, 15".....................................55.00
Plate, mayonnaise, 8" 20.00
Plate, sandwich, 13" 40.00
Plate, torte, handled, 13" or 14" 45.00
Relish, footed, 2 handled, 3 compartment.....55.00
Sugar 40.00
Sugar, individual 55.00
Tid bit, handled, 6".....................................45.00

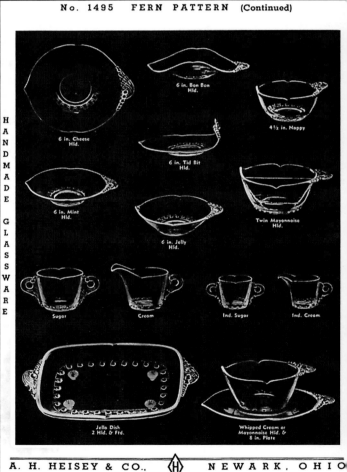

No. 1495 Fern assortment.

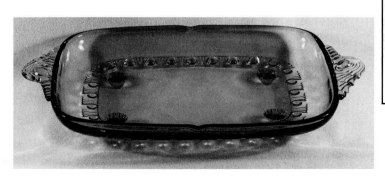

No. 1495 Fern jello dish, Zircon.

Coventry, No. 4090 — original name
Dates: 1937 to 1944. Cordial and sherry until 1947.
Colors: Crystal, Zircon

Comments: A stemware line with blown bowl and pressed stem. This line is not marked with the Diamond H. "Coventry' is the name which A. H. Heisey & Co. have given to their newest stemware shape. The long oval of the bowl is repeated in the design of the pedestal-like stem, giving the goblet a feeling of balance and symmetry. The 'Coventry' is made in full stemware, of course, and in addition to appearing in crystal it is also made in the new 'Zircon' color." *China, Glass & Lamps*, September 1937.

A variation listed in Heisey literature indicates a goblet was made with a Wabash bowl and a Coventry stem and given No. 4005.

Brandy, ¾ oz. $160.00
Claret, 4½ oz. 35.00
Cocktail, 3 oz..28.00
Cordial, 1 oz. 160.00
Finger bowl (#4080)....................................8.00
Goblet, 10 oz..40.00
Goblet, low footed, 10 oz. 40.00
Oyster cocktail, 4½ oz. 20.00
Saucer champagne, 6 oz...............................22.00
Sherbet, 6 oz. 18.00
Sherry, 2 oz. 50.00
Soda, footed, 5 oz. (juice) 25.00
Soda, footed, 12 oz. (ice tea).......................40.00
Wine, 2½ oz..48.00

No. 4090 Coventry goblet, unknown cutting.

No. 4091 Kimberly goblet with No. 1015 Dolly Madison Rose engraving.

Kimberly, No. 4091 — original name
Date: 1937 to 1957, although discontinued during World War II.
Colors: Crystal. Rare in Zircon bowl with Crystal stem and foot.

Comments: Blown bowl, pressed stem. The Diamond H is located at the top of the stem on one of the panels. Made in plain or with saturn optic bowls. Used to complement No. 1488 Kohinoor table accessories. Kimberly is the same as Kohinoor stemware but with a flared bowl.

Claret, 4½ oz........................$25.00
Cocktail, 3 oz. 20.00
Cordial, 1 oz. 70.00
Finger bowl (#3335)................8.00
Goblet, 10 oz. 25.00
Goblet, low foot, 10 oz. 25.00
Oyster cocktail, 4½ oz. (#3542).10.00

Saucer champagne, 5½ oz. ...15.00
Sherbet, 5½ oz......................12.00
Soda, footed, 5 oz. (#4091½, juice) 15.00
Soda, footed, 12 oz. (#4091½, ice tea)..............................15.00
Wine, 2 oz.............................32.00

Kenilworth, Nos. 4092, 4092½ — original name
Date: 1937 to 1941
Color: Crystal

Comments: A stemware line with blown bowl, pressed stem. Marked with the Diamond H on the upper stem just below the bowl. The same as Barbara Fritchie stemware (No. 3416) but with a flared bowl. The cordial, brandy snifter, Rhine wine, brandy, and sherry are the same shapes in both patterns. Made with wide optic.

Brandy, ¾ oz. $95.00
Brandy snifter...200.00
Claret, 4½ oz. 35.00
Cocktail, 3 oz. 20.00
Comport, 5½" 85.00
Cordial, 1 oz..80.00
Finger bowl (#3335) 8.00
Goblet, 10 oz. 35.00
Oyster cocktail, 3 oz. 15.00
Rhine wine, 6 oz. 175.00
Saucer champagne, 5½ oz............................28.00
Sherbet, 5½ oz. 10.00
Sherry, 1½ oz. 70.00
Soda, footed, 5 oz. (#4092½, juice).................20.00
Soda, footed, 12 oz. (#4092½, ice tea)............30.00
Wine, 2 oz. 55.00

No. 4092 Kenilworth goblet with No. 497 Rosalie plate etching.

Decorations Introduced in 1937
Carvings: No. 5017 Sailboat.

Cuttings: No. 887 Southampton, No. 888 Maderia, No. 889 Sheffield, No. 890 Churchill, No. 891 Pembroke, No. 892 Berkeley Square, No. 893 Carlton, No. 894 Brambleberry, No. 895 Waterford, No. 896 Sungate, No. 898 Trafalgar, No. 900 Saratoga, and No. 901 Delft Diamond.

Etchings: No. 1 Short Sailboat silhouette etching, No. 2 Tall Sailboat silhouette etching, No. 3 Motor Boat silhouette etching, No. 481 Lancaster silhouette etching, No. 490 Maytime plate etching, No. 491 Frosty Dawn plate etching/satin, No. 493 Coronation plate etching, No. 494 Swingtime plate etching, No. 495 Polo Player silhouette etching, No. 496 Skier silhouette etching, No. 497 Rosalie plate etching, No. 498 Modern Polo Player silhouette etching, No. 499 Good Morning plate etching, No. 500 Belvedere plate etching, and No. 607 Vicars (satin).

1938:

Boat, No. 1497
Dates: 1938 to 1953
Colors: Crystal

Comments: This floral bowl may be marked or unmarked with the Diamond H. It has a ground base rim. It was available with either a plain edge as shown or with a beaded rim which is an irregular edge that looks like it has cut notches but is completely pressed.

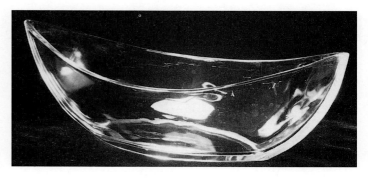

No. 1497 Boat floral bowl.

Bowl, floral, plain rim or beaded rim $25.00

Crystolite, No. 1503 — original name
Dates: 1938 to 1957
Colors: Crystal. Cigarette set in Sahara and Zircon.
Patents: There were many patents on Crystolite items, all listing T. C. Heisey as designer. The candleblock was given No. 114217 on 4-11-1939; the three-part relish No. 114895 on 5-23-1939; the three-light candle No. 115400 on 6-27-1939; the celery No. 155205; the three-part oval relish No. 115497 on 7-4-1939 and the melon candle No. 128373 on 7-22-1941. Horace King was granted patent No. 152804 on 2-22-1949 for the square candleblock.

Comments: When first introcuded in 1937, this pattern was called No. 1496 Mahabar when it was a smoking set made in Sahara and Zircon. According to Fred Bosworth, one of Heisey's salesmen, he was sent to buy a European cigarette set so that Heisey could make a similar one. Almost immediately the name was changed to Rajah and then No. 1503 Crystolite, the name it was known by from then on. This pattern kept the company in business during World War II. Many pieces were used by various companies to make new items, such as candy boxes with metal lids (some with a Crystolite candleblock as a finial), lamps, baskets, and others. The candleblock also became a cigarette lighter with a metal lighter inserted into the candle cup. The pattern also had a cigarette lighter marketed by the company using the salt shaker. Most pieces are marked with the Diamond H. The Imperial Glass Corp. made about 15 pieces in crystal, some of which were marked with the Diamond H.

Ashtray or coaster, round, 3½".....................$7.00	Bowl, 1000 Island dressing, 5", crimped or plain...24.00
Ashtray or coaster, round, 4".........................7.00	Bowl, combination salad & mayonnaise, shell, 11"...200.00
Ashtray, 4" x 6"..75.00	
Ashtray, book match, 5"................................40.00	Bowl, floral, round, 10" 55.00
Ashtray, square, 3½" or 4½" 7.00	Bowl, floral, round, 11½"..............................45.00
Ball vase (#1503½)......................................500.00	Bowl, floral, oval, deep, 13"........................60.00
Basket, 6"..300.00	Bowl, floral, shell, 12" 275.00
Bitter bottle & tube, 4 oz. 110.00	Bowl, floral, touraine, 9"..............................40.00
Bonbon, 2 handled, 7"..................................15.00	Bowl, fruit, 12" 45.00
Bonbon or relish, shell, 7"............................30.00	

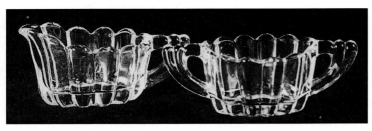

No. 1503 Crystolite individual cream and sugar.

Bowl, gardenia, square, 10"........................125.00
Bowl, gardenia or floral, shallow, 12"............45.00
Bowl, hollandaise sauce (oval) 24.00
Bowl, oval, shallow, 12"..............................50.00
Bowl, salad, round, 10" or 12" 45.00
Bowl, salad, shell, 11" 235.00
Bowl, spring salad, 10"..............................45.00
Breakfast preserve (leaf shape), 5"..............35.00
Candleblocks, 1 light, pr. (round) 35.00
Candleblocks, 1 light, (tall cylinder), pr.
  (#1503¾)...85.00
Candleblocks, melon, 1 light, pr. (#1503½) .100.00
Candleblocks, square, 1 light, pr. (#1503¼) ..65.00
Candleblocks, swirl, 1 light, pr. (#1502) 50.00
Candlesticks with 5" vase, 3 light, pr...........180.00
Candlesticks, 2 light, with bobeches &
  prisms, pr...200.00
Candlesticks, 3 light, pr..............................120.00
Candlesticks, footed, 1 light, 4", pr...............55.00
Candy box & cover, 7" 50.00
Candy box & cover, 3 footed, 6" 55.00
Candy box & cover, shell, 5½" 60.00
Candy box & cover, 3 compartment, 7" 60.00
Candy or jelly, swan, 6½"............................55.00
Celery & olive, 12" 35.00
Celery tray, 12" 35.00
Centerpiece, 11" (garden tray)....................225.00
Cheese & cracker, 2 piece, 14" 35.00
Cherry jar & cover......................................55.00
Chocolate, high footed, 5½"........................30.00
Cigarette box & cover, 4" 25.00
Cigarette box & cover, king size, 4½" 35.00
Cigarette holder, footed 25.00
Cigarette holder, oval..................................20.00
Cigarette holder, round 20.00
Cigarette lighter...75.00
Coaster, 4" 7.00
Coaster or ashtray, shell, 5" 20.00
Cocktail shaker, 1 quart. 300.00
Cologne bottle, 4 oz. 160.00
Comport, deep, footed, 5" 40.00
Conserve, 2 compartment, center handled,
  8" 60.00

Cream (#1503½)..55.00
Cream, oval..25.00
Cream, oval, individual 22.00
Cup, plain edge (#1503½) 12.00
Cup & saucer 20.00
Ice tub 70.00
Jam jar & cover 50.00
Jelly, 1 handle, 5" 25.00
Jelly, 1 handle, 3 compartment 50.00
Jelly, 2 compartment, 2 handled, 6".............18.00
Jelly, 2 handled, 6" 15.00
Jelly, high footed, 5".....................................30.00
Jelly, oval, 4 footed, 5½" 65.00
Jug, swan (#1503½ or #1556) 800.00
Lamp, electric, 1 light 150.00
Lamp, hurricane, square, 2 piece, 1 light,
  10"..220.00
Lamp, hurricane, round, 2 piece, 1 light 220.00
Mayonnaise, oval, handled, 6"......................30.00
Mayonnaise, shell, 3 footed, 5½" 40.00
Mayonnaise, 2 compartment 50.00
Mustard & cover..35.00
Nappy, 4½" or 5½"..8.00
Nappy, 8" 25.00
Nappy, 3 footed, 7" 35.00
Nut dish, handled (leaf shape), 3"..................25.00
Nut dish, individual swan, 2"..........................20.00
Oil bottle & stopper, 3 oz. 40.00
Pickle, leaf, 9" 45.00
Pickle, oval, 6" 15.00
Plate, cheese, oval, 2 handled, 8"...............18.00
Plate, coupe, 7½"...25.00
Plate, demi-torte, shell, 10½"......................180.00
Plate, dinner, 10½".....................................125.00
Plate, oval, 8"..15.00
Plate, salad, 7" or 8½" 15.00
Plate, sandwich, 12".....................................20.00
Plate, sandwich, 14".....................................25.00
Plate, shell, 7"..50.00
Plate, snack, 2 handled, 7" 20.00

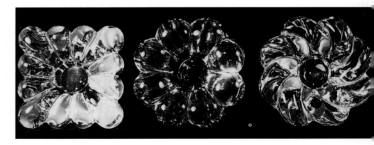

Crystolite candleblocks: No. 1503¼ square, No. 150?
round, No. 1502 swirl.

Plate, thousand island dressing, 7".............15.00
Plate, torte, 11"..............................20.00
Plate, torte, 13" or 14".......................25.00
Plate, torte, shell, 13".......................225.00
Praline, shell, 7".............................55.00
Preserve & cover, 2 handled, 6"................40.00
Preserve dish, oval, 7"........................40.00
Puff box & cover, 4¾"..........................85.00
Punch bowl, 7½ qt..............................90.00
Punch bowl plate, 20"..........................65.00
Punch or custard cup...........................8.00
Relish, 3 compartment, 8" (oblong).............35.00
Relish, 3 compartment, oval, 12" or 13"
   (#1503½)....................................35.00
Relish, 5 compartment, shell, 13"..............200.00
Relish, clover leaf, 4 compartment, 9".........45.00
Relish, round, 5 compartment, 10"..............45.00
Relish, utility, 4 compartment.................45.00
Rye bottle & stopper, 1 quart..................300.00
Salt & pepper, pr..............................40.00
Salt & pepper, pr. (#1503½ — straight sides) .90.00
Salver, cake, footed, 11"......................250.00
Sugar (#1503½).................................50.00
Sugar, oval....................................25.00
Sugar, oval, individual........................22.00
Syrup bottle with drip cut top.................110.00
Thousand Island dressing bowl, round, 5" ...25.00
Tray, for individual sugar & cream, 5½"........28.00
Tray, oval, 13"................................40.00
Tumbler, 10 oz.................................22.00

No. 1503 Crystolite shell sandwich plate.

Urn, flower, 7"................................60.00
Vase, footed, regular or flared, 6"............32.00
Vase, footed, regular or flared, 9"............165.00
Vase, short stem flower, 3"....................40.00
Vase, swing, footed, 10" to 12"................225.00
Vase, swing, footed, 12" to 15"................260.00
Vase, swing, footed, 15" to 18"................325.00
Vase, swing, footed, 18" to 21"................400.00

No. 1503 Crystolite shell bonbon or relish.

No. 1503 Crystolite oval jelly, four footed — hard to find.

● The simple lines of Heisey's celebrated CRYSTOLITE Pattern cause your eye to linger fondly on it and your touch thrills to its fine texture. The uniformity of luster and sheen in this serviceable, beautifully styled pattern make it an outstanding favorite, everywhere. It is deftly moulded and finished by expert hands to reflect lights in sparkling, shimmering beauty.

CRYSTOLITE is made in more than 200 different pieces for your selection... to set a shining table, to brighten your buffet or an occasional table.

See CRYSTOLITE in leading stores. It's open stock. Write for free, complete, illustrated folder.

A. H. HEISEY & CO., NEWARK, OHIO

No. 1503 Crystolite items. Note especially the melon candleblocks and the No. 5003 footed jelly — both very difficult to find.

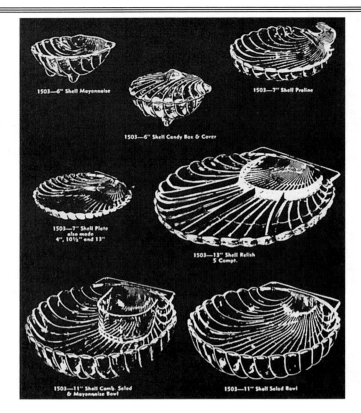

No. 1503 Crystolite shell items. Top: mayonnaise, candy box & cover, praline. Middle: plate, five-compartment relish. Bottom: combination salad & mayonnaise bowl, salad bowl.

No. 1503 Crystolite. Top: oval utility tray, gardenia bowl. Middle: punch bowl, salver. Bottom: basket, buffet plate.

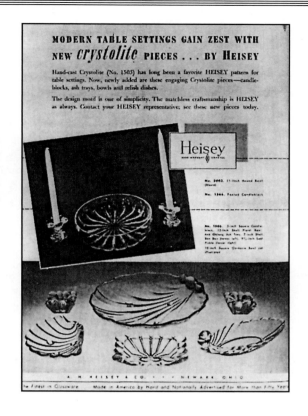

Top: No. 5003 Crystolite blown floral bowl and No. 1566 candleblocks. Bottom: No. 1503¼ Crystolite square candleblocks, 12" shell floral bowl, shell bonbon, 4"x 6" oblong ashtray, and leaf pickle, 1947 ad.

Bowl, floral, 11"	$600.00+
Claret, 3½ oz.	35.00
Cocktail, 3½ oz.	35.00
Comport, 5"	465.00
Cordial, 1 oz.	130.00
Finger bowl	15.00
Goblet, 10 oz.	30.00
Ice tea, footed, 12 oz.	25.00
Jelly, footed	500.00
Jug, ice lip, ½ gallon	145.00
Juice, footed, 5 oz.	25.00
Oyster cocktail, 3½ oz.	20.00
Sherbet or saucer champagne, 6 oz.	15.00
Soda, regular, 5 oz. (juice)	15.00
Soda, regular, 12 oz. (ice tea)	25.00
Tumbler, footed, 10 oz.	25.00
Tumbler, regular, 10 oz.	25.00

No. 5003 Crystolite blownware
Blown bowl, pressed stem, made in wide optic. The Diamond H is located at the bottom of the stem near the foot when present. Compare with No. 5077 Legionnaire.

No. 5003 Crystolite ice tea with variant of Arcadia cutting.

No. 1504 Regency cologne.

Regency, No. 1504 — original name
Date: 1938 to 1943+
Color: Crystal

Comments: When advertised, the description was sometimes called Wheat. This is appropriate when looking at the pieces and seeing the wrapped "twine" around the pieces, making a "bundle" or sheaf of wheat. It is a limited pattern with the candlesticks and puff box being pressed and the salt and cologne being blown.

Candleblocks, 1 light, pr. $135.00
Candlesticks, 2 light, pr. 140.00
Cologne & stopper 225.00
Puff box & cover 135.00
Salt & pepper, pr. 200.00

No. 1504 Regency two-light candlestick with No. 341 Old Williamsburg epergnette

Whirlpool, No. 1506 — original name
Date: 1938 to 1957
Colors: Crystal, Zircon. Other colors such as ruby, verde green, blue, and more were made by Imperial Glass Corp. after 1957.
Patents: T. C. Heisey was granted patent No. 114712 on 5-9-1939 for the tumbler. He was also granted the following patents: No. 116030 on 8-8-1939 for the two-handled jelly; No. 115818 on 7-18-1939 for the four-part relish, and No. 115819 on 7-18-1939 for the goblet. The mayonnaise was patented on 3-13-1951 and given No. 162411 and granted to T. C. Heisey.

Comments: All pressed, including stemware. Many items are marked with the Diamond H. Heisey renamed the pattern Provincial in later years when they again promoted the pattern. Add 400% to 500% for pieces in Zircon (blue-green). For Imperial colors add 15% to crystal prices.

Ashtray, square...$10.00
Bonbon, 2 handled, 7" 15.00

Bowl, beverage, 5 quart (punch bowl) 120.00
Bowl, flared, 12"..35.00

Bowl, footed flower, rolled edge, 13".............40.00
Bowl, gardenia, 13" 40.00
Bowl, nasturtium...22.00
Bowl, orange, 15" 40.00
Bowl, oval floral, deep, 4 footed, 12"............70.00
Bowl, salad, 10"...35.00
Bowl, shallow oval, 4 footed, 13" 75.00
Bowl, thousand island 15.00
Butter & cover, ¼ lb......................................50.00
Candleblock, 3", pr.......................................70.00
Candlestick, 3 light, pr..................................110.00
Candy box & cover, footed, 5½".....................75.00
Celery tray, 13"..20.00
Cigarette box & cover 45.00
Coaster, 4" 10.00
Cocktail, 3½ oz. 12.00
Cream, footed...20.00
Cream, individual..45.00
Custard or punch cup 12.00
Goblet, 10 oz. 18.00
Ice tea, 13 oz. 22.00
Jelly, 2 handled, 5" 20.00
Jelly, 2 handled, 2 compartment 20.00
Juice, 5 oz..18.00
Juice, footed, 5 oz. 20.00
Mayonnaise, 3 handled..................................25.00
Nappy, 4½" or 5½"...15.00
Nut or jelly, individual....................................22.00
Oil bottle & stopper 95.00
Oyster cocktail, 3½ oz....................................12.00

Plate, 7" or 8" 11.00
Plate, buffet, 18" (also for punch bowl)...........75.00
Plate, cheese, footed, 8"................................15.00
Plate, mayonnaise, 7" 10.00
Plate, sandwich, 14" 27.00
Plate, snack, 7"..12.00
Plate, torte, 14" 27.00
Relish, 4 compartment, 10"............................28.00
Salt & pepper, pr. 30.00
Salver, footed, 15"...65.00
Saucer champagne or sherbet, 5 oz. 12.00
Soda, footed, 12 oz. (iced tea) 24.00
Sugar, footed 20.00
Sugar, individual 45.00
Tray, for individual cream & sugar.................35.00
Tumbler, footed, 9 oz.....................................24.00
Tumbler, regular, 8 oz. 20.00
Vase, pansy, 4" 18.00
Vase, sweet pea, 6".22.00
Vase, violet, 3¼"......20.00
Wine, 2½ oz. 18.00

No. 1506 Whirlpool goblet.

No. 1506 Whirlpool individual cream and sugar.

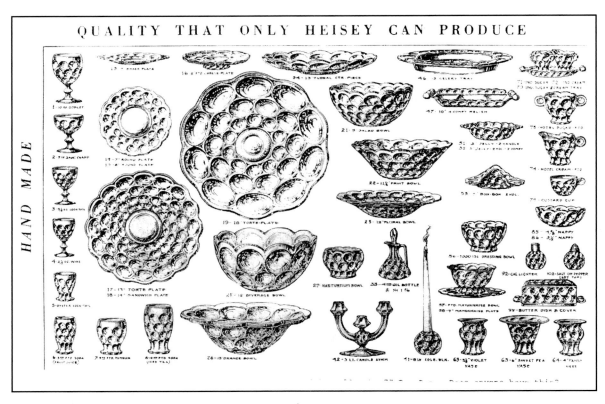

QUALITY THAT ONLY HEISEY CAN PRODUCE

No. 1506 Whirlpool items.

No. 1508 card case with 1939 World's Fair etching.

No. 1508
Date: 1938 to 1944
Color: Crystal only

Comments: "A novelty that is distinctly usable is...a card case holder in heavy crystal, just brought out by A. H. Heisey & Co. The holder is large enough for two decks of cards, and the two identical halves are made to serve as ashtrays, equipped with four snuffers and slots for cigarettes." *China, Glass & Lamps*, August 1938. The card case is not marked with the Diamond H.

Card case $100.00

Queen Ann, No. 1509 — original name
Date: 1938 to 1957
Color: Crystal only

Comments: "The 'Queen Ann' has a perpendicular optic and a fan-shaped motif at the edges. The line includes tableware and decorative pieces." *China, Glass & Lamps,* August 1938.

Queen Ann was an updated pattern developed from some old No. 1401 Empress molds. However, several pieces were newly designed and were not originally in the Empress line. Also, many of the Empress molds did not become part of Queen Ann. Many collectors become confused when trying to distinguish between the two patterns. This is made easier when remembering that items in Queen Ann were made only in crystal. Most pieces of Queen Ann also have an interior wide, swirl optic which is easily felt. Empress pieces have no optic and are smooth on the interior. Many pieces also have the dolphin feet of the Empress pieces. These are designated as d. f. in the following list. Most items are marked with the Diamond H. The dolphin footed 10" floral bowl in sunshine yellow made by Imperial Glass Corp. is often confused with Heisey.

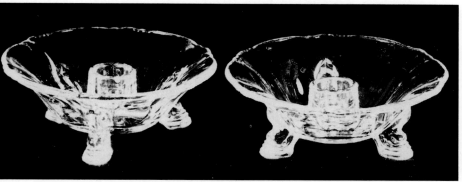

No. 1509 Queen Ann dolphin footed nappy candlesticks.

Bowl, combination dressing, 7"	$40.00
Bowl, flared, 8½"	38.00
Bowl, floral, d.f., 8½"	50.00
Bowl, floral, d.f., 11"	58.00
Bowl, floral, 12½"	58.00
Bowl, floral, 2 handled, footed, 8½"	42.00
Bowl, gardenia, 9"	40.00
Bowl, lily, 7"	40.00
Bowl, sauce, d.f., 7½"	55.00
Bowl, sunburst, 9"	40.00
Bowl, sunburst floral, 10"	40.00
Bowl, swing, 13"	60.00
Candelabra & prisms, 1 light, 7½", pr.	250.00
Candlesticks, footed, 2 handled (nappy), pr.	75.00
Candlesticks, pr., d. f. (nappy), pr.	100.00
Candlesticks, pr., d. f. (nut dish), pr.	155.00
Cheese & cracker, 2 piece	50.00
Celery tray, 13"	25.00

Comport, oval, 7"	45.00
Cream, d. f.	25.00
Cream, individual	28.00
Cream soup	28.00
Cup & saucer	35.00
Grapefruit, 6"	25.00
Ice cube bucket, d. f.	85.00
Jelly, footed, 2 handled, 6"	22.00
Jug, 3 pint, d. f.	125.00
Lemon & cover, dolphin finial, 6½"	50.00
Mayonnaise, d. f., 5½"	32.00
Mint, d. f., 5½"	20.00
Mint, footed, 6"	20.00
Mint, footed, 8"	50.00
Mustard & cover	70.00
Nappy, 4½"	10.00
Nappy, 8"	30.00
Oil bottle & stopper	60.00
Pickle & olive, 13"	20.00
Plate, round, 4½"	12.00
Plate, round or square, 6" or 7"	12.00
Plate, round or square, 8"	15.00
Plate, round, 10½"	110.00
Plate, demi-torte, 11"	35.00
Plate, sandwich, 10"	35.00
Plate, sandwich, 2 handled, round or square, 12"	32.00
Plate, sandwich, center handled, 12"	32.00
Plate, service, 10½"	110.00
Plate, snack rack & center, 16"	55.00
Plate, torte, 15" (social hour tray)	55.00
Relish, 3 compartment, 11" (5 o'clock)	35.00
Relish, triplex, 7"	28.00

Salad dressing, combination (2 part), 7".........35.00
Salt & pepper, pr. 50.00
Sugar, d. f. 25.00
Sugar, individual 28.00
Tray, for individual cream & sugar.................28.00

Detail of No. 497 Rosalie etching.

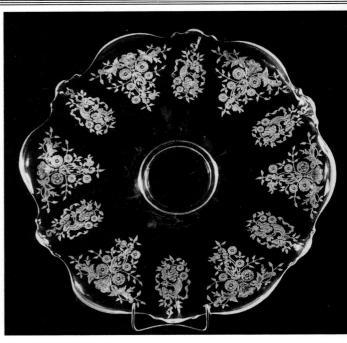

No. 1509 Queen Ann torte plate with No. 497 Rosalie plate etching.

No. 1509 Queen Ann dolphin footed cream and sugar with No. 921 Danish Princess cutting.

No. 5009 Queen Ann stemware
Blown bowl, pressed stem. Not marked with the Diamond H. Hard to find.

Claret, 4 oz..$22.00
Cocktail, 3½ oz. 18.00
Finger bowl (#3309) 8.00
Goblet, short or tall stem, 10 oz. 25.00
Oyster cocktail, 4 oz...................................10.00
Saucer champagne, 6 oz. 22.00
Soda, footed, 5 oz. (juice)............................12.00
Soda, footed, 8 oz. (tumbler) 15.00
Soda, footed, 12 oz. (ice tea)......................18.00
Wine, 2½ oz..22.00

No. 5009 Queen Ann goblet.

Sunflower, No. 7000
Date: 1938
Color: Crystal

Comments: A short pattern in which most pieces are marked with the Diamond H. Probably made as a specially priced pattern to introduce Heisey glass to customers. The motif is composed of large diamonds.

No. 7000 Sunflower tumbler.

Bowl, floral, 12".....................................$45.00
Bowl, gardenia, 13½"............................45.00
Bowl, salad, 10"......................................45.00
Butter & cover.......................................150.00
Candlesticks, 1 light, pr. 70.00
Cream..50.00
Plate, salad, 7¼"....................................20.00
Plate, 8"...20.00
Plate, torte, 15".....................................65.00
Relish, 3 compartment, 8"......................70.00
Sugar 50.00
Tumbler 40.00

Decorations Introduced in 1938
Cuttings: No. 902 Orlando, No. 903 Zeuse, No. 904 Rialto, No. 905 Rosemont, No. 906 Windemere, No. 907 Cheerio, No. 908 Rondo, No. 909 Champlain, No. 910 Copperfield, No. 911 Lyric, No. 912 Sabrina, No. 913 Everglade, No. 914 Royal Sensation, No. 915 Amarillo, No. 917 Sarasota, and No. 918 Winston.

Etchings: No. 501 Belle Le Rose plate etching.

1939:

No. 11 Punch ladle
Date: Ca. 1939
Color: Crystal

Comments: A blown ladle with applied handle. Not marked with the Diamond H. This ladle has a deep bowl and two side-pouring spouts. The bottom of the bowl is ground and polished.

Punch ladle $135.00

No. 11 punch ladle.

Old Williamsburg, No. 341 — original name

Dates: 1939 to 1957. Made until the factory closed in 1957 and then continued by Imperial Glass and later by Indiana Glass. The pattern first appeared in the early 1900s and was called Puritan.

Colors: Crystal. Rare pieces in Stiegel Blue, Dawn (gray), Alexandrite, Amber, Limelight. All other colors were made by Imperial Glass Corp. after 1957.

Patents: The Old Williamsburg epergnette candle was granted No. 153506 on 4-26-1949 to A. & M. Dillon. The footed epergne candleholder was patented by T. C. Heisey on 11-22-1949 and granted No. 156097.

Comments: All pressed. Most items marked with the Diamond H. Originally this stem line was No. 373 introduced by Heisey about 1912. Later it replaced the original No. 341 stem line and became Old Williamsburg. Pieces were also borrowed from earlier colonial patterns and made part of the Old Williamsburg pattern. T. Clarence Heisey was involved in the restoration of the glass house at Williamsburg, Virginia, during this time. This probably was the origin of the Old Williamsburg name. Numbers in brackets following piece entries refer to numbers in the catalog pages. Many pieces of Old Williamsburg were continued by Imperial Glass after 1957. The Heisey/Imperial Old Williamsburg molds are owned by Indiana Glass Co. (Lancaster-Colony).

No. 341 Old Williamsburg platter, cutting by Krall studios.

Bowl, fruit, flared, footed, 9½" [36] $90.00
Bowl, gardenia, footed, 10" [35] 75.00
Candleholder, epergne, footed, pr., 5½" [49].160.00
Celery tray, 9" 22.00
Celery tray, 13" [43]......................................25.00
Cheese & cracker, 2 piece, 11½" 50.00
Cheese & cracker, 2 piece, 13" [28] 60.00
Cheese, footed, 5½" 20.00
Claret, 4½ oz. [5]..20.00

Cocktail, 3 oz. [6]...18.00
Comport, cupped or flared, 4½" (#353) [29] ...15.00
Comport, tall footed, 5½" 20.00
Cream (#300 [23], #341 [21] or #352) 25.00
Cream, individual, 2¼ oz. (#300) 28.00
Cup & saucer, tea [34]....................................80.00
Decanter & stopper, 1 pint (#367) 140.00
Decanter & stopper, 1 quart (#367) [48]........185.00
Decanter, individual......................................32.00
Dessert or sauce dish (nappy), 3½", 4", or 4½"...8.00
Dessert or sauce dish (nappy), 6" or 7" [42] ...15.00
Dessert or sauce dish (nappy), 8" or 9" 20.00
Dessert, plain edge (nappy), 4½" or 5½"
   (#352) [40], shallow [41] 10.00
Dessert, plain edge (nappy), 7½" (#352).........15.00
Epergnette candleholders, 5½" pr. 42.00
Epergnette, 5½", pr. 37.00
Epergnion bobeche with prisms, 5½", pr. ** ..50.00
Epergnion candleholder, 5½", pr. 42.00
Finger bowl, 4½" (#341 [15] or #341½)............9.00
Goblet, 9 oz. (#373) [1]..................................22.00
Goblet, low footed [2] 22.00
Grapefruit or cereal, 6½" [39]........................15.00
Ice tea, footed, 12 oz. (#341 [10] or #300
   footed [11]) 20.00
Ice tea, footed, 14 oz. (#373) 22.00
Jelly, handled, 5" [38] 24.00
Jug, ice lip, 3 pint.......................................130.00
Jug, squat, stuck handle, ½ gallon (#341½)..160.00
Jug, squat, stuck handle, 1 pint (#341½)......185.00
Jug, squat, stuck handle, 1 quart (#341½) [19]..175.00
Jug, squat, stuck handle, 3 pint (#341½)......130.00

Juice, footed, 5 oz. (#300 [12] or #341 [9]) 15.00
Mayonnaise, 4½" [37]..................................25.00
Mustard & cover 35.00
Nappy, 3½", 4" or 4½"...............................10.00
Nappy, 6" or 7"..15.00
Nappy, 8" or 9"..20.00
Oil bottle & stopper, 4 oz. [17].....................25.00
Oyster cocktail [7] 9.00
Pickle, 6"...15.00
Plate, buffet, 19" (also punch bowl
  underplate) [33]......................................95.00
Plate, coupe, 7" or 8" [18] 30.00
Plate, coupe, 10" [26]..................................60.00
Plate, mayonnaise.....................................15.00
Plate, party (torte), star ground bottom, 11½".55.00
Plate, party (torte), star ground bottom, 13"
  [25] 60.00
Plate, sandwich, star ground bottom, 11½" ...55.00
Plate, sandwich, star ground bottom, 13" [24]..60.00
Plate, star ground bottom, 6" (#1150) 12.00
Plate, star ground bottom, 7" or 8" (#1150) 15.00
Platter, oval...85.00
Punch bowl & foot, straight, 7 quart * [32] ...175.00
Punch or custard cup, 4½ oz. [31] 12.00
Relish, 3 compartment, oval, 10" [45]............55.00
Relish, 5 compartment, 13½" (#352) [44] 110.00
Relish, oval (nappy), 8" [46] 40.00
Relish, oval, 6½" 32.00
Salt & pepper, #2, pr. [16] 40.00
Salver, cake, 11" [27] 90.00
Saucer champagne or tall sherbet, 5 oz.
  (#373) [3]...15.00
Sherbet, low, 4½ oz. (#373) [4].......................9.00
Sugar, individual, 2¼ oz. (#300) 28.00

Sugar, with (#300 [22] or #352) or without
  handles (#341) [20] 25.00
Toddy 12.00
Tray, round, 10" (#353) [47]...........................50.00
Tumbler, 8 oz. (#341 [13] or #341½)..............20.00
Tumbler, footed, 8 oz. [14]............................35.00
Wine, 2 oz. (#373) [8] 20.00

* also sold without foot
** also available threaded to fit No. 300 and No.
   301 candelabra arms. All came with rubber
   fitters

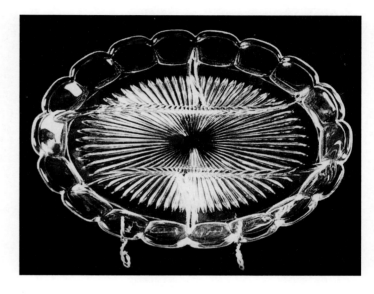

No. 341 Old Williamsburg five-compartment oval relish.

No. 341 Old Williamsburg footed tumbler — hard to find.

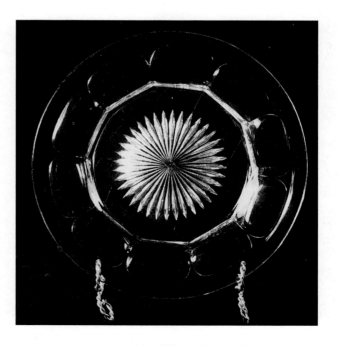

No. 341 Old Williamsburg plate.

No. 341 Old Williamsburg items.

No. 341 Old Williamsburg items.

Toujours, No. 1511 — original name
Dates: 1939 to 1953. Apple marmalade continued to 1955.
Color: Crystal only

Comments: A short tableware line. Many items are marked with the Diamond H, but some are not. The Heisey museum reproduced the apple marmalade in green.

Bowl, floral, 13"	$45.00
Bowl, oval floral, 12"	40.00
Bowl, salad, 10"	35.00
Candlesticks, 2 light, pr.	185.00
Celery, 12"	20.00
Centerpiece, vase & prisms	195.00
Comport, 7½"	32.00
Cream	22.00
Cream, individual	25.00
Floral plateau, 13"	40.00
Marmalade & cover (apple)	95.00
Mayonnaise, footed	30.00
Plate, 7" or 8"	8.00
Plate, sandwich, 15"	35.00
Plate, torte, 14"	30.00
Sugar	22.00

No. 1511 Toujours apple marmalade.

Sugar, individual	30.00
Vase, footed, 5½"	30.00

No. 1511 Toujours assortment.

Chanticleer, No. 1557 — original name
Date: 1939 to 1948
Color: Crystal only

Comments: Ground and polished bottom. While the number is out of sequence for most other items, it appears that during World War II development of designs went forward with a few new items brought into the line while many others were held back until materials were available.
Also sometimes called the Rooster vase.

Vase, chanticleer $125.00

No. 1557 Chanticleer vase.

No. 2355 Clover Leaf soda.

Base of soda showing squared bottom.

Clover Leaf, No. 2355 — original name
Date: 1939 to 1944
Color: Crystal

Comments: A blown soda line made up of various standard sodas, but made with an extra sham and hand-tooled four crimp base — a clover leaf shape. Bases are ground and polished. Hard to find today and not marked with the Diamond H. Numbers following the listings indicate the original item from which the Clover Leaf piece was made.

Bar, 2½ oz. (#2052)	$90.00		Soda, 10 oz. (#2351)	60.00
Old fashion, 8 oz. (#2351)	45.00		Soda, 13 oz. (#2351)	70.00
Soda, 5 oz. (#2351)	40.00		Soda, 16 oz. (#2351)	90.00
Soda, 6 oz. (#2401)	40.00		Tumbler, 10 oz. (#2930)	65.00
Soda, 8 oz. (#2351)	50.00		Vase, 9" (#4057)	150.00

Symphone, No. 5010 — original name
Date: 1939 to 1957
Color: Crystal

Comments: Blown bowl, pressed stem. Not marked with the Diamond H.

Claret, 4 oz.	$22.00
Cocktail, 3½ oz.	20.00
Comport, 5½"	68.00
Cordial, 1 oz.	80.00
Finger bowl	8.00
Goblet, 9 oz.	28.00
Goblet, low foot, 9 oz,	26.00
Oyster cocktail, 4½ oz.	9.00
Saucer champagne, 6 oz.	15.00
Sherbet, 6 oz.	10.00
Soda, footed, 5 oz. (juice)	10.00
Soda, footed, 12 oz. (ice tea)	15.00
Wine, 2½ oz.	35.00

No. 5010 Symphone pattern folder with No. 503 Minuet double plate etching.

When there's music in your heart, let MINUET accent those shining hours you want to remember forever. Inspired by romantic bygone days of old world elegance, this exquisite Heisey pattern of double-etched, hand-blown lead crystal has won the hearts of hostesses everywhere. MINUET is available in a complete line of stemware and accessory pieces.

Below—Stemware grouping of Footed Iced Tea, Saucer Champagne (with 8" Salad Plate), Goblet, Claret, Wine, Cocktail.

Heisey A. H. HEISEY & CO., NEWARK, OHIO
THE FINEST IN GLASSWARE, MADE IN AMERICA BY HAND

Yorktown, No. 5011 — original name
Date: 1939 to 1944
Color: Crystal only

Comments: A stem line with blown bowl, pressed stem. Marked with the Diamond H on the upper stem just below the bowl. Yorktown has a double sham, making the pieces quite heavy. Compare with No. 5024 Oxford stemware which does not have a sham.

No. 5011 Yorktown goblet with No. 925 Huguenot cutting, cordial.

Claret, 3½ oz. $22.00
Cocktail, 3½ oz......................................18.00
Cordial, 1 oz..50.00
Cordial, tall stem, 1 oz. 60.00
Goblet, 10 oz. 25.00
Liquor, footed, 1 oz................................50.00
Oyster cocktail, 3½ oz. 10.00
Saucer champagne, 6 oz. 15.00
Soda, footed, 5 oz. (juice).......................15.00
Soda, footed, 12 oz. (ice tea)..................20.00
Wine, 2½ oz. 22.00

No. 5012 Urn vase and bud vase.

Urn, No. 5012
Date: 1939 to 1957
Colors: Crystal. The bud vases were available with Sultana bases for a very short time.

Comments: This line consists of several classic forms of vases, a floral bowl, and a cigarette holder. The pieces are blown with pressed bases.

Bowl, floral $60.00
Cigarette holder 25.00
Vase, footed, 7" 55.00
Vase, footed, 9" 65.00
Vase, square footed, bud, 8" 40.00
Vase, square footed, bud, 10" 50.00

Shasta, No. 5013 — original name
Date: 1939 to 1941
Color: Crystal only

Comments: A stemware line with blown bowl, pressed stem. Not marked with the Diamond H. A similar stem was imported from Europe in the 1970s or 1980s in lead crystal which looks somewhat like Shasta.

Claret, 4 oz. $22.00	Saucer champagne, 6 oz. 15.00
Cocktail 18.00	Sherbet, 6 oz. 10.00
Comport, 5" 45.00	Soda, footed, 5 oz. 15.00
Cordial, 1 oz. 80.00	Soda, footed, 12 oz. 20.00
Goblet, 10 oz. 24.00	Wine, 2½ oz. 22.00
Oyster cocktail, 4 oz. 9.00	

No. 5013 Shasta stemware.

Decorations Introduced in 1939
Carvings: No. 5020 Lily

Cuttings: No. 844½ Cromwell, No. 919 Laurel Wreath, No. 920 Gray Laurel Wreath, No. 921 Danish Princess, No. 922 Calgary, No. 924 Daisy, No. 925 Huguenot, No. 926 George VI, No. 927 Powhattan, No. 928 Legionnaire, No. 929 Ticonderoga, No. 930 Narragansett, No. 931 Plantagenet, No. 932 Coreopsis, No. 933 Fan, and No. 934 Olive.

Etchings: No. 502 Crinoline plate etching and No. 503 Minuet double plate etching.

1940:

Clock
Date: 1940
Color: Crystal

Comments: This Heisey clock was designed for a private firm who contracted with Heisey for the glass component. The blueprint for the clock was drawn in 1940 by a Pittsburgh firm. It has 14 panels (not 12!) of geometric pattern around the face. It is not marked with the Diamond H. The small boudoir type clock is fitted into the middle of the clock. The entire clock is 5½" in diameter.

Clock .... $1,500.00+

Heisey clock.

Miter, No. 1518
Date: Ca. 1940 to 1944
Color: Crystal

Comments: Also used as a lamp base. Heisey may have tried to make this as a bowl and underplate according to an original mold list, but these never were listed in price lists or catalogs. Sometimes the pattern is cut all over. Not marked with the Diamond H.

Vase $45.00

No. 1518 Miter vase.

Waverly, No. 1519 — original name
Date: 1940 to 1957
Colors: Clear. Limited items in light amber.
Patents: T. C. Heisey was granted several patents on Waverly as follows: footed oval comport No. 156508 on 1-17-1950; center-handled sandwich plate No. 156508 on 12-29-1949; seahorse handled tall covered candy No. 157954 on 4-4-1950; Waverly lid on Lariat candy base, No. 156883 on 1-17-1950; chocolate box, No. 156884 on 1-17-1950; ice tub, No. 156885 on 1-17-1950; torte plate, No. 160860 on 11-14-1950; goblet, No. 159730 on 8-15-1950; fan vase, No. 160385 on 10-19-1950; two compartment mayonnaise, No. 162412 on 3-13-1951; cruet, No. 160386 on 10-10-1950; oval bowl from Fern pattern, No. 161179 on 12-12-1950; and vase, No. 163602 on 6-12-1951.

Comments: When first introduced this pattern was called Oceanic, but soon the name was changed to Waverly. Waverly pressed ware was used for many Heisey decorations. Horace King was the Heisey designer who developed Waverly with plumes, waves, and sea motifs. Most items are marked with the Diamond H. "It (Orchid) decorates the swirling Oceanic Pattern, a Heisey pattern which wins shoppers' instant acclaim and gives an air of 'just rightness.'" *Crockery & Glass Journal*, March 1941.

Imperial Glass Corp. continued some Waverly in a limited number of pieces. Imperial also reproduced the Lion covered trinket box in amber with also a few in crystal. Candy boxes were made in caramel slag and a few other Imperial colors. These are marked with the Diamond H and can cause confusion. The Heisey museum reproduced the seahorse handled candy jar in green and a cranberry color.

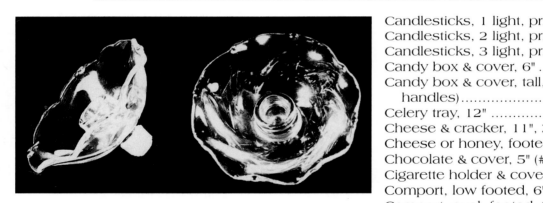

No. 1519 Waverly epergnettes.

Bowl, crimped, 10" or 12" $28.00
Bowl, dressing, oval, 2 compartment, 6½" ...24.00
Bowl, floral, 13" 28.00
Bowl, floral, 3 sea horse feet, 11" 65.00
Bowl, fruit or salad, footed, 9" 55.00
Bowl, gardenia, 10" or 13" 28.00
Bowl, oval, 11" (from Fern pattern) 65.00
Bowl, salad, 7" 38.00
Bowl, salad, 9" 38.00
Bowl, salad, footed, 9" 75.00
Butter dish & cover, square, 6" 60.00

Candlesticks, 1 light, pr. 145.00
Candlesticks, 2 light, pr. 68.00
Candlesticks, 3 light, pr. 80.00
Candy box & cover, 6" 45.00
Candy box & cover, tall, footed, 5" (seahorse handles) 55.00
Celery tray, 12" 18.00
Cheese & cracker, 11", 2 piece 38.00
Cheese or honey, footed 22.00
Chocolate & cover, 5" (#1559) 45.00
Cigarette holder & cover (seahorse handles).90.00
Comport, low footed, 6" 22.00
Comport, oval, footed, 7" 25.00
Cream, footed 25.00
Cream, individual, footed 28.00
Cup & saucer 35.00
Dish & cover, lemon, oval, 6" 40.00
Epergnette candleholder, 5" 20.00
Epergnette candleholder, cupped, 6½" 20.00
Epergnette candleholder, deep, 6" 20.00
Fruit centerpiece, 13" (candleholder center) * .150.00
Gardenia centerpiece, 13" (candleholder center) * 150.00
Ice bowl, 2 handled, 6½" 60.00
Jelly, footed, 6½" 20.00
Mayonnaise, 1 handle, 5½" (from Fern pattern) ..35.00

Mayonnaise, 1 handle, divided, 5½" (from
    Fern pattern) 35.00
Mayonnaise, footed, 5½"...............................24.00
Oil & stopper, footed, 3 oz. 85.00
Plate, demi-torte, 11".....................................35.00
Plate, dinner, 10½" 100.00
Plate, mayonnaise, 7" 10.00
Plate, salad, 7" or 8"......................................10.00
Plate, sandwich, 11" 35.00
Plate, sandwich, 14" 40.00
Plate, sandwich, center handled, 14"...........50.00
Plate, torte, 14" 40.00
Relish, oblong, 3 compartment, 11" 20.00
Relish, round, 3 compartment, 7" 24.00
Relish, round, 4 compartment, 9" 24.00

Salt & pepper, footed, pr 50.00
Salt & pepper, low, pr. 60.00
Salver, footed, 13½" 65.00
Sugar, footed 25.00
Sugar, individual, footed 28.00
Tray, for individual cream & sugar................25.00
Trinket box & cover, oval, 6½" (lion finial) ....700.00+
Vase, fan, footed, 7" 25.00
Vase, footed, 7" 25.00
Vase, violet, 3½" 30.00

* These centerpieces were also sold with either
No. 1519 epergnettes, No. 4233 6" vases, or No.
5013 5" vases in the candleholder.

No. 1519 Waverly two-light candlestick.

No. 1519 Waverly sugar with No. 507
Orchid plate etching.

No. 1519 Waverly salad plate with No. 965 Narcissus cutting.

No. 1519 Waverly 11" oval bowl with No. 980 Moonglo cutting, made from the old No. 1495 Fern mold.

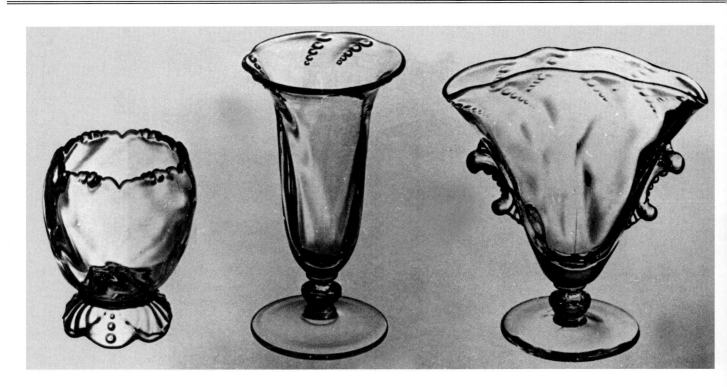

No. 1519 Waverly violet vase, footed vase, and fan vase.

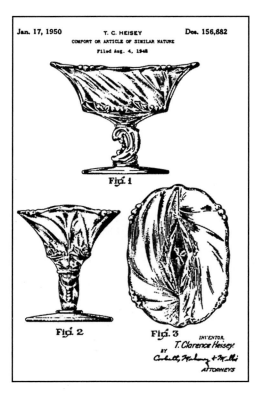

Patent drawing for No. 1519 Waverly
oval comport.

No. 5019 Waverly
blown stemware
Made from 1949 to 1957.
Blown bowl, pressed
stem. When marked with
the Diamond H, it will be
on the lower stem below
the wave.

Claret, 4 oz. $18.00
Cocktail, 3½ oz...............15.00
Cordial, 1 oz. 70.00
Goblet, 10 oz. 20.00
Ice tea, footed, 13 oz. 18.00
Juice, footed, 5 oz...........18.00
Oyster cocktail, 4 oz. 15.00
Sherbet or saucer
    champagne, 5½ oz. 15.00
Wine, 3 oz. 18.00

No. 5019 Waverly goblet with
No. 9015 English Ivy etching.

No. 4036½
Date: 1940 to 1957
Color: Crystal

Comments: A blown decanter, not marked with the Diamond H. Bottoms are usually ground and polished. Redesigned from the No. 4036 decanter with the foot eliminated.

Decanter & stopper, 1 pint.$75.00   Decanter & stopper, 2 pint..95.00

No. 4036½ decanter with unknown Heisey cutting.

Colonade, No. 1520
Date: Ca. 1940
Color: Crystal only

Comments: Made for the Colonade Restaurant in Cleveland, Ohio. Not marked with the Diamond H.

Sugar pourer $90.00

No. 1520 Colonade sugar pourer.

Graceful, No. 5022 — original name
Date: 1940 to 1943
Color: Crystal only

Comments: A stemware line with blown bowl, pressed stem. May be marked with the Diamond H near the top of the stem. Compare this with No. 5025 Tyrolean which has a different bowl shape. Some items with the Graceful shape are common to both lines. Both Graceful and Tyrolean are noted for the famous No. 507 Orchid etching.

Bell, dinner $75.00	Oyster cocktail, 4 oz. 10.00
Candy box and cover,	Saucer champagne, 6 oz..22.00
low footed, 6" 95.00	Sherbet, 6 oz. 10.00
Claret, 4½ oz. 22.00	Sherry, 2 oz. 65.00
Cocktail, 4 oz....................18.00	Soda, footed, 5 oz. 12.00
Cordial, 1 oz. 75.00	Soda, footed, 12 oz. 18.00
Goblet, short stem, 10 oz..22.00	Wine, 3 oz. 25.00
Goblet, tall stem, 10 oz.....25.00	

No. 5022 Graceful goblet with No. 947 Enchantress cutting.

No. 5023 Continental goblet with No. 946 Port Said cutting.

Continental, No. 5023 — original name
Dates: 1940 to 1944. Periodically made until 1953.
Color: Crystal only

Comments: A blown stem line with a pulled stem. Not marked with the Diamond H. This pattern is very plain and delicate, very like imported stem lines. It is difficult to find.

Claret, 4 oz. $25.00	Saucer champagne, 6 oz. ..20.00
Cocktail, 3½ oz. 20.00	Soda, footed, 5 oz. (juice)...15.00
Cordial, 1 oz. 65.00	Soda, footed, 13 oz. (ice
Goblet, 11 oz. 32.00	tea) 20.00
Pousse café 55.00	Wine, 2 oz. 30.00

Decorations Introduced in 1940

Cuttings: No. 935 Basque, No. 936 Cathay, No. 937 Donegal, No. 938 Kilkenny, No. 939 Festoon Wreath, No. 940 Westchester, No. 941 Barcelona, No. 942 Harvester, No. 943 Belfast, No. 944 Courtship, No. 945 Virginia, No. 946 Port Said, No. 947 Enchantress, No. 948 Boquet, No. 949 Evelyn, No. 950 Erin, No. 951 Holly Wreath, No. 952 Santo Domingo, No. 953 Corsica, No. 955 Polished Punties, and No. 956 Everest.

Etchings: No. 507 Orchid plate etching, No. 508 Floral plate etching, and No. 510 Tavern silhouette etching.

1941:

Standing Pony, No. 1522 — original name
Kicking Pony, No. 1527 — original name
Balking Pony, No. 1529 — original name
Dates: Standing, 1941 to 1952; Kicking, 1941 to 1945; Balking, 1941 to 1945
Colors: Crystal, Amber, Stiegel Blue
Patent: T. C. Heisey was granted patent No. 127473 on 5-27-1941 for the Standing Pony.

Comments: The ponies may be found marked or unmarked with the Diamond H. Imperial Glass reproduced all three in crystal and caramel slag. The Heisey Collectors of America reproduced the set in several colors. Original amber or Stiegel Blue ponies are very difficult to find and quite expensive, adding 700% to 1,000% to the value of crystal ones.

No. 1522 Standing Pony.

Pony, balking..$265.00
Pony, kicking 250.00
Pony, standing..110.00

Apple, No. 1523
Date: Ca. 1941
Color: Crystal

Comments: A one item pattern although Heisey also made an apple ashtray, No. 1549. This jelly is unmarked.

Jelly $85.00

No. 1523 Apple jelly.

No. 1528 Oak Leaf relish.

Oak Leaf, No. 1528
Date: 1941
Color: Crystal

Comments: A one item pattern, not marked with the Diamond H. Sometimes seen with allover satin finish.

Relish $75.00

Wampum, No. 1533
Date: 1941 to 1944
Colors: Crystal. A rare bowl is known in Stiegel Blue.

Comments: Items may be marked with the Diamond H. A small pattern line that is difficult to find. Imperial Glass reproduced the candy box and cover in pink and blue satin. No. 1521 Quilt is a similar pattern with fewer pieces.

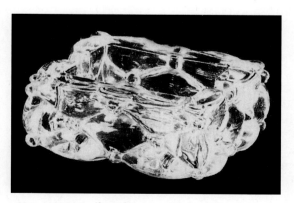

No. 1521 Quilt ashtray with beads only at intersections of diamonds.

Ashtray, individual.......................$20.00	Candlesticks, 1 light, pr. 70.00
Bowl, floral...70.00	Candy box & cover, 7"................................190.00
Bowl, gardenia...70.00	Cigarette box & cover.................................120.00

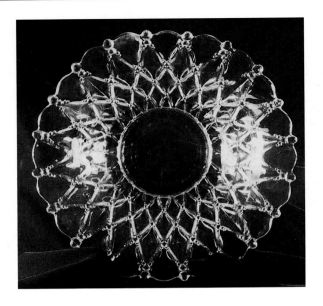

No. 1533 Wampum floral bowl.

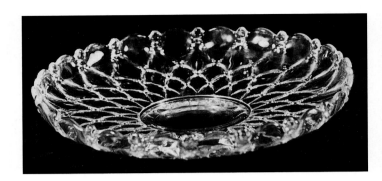

No. 1533 Wampum gardenia bowl.

Melon, No. 1534
Date: 1941
Color: Crystal

Comments: A one-item pattern, although Heisey information indicates that a bookend was made and also given No. 1534. This is an unknown piece. The Melon ribbed handled jelly is completely pressed but is not marked with the Diamond H. A copy (or the inspiration for Heisey's item!) is blown with an applied handle.

No. 1534 Melon handled jelly.

Jelly, handled...$45.00

No. 1536 Military Cap ashtray.

Military Cap, No. 1536 — original name
Date: 1941 to 1947+
Color: Crystal

Comments: Not marked with the Diamond H. Collectors have long referred to this as the McArthur hat, but Heisey called it only a military cap.

Ashtray $40.00

Rabbit, No. 1538 — original name
Date: 1941 to 1946
Color: Crystal

Comments: Not marked with the Diamond H. Base is ground and polished. Reproduced by Heisey Collectors of America in colors.

Paperweight $200.00

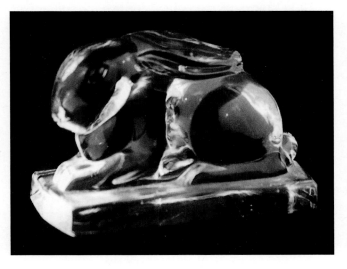

No. 1538 Rabbit paperweight.

No. 1540 Oscar.

Oscar, No. 1540 — original name
Date: 1941 to 1946
Colors: Crystal, Light Amber

Comments: A comic figurine, sometimes marked with the Diamond H. The name, Oscar, was given to the horse by the salesmen at a company meeting. Reproduced by Imperial Glass in caramel slag and other colors. This figurine has served as a convention souvenir for the Heisey club for many years and was made in a great number of colors.

Oscar..$150.00

Scottie, No. 1541 — original name
Date: 1941 to 1946
Color: Crystal

Comments: Ground and polished base. According to dog experts this is actually a Sealyham terrier, but Heisey referred to it as a Scottie. May or may not be marked with the Diamond H. Imperial Glass Co. reproduced the Scottie in crystal and several colors.

Scottie $175.00

No. 1541 Scottie.

Polka Dot, Impromptu, No. 4004 — original name
Dates: 1941 discontinued during the war years. 1952 to 1956.
Color: Crystal only
Patent: T. C. Heisey was granted No. 130432 on 11-18-1941 for the goblet.

Comments: Not marked with the Diamond H. This line was reintroduced again in 1952 as No. 4004 Impromptu with some new pieces. "A Preview of Heisey's 'Polka Dot' pattern (Pat. Applied for)...No. 4004. This new POLKA DOT Pattern achieves a 'Knotty pine' effect that is certain to excite buyer interest.... The Polka Dots reflect light in a wonderfully intriguing way — precisely like cabochon jewels. They exert an instantaneous and a universal appeal that is practically irresistible." *Crockery & Glass Journal*, September 1941.

In 1942, T. C. Heisey noted that "We have had very favorable reaction to the #4004 Polka Dot line. ...we are making several large vases, bowls, in this Spot Optic, and I am sure that your trade will like them and buy them." In 1952 the name was changed to Impromptu.

Bar, half sham, 2 oz. $25.00
Bowl, salad, 11" 55.00
Cocktail shaker..160.00
Cocktail, 4 oz..20.00
Decanter & stopper 145.00
Finger bowl 18.00
Goblet, 10 oz..45.00
Ice tea, footed, 12 oz....................................40.00
Ice tub 120.00
Jug, cocktail, 1 pint.....................................195.00
Jug, ice, ½ gallon 150.00
Martini mixer..145.00
Old fashioned, half sham, 9 oz.....................20.00
Plate, 7"..25.00
Sherbet, 6 oz...20.00
Soda, half sham, 10 oz..................................40.00
Vase, 9" 135.00

Vase, 10½"...150.00
Vase, ball..250.00

No. 4004 Polka Dot/Impromptu ball vase.

No. 4004 Polka Dot/Impromptu plate and goblet.

No. 4004 Polka Dot/Impromptu jug.

Unknown number small jug with No. 964 Maryland cutting, Polka Dot optic and plain.

No. 4004 Jacobean goblet with No. 910 Copperfield cutting.

Jacobean, No. 4004 — original name
Date: 1936 to 1939
Color: Crystal only

Comments: A plain stem line. When optic was added it was called Impromptu or Polka Dot. Pieces may be marked with the Diamond H at the bottom of the stem just above the foot.

Cocktail, 4 oz..$15.00
Cordial, 1 oz..50.00
Goblet, 10 oz..22.00
Sherbet, 6 oz..10.00
Soda, footed, 12 oz. (ice tea).................15.00
Wine, 2½ oz..22.00

Oxford, No. 5024 — original name
Date: 1941 to 1957
Color: Crystal

Comments: A stem line with a blown bowl and pressed stem. Usually marked with the Diamond H at the top of the stem just below the bowl. This is a standard shape made by many other companies. Heisey used this design earlier in their No. 5011 Yorktown which has a heavy sham in the base of the bowl. "Heisey's Oxford, the oldest type of English and Irish design, truly exemplifies simple beauty that is ageless." From Heisey pattern folder. This line was continued by Imperial after they purchased the Heisey molds. Numbers following pieces in list refer to numbers in illustration.

Claret, 4½ oz. (4)..............................$15.00
Cocktail, 3½ oz. (9)..........................12.00
Cocktail, double, 6 oz. 15.00

Cordial, 1 oz. (6)..40.00
Goblet, 11 oz. (1)..20.00
Goblet, 9 oz...20.00

Iced tea, footed, 12 oz. (8)) 18.00
Juice, footed, 5 oz. (7) 15.00

Oyster cocktail, 4 oz. (3) 8.00
Saucer champagne or sherbet, 6½ oz.
   (2) 15.00
Wine, 3 oz. (5)..18.00

No. 5024 Oxford with No. 964 Maryland cutting.

No. 5024 Oxford stems with No. 1074 Inspiration and No. 1077 Fanfare cuttings.

Tyrolean, No. 5025 — original name
Date: 1941 to 1957
Color: Crystal only

Comments: A stem line with blown bowl, pressed stem. May be marked with the Diamond H near the top of the stem. Compare with No. 5022 Graceful which has a differently shaped bowl. Some items listed below are taken directly from the Graceful line and are common shapes to both patterns. Usually found with No. 507 Orchid etching.

Bell, dinner...................$75.00
Claret, 4 oz.....................22.00
Cocktail, 4 oz. (#5022)....18.00
Cordial, 1 oz. (#5022).....75.00
Goblet, short stem, 10 oz..22.00
Goblet, tall stem, 10 oz. ..25.00
Oyster cocktail, 4 oz.
   (#5022).....................10.00

Saucer champagne,
   6 oz. (#5022)..............22.00
Sherbet, 6 oz. (#5022)....10.00
Sherry, 2 oz. (#5022)......65.00
Soda, footed, 5 oz. (juice).12.00
Soda, footed, 12 oz. (ice
   tea)............................18.00
Wine, 3 oz. 25.00

No. 5025 Tyrolean stems with No. 507 Orchid plate etching.

Decorations Introduced in 1941
Cuttings: No. 957 Oriental, No. 958 Ping Pong, No. 959 Lotus, No. 960 Atlantic City, No. 961 Versailles, No. 962 Punties, No. 963 Commodore, No. 964 Maryland, No. 965 Narcissus, No. 966 Picket, No. 967 Vivian, No. 968 Mary, No. 969 Miriam, and No. 970 Limerick.

1942:

E. Wilson Heisey died early in 1942. He was succeeded by his brother, T. Clarence Heisey as president of the company.

In 1942 Heisey introduced the "dolphin group" of figurines. Heisey collectors now refer to them simply as fish. "ROYAL HICKMAN DESIGNS THE DOLPHIN GROUP FOR HEISEY. Now he is working with crystal — Heisey Crystal — and the group illustrated above is an example of his master touch in designing. The playful dolphin candlesticks and the flower bowl offer your customers delightfully new possibilities for their table decorations. This dolphin group — and many other exciting Hickman 'figurines' to be announced later — will make the cash register jingle for you." *Crockery & Glass Journal*, May 1942.

A patriotic set for World War II was introduced in October of 1942 and highly collectible today. It consisted of a pint No. 4225 Cobel cocktail shaker and two Rooster Stem cocktails. The shaker is etched Us and the cocktails etched You and Me. "The New Victory Eagle motif is a complete Bar and Drinking Accessory line that will make a quick hit with Americans who want to combine patriotism with pleasure." *Crockery & Glass Journal*, October 1942. Another war item was a blackout lamp in Lariat.

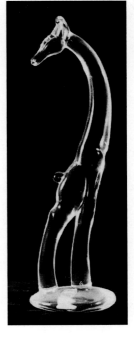

Giraffe, Head Straight, No. 1;
Giraffe, Head Turned, No. 2 — original name
Date: 1942 to 1953
Colors: Crystal, Sultana (dark amber) in 1950.

Comments: The giraffes may be marked with the Diamond H near the base. Reproduced by Imperial Glass Co. in crystal, amber, and several other colors.

Giraffe, either style...$300.00

No. 2 head turned Giraffe.

Goose, Wings Down, No. 1; Goose, Wings Half,
No. 2; Goose, Wings Up, No. 3 — original name
Dates: No. 1: 1942 to 1953. No. 2 and No. 3: 1942 to 1955.
Color: Crystal

Comments: Any of the geese may be marked with the Diamond H near the base on the side. Ground and polished bottoms. "...a series of 'swans-in-flight' figures, three different poses." *China, Glass & Lamps*, January 1942.
Imperial Glass Co. reproduced the wings half and the wings up geese in crystal.

Goose, wings down......................$550.00
Goose, wings half..........................125.00
Goose, wings up 125.00

No. 1 wings down Goose.

No. 2 wings half Goose.

No. 3 wings up Goose.

Madonna, No. 1 — original name
Dates: 1942 to 1946; 1956 to 1957
Colors: Crystal, rare in Limelight.

Comments: May be marked with the Diamond H.
Heisey Madonnas will be allover satin, including
the faces. Imperial reproduced the Madonna,
often with a clear face, but sometimes with the
allover satin like the original Heisey piece. There
is a similar Madonna of unknown manufacture
which has a slightly hollowed out base and has
coarser facial features. Any colors other than
those listed are reproductions.

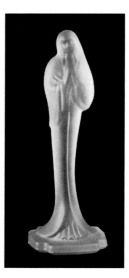

No. 1 Madonna.

Madonna $100.00

No. 1 Mother Rabbit; No. 2 Bunny, head down; No.
3 Bunny, head up.

Rabbit, Mother, No. 1; Bunny, Head Down,
No. 2; Bunny, Head Up, No. 3 — original name
Dates: Mother, 1942 to 1955. No. 2 Bunny, 1948
to 1952. No. 3 Bunny, 1948 to 1949
Color: Crystal

Comments: If marked, the Diamond H will be on
the side near the base on all rabbits. Reproduced by Imperial Glass Co. in several colors
and by Dalzell-Viking in red.

Mother rabbit..................................$1,000.00
Bunny, either style 235.00

Ringneck Pheasant,
No. 1 — original name
Date: 1942 to 1955
Color: Crystal

Comments: If marked, the Diamond H will be found near the base on the side. Reproduced by Imperial Glass Co. in crystal.

Ringneck pheasant..............$175.00

No. 1 Ringneck Pheasant.

Clydesdale, No. 2 — original name
Date: 1942 to 1948
Color: Crystal

Comments: If marked with the Diamond H, it will be found on a back leg. Reproduced by Imperial Glass Co. in crystal and several colors. Currently (2001) reproduced for Longaberger Basket Co. in many colors.

Clydesdale...........................$500.00

No. 2 Clydesdale, light amber.

Lariat, No. 1540 — original name
Date: 1942 to 1957
Color: Crystal. Rare plates in black.
Patent: T. C. Heisey was given patent No. 130368 on 11-11-1941 for the floral bowl.

Comments: Lariat is the original name although Heisey first referred to the pattern as Gordian Knot. According to Heisey material, the pattern was an instant success and more pieces were added as quickly as molds could be made with the difficulty in getting metal during World War II. Many of the molds were made with several different hand-tooled shapes, indicating a creative use of molds during a difficult time for glass factories. "Now...Lariat by Heisey (Pat. Appl. For.) Introduced at the Pittsburgh Show, Heisey's new LARIAT Pattern (No. 1540) made an instantaneous hit! Bold in conception and design, its intriguing 'rope' motif is carried, cleverly, throughout the entire line. LARIAT comes in a wide variety of hand-wrought pieces and its appeal to customers is immediate." *Crockery & Glass Journal*, February 1942.

The inspiration for this pattern was supposedly from the twisting of a heavy gold watch chain. Certainly the line was developed to compete with Imperial's very successful Candlewick pattern. Horace King was the designer for this pattern. A few pieces were made with very thick Lariat loops on the edges, designated as "heavy edge." Most items are marked with the Diamond H.

Ashtray, 4"	$12.00
Basket, handled, footed, 8½"	230.00
Basket, handled, footed, 10"	365.00
Bonbon, 7"	30.00
Bonbon, handled, 7" (basket)	120.00
Bowl, baked apple, 7"	25.00

Bowl, camellia, 9½"	35.00
Bowl, centerpiece, rolled edge, 12"	40.00
Bowl, cereal, 7"	25.00
Bowl, crimped, 13"	60.00
Bowl, dressing, 2 compartment, 7"	35.00
Bowl, flared, 13"	48.00
Bowl, floating flower, 10"	45.00
Bowl, floral, 9"	38.00
Bowl, floral, 12"	45.00
Bowl, shallow, heavy edge 13"	110.00
Bowl, floral, heavy edge, 14"	135.00
Bowl, floral, oval, shallow, 13"	55.00
Bowl, gardenia, 13"	50.00
Bowl, gardenia, heavy edge, 15"	110.00
Bowl, party salad, 2 handled, 10½"	62.00
Bowl, salad, 10½"	60.00
Candleblocks, 1 light (nappy candle), pr.	48.00
Candleblocks, 3 light, pr. (#1540½)	500.00+
Candlesticks, 2 light, pr.	85.00
Candlesticks, 3 light, pr.	100.00
Candy box & cover, 7"	90.00
Candy box & horse head cover, 7"	3,000.00+
Candy box & cover, 2 compartment, 7"	90.00
Candy box & cover, footed	125.00
Candy box & cover, small, 5"	75.00
Candy box & cover with horse head finial, 8"	3,000.00+
Candy box & cover with plume finial, 8"	175.00
Celery & olive, 13"	32.00
Celery, heart, handled	85.00
Celery, 13"	30.00

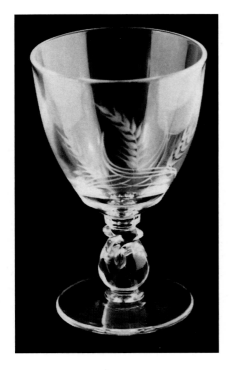

No. 1540 Lariat goblet with unknown Heisey cutting.

Cheese & cover, footed, 6" 60.00
Cigarette box & cover, 4" 55.00
Coaster, 4" 12.00
Cocktail, 3½ oz. 18.00
Comport & cover, 10" 135.00
Confection, handled, 7" (basket) 125.00
Cream..20.00
Cream soup, 2 handled 55.00
Cup & saucer...40.00
Dish, applesauce, 5"....................................18.00
Dish, candy, 7"...25.00
Dish, caramel, 7" 25.00
Dish, caramel & cover, 7".............................65.00
Dish, nut, individual, 4"...............................25.00
Dish, sauce, 6" 18.00
Goblet, 9 oz..20.00
Ice tea, footed, 12 oz..................................20.00
Ice tub, medium, 7" 75.00
Jelly, handled, 7" 38.00
Juice, footed, 5 oz.......................................20.00
Lamp, black out, with 5" globe, pr...........1,500.00
Lamp, hurricane, with 7" globe, pr 500.00
Marshmallow, rolled edge, 8"......................28.00
Mayonnaise, 5" 32.00
Mayonnaise, footed, rolled edge, 5" 40.00
Nappy, 7" 20.00
Nappy, 8" 25.00
Nougat, flat, 8" 20.00
Oil & stopper, 4 oz. (cologne).....................120.00
Oil & stopper, handled, 4 oz. 120.00
Oyster cocktail, 4½ oz. 10.00
Plate, 6" 12.00
Plate, 7" or 8"...18.00
Plate, baked apple, 8"..................................18.00
Plate, buffet, 21" 180.00
Plate, cookie, 11"...35.00
Plate, cream soup, 7" 18.00
Plate, demi- torte, rolled edge, 10"...............32.00
Plate, egg, 14" 300.00
Plate, egg, oval, 14"...................................320.00

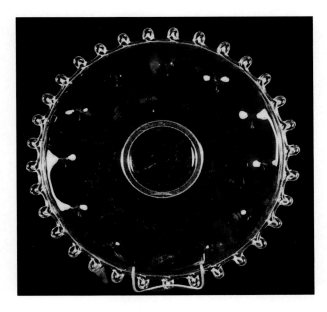

No. 1540 Lariat deviled egg plate, round.

Plate, mayonnaise, 6", 7", or 8".....................18.00
Plate, sandwich, 14" 40.00
Plate, sandwich, 2 handled, 14" 75.00
Plate, sandwich, center handled, 14" 95.00
Plate, sandwich, with cheese & cover, 14".110.00
Plate, service, 10½" 145.00
Plate, toast or cheese with dome cover, 8"...70.00
Plate, torte, 16"..50.00
Plate, torte, rolled edge, 13" 40.00
Punch bowl, 7½ qt......................................170.00
Punch cup, 4 oz. 18.00
Relish, 2 compartment 32.00
Relish, 3 compartment, round, 10" 42.00
Relish, 4 compartment, 8½".........................50.00
Relish, oblong, 3 compartment, 11" 40.00
Salt & pepper, footed, pr...........................850.00+
Saucer champagne, 6 oz.............................15.00
Sherbet, low, 6 oz...9.00
Shrimp cocktail, footed 35.00
Sugar 20.00
Sweetmeat, handled, 7" (basket).................145.00
Tray, for cream & sugar, 8"...........................28.00
Tray, oval, 14"...45.00
Urn jar & cover, 12"....................................200.00
Vase, crimped top, footed, 5" 50.00
Vase, crimped, footed, 7" 50.00
Vase, fan, footed, 6½"..................................40.00
Vase, fan, footed, 7" 40.00
Vase, square top, footed, 7" 45.00
Vase, straight, footed, 7"..............................45.00
Vase, swing, 10 to 12".................................65.00
Vase, swing, 12 to 15".................................95.00
Wine, 3½ oz. 22.00

No. 1540 Lariat salad bowl.

No. 1540 Lariat basket with No. 507 Orchid plate etching.

No. 1540 Lariat ashtray.

No. 1540 Lariat hurricane lamps with Charleton hand-painted decoration.

No. 1540 Lariat 7" straight footed vase.

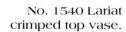
No. 1540 Lariat crimped top vase.

No. 5040 Lariat blown stemware
Date: 1947 to 1957

Blown bowl, pressed stem. May be marked with the Diamond H on the wafer just below the bowl. Imperial Glass Corp. made the blown stemware for about six years in crystal.

Claret, 4 oz. $18.00
Cocktail, 3½ oz. 18.00
Cordial, low stem, 1 oz.......................100.00
Cordial, tall stem, 1 oz. 145.00
Goblet, 10 oz. 22.00
Ice tea, footed, 12 oz. 22.00
Juice, footed, 5 oz. 20.00
Oyster cocktail, 4½ oz...........................12.00
Saucer champagne, 5½ oz. 15.00
Wine, 2½ oz. 22.00

No. 5040 Lariat goblet with No. 1003 Ivy engraving.

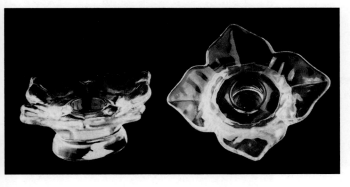

No. 1552 Four Leaf candlesticks.

Four Leaf, No. 1552
Date: 1942 to 1950
Color: Crystal

Comments: A pressed candlestick, not marked with the Diamond H. It is ground and polished on the bottom. Somewhat difficult to find.

Candlesticks, pr..................................$75.00

Chanticleer, No. 5038 — original name
Date: 1942 to 1957
Color: Crystal

Comments: The first of the Heisey rooster motif cocktails, often used with the No. 4225 Cobel cocktail shaker with Rooster Head stopper.

Cocktail, 3½ oz. $85.00
Cocktail with Victory etching...............125.00

No. 5038 Chanticleer cocktail with No. 9012 Victory etching.

No. 5039 Penguin decanter.

Penguin, No. 5039 — original name
Dates: Sherry bottle, 1942;
No. 5039 decanter, 1942 to 1944,
also as No. 5058 from 1948 to 1953.
Color: Crystal only

Comments: Blown with hand tooled wings, fitted with a pressed penguin head stopper. Not marked with the Diamond H. Designed by Royal Hickman.

Decanter $500.00
Sherry bottle 500.00

Dolphin, No. 1550 — original name
Dates: Candle, 1942 to 1946; Match holder, 1944 to 1946; Vase, 1941 to 1946
Color: Crystal

Comments: Designed by Royal Hickman. While Dolphin is the original name, most collectors refer to these simply as fish. The bowl has not been reproduced. But the candlesticks and match holder were made by Imperial Glass Co. in sunshine yellow and possibly other colors.

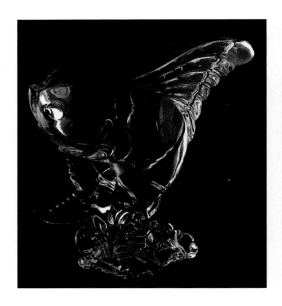

No. 1550 Dolphin bowl.

Bowl $650.00
Candlesticks, pr..400.00
Match holder 165.00

No. 1550 Dolphin candlestick, match holder.

Horse Head, No. 1551 — original name
Date: 1942
Color: Crystal

Comments: Molds for this pair of bookends were in the group purchased from Imperial Glass by Heisey Collectors of America. The number is also listed in original Heisey material. Also, one of these bookends was in the auction of the estate of Tim Heisey. However, most of the bookends found today were made by someone else and appear to be identical in design. As late as the 1980s these were available at the Corning gift shop at the Corning Museum of Glass. These bookends are made of inferior, greenish glass and have very obvious marks from the glass entering the mold while the known Heisey example is of expected Heisey quality.

Bookends, pr. ....$1,500.00+

Horse Head bookend, not Heisey and plastic model from Heisey mold.

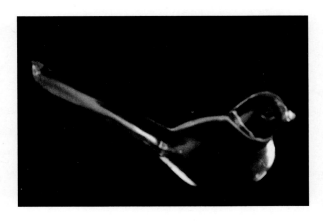

No. 1553 Sparrow.

Sparrow, No. 1553 — original name
Date: 1942 to 1945
Color: Crystal

Comments: These are not marked with the Diamond H. The base is ground and polished. Heisey made three styles designated as No. 1, No. 2, and No. 3. The only difference was in the angle at which the bases were ground. Heisey Collectors of America reproduced the sparrow in colors.

Sparrow, any style $135.00

No. 1554 Fish bookend.

Fish, No. 1554 — original name
Date: 1942 to 1952
Color: Crystal

Comments: When marked with the Diamond H, it will be located near the base on the side. Ground and polished bottom. Imperial Glass Co. reproduced the bookends in several colors in small numbers.

Bookends, pr. $375.00

Decorations Introduced in 1942
Cuttings: No. 971 Geneva, No. 972 Berne, No. 973 Ceylon, No. 974 Star Waterford, No. 975 Bow Knot, No. 976 St. George Waterford, No. 977 Diamond Waterford, No. 978 Bedford, No. 979 Tipperary, No. 980 Moonglo, No. 981 Moon Beam, No. 982 Moon Gleam, No. 983 Lady Astor, No. 984 Lancaster, and No. 985 Sheffield.

Etchings: No. 511 Gardenia plate etching, No. 9012 Victory silhouette etching, and No. 9013 You, Me, and Us silhouette etching.

1943:

With World War II curtailing the availability of gasoline, rubber for tires, and other materials used in travel, the Heisey company introduced a different marketing tool in 1943. In May, an announcement was made that four war time salesmen were now available for ordering Heisey glass. These are interesting paper collectibles for Heisey collectors today.

Announcement of Heisey's war time salesmen, 1943 ad.

Explanation of the difficulty of making glassware during the war years, 1943 ad.

Athena, No. 1541 — original name
Date: Ca. 1943 to 1948 or slightly longer
Color: Crystal only

Comments: This line was originally made for Montgomery Ward and included in their catalogs. Heisey continued some pieces later and many were cut by Susquehanna Glass. "This company will introduce a series of new cuttings, including a line of 18 popular pieces in Athena — hand wrought by Heisey, all hand cut by Susquehanna." *China, Glass & Lamps*, December 1948.

Bonbon dish	$25.00
Bowl, crimped, 11½"	45.00
Bowl, deep fruit, 10½"	45.00
Bowl, floral, 12"	45.00
Bowl, gardenia, 12½"	45.00
Candle lamp with globe	250.00
Candleblock, pr.	250.00
Candlestick, 2 light, pr.	200.00
Candy dish	45.00
Candy dish & cover	75.00
Candy jar & cover	85.00
Celery, 13"	30.00
Cigarette box, 4"	60.00
Coaster-ashtray, 4½"	20.00
Cream	22.00
Dish, preserve	25.00
Ice bucket	85.00
Mayonnaise, 5½"	35.00
Pickle dish, 9¼"	35.00
Plate, mayonnaise, 7½"	15.00
Plate, salad, 7", 7½", or 8"	15.00
Plate, sandwich, 14"	40.00
Plate, torte, 13½"	40.00
Relish, 3 compartment, oblong, 10"	35.00
Relish, 3 compartment, round, 12"	35.00
Sugar	22.00
Tray, for sugar & cream, 9¼"	24.00
Urn & cover, footed, 8"	110.00

No. 1541 Athena covered candy jar.

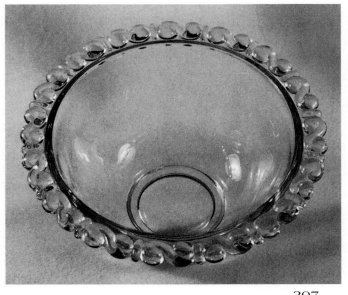

No. 1541 Athena — note figured edge.

Athena, No. 5041

Blown stemware with pressed stem.
Not marked with the Diamond H.

Cocktail, 3 oz. $22.00
Goblet, 9 oz. 40.00
Ice tea, 10 oz. or 12 oz. 32.00
Sherbet, high, 7 oz. (saucer
    champagne) 32.00
Wine, 4 oz. 40.00

No. 5041 Athena goblet.

Columbia, No. 1559 — original name
Date: 1943
Color: Crystal

Comments: This short line was used as a sales leader for the Heisey line in department stores. The items were inexpensively priced and used to stimulate sales of other Heisey glass. Items are not marked with the Diamond H. Only two molds were used to make all the items in the line. "Columbia is the name of this glassware pattern from A. H. Heisey. Graceful bowl and matching candlesticks...make an effective set — popularly priced, and a good gift suggestion." *Crockery & Glass Journal*, March 1943.

Bowl, crimped $70.00
Bowl, gardenia 70.00
Bowl, salad, deep..70.00
Bowl, salad, shallow.....................................70.00

Candlesticks, 1 light, pr. (plain or crimped
    foot) 95.00
Plate, sandwich 70.00
Plate, torte 70.00

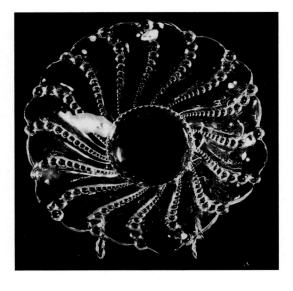

No. 1559 Columbia crimped bowl.

No. 1559 Columbia torte plate.

Victorian Belle, No. 1560
Date: 1944 to 1948
Color: Crystal only

Comments: May not or may be marked with the Diamond H on the bustle. The belle is found with either a shiny or satin finish. Highly reproduced in many colors.

Belle $95.00

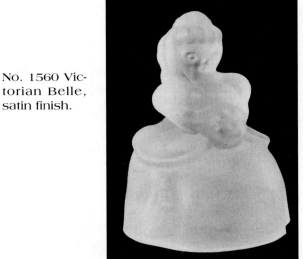

No. 1560 Victorian Belle, satin finish.

No. 4042 Johnson colognes with No. 4301 blown powder box, special Heisey cutting done for Paul Fairall, long-time Heisey employee, for a gift to his sister.

Johnson, No. 4042
Date: 1942+
Color: Crystal

Comments: The stoppers shown in the photo are unusual as Heisey did not normally make stoppers with trapped bubbles. Usually the smooth, teardrop stopper was used in these colognes. The powder box was made in early Heisey years, probably as soon as the blownware department was opened. Neither the cologne nor the powder box is marked with the Diamond H.

Cologne $110.00
Powder box (#4301)....................................135.00

No. 5012
Date: 1943
Color: Crystal

Comments: Three items were introduced in 1943 and given the number 5012, the same as the earlier Urn pattern. These pieces seem entirely unrelated to Urn, so we are listing them separately. We have never seen the marmalade, and the table salt is the bottom to the mustard. The pieces are blown and not marked with the Diamond H.

Marmalade ....$100.00   Salt, table 35.00
Mustard & cover ...90.00

No. 5012 covered mustard.

Decorations Introduced in 1943
Cuttings: No. 988 Serenade, No. 990 Mystic, No. 991 Laurel Gray, No. 997 Maytime, No. 998 Alexander, No. 999 Carolina, No. 1000 Rosemary, No. 1001 Louis XVI, No. 1002 Mediterranean, and No. 1004 Spray.

1944:

The Heisey Company, ever attuned to the times in which it existed, prepared for the 1944 Presidential election by introducing a donkey and an elephant representative of the political parties. "DID YOU PICK THE RIGHT ONE? You can win or you can lose on elections, but when you buy War Bonds, you're putting your money on a sure thing.... Incidentally, the Republican Elephant and the Democratic Mule illustrated here — both fine examples of Heisey figurine craftsmanship — are available in limited quantities." *Crockery & Glass Journal,* November 1944.

Both these animals were Royal Hickman designs. Heisey again advertised these for the 1952 Presidential campaign.

No. 1 Donkey.

Donkey, No. 1 — original name
Date: 1944 to 1955
Color: Crystal

Comments: This item may or may not be marked with the Diamond H. The donkey was reproduced by Imperial in caramel slag and called Wild Jack. Imperial also made it in green with a carnival finish and several other colors.

Donkey..................................$425.00

Elephant, Large, No. 1; Elephant, Middle, No. 2; Elephant, Small, No. 3 — original name
Date: 1944 to 1955
Color: Crystal

Comments: The Diamond H is located on the sides near the bases on all elephants, if marked at all. Imperial Glass Co. reproduced all the elephants in many colors.

Elephant, large $500.00
Elephant, middle 500.00
Elephant, small 300.00

No. 1 Large Elephant, No. 3 Small Elephant, No. 2 Middle Elephant in Sultana (dark amber).

Toy Horse Head, No. 1 — original name
Date: 1944 to 1945
Color: Crystal

Comments: Same as the horse head used on the No. 1489 Puritan ashtray, but ground and polished on the bottom and sold as a toy. Hard to find as it was made such a short time. Not marked with the Diamond H.

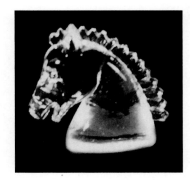

No. 1 Toy Horse head.

Toy horse head $75.00

No. 2 Madonna.

Madonna, No. 2 — original name
Date: 1945 to 1952
Color: Crystal

Comments: A large madonna, pressed, usually with allover satin finish. A very few were made by Imperial Glass. Very difficult to find. Despite being listed in catalogs for seven years, it is doubtful that many were made. The catalog listing was probably due to stock on hand.

Madonna...$900.00+

Asiatic Pheasant, No. 100 — original name
Date: 1945 to 1955
Color: Crystal

Comments: Imperial Glass made this in crystal and amber. The Asiatic Pheasant is usually marked with the Diamond H near the base. Reproduced by Heisey Collectors in color.

Asiatic pheasant $450.00

No. 100 Asiatic Pheasant.

311

In 1949, Jane Phillips, a student of Horace King's who also worked for Heisey as a designer, developed the popular etching, Heisey Rose. "never a rose like HEISEY ROSE.... Here is Heisey's famed artistry, translated into the loveliest of all flowers, the rose...a new etching on a completely new, hand-blown line of stemware, plus matching hand-cast tableware and gift items." *Crockery & Glass Journal*, February 1949.

The Metropolitan Museum of Art again sponsored a special exhibit, this time of outstanding American and European glassware. Heisey's exhibit included the Lariat candlestick, the Horse Head bookends, the Tropical Fish, and several other items including stemware and tableware.

The Glass Menagerie was a successful stage play and Heisey's animals were prominently featured in the play. When the Heiseys attended a performance, they were recognized from the stage for their contribution. In 1950 the company advertised its animals as being featured in the movie, *The Glass Menagerie* starring Jane Wyman.

Attempts were made in 1950 to tie-in glassware, china, and movies. Heisey produced Winchester '73 etching to be promoted with the movie of the same name starring James Stewart. Another tie-in was with Pan American Air Lines and Vernon Kilns dinnerware called Pan American Lei. Heisey's etching Pan American Lei was made to match this dinnerware. Neither Pan American Lei nor Winchester '73 seems to have been popular at the time because both are difficult to find today, although Winchester '73 is somewhat available.

Shortly before Christmas in 1952 Heisey opened a gift shop on the premises of the factory: "It is not only a good spot for the public in selecting their Christmas presents but also gave the workers a chance to see a lot of their finished ware on display, and to see the fine quality after it is finished and ready for the buyers." *American Flint*, 1952.

The year 1952 also saw the introduction of Sultana, a deep amber color. This attractive color was made for only a short time and is eagerly sought today.

The factory closed in December 1957 for the traditional Christmas vacation, but it never reopened after this. In early 1958 all assets including trademarks, molds, patterns, etching plates, records, patents, formulas, and any other items of value were sold to the Imperial Glass Corporation of Bellaire, Ohio. Imperial began producing some of the Heisey lines. Some of the remaining stock of Heisey glass was sold at an outlet store at the Heisey factory for several months following the closing.

1946:

Few new patterns were introduced in the Heisey line after war's end. This may have been intentional, as several glass companies had agreed not to introduce new lines during these years.

However, Heisey did begin making its No. 503 Minuet double plate etching in 1946, described in ads as "MINUET, a pattern inspired by history's gracious days of curtsies and Beethoven, light music and light laughter. Chic...charming...enchanting...." *Crockery & Glass Journal*, July 1946.

> **Hydrangea, No. 5064**
> **Date:** 1946
> **Colors:** Crystal, Crystal with applied lavender color.
>
> **Comments:** A short stemware line designed by Dorothy Thorpe, the noted California designer, and made for her by Heisey. Heisey made the glass and satin finished the flower form bases, and Thorpe's studios added the lavender color to the bases. Any Hydrangea item is valued at $250.00+. The pieces are not marked with the Diamond H.

No. 5064 Hydrangea goblet, saucer champagne, claret.

312

1947:

Heisey expanded its figurine line with more Royal Hickman designs including the pouter pigeon and the three mallard ducks. Other Hickman figurines featured in 1947 ads include the dolphin (fish) candlesticks (made earlier), swan, cygnet, gazelle, Asiatic pheasant, and wood duck and ducklings.

No. 1 Gazelle bookend.

> **Gazelle Bookend, No. 1 — original name**
> **Date:** Unknown
> **Color:** Crystal
>
> **Comments:** When marked, the Diamond H will be on the side near the base. Most collectors refer to these as doe head bookends, but Heisey called them Gazelle. Designed by Royal Hickman. A small number of these were reproduced in crystal.

Gazelle bookends, pr. ....$2,000.00+

No. 4 Swan, No. 5 Cygnet.

> **Swan, No. 4, Cygnet, No. 5 — original name**
> **Dates:** Swan, 1947 to 1955;
> Cygnet, 1947 to 1949
> **Color:** Crystal
>
> **Comments:** The swan and cygnet may be marked on the side near the base. The swan was reproduced by Imperial Glass Co. in crystal, horizon blue, and black, but in very limited quantities. The cygnet was reproduced in several colors by Imperial and others.

Swan................................$950.00
Cygnet 250.00

> **Mallard, Wings Down, No. 10; Mallard, Wings Half, No. 11; Mallard, Wings Up, No. 12 — original names**
> **Dates:** No. 10 and No. 11, 1947 to 1957; No. 12, 1947 to 1955
> **Color:** Crystal
>
> **Comments:** These mallards may be marked on the side near the base. They have been extensively reproduced by Imperial Glass Co. in crystal, caramel slag, and other colors.

Mallard, wings down ....$365.00   Mallard, wings up 225.00
Mallard, wings half.........265.00

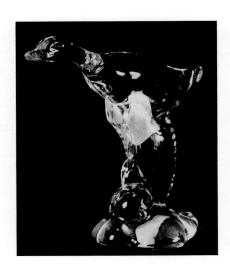

No. 10 Mallard, Wings Down.

Mother Wood Duck, No. 20; Resting Wood Duckling, No. 21;
Walking Wood Duckling, No. 22 — original names
Date: 1947 to 1949
Color: Crystal only

Comments: Designed by Royal Hickman. These three ducks may or may not be marked with the Diamond H. Heisey made the set only in crystal but Imperial made them in caramel slag and the Heisey club has used these as sale items in several colors.

Mother wood duck $450.00
Resting wood duckling 190.00

Walking wood duckling 190.00

No. 20 Mother Wood Duck.

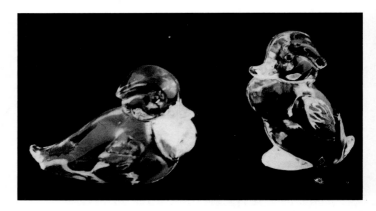

No. 21 Resting Wood Duckling and No. 22 Walking Wood Duckling.

Pouter Pigeon, No. 1 — original name
Date: 1947 to 1949
Color: Crystal

Comments: May be marked with the Diamond H on the side near the base. Reproduced by Imperial in crystal.

Pouter pigeon $1,000.00

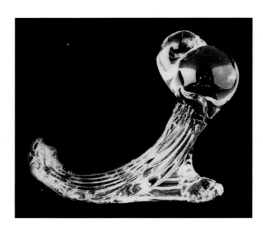

No. 1 Pouter Pigeon.

Gazelle, No. 104 — original name
Date: 1947 to 1949
Color: Crystal

Comments: The gazelle may be marked with the Diamond H near the hoof at the base. This animal was also used as a lamp base. Designed by Royal Hickman. Imperial Glass Co. reproduced the gazelle in crystal and cobalt blue using the Diamond H.

Gazelle.....................................$2,200.00

No. 104 Gazelle.

No.1565 Dawn leaf jelly.

Leaf, No. 1565
Dates: 1947. In Dawn from 1955 to 1957.
Colors: Crystal, Dawn

Comments: May or may not be marked with the Diamond H. Ground and polished bottoms. Dawn items are valued at 100% above crystal.

Jelly $45.00

Lotus Leaf, No. 1570
Date: 1947
Color: Crystal

Comments: A one-item pattern, pressed and marked with the Diamond H on the base. Somewhat difficult to find.

Candlesticks, pr................$85.00

No. 1570 Lotus Leaf candlestick.

No. 1591 Elephant handled beer mug

Elephant Handled Mug, No. 1591
Dates: Baby cup, 1947 – 1950. Beer mug, 1952
Colors: Crystal. Beer mug in Amber — rare

Comments: These items were designed by Horace King. They are pressed and marked with the Diamond H. Mr. King also designed a child's bowl to match the cup but there is no evidence that it was ever made. The baby cup has nursery rhyme characters in the panels of the mug. The beer mug has plain panels.

Baby cup ....$250.00+
Beer mug ....400.00+

Rooster Head, No. 5048 — original name
Date: 1947
Colors: Crystal, Crystal bowl with Amber stem

Comments: This the easiest to find of Heisey's animal stems. It was sold with Heisey's No. 4225 Cobel cocktail shaker or the No. 4036 shaker with Rooster Head stopper. There are similar Rooster Head cocktails of unknown maker which are not as finely modeled and come in various colors.

Cocktail, 3½ oz. $55.00

No. 5048 Rooster Head cocktail with elaborate unknown cutting.

Washington Square, No. 5060 — original name
Date: 1947 to 1950
Color: Crystal
Patent: T. C. Heisey was granted No. 154432 on 4-19-1949 for the soda.

Comments: This is a blown barware line. Not marked with the Diamond H. The defining feature of this line is a square ground pontil in the heavy double sham base. The decanter is the same shape as the cocktail shaker but does not have the strainer and is fitted with a smaller stopper. "New 'Washington Square' line of double sham, lead crystal glassware is shown at A. H. Heisey." *Crockery & Glass Journal*, March 1947.

Bar, 2 oz. $35.00
Cocktail shaker, 3 pint................................150.00

Decanter, 27 oz. 185.00
Ice tub 100.00

Jug, ice, ½ gallon 185.00
Martini mixer, ice lip, handled, 40 oz..........135.00
Old fashion, 9 oz. 22.00

Soda, 10 oz. 25.00
Soda, 14 oz. 30.00
Soda, 18 oz. 45.00

Detail of square punty on base of soda.

No. 5060 Washington Square soda.

Decorations Introduced in 1947
Etchings: No. 9014 Rose of Peace plate etching.

1948:

In January, Heisey announced it was bringing back a popular feature from years past — saturn optic. The Saturn pattern was reintroduced at this time, but in a limited number of pieces. Some Saturn pieces were redesigned at this time. The same proved true of the old No. 1506 Whirlpool pattern which was advertised again in April of 1948. June featured the introduction of No.1567 Plantation, which had been designed many months earlier but appeared on the market in mid 1948.

Heisey epergnettes were introduced in 1948. These were small peg candleholders with nappy-shaped bowls to hold tiny arrangements of flowers around candles. These were the inspiration of Mrs. Annie Dillon, a Southern society lady, who wanted this type of accessory to use at her garden teas and formal dinner tables. She contacted the Heisey Company, and an agreement was reached to produce them. The epergnettes were covered by patent numbers 153506 and 2478864.

Show Horse — original name
Date: 1948 to 1949
Color: Crystal

Comments: If marked with the Diamond H, it will be on the back hoof near the base. This animal is a glass representation of T. Clarence Heisey's show horse, Goodness Gracious. Imperial Glass Co. reproduced this animal in crystal and amber.

Show horse......................$1,800.00

Show Horse.

Rearing Horse bookend.

Rearing Horse Bookend

Comments: Very little is known about this animal except that the Heisey company did produce a very few of them. They are not listed in Heisey catalogs or price lists. Imperial reproduced these in crystal and black and possibly other colors, but in very limited quantities. Genuine Heisey Rearing Horse bookends are known only in crystal. The bookend has a hollow area in the base near the back hooves. They are not marked with the Diamond H. Rarity prohibits accurate pricing.

Airedale, No. 1 — original name
Date: 1948 to 1949
Color: Crystal

Comments: If marked with the Diamond H, it will be on a back foot near the base. The Airedale was reproduced by Imperial Glass in several colors including caramel slag.

Airedale $650.00

No. 1 Airedale.

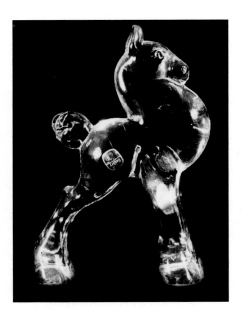

No. 1 Filly, head forward.

Filly, Head Forward, No. 1
Filly, Head Turned, No. 2 — original name
Date: 1948 to 1949
Color: Crystal

Comments: The Diamond H, if present, will be near the underside of the abdomen. Imperial reproduced the Filly in lead crystal and colors.

Filly, either $1,600.00

Rooster, No. 1; Hen,
No. 2; Chick, — original names
Head Up, No. 3; Chick, Head Down, No. 4
Date: 1948 to 1949
Colors: Crystal. Rooster rare in Sultana.

Comments: When marked with the Diamond H, the mark appears near the base on the side. All have been reproduced by Imperial in milk glass.

Rooster $450.00
Hen 500.00
Chick, either style........................100.00

Chicken family.

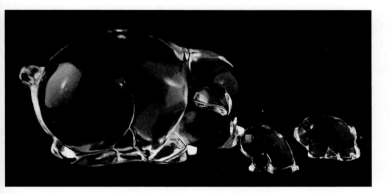

No. 1 Sow, No. 2 Walking Piglet, No. 3 Resting Piglet.

Sow, No. 1; Piglet, Walking, No. 2;
Piglet, Resting, No. 3 — original names
Date: 1948 to 1949
Color: Crystal

Comments: If marked, the Diamond H will be on the side near the base. Reproduced by Imperial Glass and others in many colors (all three pieces).

Sow.......................................$800.00
Piglet, either style.................. 130.00

Tropical Fish, No. 101 — original name
Date: 1948 to 1949
Color: Crystal

Comments: When this piece was satin finished, it was given No. 1. When present, the Diamond H will be on a side near the base. Very limited reproduction by Imperial Glass Co. in crystal and amber. Reproduced by the Heisey museum in colors.

Tropical Fish $2,000.00

No. 1 Tropical Fish.

Plantation, No. 1567 — original name
Dates: 1948 to 1957. Some early molds made in 1944.
Color: Crystal

Comments: Designed by Horace King. The inspiration for Plantation was from an old pressed glass pattern resembling pineapples. Pineapples are a symbol of hospitality and are prominently featured on most pieces of Plantation. Plantation contains both all-pressed and pressed-and-blown stemware. Most pieces are marked with the Diamond H. "FOR A NEW SENSATION SEE HEISEY 'PLANTATION.' And now Heisey captures charm...good will...and hospitality itself in a brand new pattern called 'Plantation' Yes, 'Plantation' says 'Welcome guest,' because its very design was inspired by the fabulous pineapple, traditional symbol of hospitality. Legend traces the friendliness of pineapple, first known as 'Queen Pine,' way back to 1657 when Oliver Cromwell received with ceremony the first 'Queen Pine' ever brought to England. Succeeding years of gracious, leisurely plantation life have firmly established the luscious fruit as a synonym for hospitality." *Crockery & Glass Journal*, June 1948.

Unusual pieces are those which normally have pineapples but lack them in some cases, such as the oil, salts and a few others. Some pieces were used with the Domesti-cater line. Reproductions: Imperial Glass Corp. made the covered marmalade in milk glass, marked with the Diamond H. Imperial also made the oval five-part relish in crystal. Numbers in brackets refer to items shown in catalog page.

No. 1567 Plantation salt shaker.

Ashtray, 3½"	$30.00
Bowl, dressing, 2 compartment, 8½"	55.00
Bowl, floral, 12"	65.00
Bowl, fruit or flower, crimped, 9½"	40.00
Bowl, fruit or flower, crimped, 12"	65.00
Bowl, gardenia, 9½"	35.00
Bowl, gardenia, 13"	65.00
Bowl, gardenia, footed, 11½"	80.00
Bowl, salad, 9"	50.00
Butter & cover, oblong (¼ lb.)	110.00
Butter or candy & cover, round	115.00
Candelabra, 3 light, pr.	350.00
Candleblocks, 1 light, pr. (pineapple shape)	210.00
Candleholder, epergne, footed, 5" pr.	275.00
Candlesticks, 1 light, pr.	220.00
Candlesticks, 2 light, pr.	220.00

Candlesticks, 3 light, pr.	245.00
Candy box & cover, 7"	400.00
Candy jar & cover, tall, footed, 5"	300.00
Celery & olive, 13"	42.00
Celery tray, 13"	40.00
Cheese & cracker, 14", 2 pc.	100.00
Cheese & cracker & cover, 14", 3 pc.	185.00
Claret, 4 oz. [14]	60.00
Coaster, 4"	15.00
Cocktail, 3½ oz. [15]	35.00
Comport & cover, deep, 5"	65.00
Cream, footed	35.00
Cup & saucer, tea	50.00
Goblet, 10 oz. [13]	55.00
Honey, cupped, footed, 6½"	40.00
Ice tea, footed, 12 oz. [19]	45.00
Jelly, 2 handled, 6½"	25.00
Jelly, flared, 6½"	25.00
Jug, ice lip, ½ gallon (blown) [12]	650.00
Juice, footed, 5 oz. [18]	40.00
Lamp, hurricane, 13" globe, pr.	1,700.00
Marmalade jar & cover (pineapple shape)	225.00
Mayonnaise, 5¼"	42.00
Mayonnaise, rolled foot, 4½"	70.00
Nappy, 5" or 5½"	18.00
Oil bottle & stopper, 3 oz.	165.00
Oyster cocktail, 3½ oz. [17]	25.00
Plate, buffet, 18"	200.00
Plate, coupe, native figure design	250.00
Plate, demi-torte, 10½"	65.00
Plate, mayonnaise, 7"	28.00
Plate, punch bowl, 18"	225.00
Plate, salad, 7" or 8" [10]	45.00

Plate, sandwich or torte, 14" 100.00	Sherbet or saucer champagne, 5 oz. (16)......25.00
Punch bowl, Dr. Johnson shape, 9 quart.....600.00+	Sugar, footed..35.00
Punch cup...25.00	Syrup bottle with drip cut top 200.00
Relish, 3 compartment, 11"...........................42.00	Tray, condiment, 8½".................................150.00
Relish, oval, 5 compartment, 13" (#1567½) .145.00	Tumbler, 10 oz. 130.00
Relish, round, 4 compartment, 8".................80.00	Vase, flared, 5"..65.00
Salt & pepper, pr..140.00	Vase, flared, 8"..125.00
Salver, footed, 13" 200.00	Wine, 2 oz. 60.00

No. 1567 Plantation marmalade.

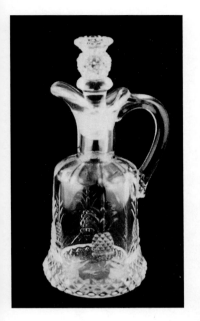

No. 1567 Plantation oil.

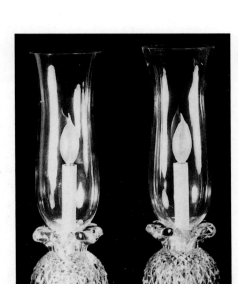

No. 1567 Plantation hurricane lamps.

No. 1567 Plantation tumbler.

No. 1567 Plantation rolled foot mayonnaise.

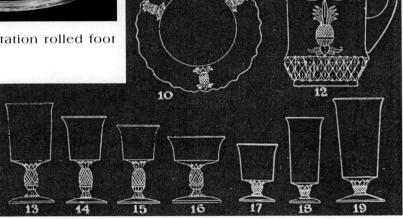

Catalog Illustration: No. 1567 Plantation pressed stems.

No. 5067 Plantation stems with No. 516 Plantation Ivy etching.

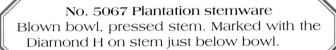

No. 5067 Plantation stemware
Blown bowl, pressed stem. Marked with the Diamond H on stem just below bowl.

Claret $32.00
Cocktail, 3½ oz. [5].........................22.00
Cordial, 1 oz. [6]............................140.00
Goblet, 10 oz. [1].............................35.00
Oyster or fruit cocktail, 4 oz. [7]........18.00
Sherbet or saucer champagne,
   6½ oz. [4] 20.00
Soda, 5 oz. (juice) [8].......................22.00
Soda, 12 oz. (ice tea) [8]..................25.00
Wine, 3 oz. [3] 30.00

Leaf, No. 1571
Date: 1948
Color: Crystal

Comments: Hard to find. Not marked with Diamond H.

Nut dish, individual $90.00

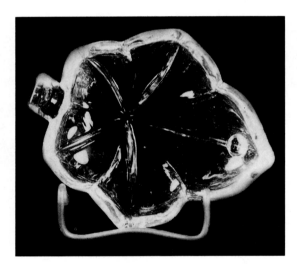

No. 1571 Leaf nut dish.

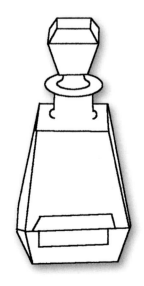

No. 1589 rye decanter.

No. 1589
Date: 1948 to 1950
Color: Crystal

Comments: Due to its short life span, this is difficult to find today.

Decanter, rye $150.00

Ashtray (any size) ....$45.00 to 55.00
Cigarette box & cover 125.00
Marmalade & cover.....................250.00
Rye bottle & stopper...................350.00

Prism, No. 1593
Date: 1948 to 1955
Colors: Crystal. Rare ashtrays in Dawn.

Comments: This pattern consists of various ashtrays in either square or rectangular shapes plus a few other items. There were seven sizes listed in price lists. The 8" square ashtray was also listed with a horse head finial in the center, but this is so rare as to be impossible to price. Not marked with the Diamond H.

No. 1593 Prism rectangular ashtray.

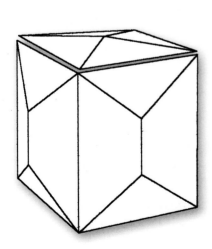

No. 1593 Prism marmalade & cover.

No. 1593 Prism cigarette box & cover and rye bottle.

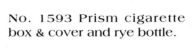

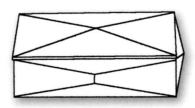

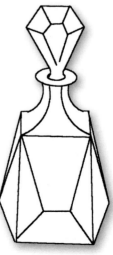

No. 1598 Cockade crimped floral bowl with Krall Studios cutting.

Cockade, No. 1598
Date: 1948+
Color: Crystal

Comments: Not marked with the Diamond H. Somewhat hard to find.

Bowl, floral...........................$75.00

Goose, No. 5058 — original name
Date: 1948
Colors: Crystal. Rare with Amber stem, Crystal bowl

Comments: Stems have blown bowls and pressed stems. Not marked with the Diamond H. Heisey made a matching Goose decanter which is blown and not marked with the Diamond H. On stems, the goose may be satin finished; on decanters the stopper and the tail may be satin finished.

Cocktail, 4 oz. $190.00
Cordial, 1 oz. 375.00
Decanter & goose stopper 600.00
Sherry, 2 oz. 375.00
Wine, 3 oz...240.00

No. 5058 Goose decanter and cordials.

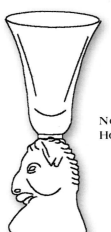

No. 5066 Horse Head sherry.

Horse Head, No. 5066 — original name
Date: 1948
Color: Crystal only

Comments: Blown bowl, pressed stem. Not marked with the Diamond H. Made to match the No. 4225 Cobel cocktail shaker with a horse head stopper or the No. 4036 Marshall cocktail shaker.

Cocktail $450.00
Sherry...525.00

1949:

In mid-1949, Heisey introduced blown stemware to match two of its popular patterns: Lariat (No. 5040) and Waverly (No. 5019). In August, blown stemware was added to the Plantation pattern (No. 5067).

The company announced several new cuttings in September of 1949. These were designed specifically to match various dinnerware or silver patterns then on the market. Dolly Madison Rose engraving matched Castleton China's Dolly Madison Rose; Botticelli cutting matched Whiting Silver's Botticelli sterling silver; Belvidere cutting matched Lenox China's Belvidere pattern; Melrose cutting matched Gorham Silver's Melrose pattern; Peachtree cutting matched Lenox China's Peachtree; Burgundy cutting matched Reed & Barton's sterling silver pattern; and Lyric cutting matched Lenox China's Lyric pattern.

Bull, No. 1 — original name
Date: 1949 to 1952
Color: Crystal

Comments: If marked, the Diamond H will be found on the abdomen. Imperial Glass reproduced this animal in crystal and several colors.

Bull......................................$1,800.00

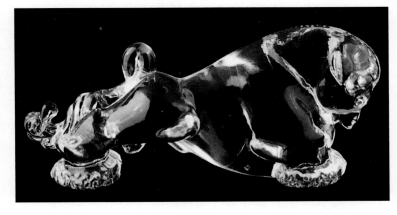

No. 1 Bull.

No. 103 Tiger paperweight.

Tiger Paperweight, No. 103 — original name
Date: 1949
Color: Crystal

Comments: When marked with the Diamond H it is near the base on the side. Reproduced by Imperial Glass in jade and black and a few in crystal. Reproduced for the Heisey Museum in several colors.

Tiger paperweight..................$1,300.00

Ashtray, square, 3 ½" $12.00
Bowl, flower, 12 sided, 11" 50.00
Candlestick, 2 light, pr. 200.00
Candy jar & cover, footed........70.00
Claret, 4 oz.............................15.00
Coaster, 3½" 12.00
Cocktail, 3½ oz. 15.00
Comport, 6"............................30.00
Cream, footed 20.00
Goblet, 10 oz. 20.00
Ice tea, footed, 12 oz. 20.00
Nappy, 4½" 8.00
Oyster cocktail, 4 oz. 9.00
Plate, 8"..................................15.00
Plate, sandwich, 13"..............125.00
Relish, 4 compartment, 8"........35.00
Relish, oval, 2 compartment,
    10"......................................35.00
Salt & pepper, pr.......................45.00
Saucer champagne, 5 oz. 15.00
Sherbet, 5 oz............................10.00
Soda, tapered, 5 oz..................10.00
Soda, tapered, 8 oz..................12.00
Soda, tapered, 12 oz................15.00
Sugar, footed...........................20.00

Zodiac, No. 1590 — original name
Dates: 1949. Discontinued in 1950.
Candy jar continued until 1955.
Color: Crystal only

Comments: This small tableware line was designed by Horace King, Heisey's designer in the 1940s and 1950s. The 12 signs of the Zodiac make up the panel designs. Some pieces, such as the cream and sugar each contain only six of the signs. The ashtray was used as a commemorative of the Newark Sesquicentennial. "The Zodiac, ancient symbol of destiny ruled by the stars, provides the motif for Heisey's latest triumph in hand-wrought crystal — a creation that foretells a bright future for informal entertaining. Classical charm of the Zodiac sign and the twinkling brilliance of the stippling are combined with styling of striking simplicity, designed to win wholehearted approval of clever hostesses everywhere." *Crockery & Glass Journal,* January 1949.

Prices are for items in crystal by Heisey. Most of the pieces are marked with the Diamond H, but often in hard to find places. Reproduced by Imperial Glass Corporation from 1969 to 1971, in crystal, amberglo, and verde. The footed candy and cover was made in nine or more colors by Imperial. Some pieces were also made in Imperial's rubigold and peacock carnival.

No. 1590 Zodiac sandwich plate.

No. 1590 Zodiac ashtray with Newark Sesquicentennial center design.

No. 1590 Zodiac goblet, sherbet, juice, ice tea, covered candy.

Suez, No. 5057 — original name
Dates: 1949 to 1953. Limited availability to 1957.
Molds were made in 1945.
Colors: Crystal; Amber stem with Crystal bowl.
Very rare in Experimental Blue.

Comments: A stemware pattern with blown bowl and pressed stem. Stems are marked with the Diamond H on the stem just below the bowl. Primarily this line was used for decorations. Amber stemmed pieces are sought eagerly. Prices are for crystal. For amber stemmed pieces, add 500%.

Claret, 4 oz. $17.00
Cocktail, 4 oz..................15.00
Cordial, 1 oz. 50.00
Goblet, low or tall, 9 oz. ..24.00
Ice tea, footed, 12 oz.......24.00
Juice, footed, 5 oz. 18.00

Oyster cocktail, 4½ oz. 12.00
Saucer champagne or
    tall sherbet, 6 oz. 20.00
Sherbet, low, 6 oz............15.00
Wine, 3 oz. 20.00

No. 5057 Suez goblet with No. 1017 Peachtree cutting.

No. 5072 Rose goblet.

Rose, No. 5072 — original name
Date: 1949 to 1957
Color: Crystal only

Comments: A stemware line with blown bowl and pressed stem. Usually found with wide optic. When marked, the mark may be in different places depending on the piece — sometimes on stem under bowl and other times on one of the leaves of the rose. Imperial Glass Corp. also continued to make Rose stems, both plain and with Heisey Rose etching.

Bell, dinner..........................$70.00
Claret, 4 oz............................24.00
Cocktail, 4 oz. 20.00
Cordial, 1 oz...........................80.00
Goblet, 9 oz. 30.00
Ice tea, footed, 12 oz. 30.00

Juice, footed, 5 oz..................22.00
Oyster cocktail, 3½ oz. 15.00
Saucer champagne (tall
    sherbet), 6 oz. 17.00
Sherbet, low, 6 oz. 15.00
Wine, 3 oz. 25.00

Decorations Introduced in 1949
Cuttings: No. 1003 Ivy, No. 1004 Rose, No. 1006 Londonderry, No. 1007 Galway Bay, No. 1008 Georgetown, No. 1009 Mexicali Rose, No. 1015 Dolly Madison Rose, No. 1016 Botticelli, No. 1017 Peachtree, No. 1018 Belvidere, No. 1019 Lyric, No. 1020 Burgundy, No. 1021 Melrose, No. 1022 Darlington, and No. 1025 Arcadia.

Etchings: No. 515 Heisey Rose plate etching and No. 9015 English Ivy plate etching.

1950:

Following the cuttings to match dinnerware in 1949, the Heisey company brought out several more in early 1950: Hibiscus gray cutting to match Vernon Kilns Hibiscus dinnerware, Evening Star cutting to match "many modern patterns," Fremont cutting to match Gladding-McBean's Fremont dinnerware, Bellevue cutting to match Lenox's Bellvue dinnerware, and Arcadia gray cutting to match Gladding-McBean's Arcadia dinnerware.

In June, Heisey took advantage of the fact that many of their glass animals were used in the Tennessee Williams' play when on Broadway and later in the movie, *The Glass Menagerie.* "Beautiful crystal animals hand-wrought by Heisey are prominently featured in a heart-warming new movie, 'The Glass Menagerie,' starring Jane Wyman and Gertrude Lawrence." *Crockery & Glass Journal*, June 1950.

No. 5074 Sea Horse cocktail.

Sea Horse, No. 5074 — original name
Date: 1950
Colors: Crystal, Crystal bowl Amber stem.

Comments: Blown bowl, pressed stem. Occasionally found with a wide swirl optic in the bowl. Marked with the Diamond H at the top of the stem just below the bowl.

Cocktail, crystal...................................$175.00
Cocktail, amber stem 1,000.00

Legionnaire, No. 5077 — original name
Date: 1950 to 1957
Colors: Crystal, Crystal bowl with Amber stem.

Comments: A stemware pattern with blown bowl, pressed stem. Marked with the Diamond H on the stem below the knop. Compare with Crystolite blown stemware, No. 5003. For pieces with amber stems, add 150+%.

Claret, 3½ oz. $17.00
Cocktail, 3½ oz................................12.00
Cordial, 1 oz. 45.00
Goblet, 10 oz. 15.00
Ice tea, footed, 12 oz. 14.00
Juice, footed, 5 oz............................12.00
Oyster cocktail, 3½ oz.......................8.00
Sherbet, 6 oz. 7.00

No. 5077 Legionnaire goblet with No. 1026 Bellevue cutting.

Park Avenue, No. 5078 — original name
Date: 1950
Color: Crystal only

Comments: A stemware line with blown bowl, pressed stem. Marked with the Diamond H on wafer just below the bowl. Models for this pattern were made as early as 1945. Volumes are larger than most Heisey stemware patterns. All pieces in this pattern have tall, elegant stems. This is a very similar line to Libbey's Embassy line. Price lists say "See Mid Century Pattern No. 5082 for 5 oz. Ftd. Juice and 12 oz. Ftd. Ice Tea."

Claret, 4 oz. $55.00
Cocktail, 4½ oz. 45.00
Cordial, 1½ oz. 150.00
Goblet, 12 oz...............85.00

Saucer champagne,
6 oz. 65.00
Sherry, 3 oz. 95.00

No. 5078 Park Avenue cordial.

No. 5078 Park Avenue sherry and saucer champagne.

Pan American, No. 5079 — original name
Date: 1950
Color: Crystal only

Comments: A stemware line with blown bowl, pressed stem. Marked with the Diamond H on the top of the stem just below the bowl. The stem appears to be twisted, but is actually a pressed pattern made to simulate a true twist. Compare this with No. 5083 El Rancho which has the same stem design but in a taller version and with a differently shaped bowl. This pattern is difficult to find today, indicating it was probably not a good seller.

No. 5079 Pan American goblet with No. 1033 Patio cutting.

Claret, 4 oz. $45.00
Cocktail, 4 oz.....................32.00
Cordial, 1 oz. 150.00
Goblet, 10 oz.....................65.00
Ice tea, footed, 12 oz.........60.00

Juice, footed, 5 oz. 50.00
Oyster cocktail, 3½ oz. 20.00
Saucer champagne,
5½ oz. 55.00

No. 5082 Mid Century ice tea and goblet, Limelight.

Mid Century, No. 5082 — original name
Date: 1950 to 1956
Colors: Crystal. Limelight bowl with Crystal stem. Very rare in pale Amber.

Comments: A stemware line with blown bowl and pressed stem. Marked with the Diamond H on wafer just below the bowl. For Limelight pieces, add 250 – 300%.

Claret, 4 oz. $22.00
Cocktail, 4½ oz. 18.00
Cordial, 1 oz. 60.00
Goblet, low, 10 oz. 22.00
Ice tea, footed, 12 oz.......................22.00
Juice, footed, 5 oz. 18.00
Oyster cocktail, 4 oz. 10.00
Sherbet, 5½ oz. 9.00
Sherry, 2 oz. 22.00

El Rancho, No. 5083 — original name
Date: 1950 only
Color: Crystal

Comments: A stem line with blown bowl, pressed stem. Marked with the Diamond H at the top of the stem just below the bowl. Apparently this did not sell well as it was made only in 1950, making examples difficult to find today. The stem appears to be twisted, but is actually a pressed pattern made to simulate a true twist. The same stem design is used for No. 5079 Pan American. "El Rancho stemware pattern has a new twisted effect although the stem is perfectly straight. Of handblown lead crystal, the new design will blend with modern table appointments where the emphasis is simplicity." *Crockery & Glass Journal*, September 1950.

No. 5083 El Rancho goblet.

Claret, 4 oz. $50.00
Cocktail, 3½ oz. 37.00
Cordial, 1 oz. 170.00
Goblet, 10 oz. 75.00
Oyster cocktail, 4 oz. 25.00
Saucer champagne, 5½ oz. ..65.00
Soda, 5 oz. (juice) 60.00
Soda, 12 oz. (ice tea) 70.00

Country Club, No. 6060 — original name
Dates: 1950 to 1957. Cocktail shaker as early as 1948.
Color: Crystal, rare sodas in Limelight and Dawn.

Comments: A blown stemware and bar line, unmarked with the Diamond H. It has not been reproduced. Rare large sodas are known in Limelight and Dawn with a swirled screen optic. Most items have a sham bottom, making them sturdy. "One of two new handblown stemware lines designed for moderns, the graceful holiday pattern blends with modern or traditional types of home furnishings." *Crockery & Glass Journal*, October 1950.

Bar bottle & stopper	$95.00	Ice tea, footed, 12 oz.	20.00
Bar, sham, 2 oz.	18.00	Ice tub	40.00
Beverage, sham, 10 oz.	15.00	Jug, ice lip, ½ gallon	75.00
Beverage, sham, 14 oz.	18.00	Juice, footed, 5 oz.	15.00
Claret, 4 oz.	15.00	Martini mixer, handled, 40 oz.	65.00
Cocktail shaker, 3 pint	90.00	Old fashion, sham, 8 oz.	15.00
Cocktail, 4 oz.	15.00	Old fashion, sham, double, 13 oz.	20.00
Decanter & stopper, 27 oz. (#4036½)	85.00	Sherbet, 6 oz.	10.00
Goblet, low, 12 oz.	20.00	Soda, sham, 18 oz.	20.00

No. 6060 Country Club ice lip jug, No. 1083 Jungle Flower cutting.

No. 6060 Country Club ice tub with Eva Zeisel designed cutting.

No. 6060 Country Club soda with No. 517 Winchester '73 etching.

Decorations Introduced in 1950
Cuttings: No. 1024 Hawthorne, No. 1026 Bellevue, No. 1027 Fremont, No. 1028 Hibiscus, No. 1029 Evening Star, No. 1030 Bandoleer, No. 1031 Greenbriar, No. 1032 Heirloom, No. 1033 Patio, and No. 1033 Corral.

Etchings: No. 516 Plantation Ivy plate etching, No. 517 Winchester '73 silhouette etching, No. 518 Pan American Lei plate etching, and No. 9016 Poppy plate etching.

1951:

Flying Mare, light amber.

Flying Mare
Date: 1951 to 1952
Colors: Crystal, rare in Sultana (amber) or light amber

Comments: May be marked on the side of the base. Original Heisey flying mares are very hard to find and expensive to buy. Imperial Glass reproduced this animal in crystal, amber, and sunshine yellow.

Flying mare $3,800.00

Patio, No. 1624 — original name
Date: 1951 to 1955
Colors: Crystal, Sultana (amber)

Comments: A very short, modernistic tumbler line. Often not marked. Very sleek and modern in appearance. Prices are for crystal items. For Sultana add 100%.

Ice tea, 15 oz. $50.00
Juice, 5 oz. 35.00
Sherbet, 6 oz. 18.00
Tumbler, 10 oz. 48.00

No. 1624 Patio juice, Sultana.

No. 1624 Patio tumbler.

Cabochon, No. 1951 — original name
Date: 1951 to 1957
Colors: Crystal. Some production in Dawn (charcoal gray). Limited items in Amber.
Patent: Horace King was granted patent No. 168795 on 2-10-1953 for the footed jelly.

Comments: The last major pattern made by Heisey. Cabochon is the original company name and was designed by Horace King. "The Circle and the Square are the two perfect shapes that are basic to all design. CABOCHON is the ideal combination of these two perfect shapes." *Crockery & Glass Journal*, March 1951.
    Imperial Glass Corporation made pieces in the pattern after 1957, including the blown stemware.

Bonbon, handled, 6¼" $15.00
Bowl, cereal, 7" 8.00

Bowl, floral, fruit or salad, 13" 25.00
Bowl, gardenia, 13" 25.00

Butter & cover, ¼ lb. 35.00
Candelette, 1 light, pr. 50.00
Candlesticks, 2 light, pr. 200.00
Candy & cover, 6¼" 50.00
Cheese & cracker, 2 piece, 14" 38.00
Cream 15.00
Cream, cereal, 12 oz. 50.00
Cup & saucer 20.00
Jelly, handled, 6" 15.00
Juice, 5 oz. 20.00
Mayonnaise, 6" 15.00
Mint, footed, 5¾" 15.00
Nappy, 4½" or 5" 8.00
Oil bottle & stopper, 3 oz. 70.00
Pickle tray, 8½" 15.00
Plate, mayonnaise, 8" 9.00

Plate, salad, 8" 9.00
Plate, sandwich, 14" 25.00
Plate, sandwich, center handled, 13" 50.00
Plate, torte, 14" 25.00
Relish, oblong, 3 compartment, 9" 20.00
Relish, square, 3 compartment, 9" 22.00
Salt & pepper, pr. 100.00
Salver, footed, 13" 75.00
Sherbet, 6 oz. 7.00
Sugar 15.00
Sugar & cover 40.00
Tidbit, 7½" 8.00
Tray, for sugar & cream, 9" 15.00
Tumbler, 12 oz. 50.00
Vase, flared, 3½" 20.00

No. 1951 Cabochon plate, amber.

No. 1951 Cabochon oil.

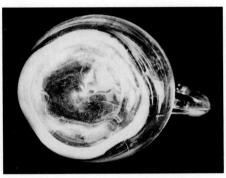

Detail of base of Cabochon oil.

No. 1951 Cabochon
tumbler.

No. 1951 Cabochon cream and covered sugar.
Later sugars did not have covers.

No. 1951 Cabochon.

333

Pattern folder: No. 6091 Cabochon stem line.

Cabochon blown stemware, No. 6091
Color: Crystal

Comments: Stemware with blown bowl, pressed stem. Marked with the Diamond H at the top of the stem just below the bowl.

No. 6091 Cabochon goblet with Lily etching.

Cocktail, 4 oz.	$12.00
Cordial, 1 oz.	80.00
Goblet, 10 oz.	20.00
Ice tea, footed, 12 oz.	20.00
Juice, footed, 5 oz.	15.00
Oyster cocktail, 3 oz.	10.00
Sherbet, 5½ oz.	8.00
Wine, 3 oz.	18.00

Cabochon, No. 6092
Date: 1952 to 1954

These blown tumblers with solid cabochon bases were made with crystal bowls and Sultana (amber) bases and are priced as such.

Beverage, 10 oz.	$95.00
Ice tea, 12 oz.	110.00
Juice, 5 oz.	75.00
Sherbet, 6 oz.	75.00
Soda, 14 oz.	130.00
Tumbler, 10 oz.	95.00

No. 6092 Cabochon juice, beverage, tumbler, ice tea, crystal with Sultana bases.

Bantam Rooster, No. 5063 — original name
Date: 1951
Color: Crystal

Comments: Not marked with the Diamond H. One of three rooster stems made to match No. 4225 Cobel cocktail shakers and the No. 4036 Marshall with rooster head stoppers.

Cocktail..$500.00

No. 5063 Bantam Rooster cocktail.

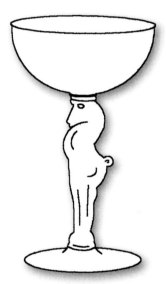

No. 5065 Colt cocktail.

Colt, No. 5065 — original name
Date: 1951
Color: Crystal

Comments: Not marked with the Diamond H. Used with the No. 4225 Cobel cocktail shaker and the No. 4036 Marshall cocktail shaker with horse head stopper.

Cocktail $500.00

Decorations Introduced in 1951
Cuttings: No. 1034 Maytime, No. 1035 Cornflower, No. 1036 Beau Knot, No. 1037 June, No. 1038 Pine, No. 1039 Desert Rose, No. 1040 Iris, No. 1041 Lily, No. 1042 Wood Lily, No. 1043 Heritage, No. 1044 Laurel, No. 1045 Sagamore Hill, No. 1046 Pussywillow, No. 1047 Autumn Rushes, No. 1048 Crocus, No. 1050 Skyline, No. 1051 Holly-Hock, No. 1052 Silver Iris, No. 1053 Cat-Tail, No. 1054 Gothic, No. 1055 Westminster, No. 1056 Bermuda, No. 1057 Florida, No. 1058 Southland, and No. 1060 Starlight.

1952:

Heisey reintroduced its old No. 4004 Polka Dot pattern in 1952 and renamed it No. 4004 Impromptu. "Formerly called Polka Dot, this hand-blown crystal has been renamed Impromptu in keeping with today's trend towards more informal entertaining. The company feels that the new name is more in keeping with the decidedly casual pattern of the glass, a low-stem and goblet line with many accessory pieces." *Crockery & Glass Journal*, December 1952. See No. 4004 Polka Dot for list of items and prices.

Lodestar, No. 1632 — original name
Dates: 1952. 1955 to 1957
Colors: Lodestar, Dawn; Satellite, Crystal.

Comments: In crystal, this pattern is called No. 1626 Satellite. The patterns have many pieces common to both but also have some different. However, if the same description and size appears in both lists the pieces are the same in both patterns. The old No. 120 tumbler mold was modified to have an internal five-point star similar to the stars on Lodestar pieces, but is not part of the Lodestar pattern. A tumbler and cream and sugar are known with this internal star, all made from the same mold and all very rare. The two-light candlesticks are from the No. 1510 Square on Round pattern and the four-part tray is from No. 500 Octagon (the variety tray). Numbers in brackets below refer to numbers in the catalog illustration.

Ashtray, 5½" $120.00	Jar & cover [6] 250.00
Bowl, 8" [3]..165.00	Juice or cocktail, 6 oz. 55.00
Bowl or nappy, 5" 45.00	Mayonnaise bowl, 5" 110.00
Bowl, crimped, 11" 190.00	Pitcher, juice or cocktail, 1 quart.................200.00
Bowl, deep fruit or floral, 12" 190.00	Plate, party, 14" 165.00
Candle centerpiece, 1 light, pr. (nappy) [7] ...195.00	Relish, 3 part, 7½" 95.00
Candleblocks, star, 1 light, pr. (#1543) 350.00	Sugar 60.00
Candlesticks, 2 light, pr. (#1510) [8]..............500.00	Tray, 4 compartment, 12" (#500) [9] 250.00
Candy box & cover 160.00	Tumbler (internal star) 185.00
Celery tray, 10"..110.00	Vase, 8" [5]..145.00
Cream...60.00	Vase, crimped, 7½" [4] 145.00

No. 1632 Lodestar cream, Dawn.

No. 1632 Lodestar ashtray, Dawn.

No. 1632 Lodestar mayonnaise, Dawn.

No. 1632 Lodestar cocktail, Dawn.

No. 1632 Lodestar divided relish, Dawn.

No. 1632 Lodestar items.

No. 120 tumbler modified to have an internal
five-point star, Dawn, $250.00.

Satellite, No. 1626 — original name
Date: 1956
Color: Crystal

Comments: The star-shaped bottoms of this pattern make it easily identifiable and are usually satin finished. Heisey ads described it as "double star pattern crystal." Most pieces are marked with the Diamond H and have ground and polished bottom rims. Catalog notes state: "Frosted Star Appears to be Carved from Solid Glass..." When made in Dawn, the pattern is called No. 1632 Lodestar. Numbers in brackets refer to catalog illustration.

Ashtray, 5¼" $50.00
Bowl, 8" 70.00
Bowl or nappy, 5"..25.00
Bowl, crimped, 7½" 70.00
Bowl, crimped, 11" [8] 120.00
Bowl, cupped, 4" [6] 25.00
Bowl, fruit or floral, deep, 12" [7] 90.00
Candleblocks, star, 1 light, pr. (#1543) [12]...200.00

Candy box & cover, 5" [18].............................75.00
Celery tray, 10"..60.00
Cigarette urn 32.00
Cocktail or juice, 6 oz...................................32.00
Cream [17]...32.00
Mayonnaise, 5"..70.00
Pitcher, juice or cocktail 110.00
Plate, party, 14" [1]......................................85.00
Plate, torte, 8½" 35.00
Relish, 3 part, 7½" 45.00
Sugar [16]..32.00
Vase, crimped, 8½" [5]...................................75.00

No. 1626 Satellite pitcher, unknown Heisey cutting.

No. 1626 Satellite cocktail, frosted base.

No. 1626 Satellite items.

Plantation Ivy, No. 5086
Date: 1952 to 1956

Comments: A blown stemware line with pressed stem. Marked with the Diamond H on upper stem just below the bowl. Numbers in brackets correspond to numbers in illustration.

Claret, 4½ oz. (4) $15.00
Cocktail, 3½ oz. (7)..............................12.00
Cordial, 1 oz. (6)..................................40.00
Goblet, 10 oz. (1) 18.00
Ice tea, footed, 12 oz. (9) 18.00
Juice, footed, 5 oz. (8)........................14.00
Oyster cocktail, 2½ oz. (3)....................8.00
Saucer champagne or tall sherbet, 6 oz.
   (2) 15.00
Wine, 2½ oz. (5) 15.00

No. 5086 Plantation Ivy stems with No. 1069 Lilyvale cutting.

No. 5087 Comet bar ware.

Comet, No. 5087 — original name
Date: 1952 to 1954
Color: Crystal only

Comments: A bar ware line which is blown and so not marked with the Diamond H. This line has a unique sham, called a torpedo sham by Heisey. Basically this is a nearly solid base with a hollow cone inside. Bottoms are ground and polished. "The new Comet pattern is aptly named for it is streamlined crystal with torpedo sham and ground bottom." *Crockery & Glass Journal,* April 1952.

   Numbers in brackets refer to catalog illustration.

Bar, 2 oz. (1).............................$20.00
Beverage, 14 oz. (4)....................30.00
Ice tea, 12 oz. (3).......................27.00
Old fashion, 9 oz. (2) 18.00
Soda, 18 oz. (5).........................30.00

Princess, No. 5089 — original name
Date: 1952 to 1956
Color: Crystal

Comments: A stemware line with blown bowl, pressed stem. Marked with the Diamond H at the top of the stem just below the bowl. This pattern had limited success. When found, it is usually decorated. Numbers following items in list refer to numbers in illustration. No. 10 is the No. 1609 salad plate which is used with many later cuttings.

Claret, 4 oz. (4).........................$15.00
Cocktail, 3½ oz. (9).....................12.00
Cordial, 1 oz. (6)..........................30.00
Goblet, 10 oz. (1)........................18.00
Ice tea, footed, 12 oz. (8) 18.00
Juice, footed, 5 oz. (7) 15.00
Oyster cocktail, 2½ oz. (3) 8.00
Saucer champagne or sherbet,
    5½ oz. (2) 14.00
Wine, 2½ oz. (5).........................15.00

No. 5089 Princess stems with No. 1076 Nonchalance cutting.

Empress Lily, No. 5092
Date: 1952
Color: Crystal

Comments: A blown stemware line with pressed stems. Marked with the Diamond H at the top of the stem just below the bowl or at the bottom of the stem. Factory information indicates that the No. 4090 Coventry bowls were used for most items. Variations of the bowl shapes exist which were probably experimental for the most part. The most commonly seen of these is now called Princess Lily and has a bowl slightly flared at the top.

No. 5092 Empress Lily saucer champagne, also same item with bust off.

Claret, 4½ oz. $60.00
Cocktail, 3 oz.....................................50.00
Goblet, 10 oz.....................................70.00
Saucer champagne or tall sherbet,
    6 oz. 60.00
Soda, footed, 5 oz. (juice)...................50.00
Soda, footed, 12 oz. (ice tea)...............65.00

Louisa, No. 5098
Date: 1952 to 1956
Color: Crystal only

Comments: A stemware line with blown bowl and pressed stem. Marked with the Diamond H at the top of the stem just below the bowl. This pattern is very similar to No. 5024 Oxford and No. 5011 Yorktown.

Claret, 4 oz.	$15.00
Cocktail, 3½ oz.	12.00
Cordial, 1 oz.	45.00
Goblet, 10 oz.	25.00
Ice tea, footed, 12 oz.	25.00
Juice, footed, 5 oz.	18.00
Oyster cocktail, 2½ oz.	8.00
Saucer champagne or sherbet, 5½ oz.	15.00

No. 5098 Louisa goblet.

Decorations Introduced in 1952
Cuttings: No. 1059 Midwest, No. 1061 Primrose, No. 1062 Bridal Lace, No. 1063 Wood Violet, No. 1064 Provincial Wreath, No. 1065 Baroness, No. 1066 Debutante, No. 1067 Yorktown, No. 1068 Victoria, No. 1069 Lilyvale, No. 1070 Bel-Air, No. 1071 Baroque, No. 1072 Southwind, No. 1073 Serenade, No. 1074 Inspiration, and No. 1075 Radiant.

1953:

No. 1633 bonbon.

No. 1633
Date: 1953
Color: Crystal

Comments: This bonbon is pressed but is not marked with the Diamond H. It is similar in design to Duncan's Flair pattern.

Bonbon, 1 handle, 6" $65.00

No. 5044 Constellation soda.

Constellation, No. 5044 — original name
Date: 1953 to 1957
Color: Crystal only

Comments: A bar ware line of only a few pieces. It is blown and thus not marked with thte Diamond H. This pattern may have been made slightly earlier than 1953. Somewhat difficult to find. Usually has ground and polished bottoms with a crimped base and a sham.

Bar, 2 oz. $28.00
Beverage, 10 oz. 24.00
Ice tea, 12 oz. 24.00
Old fashion, 6½ oz. 18.00
Old fashion, double, or tumbler,
   14 oz. 28.00

Celestial, No. 6000 — original name
Date: 1953 to 1956
Color: Crystal only

Comments: Only two pieces comprise this short blown bar line which is not marked with the Diamond H. This pattern is unique in Heisey because of the bubble in the base. On other lines, Heisey used solid bases or stems. Very difficult to find although listed in catalogs for three years. Described as "heavy sham base with bubble" in Heisey catalogs.

Cocktail, 4 oz. $100.00
Hi-ball, 11 oz. 135.00

No. 6000 Celestial cocktail.

No. 6003 Tempo goblet, claret, sherbet.

Tempo, No. 6003 — original name
Date: 1953 to 1957
Color: Crystal

Comments: A stemware line with blown bowl and pressed stem. Marked with Diamond H at the top of the stem near the bowl.

Claret, 4 oz. $15.00
Cocktail, 3½ oz. 12.00
Cordial, 1 oz. 40.00
Goblet, 11 oz. 24.00
Ice tea, footed, 12 oz. 24.00
Juice, footed, 5 oz. 15.00
Sherbet, 7 oz. 9.00

Domesti-Cater — original name
Date: 1953 to 1955
Color: Crystal only

Comments: An unusual line made of various Heisey items borrowed from other patterns and combined with wooden and wire racks and holders. Interestingly, it is quite difficult to find the wire racks today, and almost impossible to find complete sets. "Heisey proudly presents eight gifts in crystal that made bold black headlines at the recent shows. Created for carefree entertaining, the exciting Domesti-Cater line, available in natural finish wood, black wire or ebony finish with polished wire leads the profit parade of Heisey gifts for spring and summer." *Crockery & Glass Journal*, March 1953. Any complete set should be valued at $100.00 to $150.00.

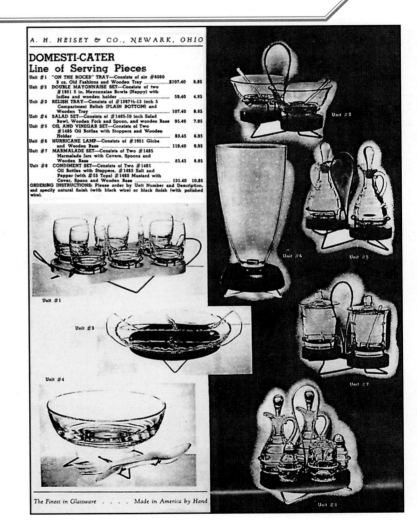

Domesti-Cater items, 1953

On the Rocks tray: six No. 6060 Country Club old fashions and wooden tray

Double mayonnaise set: two No. 1951 Cabochon 5" mayonnaise bowls with ladles and wooden holder

Relish tray: No. 1467½ Plantation 13" five-compartment relish with plain bottom and wooden tray

Salad set: No. 1485 Saturn 10" salad bowl with wooden fork, spoon, and wooden base

Oil & vinegar set: two No. 1485 Saturn oil bottles and wooden holder

Hurricane lamp: No. 1951 Cabochon globe with wooden base

Marmalade set: two No. 1485 Saturn marmalade jars with lids, spoons, and wooden base

Condiment set: two No. 1485 Saturn oil bottles, salt and pepper, and mustard and lid with wooden base

Decorations Introduced in 1953
Cuttings: No. 1076 Nonchalance, No. 1077 Fanfare, No. 1078 Bellflower, No. 1079 Garland, and No. 1080 Fern.

1954:

In December of 1953 Heisey announced that the noted industrial designer, Eva Zeisel, was joining the Heisey team to design new lines for the company. Her official title was art director. While she was highly regarded in her field, most of her designs for Heisey were commercial failures, making them very hard to find today. She designed several lines for Heisey and also several etchings and at least a few cuttings. The new color, Dawn (a charcoal color with distinct purple highlights), was also introduced in 1954. Several of Zeisel's designs, along with other Heisey patterns, were made in the new color.

Several items in original Verlys molds were made by Heisey in 1954. These were available in crystal and some in Limelight. None were marked with either the Diamond H or the Verlys script signature.

Tassels bowl
in Verlys mold.

Town & Country, No. 1637A
Date: 1954 to 1957
Colors: Dawn. Rare 6" plates are known in Black.

Comments: Designed by Eva Zeisel. Received the Good Design award. Zeisel described Town & Country like this:

"Pressed ware is often designed as thin as possible to make it look like blown ware. The elegance and 'snob appeal' of the 'Town and Country' line lies in the heavy, clear glass, in the weight, in the fact that they are not shells but have a bodily feeling to them...

"Although the edge is fine, the objects are almost soft to touch. What I mean is this. It is in the designer's power to design objects that look hard and brittle or soft and pliable. This group illustrates the latter. For maximum effectiveness in displaying it, a white background should be used. This will point up the lighter and darker shades of the glass...."

TOWN AND COUNTRY—Pattern No. 1637A in "Dawn" Color

No. 1637A Town & Country items.

Prices are for Dawn items.

Bowl, salad, flared, 10"	$200.00	Pitcher, ice lip, optic, 54 oz.	400.00+
Ice tea, 12 oz.	65.00	Plate, 6"	25.00
Juice, 5 oz.	45.00	Plate, 8"	35.00
Nappy, 4"	35.00	Plate, sandwich, 14"	175.00
Nappy, flared, 6"	45.00	Plate, service, 10"	175.00
Nappy, flared, 8"	65.00	Tumbler, 9 oz.	55.00

Classic, No. 6004 — original name
Date: 1954 to 1957
Colors: Crystal. Very rare in Experimental Blue.

Comments: A stemware pattern with blown bowl and pressed stem. Marked with the Diamond H on the narrow portion at the top of the stem above the knop.

Claret, 4 oz. $15.00
Cocktail, 3½ oz. 12.00
Goblet, 12 oz. 28.00
Ice tea, 12 oz. 28.00
Juice, footed, 5 oz. 15.00
Sherbet, 7 oz. 10.00

No. 6004 Classic goblet, claret, sherbet.

No. 6006 Hourglass juice and sherbet.

Hourglass, No. 6006 — original name
Date: 1954
Color: Crystal

Comments: A blown tumbler line designed by Eva Zeisel. The original ad uses the company name "Hourglass" and a description: "This latest of 'new horizons at Heisey' is bound to intrigue those with a flair for things modern. Eva Zeisel has lent her fresh, deft touch to a thrilling new line of hollow-bottom glasses we've christened Hourglass. Shown above are the ice tea, goblet, claret and cocktail in this exciting line. And this is just one of several new patterns designed for Heisey by Eva Zeisel. You'll want to cash in on the proven appeal of these designs."

While Heisey promoted this line with utmost enthusiasm, it apparently did not appeal to buyers, and it never appeared in Heisey catalogs. Thus it is very difficult to find today. Four molds are known: 5 oz. sherbet, 5 oz. juice, 10 oz. tumbler, and 12 oz. ice tea. (Note these differ from the items listed in the quote.) Items are not marked with the Diamond H. Any item is valued at $150.00 to $200.00 each.

NEW HORIZONS AT HEISEY

It's the New Hourglass!

This latest of "new horizons at Heisey" is bound to intrigue those with a flair for things modern. Eva Zeisel has lent her fresh, deft touch to a thrilling new line of hollow-bottom glasses we've christened Hourglass. Shown above are the ice tea, goblet, claret and cocktail in this exciting line.

And this is just one of *several* new patterns designed for Heisey by Eva Zeisel. You'll want to cash in on the proven appeal of these designs.

Original ad for No. 6006
Hourglass from 1954

Crystal Buds, No. 6007A — original name
Date: 1954
Color: Crystal

Comments: This blownware short line was designed by Eva Zeisel. Not marked with the Diamond H. In an interview at the time, Eva Zeisel described Crystal Buds as follows:

"In 'Crystal Buds' I've tried to produce four dainty flowery bubbles, thin edged, light sham. Like flowers in various stages of growth, the smallest glass is mostly a bud. The sherbet is just about to lose its petals. Each glass has a different contour, a different swing...

"The usual way of designing a group of glasses is to adhere strictly to the same contour, changing only the proportions. Here, however, I have introduced the notion that a much livelier group of designs results from a variation on the same theme, yet with all pieces belonging together like members of a family. The more informal a line is, the wider the variety allowed...

"I designed this line for touch appeal as well as eye appeal. I have played up a sculptural feeling, catering to the pleasure of cuddling the glasses and the urge to wrap both hands around them. The glasses have a very fleshy roundness as well as the appearance of a dainty shell, extremely fine, fragile, pure...."

Ice tea or hi-ball, 15 oz.	$40.00	Sherbet, 9 oz.	25.00
Juice or cocktail, 7 oz.	35.00	Tumbler or old fashion, 12 oz.	40.00

Company ad for No. 6007A Crystal Buds items.

Unknown Heisey goblet with unusual twisted stem and with cutting similar to those found on Crystal Buds items.

Roundelay, No. 6009A — original name
Date: 1954
Colors: Dawn. Limited in Crystal.

Comments: A blown ware line designed by Eva Zeisel. Not marked with the Diamond H. She explained the design of Roundelay as follows:

"I have been asked why the bowls in the 'Roundelay' line are not flat at the bottom. I feel there is a certain pleasure in holding or looking at a full, complete shape, like one that nature produces, a form from which nothing has been cut away — a sea shell or a piece of fruit, for instance....

"I don't feel that it is necessary that a bowl have a strictly defined base that disturbs its completeness. Without such a base it becomes livelier, more amusing, a bowl that seems to 'dance.'

"Of course, if because of the difference in the thickness of the glass on the different sides of the bowl it does not stand straight, we must flatten the bottom a little. But a perfectly round-bottomed salad or fruit bowl expresses the feeling of blown glass better and has the appeal of a complete shape..."

Many of the items are based on a ball shape modified from the No. 4045 Ball vases, including the cream and sugar and the cocktail shaker. The ashtray was made from the No. 4301 puff cover. The salad bowl was made from an electroportable lamp shade.

Ashtray, 3"	$125.00	Marmalade & cover	195.00
Bitters, 6 oz.	300.00	Mayonnaise, 4"	125.00
Bowl, gardenia, 10"	250.00	Oil bottle & stopper, 8 oz.	350.00
Bowl, salad, 8"	185.00	Pitcher, 16 oz.	300.00
Bowl, salad, individual, 4½"	60.00	Pitcher, ice lip, 54 oz.	600.00
Candle centerpiece, 6"	195.00	Salt & pepper, pr.	300.00
Cigarette holder	125.00	Saucer champagne, 6 oz.	110.00
Cocktail, 5 oz.	125.00	Soda, footed, 5 oz.	60.00
Cocktail shaker, 54 oz.	700.00+	Soda, footed, 12 oz.	90.00
Cream, no handle	125.00	Sugar, no cover, 3"	125.00
Decanter & stopper	750.00+	Vase, bud (oil bottle, no stopper)	225.00
Finger bowl (#3306)	70.00	Water bottle (#2 & #3)	250.00
Goblet, 10 oz. (#5092 bowl)	120.00		

No. 6009A Roundelay oils with stoppers, gardenia bowl, salad bowl, salt & pepper.

No. 6009A Roundelay ashtray, Dawn.

Decorations Introduced in 1954
Cuttings: No. 1081 Wedding Band and
No. 1082 Rosebud.

1955:

In 1955, the Heisey company entered into an agreement with the Holophane Company of Newark to reissue several of the Verlys designs which Holophane had made in the past. The items made by Heisey include Mandarin vase, Tassels bowl, Chrysanthemum bowl, Love Birds vase, Poppies bowl, Rose bowl, Wild Ducks bowl, Flowers bowl, Cupidon bowl, Thistles bowl, Pine Cones bowl, Water Lilies bowl, Gems vase, Rose candy & cover, Sacred Mountain bowl, Sacred Mountain party plate, the two Seasons vases, and Swallows ashtray. Heisey made these pieces in crystal frosted and a few were made in turquoise (Limelight). Original Verlys pieces are marked with a script diamond point signature, but those made by Heisey bear no signatures.

Heisey introduced its last color, Limelight in 1955. Actually, Limelight is very similar to the earlier Zircon, but, for the most part, made in different pieces and patterns.

Decorations Introduced in 1955

Cuttings: No. 1083 Jungle Flower, No. 1084 Spring, No. 1085 Forget-Me-Not, No. 1086 American Beauty, and No. 1087 Comet.

1956:

No. 6010 Finesse goblet.

Finesse, No. 6010 — original name
Date: 1956 to 1957
Color: Crystal only

Comments: A stemware line with blown bowl and pressed stem. Not marked with the Diamond H. The stem portion is a tapered square column.

Claret, 5 oz.	$30.00
Cocktail, 4 oz.	20.00
Cordial, 1 oz.	100.00
Goblet, 11 oz.	40.00
Ice tea, 12 oz.	40.00
Juice, footed, 5 oz.	20.00
Sherbet, 6 oz.	15.00

Omega, No. 1E92
Date: 1956 to 1957
Color: Crystal only

Comments: Heisey's last stemware pattern. It is all pressed and marked with the Diamond H on the lower part of the stem near the foot.

Claret	$15.00	Sherbet, 6 oz.	8.00
Cocktail, 4 oz.	12.00	Soda, 5 oz. (juice)	15.00
Goblet, 10 oz.	18.00	Wine, 3½ oz.	15.00
Ice tea, 12 oz.	18.00		

No. 1E92 Omega goblet with No. 1100 Waltz cutting.

Decorations Introduced in 1956

Cuttings: No. 1083½ El Dorado, No. 1088 Aurora, No. 1089 Silver Leaves, No. 1090 Radiance, No. 1091 Wheat, No. 1092 Melody, No. 1093 Flight, No. 1094 Ultronic, No. 1095 Tea Rose, No. 1096 Wreath, No. 1097 Wildflower, No. 1098 Starflower, No. 1099 Festoon, No. 1100 Waltz, and No. 1103 Hi-Fi.

1957:

In late December of 1956, the Heisey Co. had several pieces of glass with Heisey cuttings and etchings encrusted in gold by Lotus Glass Co. The only line ever to be added to price lists was the No. 1083 Jungle Flower cutting which when gold encrusted became No. 1083½ El Dorado. Fifteen items were listed with this decoration. Other known gold encrusted decorations are No. 515 Heisey Rose etching and No. 1015 Dolly Madison Rose cutting. It is quite likely that most, if not all, of these pieces were never produced beyond the samples done by Lotus. An announcement appeared in the December 1956 issue of *Crockery & Glass*: "A. H. Heisey & Co. will introduce a new line of crystal accessories with a cut and gold-filled decoration in a semi-contemporary vein."

 # Epilogue

Following the Christmas 1957 close of the factory and the purchase of all assets by Imperial Glass Corporation of Bellaire, Ohio, the Imperial factory continued to make several Heisey patterns. Some of these include Old Williamsburg, Revere, Cabochon, some Heisey Rose and Orchid etchings. They also made numerous reproductions of the animals in crystal, caramel slag, and various other colors.

When facing bankruptcy itself, Imperial made short runs of animals and other items in various colors and sometimes satin or carnival finishes. Upon the closing of Imperial, the Heisey club was able to purchase all existing Heisey molds and other Heisey material from Imperial. The major exception to this was the Old Williamsburg molds and a few other colonial items.

Since the purchase of the molds, the Heisey club and museum have continued to reproduce items from the molds, usually in colors not conflicting with the original production. However, these pieces can be confusing to the beginning collector, so be wary of unusual colors or colors not listed as original Heisey production. Noteworthy are the series of many animals made in Fenton's Rosalene and Viking's Lavender Ice (which is close to Alexandrite to the untrained eye). The club is also making a multitude of animals in many colors and also leasing the molds to various organizations, such as Longaberger Basket, for their use in limited run items.

So the Heisey designs are continuing to be used, although it is debatable as to the whether this policy is to the advantage of the collector of Heisey glass.

Index

Schroeder's
ANTIQUES
Price Guide

. . . is the #1 bestselling antiques & collectibles value guide on the market today, and here's why . . .

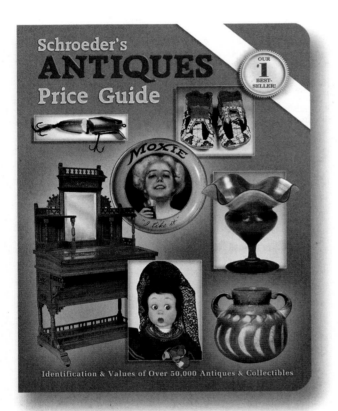

8½ x 11, 608 Pages, $14.95

• *More than 400 advisors, well-known dealers, and top-notch collectors work together with our editors to bring you accurate information regarding pricing and identification.*

• *More than 50,000 items in over 500 categories are listed along with hundreds of sharp original photos that illustrate not only the rare and unusual, but the common, popular collectibles as well.*

• *Each large close-up shot shows important details clearly. Every subject is represented with histories and background information, a feature not found in any of our competitors' publications.*

• *Our editors keep abreast of newly developing trends, often adding several new categories a year as the need arises.*

If it merits the interest of today's collector, you'll find it in *Schroeder's*. And you can feel confident that the information we publish is up to date and accurate. Our advisors thoroughly check each category to spot inconsistencies, listings that may not be entirely reflective of market dealings, and lines too vague to be of merit. Only the best of the lot remains for publication.

Collector Books
P.O. Box 3009
Paducah, KY 42002-3009
1-800-626-5420
www.collectorbooks.com

COLLECTOR BOOKS
A Division of Schroeder Publishing Co., Inc.